John James Lias

The First epistle of St. John:

With exposition and homiletical treatment

John James Lias

The First epistle of St. John:
With exposition and homiletical treatment

ISBN/EAN: 9783337729929

Printed in Europe, USA, Canada, Australia, Japan

Cover: Foto ©ninafisch / pixelio.de

More available books at **www.hansebooks.com**

THE
FIRST EPISTLE OF ST. JOHN.

WITH

Exposition and Homiletical Treatment.

BY THE

REV. J. J. LIAS, M.A.

VICAR OF ST. EDWARD'S, CAMBRIDGE,
LATE HULSEAN LECTURER AND PREACHER AT THE
CHAPEL ROYAL, WHITEHALL.

LONDON:
JAMES NISBET & CO., 21 BERNERS STREET.
MDCCCLXXXVII.

PREFACE.

THE present Commentary has been reprinted, almost without alteration, from the pages of the *Homiletic Magazine*, in which it appeared from time to time during a period of nearly six years. The author readily acceded to the proposal for the reprinting, from the hope that as it had been already found useful by some, it might be useful to more. At the same time, he is fully aware that the circumstances under which it was originally produced have precluded any careful independent investigation of the Epistle for himself. His task has simply been to select from the various commentaries before him such matter as seemed to him most likely to be useful to those for whom his own was originally designed. Full and thoughtful as are many of the recent German commentators, their style is too diffuse to make their works of much value to the hard-worked parish clergyman, who has too little time to extract the many grains of gold scattered here and there in their writings, and who frequently loses his way amid the disquisitions into which they enter on points—to him at least—of comparatively slight importance.

The author regrets that the valuable works of Professor Westcott and Mr. Plummer had not appeared when he commenced his task. He has therefore only been able to consult them from ch. iii. onwards. Any coincidence of thought in the earlier part of the Commentary has been independently arrived at. Of the admirable work of Haupt, which may be said to mark an epoch in the exegesis of this Epistle, it is impossible to speak too highly.[1] In one or two instances only (especially in ch. v. 6–8) has the present writer ventured on a line of his own, and even then he has but expanded and developed the hints of those who have gone before him.

It may be well to remark that the more the Epistle is studied the more clearly it comes out that anything like a literal application of the strong statements in ch. ii. 20, 27; iii. 9, to the actual present condition of any individual Christian is impossible. It is absolutely necessary in interpreting St. John's meaning to bear in mind the perpetual oscillation throughout the Epistle between the ideal and the practical condition of Christians, between the believer as he might be and the believer as he is. The whole character of the Epistle, in fact, is indicated by ch. ii. 1. "These things we write to you, that ye sin not. And *if any man sin*, we have an Advocate with the Father, Jesus Christ the Righteous."

The repetitions which will be found in some portions of this Commentary were rendered necessary by the circumstances of its original appearance. It is hoped that though they may to some extent injure the form of the work, they will in no way interfere with its usefulness. Such repetitions as are found in the Homiletic section are due to the necessity of producing sketches for single sermons on particular passages.

With these few words of explanation the Commentary is given to the world, in the hope that if it has no other merit, it may at least be found to have made some of the best thoughts of other men, on this most deep and weighty portion of God's Word, more accessible than before.

---

[1] This work has been translated in Messrs. T. & T. Clark's series.

CONTENTS.

		PAGE
I.	INTRODUCTION	1
II.	THE WORD OF LIFE	8
III.	THE MESSAGE	29
IV.	THE FORGIVENESS OF SINS, AND ITS RESULTS	54
V.	DARKNESS AND LIGHT	75
VI.	THE APPEAL TO THE CHRISTIAN	100
VII.	THE OBJECT OF THE APPEAL—LOVE NOT THE WORLD	113
VIII.	THE WORK OF ANTICHRIST	123
IX.	THE EFFECTS OF BELIEF IN THE TRUTH	144
X.	REJECTION AND ACCEPTANCE OF GOD'S REVELATION	153
XI.	THE BLESSING OF ABIDING IN THE TRUTH	165
XII.	THE RIGHTEOUSNESS OF CHRIST TO BE MANIFESTED IN US	177
XIII.	THE PRIVILEGES OF THE CHRISTIAN	191
XIV.	THE FUTURE OF THE CHILDREN OF GOD	202
XV.	PURITY BY ABIDING IN CHRIST	210
XVI.	TRUE HOLINESS	227
XVII.	LOVE THE SIGN OF THE BELIEVER	242
XVIII.	PASSING FROM DEATH UNTO LIFE	257
XIX.	CHRISTIAN ASSURANCE	270
XX.	SPIRITUAL INFLUENCE	287
XXI.	LOVE A DIVINE GIFT	304

	PAGE
XXII. TEACHING OF CHRISTIAN EXPERIENCE	324
XXIII. CHARACTER OF CHRISTIAN EXPERIENCE	335
XXIV. SOURCE OF THE LIFE OF LOVE	349
XXV. UNION WITH CHRIST	363
XXVI. THE THREE WITNESSES	379
XXVII. CONCLUSION OF THE EPISTLE	398

THE FIRST EPISTLE OF ST. JOHN.

I.

INTRODUCTION.

THE genuineness of this Epistle has never been disputed, save in the very wantonness of criticism. Those who desire to see what arguments have been advanced to support foregone conclusions may consult the works of Dean Alford, or, better still, of Dr. Davidson. The absence of any traces, not only of later theological ideas, but even of Pauline influences, the strong similarity between the language of the Epistle and the Gospel, are arguments of the strongest kind for the genuineness of the former. He who by his nature was evidently of a strongly affectionate and meditative disposition, who leaned on his Master's breast at supper, who enjoyed his Master's special and peculiar affection, was sure to reflect, as far as mortal could, the very voice and tone, manner and style, of that Master, and Him alone. Add to this the fact, that the style suggests most strongly the calm repose of age, a repose mingled with an affectionate anxiety (1) that his younger disciples should not listen to the voice of seducers, and (2) should be firmly built up in the Life which flows from the truth and light and love of God; and that it is as far removed from the argumentative mobility of St. Paul as from the business-like (if we may use the term) and practical wisdom of the energetic St. Peter; and we are irresistibly led to the conclusion that none but the beloved disciple could have penned this work, nor even he, except at an advanced age, mellowed and purified by a lifelong meditation on the words and deeds, and looks and tones, of the "Eternal Life, which was with the Father," but was "manifested unto" men. This view is supported by a glance at the Apocalypse. It is outside our province to enter into an examination of the coincidences and differences between the Apocalypse and the acknowledged writings of St. John. Suffice it to say, that a careful examination of the Apocalypse discloses the fact that though it is written in less polished Greek (for even the miraculous gifts of the Apostles were capable of improvement by use), it is yet filled with phrases and turns of thought peculiar to it and the rest of St. John's writings; while the greater animation of the style, and the absence of redundancies such as are frequent in the Gospel and Epistles, betray the less advanced age of the writer.[1] Above all, the fact that in the Gospel and Epistles of St. John and in the Apocalypse only is the significant term Logos applied to our Lord is a strong argument for all having come from the same pen. This confirms the view which has been taken, that the Epistles and Gospel are the product of the very advanced age of the writer. The internal evidence that this Epistle is by St. John is confirmed by the strongest external testimony. Polycarp, St. John's own disciple, quotes, as it is natural he should, his revered teacher's words in his Epistle to the Philippians. And Irenæus, who relates at length in his treatise against heresies his recollections of the

---

[1] Professor Milligan, in his recent able work on the Revelation, takes the opposite view.

venerated and Apostolic man Polycarp, whom he well remembered in his youth, also quotes the Epistle as genuine. It is true that modern critics have denied the genuineness of Polycarp's Epistle; but they have done this with an object, and that object the getting rid of inconvenient early testimony to the genuineness of the Scriptures themselves. Boldly deny the genuineness of every early document which quotes the canonical Scriptures as genuine, and you have disposed of every argument by which the authenticity of those Scriptures can be maintained. The course is perhaps not strictly honest; but it serves the purpose, as can plainly be seen in the current literature of the day, of "beguiling unstable souls," and spreading abroad a vague impression among the indifferent and inexperienced, that the cause of Scripture cannot be defended. Those, however, who desire to see the evidence for the genuineness of the Epistle of Polycarp may consult the masterly papers of the present Bishop of Durham in the *Contemporary Review*, against the pretentious but hollow assertions contained in the volume known as "Supernatural Religion." These will show that even this wholesale method of disposing of the witnesses to Scripture is not without its difficulties, and that the scanty remains of early ecclesiastical literature are sufficient, in the hands of a competent scholar, to dispose of the baseless assumptions and confident assertions of the enemies of Holy Writ.

The object of the Epistle of St. John is clear enough from a perusal of its contents. Yet it is interesting to remark that an early writer (Clement of Alexandria) has confirmed this view of it from tradition in reference to the Gospel, the prologue of which has obviously the same purport. It was the desire of St. John, he says, to confirm his converts in the faith which had been delivered to them, and to preserve them from all who would seduce them from it. And this he did by leaving behind him a record of the authentic teaching of Jesus Christ, such as he had verbally imparted to those who heard him for many years. A similar object is declared in this Epistle. It was to preserve his younger disciples in the Light which God had given. It was to secure them against the fatal Antinomian error, which had begun to spread itself abroad, that men might be disciples of light and yet do the deeds of darkness (ch. iii. 7); it was to warn them of the antichrists whom Jesus had foretold, and who were already come (ch. ii. 18, iv. 3); it was to declare the truth that Jesus and He alone was the Saviour of the world, and that He saved the world only by taking on Him our flesh (ch. iv. 3, 14); and it was to deepen their conviction that the result of the reception of the Life and Light that was in Jesus Christ must be a life of love like His. So close is the resemblance between the Epistle and the prologue to the Gospel that it has led some theologians (Hug, for instance) to suppose that the former was an encyclical Epistle intended as an introduction to the Gospel. For this view, however, there would seem to be little ground. The Gospel is not mentioned. Its contents are nowhere referred to; and the only similarity between the two writings is a similarity of aim, such as might well be found in the works of one whose fundamental doctrine was that Jesus Christ was the Logos or Revelation of God, come down from heaven to cleanse mankind from sin, and restore them to fellowship with God. When this commentary was commenced in 1881 the priority of the Gospel was here maintained. A careful study of the Epistle, and a comparison of ch. v. 13 with John xx. 31, have suggested a different conclusion. The Gospel may, to a certain extent, have been written for those without. The Epistle is clearly addressed to those who are within. Nothing is established, of course, from internal evidence concerning priority of composition. But inasmuch as the Epistle takes the truths contained in the Gospel as its starting-point, and assumes the belief the Gospel endeavours to produce in order to establish the believer more firmly in the truth, the former can hardly have been an introduction to the latter, and may have been the fitting sequel to it.[1]

The precise course of the argument in the Epistle is hard to trace; and yet that there is a meaning in its reiterated repetitions will not be denied by those who study it. Commencing with a brief introduction, the object of which is to show that what the Apostle writes he writes from personal knowledge, he lays down the principle (1) that God is light, and the precise opposite of darkness. He proceeds to explain that the light and darkness he speaks of are not intellectual but moral qualities, and insists (*a*) upon our actual sinfulness; (*b*) upon the duty incumbent upon us of shaking off that sinful condition; and (*c*) upon the fact that there is a propitiation for the sins we *do* commit in Jesus Christ.[2] It will be seen in the notes, we may remark by the way, how exactly the doctrine of St. John corresponds with that of St. Paul, in spite of the extremely different way in which it is stated. In the passage ch. i. 8–ii. 2 we have the doctrine of Justification set forth, as it is more briefly in ch. i. 7. The Apostle now proceeds (2) to insist upon the necessity of justification being no mere formal or forensic process, but the parent of holiness of

---

[1] "The substance of the Gospel is a commentary on the Epistle: the Epistle is, so to speak, the condensed moral and practical application of the Gospel."—Westcott, Introduction.   [2] i. 5–ii. 2.

life. We must keep the commandments; and this involves the expulsion of all feelings of hate against our brother man.[1] We are then (3) warned against exactly the opposite form of evil. We are not to hate our brother, but we are not therefore necessarily to love the principles by which he is actuated. We are not to love the world; still less the denials of Christ which are so prevalent in the world in our time.[2] And then (4) we are invited to behold our sonship and its results, purification from— righteous hatred of—sin.[3] We advance (5) to a consideration of the result of this purification—love. Hate is a passion of the world we have left; a Divine tenderness and compassion is the sign that we have quitted it. Thus, then, we are led to a higher point of view than before. To fulfil God's commandments is to cultivate a spirit of love.[4] A *Spirit*, the Apostle goes on (6). It is a blessed influence breathed in us from above, which we must carefully distinguish from the many evil influences breathed into us from below. That Spirit is the Spirit of love.[5] And (7) He is the Spirit of Christ. He comes to us by a new birth from God. The life we possess, if by the Spirit, is in the Son, and from the Father; so that Father, Son, and Holy Ghost dwell in us.[6] In conclusion, (8) the Apostle gives some practical advice for the realisation of this great truth in ourselves and others. He would have us observe (*a*) that the result of our fellowship with God is the fulfilment of our petitions; (*b*) that *every* sin is not of sufficient gravity to cut men off from the blessed privileges which, as Christians, they enjoy; (*c*) that there *are* sins of sufficient gravity to do so. And he concludes

---

[1] ii. 2-14.   [2] ii. 14-27.   [3] ii. 27-iii. 10.
[4] iii. 11-24.   [5] iv. 1-13.   [6] iv. 14-v. 12.

by a brief summing-up of all that has been said. He that is born or begotten of God is safe from evil, if he will. Others possess not this blessedness; but for ourselves we may rejoice in the thought of our union with the Eternal Truth in Jesus Christ. Rest secure, he says, in this blessedness: reject those vain imaginations of man's fancy which would rob you of the inestimable privileges in your possession; walk warily in these dangerous days, and hold fast the truth. Such is a brief and inadequate summary of the contents of the Epistle. From this brief analysis of the Epistle it appears that the main object of the Apostle's teaching is summed up in two heads. God is LIGHT and God is RIGHTEOUSNESS. That is to say, the moral and spiritual illumination obtained by fellowship with God must issue in holiness of life. This holiness of life, to give a short summary of the second portion of St. John's argument, is to be manifested (1) by active love, and (2) by active resistance to evil influences. And we may best carry out these precepts by remembering (1) that our life as Christians is a new birth from above, which (2) conveys a new principle of life breathed into us by God, through Jesus Christ.

II.

THE WORD OF LIFE.

EXPOSITION.

VER. 1.—**That which was from the Beginning.** We have here an introduction to the Epistle, consisting of the first four verses. The Apostle explains (1) what his *intention* is, to declare the truth concerning the Word of Life. He further insists (2) on his *qualifications* for so doing. He had "heard," had "seen with his eyes," had "looked upon," and his "hands had handled" that which he proposed to proclaim to them. Then (3) he states what is his *object* in making this proclamation. It was that they might share in the blessings which he and other believers in Christ possessed, namely, fellowship (see this word explained below) with the Father and with His Son Jesus Christ. A further result he mentions in ver. 4—the joy resulting from so precious a possession. Before we proceed to explain the words at

---

HOMILETICS.

I. THE WORD OF LIFE THE CENTRE OF THE GOSPEL. 1. *Introduction.* The nature of the Epistle. Addressed to no particular Church. A *Catholic* Epistle, as it is called, addressed generally to any one into whose hands it may fall. Designed specially to meet the needs of Asia Minor at that period; but cast into such a form, by the help of the Holy Spirit, that it has satisfied the needs of Christians ever since. No one can read the Epistle and doubt that here

the head of this paragraph, it may be well to explain the *form* of the introduction. The second verse is parenthetical and explanatory. It contains a more direct mention (1) of what is meant by the words Word of Life, and (2) of the fact that the Apostle was writing from personal observation of that on which he wrote. The next point to which our attention must be directed is, the reason for the neuter gender here. We have not ὅς but ὅ, not *Who*, but *that* or *what*. The explanation must be found in the word περί. The Apostle desires to declare what he knows to be true, what he has heard and seen, *concerning* the Word of Life. Alford explains the form of the sentence as depending loosely upon the rest of the sentence, strictly on ἀκηκόαμεν. Perhaps it would be more true to say that the sentence will not bear strict grammatical analysis, though its scope and meaning is clear enough. St. John desires to bear testimony concerning the Logos; concerning His eternal essence and His manifestation in the Person of the Man Christ Jesus. This is the interpretation of Ebrard and Haupt (whose thoughtful commentary will be often referred to in these pages) as well as of Calvin, Beza, and Düsterdieck. Why does the Apostle, it may be asked, say that he declares something *about* the Logos, and not the Logos Himself? Simply, it may be replied, because the latter is just what he does *not* do. In the Gospel he declares to us the Logos Himself. In the Epistle, though the Logos

---

he has the *essentials* of the faith of Christ. And how is it that the Epistle is Catholic in this sense, that it meets the needs of all classes of men, for all time? This leads us to—

2. *It is the revelation (a) of a Person, (b) of a Life.* (*a*) *Of a Person.* This person is the Logos, or Word of God (cf. St. John i. 1-14). The term Word is insufficient to express St. John's meaning. Logos signifies (1) reason, (2) discourse. The Word subsisted from all eternity as the eternal mind or reason in the bosom of the Father (John i. 1,

is the subject-matter of the whole work, yet it is not strictly the personal Logos whom he sets forth, but the doctrine concerning Him which he knows to be true. We now proceed to observe *what* it is that he so delivers. First of all, he delivers the truth of the eternal existence of Him of whom he is speaking. He proclaims " what *was* from the beginning" concerning Him. We have here not ἐγένετο but ἦν. That these words are not identical is shown by a comparison of St. John i. 1, 2, with 3, 10, 14. The former word refers to things which have a beginning; the latter implies continued existence. He was existing *at* the beginning, we learn from St. John i. 1. He was existing *from* the beginning, we learn here. Not that at any particular time He began to be. No, at any particular time, whenever it might be, He *was*. But the Apostle here says, We declare to you what was the fact about Him from the beginning, a phrase which does not necessarily imply what the Gospel plainly asserts, that He was from all eternity. We next proceed to inquire the meaning of the word **Beginning.** In St. John i. 1 the phrase is equivalent to the Hebrew בְּרֵאשִׁית. Hence it means the very first starting-point of all creation (Ebrard would make the ἀρχή anterior to all creation)—the primeval moment when the idea of self-impartation which dwelt in the Divine Mind from all eternity became a realised fact. This is a more satisfactory meaning than Haupt's alternative

---

2, 18; xiv. 10, 20; Col. i. 15; Heb. i. 3). His first revelation of the Father—He thus becoming the *spoken* Word—was in the act of creation (John i. 3; 1 Cor. viii. 6; Eph. iii. 9; Col. i. 16; Heb. i. 2, ii. 10). His last was in the Dispensation of Restitution, whereby He imparted His Spirit to man to breathe into him the Divine Life. None but a Divine person possessing God's attribute of Omnipotence could save mankind from the condition into which they were fallen: for (*a*) He had to fulfil for man the ideal of perfection he was designed to attain;

suggestion that it may mean "the starting-point of human thought in its way over the creaturely universe." The Epistle does not, we must not fail to observe, here rise to the height of the Gospel. There the eternal pre-existence of the Logos is stated in the clearest possible form. St. John contents himself here with the simple statement that he desires to speak of His existence from the beginning, to represent Him as having been concerned with life and its manifestations throughout all time. Whatever may be the reason for this comparatively meagre statement of the doctrine of the Logos (and it may simply be a desire to avoid repetition) we are not to suppose, with the sceptical school, that the apotheosis of Jesus Christ was the result of an afterthought, the fruit of a long brooding on the beauty and majesty of the character of Jesus, which at last found form in the fourth Gospel. We find as clear statements of the doctrine in Col. i. 15 and Heb. i. 3, 8. St. John was here concerned with the Life that was manifested in Jesus rather than with His Person. When the time came for him to speak of His Person, he states in all its fulness the doctrine he did but dimly indicate before. St. John viii. 44, which may be compared with this passage, does not disprove the view taken above. The devil was "a murderer" from the beginning, *i.e.*, from the time when he began to be (cf. also ch. ii. 13, 14).—**which we have heard.** "What we have *heard, seen, gazed*

---

and (β) He had to translate man from the region of infirmity and failure into that of hope and perfectibility. And this He did by making him partaker of the Divine (cf. θείας κοινωνοὶ φύσεως, 2 Pet. i. 4). In that Divine Person, in the possession of His nature alone, can we escape the sins and infirmities to which our flesh is heir—can we reach that glorious purity and perfection which He alone has rendered or can render possible for us. In ourselves we can but be sinners evermore (W. B. Pope). In Him we are delivered from sin's guilt, from sin's

upon, handled, is a rising gradation," says Braune in "Lange's Commentary." "That which has thus its essence in the eternities has become, to the Apostle and his fellow-apostles, the object of personal and most interior experience" (Haupt). Personal, in that they heard His voice, saw Him with their eyes, touched Him with their hands. Interior, in that what they heard penetrated their souls, and in that the act of perception involved in ἐθεασάμεθα perhaps involves more than mere bodily vision (see below). *We* of course refers to the body of believers, and especially to the "witnesses chosen before of God." So St. Paul, who sometimes speaks of himself personally, more frequently merges his personality in that of the body of men who were engaged in disseminating the Gospel. See 2 Cor. i. 13–20, where he alternately uses the singular or the plural, according as he is speaking of himself personally, or of himself as a minister of Christ. Also the second chapter of that Epistle, where the first person is steadily maintained till the fourteenth verse, where the individual is lost in the messenger of Christ. So St. John here speaks of no individual experience, but, as he explains in verse 3, of an experience common to all believers in Christ.—**which we have seen with our eyes.** St. John's Epistles and Gospel, we are told *ad nauseam* by literary sceptics (in the *Nineteenth Century* for August 1880 this statement was repeated with as much confidence as if scholars like

---

dominion; in Him we become what by nature we are not, "perfect," though only "perfect in Christ Jesus."

(*b*) *Of a life.* (1) We all know that example is better than precept. We may *tell* people how to do things for ever, and they will hardly understand; but let us once *show* them, and all becomes clear. So Jesus Christ did not merely preach to men; He lived the life they were to live, and thus they learned to live it also. But (2) it was not only *a* life, but *the* life, or *life*—the only true or genuine life. Our life apart

Bishop Lightfoot, Drs. Westcott and Sanday had not lately given this theory the *coup de grace*), are forgeries of the second century by men alien to the Jewish school of thought. The fact is that this Epistle, as well as the Gospel (see also my "Doctrinal System of St. John," Appendix iv. p. 272, *sqq.*), literally teems with Hebraisms. Such is the form of expression found here, which, continually as we meet it in the Old Testament, does not occur elsewhere in the New. This appeal to personal vision of the Lord is insisted upon in the most emphatic manner by all the apostles. (See Acts iv. 20, xxii. 15.) And we may infer from 1 Cor. ix. 1, that the absence of such a credential of his ministry was sometimes objected against St. Paul. (See also 1 Cor. xv. 8; and cf. John xx. 8, xxi. 24.)—**which we have looked upon.** "These four members of the sentence form a ladder of three steps" (Ebrard), "a thoroughly fitting climax." The tense is here altered. Nor is this altogether without meaning. We perhaps may not press in Alexandrian Greek the strict classical force of the tenses (see an able article in the *Expositor* by the Dean of Peterborough on this point), though on the other hand we can hardly regard the aorist as the precise equivalent of the perfect. A glance at the Hebrew language may explain in what sense these tenses were to be used. That language had two tenses, a perfect and an imperfect, and the former is used of absolutely completed action, while of uncompleted

---

from God is but a living death—the death first of the spirit, then of the soul, then of the body, so that the nobler part of man first decays, and then the humbler. The only true life is the life of God. And Jesus Christ was the Word who spake that life to us—told us what it was. And as a word once spoken abides in him to whom it is spoken so Christ's revelation of life is an eternal inward possession to him who has heard it with the ears of faith. And thus we come to—

3. *It is not a life external to us, but communicated to us.* Some

action, whether in the past or future, the imperfect was used. In Greek the writer, accustomed to the Hebrew idiom, had a wider choice of tenses, but his Hebrew instincts did not altogether fail him. Thus the perfect is used still of an action which has passed over into the region of things completed and done with. The aorist is used of things which, though now past, extended over an indefinite period of considerable length. Thus their eyes had seen Jesus Christ. That was a completed fact, whether they had seen Him once or a thousand times. But in what follows the reference is to *repeated* action. They saw Him again and again. They gazed upon Him. They filled their souls with His fulness. They saw Him in various circumstances and under various conditions. They saw Him in hunger and thirst and weariness. They also saw Him in the plenitude of His Divine Power, as the worker of miracles, the controller of things seen and things unseen. They saw Him fainting and dying on the Cross. They also saw Him transfigured before His Passion, risen and ascending after it. Thus the tense as well as the meaning of the verb θεάομαι— which, if it does not strictly (with Haupt after Theophylact and Œcumenius) imply wonder or astonishment, has at least the sense of beholding with interest and attention, as in Matt. vi. 1, xxii. 11 ; John i. 14, 32—can hardly be held to exclude a certain idea of mental and spiritual vision, the result of the long con-

---

would have us believe that all Christ did for us was to set us an example. This is the Socinian theory. So far as it is true we gladly accept it. But the poet warns us that "a truth which is half a truth is the greatest lie of all." And Socinianism lands us in one of the most dangerous of half-truths. We must not forget that the New Testament does not fail to proclaim with the utmost emphasis, that the life of Christ is not merely an example offered *to* us, but a principle implanted in us. Our version of the Bible obscures our view of this

templation of His visible Presence on earth. (See, for use of the aorist in this sense, John xvii. 4, 6.)—**which our hands have handled.** One of the minute touches which are evidences of authorship is to be found here. No one could have been a witness of the scene between our Lord and St. Thomas without having the whole event indelibly impressed upon his mind. So here we have a striking reference to that scene; but not to that scene only. In St. Luke xxiv. 39 our Lord invites the disciples to "handle" Him, using the same word that is used here. See also the LXX. in Gen. xxvii. 12, 22. Often must the hands of the disciples have touched the sacred Body of their Lord. And it is to this *repeated* action, no doubt, that the aorist refers.— **of the Word of Life.** St. John, as has already been stated, in his Gospel and Epistle, and in the Apocalypse, is the only one who speaks of Jesus Christ by this term. This fact is itself of extreme significance as implying the common authorship of all three. Of the history and meaning of the expression little can be said here. Those who wish to study it fully will find it discussed in the Prolegomena of almost every writer who treats at any length on the Gospel of St. John. Such books as Neander's "History of the Christian Church" and his "Planting of Christianity" contain much useful information. Dorner, in his "Person of Christ," treats on the subject, and in Canon Liddon's "Bampton Lectures" it

---

truth sometimes by rendering (as in Rom. vi. 23) the Greek *ἐν* by the English *through*. In the Epistle, however, as in the Gospel, the more accurate rendering *in* is maintained. In the Gospel we find this truth enunciated throughout, but especially in chapters vi., xv., xvii. We find it in the Epistle from ch. ii. 24 onward, with ever-increasing definiteness (cf. ch. iv. 4, 15, 16; v. 11, 12, 20). Nor is it absent from our own version of St. Paul's Epistles. (See Eph. i. 23, v. 30; Col. i. 27, iii. 3).

is elucidated with learning and eloquence combined. I
have given a short sketch of the history of the expression
in the "Doctrinal System of St. John," Part i. ch. ii.
As regards its meaning, it would seem to be the only
expression which could embody what it was St. John's
desire to convey. For the word Logos signifies both
thought itself and the expression of thought. It is
both *reason* and *discourse*. Thus therefore it involves
in itself the two ideas which theologians learned to
express by the terms λόγος ἐνδιάθετος and λόγος
προφορικός, that is to say, the Son as He subsists in
the bosom of the Father, and as He streams forth thence
to impart Him in creation, and to reveal Him to those
who do not yet perceive Him as they ought. (See Suicer,
Thesaurus, s. v. λόγος.) And we have here not merely
the remarkable term Logos—referring to the twofold
aspect of the Logos as being Himself very and Eternal
God, and the means whereby the Divine Essence imparts
itself (no words are adequate to explain or even to express this mystery) beyond itself—but the words "Logos
of Life." We must not forget that we are here dealing
with Hebraistic Greek. Commentators like Alford, in
protesting against the "miserable hendiadys," have forgotten that the genitive in Hebrew is more intimately
associated with the noun on which it depends, as quali-
fying its meaning, than in Greek or any modern language.
It usually stands in the place of the adjective, for there

---

4. *It is communicated to us by certain means.* The one primary
means is faith, without which all other means are useless. Faith is
the medium whereby we place ourselves *en rapport* with the celestial
impulse. Faith is the electric wire which connects heaven with earth,
and makes our lives sensitive and responsive to influences from above.
Without faith, what are known as the means of grace are like the
apparatus of the telegraph when the electric current is absent—mere
dead, lifeless machinery. Yet without these means the electric current

are comparatively few adjectives in Hebrew. If, therefore, the expression the "Logos of Life" be not the precise equivalent of "the living Logos" (as Grotius, De Wette, and Ewald interpret), it must mean the Logos whose chief function it is to impart life, the Logos between whom and life there exists a peculiar and inseparable relation. This is the leading idea of St. John's Gospel. Life was the essential principle of the Logos (John i. 4). It was to give life that Christ came (ch. x. 10), to give life to His sheep (ch. x. 28). He gave it to whom He willed (ch. v. 21); for He was Himself the Life (ch. xi. 25, xiv. 6). The phrase "the Logos of Life," as signifying His impartation of life, is compared by Alford and Haupt with the phrase, the "Bread of Life," in John vi., where the genitive clearly means the bread which possesses the property of giving life. It is not, as we have seen, with the Person of the Logos that St. John is here concerned, except so far as it is connected with the life which is the subject of his whole Epistle.

Ver. 2.—**For the life was manifested.** This verse is parenthetical, as is at once seen by those familiar with the Hebrew construction, in which dependent sentences are frequently introduced by the simple copulative. The καί here, therefore, is not altogether incorrectly rendered in our version by *for*. St. John now explains what he

---

would be wasted, would not be able to make itself felt. And so, without the means Christ has blest, faith itself would fail to exert its influence. And these means are threefold, *prayer, sacraments,* and the *study of God's oracles.*

5. *It issues in actions consonant to the will of God.* We need not enter into the endless controversy concerning faith and works, but simply state that if what we call faith do not produce results in conformity with Him in whom we believe, it is not faith at all. The life of Christ, if it dwell in us, must show its presence by *being* the life of

means by the allusions in the last verse to seeing and hearing about the Word of Life. We have seen and heard about it, because it was manifested in the Person of Jesus Christ. It was manifested primarily in His earthly life and conversation; but secondly and chiefly by the incontrovertible proof given that He was the Word of Life by His Resurrection from the dead. It is not said that the life became flesh (Haupt), for life was not the Logos or Divine Person, but simply one of His attributes. But through the incarnation of the Logos it was (John i. 14) that men were able to discern the glory of the life that He gave. We may observe, by comparing John i. 4 with this chapter, how closely the train of thought here is connected with that of the Gospel. Light is an attribute of life, as life of the Logos. And the result of the life is the enlightenment of the conscience, as we see in a later portion of this chapter. Bishop Wordsworth remarks on the similar expression relating to the incarnation in 1 Tim. iii. 16.—**and we have seen it, and bear witness and shew unto you.** The word *it* should not be inserted. All three verbs are closely connected with the words *that eternal life*. There is a threefold gradation here. First the Apostle sees the life himself; then he bears general testimony to it wheresoever he goes; lastly he declares it specially to those to whom the Epistle is addressed. These words $\mu\alpha\rho\tau\upsilon\rho\acute{\epsilon}\omega$,

---

Christ in us; if not, there is no life of Christ dwelling in us. Its free course will no doubt be hindered by the antagonistic influences of our lower nature; but if it be in us it must be destroying those hindrances and bringing us every day nearer to what Christ is. Thus, then, we look for the evidence of Christ's presence in the heart to the signs of His directing and controlling influence producing a likeness to Him in thoughts, opinions, actions, motives, character. This is the only result that can be produced by a true faith in the Word of Life.

II. THE BELIEVER MUST HAVE EXPERIMENTAL PROOF OF THE

μαρτυρία, are eminently characteristic of all St. John's writings, as the most cursory perusal will show. They occur more often in his writings than in the whole of the rest of the New Testament. We may compare John xxi. 24 with Rev. xxii. 20. (See also Rev. i. 2, 9, vi. 9, xi. 7, xii. 11, &c., and compare with the Gospel *passion* and with ch. v. 9–11 of this Epistle.) The word *shew* is frequently used to translate the derivatives of ἀγγέλλω (as in 1 Cor. xi. 25), but the more correct translation would be *declare*. *Shew*, however, had this meaning when our version was made, as, for instance, "Shew these things unto James and to the brethren" (Acts xii. 17).—**that eternal life.** More literally, perhaps, *the life which is eternal*—the life whose principal attribute it is to be eternal, or rather ever-being, the word αἰώνιος denoting not so much the endlessness of life as its stability, its fixedness, its vastness from every point of view, that of endurance and every other, its unchangeableness as contrasted with the shifting conditions of everything in time.—**which was with the Father,**—literally, *which existed towards the Father.* It is impossible to give the force of the preposition in English. The verb signifies, as we have seen above, continued existence; but the use of πρός here, which is distinct from παρά or σύν, contains a great meaning in itself. It has been rightly held to imply a distinction of Persons in the

---

TRUTH OF THE GOSPEL. St. John speaks of what he has heard and seen and his hands have handled. Is there no such possibility for us? Has the believer of later times no evidence to which he can personally appeal before he proclaims to others that communion with God that he himself enjoys? Far from it. The experience of every one who has striven to serve Christ will supply him with abundance of argument.

1. There is *what we have heard*. "We have heard with our ears, O Lord, and our fathers have told us, what Thou hast done in their

Trinity; but it also casts light upon the mutual relations of those Persons. It not only means (as Bishop Wordsworth *in loc.*), "united to the Father and ever abiding *in* and *with* Him." It involves the truth that "the Face of the Everlasting Word, if we may dare to so express ourselves, was ever *directed towards* the Face of the Everlasting Father" (Liddon, "Bampton Lectures," v. p. 342). It indicates "the significant fact of perpetual intercommunion" (*Ib.*) It teaches the truth of a "perpetual turning to Him" (Haupt). In fact, it sums up in one striking and pregnant word the whole teaching of John xvii. See John i. 1, and note the fact that the use of this preposition in each, in this particular connection, is sufficient to establish the common authorship of the two books, since St. John himself often uses παρά (see ch. vi. 46, xvii. 5).—**and was manifested to us**—in order to bring mankind within the sphere of that Eternal Unity and Love.

VER. 3.—**That which we have seen and heard declare we unto you.** It is one of the shortcomings of our version that it renders the same Greek word by different English ones, sometimes without adequate cause, and thus frequently obscures the sense. This is the case here. The word here translated *declare* is the same as that translated *shew* in the last verse. The Apostle, in a different manner to St. Paul, but with the same intent, resumes the main current of thought, yet at the same time in-

---

time of old." Under this head the whole of the treasures of history and biography are open to us, and the treasures of illustration regarding what the Word of Life has done for others are practically infinite.

2. There is *what we have seen*, what we know from our own experience.

3. *Our hands have handled the Word of Life.* The contact is no longer physical but spiritual, but contact there is. We lay hold of Christ with the hands of faith. In prayer, in praise, in meditation, in spiritual communion with Him in the Sacrament of His love, we feel

cluding the subsidiary idea introduced in his parenthesis. Many of the old MSS. read καί after ἀπαγγέλλομεν, *declare we also unto you*, not, as Alford would suppose, that the Epistle was addressed to any special circle of readers, but that St. John felt himself impelled by a necessity not to keep to himself what he had seen and heard, but to declare it to others also (cf. Acts iv. 20). The position of καί in the sentence is explained by the fact that if it had been placed before the verb it would have been the simple copula. Or we may hold with Haupt, "that the first καί" (the one of which we are now speaking) implies "the community of the *announcement*," as the second, that before ὑμεῖς, "implies the community and equality of the *blessing* which should be the fruit of the announcement."—**that ye also may have fellowship with us.** The invariable object of all true Christians is to communicate to others the blessings they possess. This was the Divine object in creation; this is the object of Jesus in redemption; this is the one unfailing characteristic of the true disciple of Christ, as contrasted with mere external professors of His religion. The word *fellowship* or *communion* (it is a pity it is translated by two different words, and the verb formed from it yet more loosely, *e.g.*, Rom. xii. 13, xv. 27) is one of the most important words in the New Testament. It is therefore essential that it should be fully under-

---

Him near us.[1] "We stretch lame hands of faith and grope," and we hear His voice bidding us put our finger into the print of the nails, and to thrust our hand into His side, and not be faithless, but believing. Thus in many ways we

"'scan His features well;'
And know Him for the Christ by proof—
Such proof as they are sure to find
Who spend with Him their happy days."—*Keble, Christian Year.*

[1] "Here, O my Lord, I see Thee face to face;
Here would I touch and handle things unseen."—*H. Bonar.*

stood. Some have asserted that it is confined in the New Testament to communion with God; but this, as Haupt remarks, is refuted by Acts ii. 42. What is meant by it is the *common possession* of anything by various persons. Aristotle ("Ethics," iv. 8) uses it as almost equivalent to *interchange*. St. John here states that he declares what he has seen and heard to those whom he is addressing that it may henceforth be a common possession between him and them. The use of $\mu\epsilon\tau\acute{\alpha}$ rather than $\sigma\acute{\upsilon}\nu$ here implies that this common possession is placed as it were *between* those who share it; and does not involve here the idea of combination or conjunction, which is, however, inseparable from the idea of a common life, but rather that of *equality* in the possession.—**and truly our fellowship.** Our version is here strictly accurate in its rendering of $\kappa\alpha\acute{\iota}$ $\delta\acute{\epsilon}$. Wordsworth paraphrases by *and, remember*. The word *our* is emphatic, and may either refer to the apostles and ministers of the Word or to the whole Christian community. Ebrard explains, "The communion in which we already stand, and into which we desire to introduce you."—**is with the Father and with His Son Jesus Christ.** Here the same preposition is used, and suggests the amazing condescension of the Father and the Son in putting us in a way on a level with themselves, in condescending to share with us their privileges. The

---

III. WHAT WE KNOW OURSELVES WE MUST IMPART TO OTHERS. "What we have seen and heard declare we unto you," says St. John. Here we learn two truths—

1. *The Word of Life is free and expansive.* The word spoken must be for others to hear. It were useless to speak it otherwise. Therefore the Word of God must be spoken, must be the revelation of God, that is, to all to whom He has given ears to hear it, to all mankind. It is its essential character to be diffused and diffusing. If it be in us at all, it cannot be kept within our own hearts. It must burn, it must

double repetition of μετά, as Alford reminds us, declares the eternal distinction of person between the Father and the Son, their association together here, the equality of their Divine Essence. He goes on to ask why the Holy Spirit is not here mentioned. But he does not give, we venture to think, the right reply, which is, that this would be to anticipate the teaching concerning the Spirit, which is introduced in ch. iii. 24 (cf. John xvii. 21 and ch. ii. 24). The doctrine here laid down, or rather indicated —it is not taught explicitly till ch. v. 11—is the central doctrine of the Gospel, which is the source whence the morality of the three Synoptic Gospels is derived, which permeates all the Epistles, which flows from the lips of Jesus Christ Himself, as St. John tells us in his Gospel, and especially in ch. xvii. God is pleased to communicate to us, through His Son and by His Spirit, His *own life*. This He did in a degree by creation. But He has now been pleased through a second creation, the Incarnation of Jesus Christ, to impart to us that life in a far higher degree of perfection; so that, in a moral and spiritual sense that was not true before Christ came, we are partakers of the life that dwells in the Father and in His Son Jesus Christ.

VER. 4.—**And these things write we unto you.** The *we* here relates to the Apostle as one of a body, and that body composed of the ministers of Christ. He does not

---

struggle to communicate itself to others. We cannot rest satisfied without endeavouring, according to our circumstances and opportunities, to bring others to the knowledge of what we know ourselves. If there be no such ardent feeling, we have not yet appropriated the Word of Life by faith. If we have, we must in our measure feel with St. Paul that "necessity is laid upon us, yea, woe unto us if we preach not the Gospel." Our call is in various ways. Some have the humbler task of aiding relations and friends to live the new life. Some have a wider influence over scholars, or workmen, or dependents. Some as

stand alone, either in the life which he shares with the Father and the Son, or in the message he delivers, which was entrusted by Jesus Christ to no one individual, but to His Church. Alford reads here ἡμεῖς for ὑμῖν, and ἡμῶν for ὑμῶν in the second member of the sentence. The rule that the harder reading should be preferred is no doubt, on the whole, a sound one; but to apply it universally would lead to serious mistakes. The mistake of a careless copyist, reading H for Y and the like, would force us to rob a passage like this of all its meaning. Thus what force has the emphatic ἡμεῖς here, where St. John is not drawing a contrast between himself and some one else? And why should he write in order to fulfil his *own* joy, when, as we have seen in the last verse, his object was to impart to others what he himself enjoyed? The substitution of ἡμεῖς and ἡμῶν for ὑμῖν and ὑμῶν is a common one, and easily made—more easily made still if, as is not improbable, the scribe were writing from dictation. We should, therefore, hesitate to sanction an alteration which, though it has high MS. authority, seems unsupported by the still higher authority of the earlier versions, and certainly renders a much worse sense. A similar difficulty occurs in 2 Cor. vii. 12, where some editors read, "That *your* care for *us* might appear unto you."[1]

[1] This note has been printed as originally written. The great authority of Professor Westcott has declared in favour of the reading rejected, but

---

persons of education and position have a wider sphere still. Some undertake the special care of the young, or the evangelisation of the wicked and degraded, or the reclaiming of the fallen. Some, again, are ministers of Christ, some His messengers to the heathen. But all in their appointed place must impart to others the knowledge they have received. But—

2. *We cannot speak of what we have never known.* If the life and peace of the Gospel, the sense of being reconciled to God and in His favour, the sense of a power within us which is superior to sin, be

that your joy may be full. It is impossible to render this passage otherwise, unless, perhaps, we substitute *fulfilled*, as a more emphatic term, for *full*. Yet the use of the perfect participle in Greek gives a sense which nothing but a paraphrase can convey. The Collect in the Morning service of the Church of England says, "In whose service is perfect freedom." It is some such idea as this that the words at the head of this note convey in the original. In the knowledge of God's truth there is fulness of joy. Hitherto the joy of those to whom St. John writes had not been "full," because, as the Epistle throughout implies, they had as yet been but partially instructed in the Gospel. But when they had fully learned the truth "as it is in Jesus," the result would be a joy perfected and fulfilled, as of men living from henceforth in the full possession of Him, "in whose presence is fulness of joy, and at whose right hand there are pleasures for evermore" (Ps. xvi. 11). It will be observed that St. John goes on to explain in the next verse *how* their joy will attain this condition of perfect fulness. It is through the truth, briefly enunciated there, and then pursued in detail up to ch. ii. 11, that

---

with the admission that "the confusion of ἡμ- with ὑμ- in the MSS. is so constant that a positive decision is impossible." Internal evidence is strong (see last verse) in favour of ὑμῶν. But ἡμεῖς is very probably the true reading. "These things *we* write, that *your* joy may be fulfilled."

---

absent, how can we take upon ourselves to proclaim Christ at all? Better be eternally silent than to speak what we do not know to be true. We must have heard Him and seen Him, and our hands must have handled Him, before we can communicate Him to others. What sin and shame, then, were it to undertake the solemn duty of teaching the young the truths of religion, the proclaiming Him from a Christian pulpit, from any other motive than our personal knowledge of Him as a living God, a Word of Life! A mere theoretical acquaintance with Christian doctrine, a familiarity with the Bible, an intellectual know-

God is *absolute light*, in the fullest sense of the term. In the Gospel St. John wavers between the aor. and the perf. in this phrase (cf. ch. iii. 29, xvi. 24, with xv. 11). In the two former passages it signifies the *perfection*, in the latter (see the view maintained of the aorist above) the *abiding nature* of the joy. Joy (Gal. v. 22) is one of the necessary fruits of the Spirit. St. Paul's writings are as full of it as St. John's. And this may well be, as it formed a considerable part of the Saviour's message, as of its foreshadowing in the prophets. And how should it be otherwise? How should the inestimable blessing that our sins are covered and not imputed to us, that there is henceforth no condemnation for us, that we are accepted in the beloved, be any other than a fount of joy? It is wonderful that the religion of Christ should ever have been allied with sourness, gloominess, or austerity. Such an alliance can only have been due to a remarkable perversion of its nature. For the Christian should have joy within as a consequence of the reconciliation with God in Christ Jesus; joy without in consequence of that reconciliation; joy in the external universe, because it, too, has been sanctified through Christ; joy in science and philosophy and literature and art (so far as these last are pure), because all these are various phases of the revelation of God. An inner fount

---

ledge of the deep things of theology, will not satisfy souls hungering for the Bread of Life.

IV. JOY IS THE RESULT OF THE PROCLAMATION OF THE GOSPEL. The knowledge of Christ must needs produce a heavenly joy; for it is the knowledge (1) of the forgiveness of our sins, original and actual, (2) of our reconciliation to God, (3) of the power which enables us to tread sin and Satan under foot; (4) it is the knowledge of a future life; and (5) it is the knowledge of Him "in whose presence is fulness of joy, and at whose right hand there is pleasure for evermore." Thus

of joy, continually welling up from within, and overflowing to refresh all without who come within the sphere of its influence—this should be the unfailing effect of all genuine Christianity.

Before we leave the subject of this introductory portion of the Gospel we should not fail to observe, with Braune, on the close resemblance in form between this prologue and that of the Gospel. Not only have we, as has been observed, the use of the word Logos here, and the statement that He subsists πρὸς τὸν πατέρα. Not only have we the ἀπ' ἀρχῆς here as the correlative of the ἐν ἀρχῇ there. But if here we have ἐθεασάμεθα, we find the same word in John i. 14. If here the life ἐφανερώθη, and God (ver. 5) is φῶς or Light, there we read that the life was the light of men, and that the light φαίνει, in a darkness which does not comprehend it. Here is proof enough of common authorship. The similarity of thought is evident enough, and yet there is no exact copy of the phrases such as betrays the imitator. Bishop Wordsworth, we may remark before dismissing the subject, leads us farther. He shows, from the style of the phrases in this chapter (especially in ver. 5 and vers. 8–10), that the writer was permeated with the style of the Hebrew poetry. Perhaps this line of argument has been carried too far, but the verses which have been quoted

---

joy is one of the fruits of the Spirit. Thus the Saviour prophesies that we shall rejoice in Him (John xv. 11, xvi. 20, 22). Thus his Apostle bids us "rejoice evermore" (1 Thess. v. 16; cf. Phil. iv. 4). And another Apostle bids us count it all joy when we fall into divers temptations (James i. 2). Nothing was so characteristic of the first Christians as the fulness of joy they ever carried about with them; not the noisy mirth which is "as the crackling of thorns under a pot," but the serene, tranquil joy of a heart that is filled with His sweetness, who is life for evermore.

have the true ring of the Hebrew parallelism in them. We have thus strong presumptive evidence that the writer was the person he represents himself to be, a Jew familiar with the writings of his nation, and imbued with their spirit.

III.

THE MESSAGE.

EXPOSITION.

THE introduction completed, which states (1) the subject, (2) the purpose of the Epistle, the Apostle proceeds to unfold with greater fulness the message with which he is charged. He then commences the explanation of this message. Light and darkness, he explains, are *moral* rather than *intellectual* qualities. The light is not that of *reason*, but of *holiness*. The fellowship of which he has spoken is consistent only with a life of purity (ver. 6). That life of purity not only affects the future, but the past; for he who lives it obtains the pardon of past sin through the blood of Christ (ver. 7). It involves the consciousness of past sin, from which none can be free (vers. 8, 10); and the acknowledgment of this constitutes in the Christian a title to forgiveness (ver. 9).

VER. 5.—**This, then, is the message.** The received text has *promise* (ἐπαγγελία), but as our version has translated

---

HOMILETICS.

VER. 5.—*The Christian Message.* We are to observe—
I. THAT IT IS A MESSAGE. (1.) The philosophers of old, with some noble exceptions, used their doctrine as a means of enriching themselves. Justin Martyr has left it on record how general this conduct

message (ἀγγελία) no obscurity has arisen from the difference of reading. It will be observed how entirely the Apostles of Christ, like His forerunner (Matt. iii. 11; Mark i. 8; Luke iii. 16; John i. 20, 27, iii. 28, 30), sunk their personality in that of their Master. No desire for their own advantage animates them. Theirs is a message concerning Another. The wisdom they preach is not their own, but His that sent them. The kingdom they come to found exalts Him above measure, but does not exalt them in the least in a worldly sense. The only pre-eminence they claim is a pre-eminence in labours and sufferings (1 Cor. iv. 9; 2 Cor. vi. 5, xi. 23–28). This humility and unselfishness is a necessary characteristic both of Christ's ministers and of His disciples. "*This*" is rightly made emphatic in our version. The Apostle desires to call special attention to the message.—**which we have heard of him.** "*Of* Him" is the usual expression in our version for "by Him." (Cf. "seen of Cephas," 1 Cor. xv. 5.) Here it is equivalent to "from Him," as in Gal. i. 12, iv. 4. The Greek shows that it is not a message *about* Christ, but received *from* Christ. Here again we see the exaltation of Christ. They could not speak without His authority. Their highest teaching was a message from Him. And this was quite consistent, for they believed Him to be no mere messenger sent from God, but the Word of God Himself, who had subsisted in the bosom of the Father from all eternity. The only claim their doctrine had upon the attention of

---

was in his time. (2.) The teachers of the Christian Church have at various times regarded their position in a similar light. They have (*a*) treated it as an avenue to preferment, power, and influence—have sought to become temporal princes, to amass wealth, to stand high in the favour of kings, to exercise temporal authority. Or (*b*) they have sought to gain favour with their flocks by preaching such doctrine as

those to whom it was delivered was this. It was no evolution of their own reasoning faculties; it was a message from Eternal Wisdom itself.—**and declare unto you.** Or rather, perhaps, "*report* we unto you" (Erasmus, in his paraphrase, explains by *renuncio*). The distinction is not of much importance, but the Greek is more vivid than our version, and gives the idea of a message received and transmitted.—**that God is light, and in him is no darkness at all.** The form in which this sentence is cast is essentially Hebraic; compare, for instance, such a passage as Judges viii. 11, 12. When a Hebrew desired to attract special attention to what he said, he was accustomed to repeat the words a second time in an altered form. In fact, this passage, like all impassioned utterances in the Hebrew Scriptures, presents the phenomenon familiar to us in the parallelism of Hebrew poetry. So utterly without foundation is the popular assertion, that the writers of the works going by St. John's name were evidently Ephesine Gentiles! The most cursory examination of these writings proves them to be literally saturated with Hebrew peculiarities. Proceed we to unfold the meaning of this saying, and here we observe (1) *that this doctrine is a special characteristic of revealed religion.* It permeates the Old and New Testament alike. It appears only by inference in the Mosaic writings, though light or fire was a continual concomitant of the Divine appearances. But we meet it everywhere in the Psalms. "In Thy light shall we see light" (Ps. xxxvi. 9);

---

was agreeable to them—softening down the unpalatable features of the Gospel, doctrinal or practical, suppressing its testimony against wrong-doing, concealing their own convictions when they knew they would be unpopular, joining the cry against unpopular doctrines because they knew it was expected of them—generally, like the false prophets of old, giving in to the cry ever ready to be raised, "Speak

"O send out Thy light and Thy truth" (Ps. xliii. 3). In the Book of Job we read, "enlightened with the light of the living" (ch. xxxiii. 30; cf. ver. 28). Christ's coming is to the prophets the coming of the light. "The people that walked in darkness saw a great light" (Isa. ix. 2). He bids men "arise, shine, for their light is come" (ch. lx. 1). Here, too, we may see the prevalence of Hebrew ideas in this alleged non-Judaic writer. And the New Testament, written, as is admitted (perhaps with the exception of St. Luke's Gospel), by Jews, furnishes us with the same imagery in every one of its writers. To take one instance out of many from St. Paul, we may cite 1 Thess. v. 5: "Ye are all the children of light, and the children of day: we are not of the night, nor of darkness." Nor can we omit to notice the passage (1 Tim. vi. 15) where God is said to "inhabit the unapproachable light." St. James carries the idea still farther. In speaking of God as the "Father of the lights" ($\tau\hat{\omega}\nu$ $\phi\acute{\omega}\tau\omega\nu$) he must surely mean of all kinds of light, physical, intellectual, moral, and thus in one deep and pregnant sentence to include all the teaching we have here. A no less striking passage is to be found in St. Peter's First Epistle (ch. ii. 9), where he speaks of men as being "called out of darkness unto God's marvellous light." And all these are connected with, and dependent on, Christ's own repeated declaration that He was the light of the world (cf. also John i. 4). We may observe here how we owe to St. John three pregnant

---

unto us smooth things, prophesy deceits." Or (c) they may make it an opportunity of gaining renown for themselves by enunciating startling paradoxes, dangerous novelties, opposed to the simplicity of the Gospel, savouring of this world's wisdom, rather than the things which the Holy Ghost teaches, like the teachers at Corinth. The Christian preacher must be none of these. He must be sustained (and

sentences, each summing up in the briefest possible form some essential attribute of God: "God is Spirit" (John iv. 24; not *a* Spirit, as in our version), "God is light," and "God is love."[1] We next note (2) *the glorious conception which we thus learn to form of God.* Whether we consider natural light in itself, or in its effects, it is the grandest thing in nature. Nothing is purer, lovelier, more beautiful, more brilliant in its essence. (See Dean Alford's note here.) And when we come to consider it in its effects, we are still more struck by its universality, its power, its energy, as a type of Him from whom it emanates. Without it knowledge, even life itself, would be impossible. When we see the sun rising in his brightness, and waking all nature into life and activity, we seem to see an image of the glory of the Creator when He called the worlds into being. When we reflect on the threefold nature of light, its enlightening, its warming, its chemical powers, we are reminded of the Holy Trinity —the unapproachable Light Himself, His Eternal revealer, bringing light to earth and quickening by His genial warmth the frozen hearts of men, and the Eternal Spirit, dwelling in their hearts, and slowly bringing His healing influences to bear upon their diseased souls. And (as Braune remarks in his Commentary) without light we could not even think. We could not discern those distinctions of things without which thought is impossible.

[1] See Dr. Westcott's Commentary *in loc.* It may be necessary to add that the words in the text stand as they were printed in 1881.

---

we may instance Edward Irving, whatever we may think of his eccentricities, as a remarkable modern instance of a man of this character) by a lofty conviction that he has a message to deliver from God. He must seek conference with those who "were apostles before him," "lest by any means he should run, or had run, in vain"—that is, he must be careful to base his teaching on the Scriptures. But he must

And thus physical light is the very source of intellectual light, and upon it are based those triumphs of human reason on which man is apt sometimes to vaunt himself. But (3) we must not confine our conceptions of light to intellectual illumination. *The light of which revelation speaks is moral and spiritual.* "John's speculation or mysticism is so thoroughly ethical that he is solely concerned with the practical working out of the truth, 'God is light'" (Braune, in Lange's Commentary). The ancient Greeks thought of light as a quality of the reason simply, and as being obtained through argument and discussion; and many a modern philosopher, when he speaks of enlightenment, means such enlightenment as education and scientific research have been able to attain. But the Scriptures have from the beginning regarded that as the highest light which taught us the distinction between right and wrong—which displayed us the Father of the Lights upon His throne, enabled us to see Him—at least in a measure—as He is, and to discern as right what is in harmony with Him, and as wrong what is out of harmony with Him. And of this much we may be sure, that intellectual light without moral is darkness; that knowledge is profitless unless the heart that possesses it is sanctified by the Presence of the Eternal, and that, therefore, the light which above all others is most necessary for us is that which we obtain in His Son Jesus Christ. One final characteristic of light claims our attention. It is one of its essential properties to com-

---

make it his own by diligent prayer and study. Fully convinced that in God's Holy Word the truth is to be found, he must saturate himself with its contents, and go forth and proclaim its message to the world.

II. THAT IT IS TO BE DECLARED TO OTHERS. That (1) it must be declared by God's ministers is an obvious truth, which requires no

municate itself. It cannot remain self-enfolded. So in the beginning God began the work of creation, of self-impartation. And so for ever He gives Himself to His creatures, creating, sustaining them, filling them with Himself. This also cannot be neglected in the explanation of a passage which, as Haupt remarks, is intended to convey to us a conception of the Divine Essence. On the other hand, we should not fail to observe that darkness is the precise opposite of all this. It is the absence of warmth, motion, life. It is the blackness of utter nothingness. It is impossible even for misery to exist in its chill embrace; misery is but the premonitory symptom of its approach. And therefore it is utterly incompatible with the Being of Him, who is all joy and warmth, boundless energy and unceasing love. And once more, darkness is the opposite to light in its communicative property. Darkness cannot communicate itself; it has nothing to communicate. And so, though evil example has in a sense a tendency to spread, yet the children of darkness have in reality nothing to give, or if they had, they would not give it. A cold, hard, barren selfishness, which frets at another's good, and rejoices only in his misfortune, is characteristic of the kingdom of evil. It is the incarnation, if incarnation it can be called, not of love, but of hate.

VER. 6.—**If we say that we have fellowship with him.** Rather, if we *should* say. St. John does not mean to imply that it is likely that those he addresses would say

---

enforcement, at least theoretically, though practically some of them fail to realise it in any but a purely formal sense. But (2) it is not so generally accepted that upon *every* Christian lies this responsibility. In choosing times and places, a spirit of prudence must be sought from on high. That spirit of pride which assumes to itself the right to question and to lecture everybody on matters of the deepest privacy

this, though (see next note) it often was said. The construction, as Alford reminds us, is continued as far as ch. ii. 1. For "fellowship" see note on ver. 3. Cf. also, for the expression, ch. ii. 4.—**and walk in darkness**,—in the unprofitable, selfish, useless, worthless life that has been mentioned. As Bishop Wordsworth (whose Commentary is valuable for the light it throws upon the historical aspect of this Epistle) reminds us, there were many who did say this. The earlier Gnostics, the followers of Simon and of Nicolaus (Rev. ii. 6, 15, &c.; cf. 2 Peter ii. 15; Jude 11, remembering that Balaam is the Hebrew equivalent for Nicolaus), were continually saying it. It was their favourite doctrine that the flesh was so corrupt that no filthiness of life could affect it, and that the Gnostic who gave his soul to philosophic and mystical contemplation might safely do what he pleased with his body. They even went so far, in their capacity of seekers after knowledge (Gnostics), as to affirm that practical experience of wickedness was necessary to true enlightenment—an argument which it is to be feared has not been confined to their day. What is meant by walking in darkness is further explained in ch. ii. 11 (see also John xii. 35). The word *walk*, as is well known, is a Hebraism for the whole life. Cf. Ps. cxix. 3: "For they who do no wickedness *walk* in Thy ways." So also Ps. i. 1.—**we lie.** The most emphatic contradiction is here given to this doctrine. It is a *lie*, and comes from the father of lies (cf. ch. iii. 7). There

---

or the highest moment, savours rather of Pharisaic pride than of Gospel humility. Yet on every one there lies the duty, at proper times, of handing on to others the message we have received. And let it not be forgotten that one most effectual way of doing this is by aiding, to the utmost of our power, the efforts that are being made to spread Christianity at home or abroad.

is no other way of attaining fellowship with God than by purifying our hearts from evil, and inclining them to obey God's laws. Cf. 2 Cor. vi. 14, where the same idea finds a different expression.— **and do not the truth.** As Ebrard says, we are not only said not to *say*, but not to *do*, the truth. The expression is a remarkable one, yet it is not without warrant elsewhere. St. Paul speaks of "obeying the truth" (Gal. iii. 1). And it admits of a clear explanation when we remember that Christ is the truth (John xiv. 6; cf. viii. 46). Thus, then, the truth must not only be spoken, but acted. For, after all, truth is no other than that which is actually existing. To do the truth, therefore, is to live the life of Christ, to conform oneself to the eternal type of righteousness existing in heaven. See also John iii. 20, 21, where to do the truth is opposed to doing evil. Nothing could more clearly show how truth is to be a principle permeating our very lives. It is not to be displayed in words, but in action. Our whole lives are to be consistent and sincere, challenging the closest inspection, even as St. Paul bids us "keep our continual feast with the unleavened bread of transparent purity and truth" (1 Cor. v. 8). We may observe here how utterly abhorrent to the mind of Christ is that casuistry which makes truth worthless, save so far as it conduces to the cause of the Church. Falsehood *cannot* serve God's cause, because it is the denial of Him. The distinction suggested by Haupt between $\pi o \iota \epsilon \hat{\iota} \nu \; \tau \grave{\eta} \nu \; \grave{a} \lambda \acute{\eta} \theta \epsilon \iota a \nu$

III. WHAT THE MESSAGE IS. For the treatment of this point see Exposition.
IV. PRACTICAL CONSEQUENCES OF THIS. The duty of (1) honouring the great and glorious Being who is thus declared to us; (2) valuing as we ought the Revelation which makes Him known; (3) seeking the intellectual, moral, and spiritual light thus given.

and ποιεῖν τὰ ἀληθῆ is perhaps well founded. The Apostle, by using the former expression, probably means to imply that the actions of him who walks in darkness are not merely individually irreconcilable with truth, but are as a whole founded on a negation of the eternal verities of existence.

VER. 7.—**But if we walk in the light, as he is in the light.** The most remarkable point in this verse seems to have been lost sight of by every recent commentator but Ebrard, who rightly points out the difference between the finite being *walking*, changing his place from day to day, in the light, and God *existing* in the light.[1] Light, in ver. 5, is identified with God. Here, as in 1 Tim. vi. 15, it is regarded as the atmosphere in which He dwells. Doubtless there is here an accommodation to the nature of the thought. We are regarded as dwelling in an atmosphere of light; and as our fellowship with God is the root-idea of the passage, God is described as likewise dwelling in the light, to bring out more clearly the fact that we are made one with Him. —**we have fellowship one with another.** What might have been expected was, "we have fellowship with Him." So clear is this, that some MSS. and Versions have ventured to correct the text here to αὐτοῦ. But the Apostle's object is intensely practical (see ch. iii. 17).

[1] Professor Westcott has traced this thought to its true source, namely, Bede. The just *walk* in light because "ad meliora proficiunt. Deus autem *sine aliquo profectu* semper bonus, justus, verusque existit."

VER. 6.—*The Necessity of Holiness.*
I. WE MAY DECEIVE OURSELVES CONCERNING OUR RELATION WITH CHRIST. (1.) Christ warned us of this danger (Matt. vii. 22, 23, xxv. 44). (2.) His apostles have also warned us (Rev. iii. 17; 1 Cor. iii. 18; Gal. vi. 7, 8; Phil. iii. 18, 19). Many deceive themselves still, resting in outward observances, in membership of a particular society,

His main theme is, "walk in love;" and how can he enforce this unless he lays down the foundation on which such an exhortation must always rest?—that of a Divine life, imparted to all Christians alike, and knitting them together in a holy bond to God and to each other. Thus, then, if we walk in the atmosphere of beauty, purity, and truth which encircles God as well as ourselves, we are introduced into that holy fellowship or communion which is known as the communion of saints, which is described in Eph. iv. 15 and Col. ii. 19, and which consists in the continual interchange (see note on κοινωνία, ver. 3) of all the gifts and blessings God has vouchsafed to us.—**and the blood of Jesus Christ his Son cleanseth us from all sin.** This is not, again, exactly what we should have expected; consequently Theophylact, Beza, and other commentators have made this part of the sentence the reason for the former, and have translated καί by *for*. No doubt the ground of our reconciliation with God in the first instance is the death of Christ. But here, without wresting Scripture, we cannot interpret it of our being *accounted* righteous. The Apostle distinctly regards this cleansing effect of the blood of Christ not as a cause, but as a consequence, of our walking in the light. The truth is, that what is usually known as the justifying effect of the blood of Christ has been so pressed as to lead us to neglect its sanctifying effect. We have, therefore, reason to be thankful to a commentator like Haupt, who has placed

---

in belief of certain doctrines, or in certain feelings or experiences in the present or past. Such grounds of acceptance, in the absence of the one necessary characteristic, are simple deceptions.

II. THE ONLY TEST OF PRESENT ACCEPTANCE IS THE WALKING IN LIGHT. (I.) Nothing can be clearer than St. John's statement of this truth. Not only does he say "we lie," if we claim fellowship

the question upon a less traditional basis, and has given us wider conceptions of the merits of Christ's blood than most expositors have led us to entertain. Christ was undoubtedly the Sacrifice slain for the sins of the world. But He is also the Paschal Lamb, whose flesh is the support of mankind. Haupt therefore rightly directs us to the sixth chapter of St. John, where this truth is presented to our notice. But there is one point in which Christ's mystical exposition of the passover, there given, departs in a startling manner from the type. The blood of the paschal lamb, as of all other animals used for food, was not to be partaken of (Lev. iii. 17, vii. 26, 27), because "the blood is the life" (Deut. xii. 23; see Lev. xvii. 10–14 and Gen. ix. 4). But for this very reason the blood of Christ, the true Paschal Lamb, *was* to be drunk by His disciples. "Thus, then," says Haupt, "the καθαρισμὸς ἀπὸ πάσης ἁμαρτίας is possible only in consequence of the blood of Christ entering into our life as a new life-principle. There is absolutely no Christian sanctification imaginable which does not take place through the blood, that is, through the Redeemer's power of life working its effects and ruling within us" (Haupt). Christ's life, offered to God and accepted by Him as a perfect sacrifice, is communicated to our life as a daily fact. This view of Christ's blood, however, cannot be severed from His death. The words "blood of Christ" invariably in Scripture mean His blood *shed* (Rom. iii. 25; Eph. ii. 13; 1 Peter i. 19;

---

with Christ, and walk in darkness, but we "do not the truth," *i.e.*, (see Exposition), we do not merely make a mis-statement, but we act the lie we speak. We deny the Eternal Verities, and act as though they were not in existence. Our lives are a perpetual defiance of God and His Son Jesus Christ. (2.) This is the Gospel doctrine, which rests on the indwelling of Christ in the believer, proclaimed

Rev. v. 9, &c.) If His blood be a source of life at all, it is as the blood of the Lamb that was slain, offered in sacrifice to God, as well as partaken of by the believer. The spirit of this sacrifice enters into our every action. Thus, day by day, as we walk in the light and have fellowship with one another, we are cleansed from every tendency of the natural man, and brought ever into more perfect union with the life of truth. Braune has supplied us with a valuable corroboration to this interpretation by calling attention to the fact that we have here the present tense—$καθαρίζει$. It is not "hath cleansed," but "is cleansing" us. The cleansing is a continual present fact in the life of the believer, whereby he is knit still more closely in fellowship with Christ (see also Rev. vii. 14, &c., and Titus ii. 14). Before proceeding to the next verse, we must ask why the words "His Son" are introduced here. We may assume that no single word in Scripture is without its purpose, and we may here discern (1) the certainty of the acceptance of the sacrifice, by reason of the eternal harmony and union between the Father and the Son, and (2) the intimation of the loving purpose of God from all eternity, in that (Rom. viii. 32) He "spared not His own Son, but delivered Him up for us all" (cf. John iii. 16).[1]

VER. 8.—**If we say that we have no sin.** The use of the word *have* as an auxiliary verb somewhat weakens the force of this sentence in English. Here it has the

[1] See also Professor Westcott's additional note on this verse.

---

throughout this Epistle as elsewhere in the New Testament. So our Lord teaches (Matt. vii. 16), the expression, continually used throughout the New Testament, signifying the presence of an inner life (see especially St. John xv. 1-8). St. Paul limits the freedom from condemnation to those who are walking (this is the force of the present tense in Rom. viii. 1) after the Spirit, and thus (ver. 4) fulfilling the

same sense as in the words "to have and to hold" in the Marriage Service, *i.e.*, to *possess*. The expression is only to be found elsewhere in St. John's Gospel (ch. ix. 41, xv. 22, xix. 11). Elsewhere we find the expression *commit* sin, but not *have* it. It is a remarkable one, since the New Testament word for sin means *error*, or rather *missing the mark*. What is meant clearly is, that this habit of swerving aside from our highest good has become so inherent in us that it is practically a possession— something closely connected with and belonging to us. Now what St. John says is, that we deceive ourselves if we imagine for a moment that in this life, in spite of our redeemed and sanctified condition, we shall ever attain to perfect freedom from sin. For $ἔχομεν$ is in the present tense, and therefore must refer to the present condition of those who are addressed, in spite of the high and blessed privileges they are said in the last verse to have possessed. This must be carefully remembered when we come to expound passages like ch. iii. 6–9. In this and the following verses we have St. John's doctrine of justification. It is remarkable that he avoids the use of the word. Nothing is more striking than the diversity in temper and intellect and form of thought among the human instruments chosen by Christ to diffuse His Gospel. And yet, with all the variety in their mode of stating it, the doctrine they preached was substantially the same. Thus here we have no mention of righteousness being "reckoned," or "accounted," or "imputed,"

---

righteousness of the law. (3.) *What it is to walk in darkness and in light.* To walk in the light is to (*a*) acknowledge the truth revealed in Jesus Christ; (*b*) this revelation makes known to us God's will, and especially—the point we are at present considering—in what true holiness consists; (*c*) true holiness consists, as we have just seen, in fulfilling the righteousness of the law, by virtue of the illumination

no verb δικαιόω, to "proclaim," or "render, righteous." And yet the great Gospel truth indicated by those words is laid down in a manner which cannot be mistaken. It is stated thus, rising from one doctrinal statement to another, until it culminates in the mention of Jesus Christ as the Propitiation for sin. God is light. By walking in the light which He gives we attain to fellowship with Him, and are daily cleansed from sin. But this cleansing from sin implies sinfulness. We are not to suppose that we attain to this fellowship with God by our own works or deservings; quite the contrary. We sin continually, and to deny this fact is really to break off our fellowship with God, while to acknowledge it is to live in the light of that fellowship. And, in fact, it is the only way to avoid sin. We cannot lead pure and sinless lives unless we first of all confess that we are sinners, and recognise Jesus Christ as our Advocate with the Father and the Propitiation for our sins. Thus we clearly see the truth (1) that our acceptance with God is the work of another, not our own, and (2) that it is only upon this acceptance for the sake of One who has made propitiation for the sins of the whole world that the fabric of the personal holiness of the individual can be built. Here, then, in phrase very different to that of St. Paul, yet (cf. Rom. i.–iii.) travelling on precisely the same lines, do we find the doctrines universally accepted in the Christian Church of Justification and Sanctification. The terms we owe to St. Paul—the doctrine to

---

we have received, which enables us to distinguish right from wrong, to set up before us a higher standard of purity and perfection. To "walk" in the light is to press daily forward towards the realisation of this ideal, which is clearly perceived by the illumined soul, as well as all the steps which lead to it. To walk in darkness is, of course, the exact opposite of all this.

Jesus Christ.—**we deceive ourselves and the truth is not in us** (cf. ch. ii. 4). Unless we are ready to acknowledge our present sinfulness, if we are inclined to maintain that we "have already attained, or are already perfect," we are in the same condition as if we were walking in darkness while maintaining that we have fellowship with God. For the expression "the truth is not in us" is practically equivalent to "we do not the truth." The truth, that which is, practically means God Himself. So Jesus Christ calls Himself "the truth." And we cannot possess the life of Christ without its teaching us our own unworthiness and sinfulness, and producing in us an earnest yearning for its purifying influences. For ἁμαρτία see notes on ch. iii. 4 and v. 17.

VER. 9.—**If we confess our sins** (cf. Ps. xxxii. 5, xxxviii. 18, li. 3). The word here translated *confess* means in Greek to *speak together*, hence to *agree*. Here it means not only to accept and thoroughly recognise the fact that one is a sinner, but to acknowledge it publicly. We may observe that the Apostle does not confine himself here to the words "if we say that we have sin," the precise converse of what has gone before. He goes farther. "If we *confess* our sins," that is, make specific confession of our individual acts of sin. Well has Ebrard remarked here, that it is much easier to make pious speeches to the effect that we are sinners in a general way, and expressive of general deep contrition, and of the misery engendered by sin, than to acknowledge the

---

VER. 7.—*The Results of walking in Light.*
I. COMMUNION WITH EACH OTHER. This (see Exposition) is an unexpected result. But it is also unexpected in another way. It comes *before* the cleansing with the blood of Christ. The reason of this may be that the Apostle would set the consciences of his disciples at rest. In their communion with each other there were many failures

particular wrong that we have done, and to endeavour as far as possible to repair it. Many who are ready enough to admit generally that they are sinners would be the first hotly to repel a charge of sinfulness on any one special point, so deep is the self-deception of the human heart, which is often farthest from God when the lips are busiest in honouring Him. We have next to inquire to whom confession is to be made. Obviously to God, and, in certain special cases, to man. What these last cases are may be best seen by a reference to such passages as Matt. v. 23-25; Luke xvii. 4. The idea of auricular confession does not seem to have any connection with the argument, which concerns only our general readiness to acknowledge candidly any wrong which we have done, to the person to whom we have done it, instead of justifying or excusing it.—**he is faithful.** Almost all the commentators agree here. It is "faithful to His plighted word and promise" (Alford); of course by He God is meant.—**and just.** The word here used is translated indifferently by *just* and *righteous* in the New Testament. The original Greek idea is unquestionably that of justice (see Aristotle, "Ethics," v. 1). But the word and its correlatives are used as the translation of the Hebrew *tzedek* and *tzaddik*, which involves a higher moral idea than mere fairness between man and man, and rather implies what is abstractedly right. Thus it becomes, by its LXX. usage, a fit word to express that abstract justice of God which, and not mere human ideas of what is fair

---

in duty. But by reason of their acceptance with Christ these daily sins of infirmity were daily cleansed. It is to be observed, that in the results of the Christian life the Apostle (following his Master's example, Matt. xxv. 31-46) puts the visible before the invisible (ch. iii. 14-17, iv. 20, 21), thus reversing strangely the order of the Gospel, which sets the invisible before the visible. But the reason is clear.

or right to one another, is the basis of all true Christian integrity. Here again, though differently expressed, we have the true Pauline doctrine of the harmony between God's justness and His forgiveness (Rom. iii. 26), as well as the doctrine (cf. Rom. i. 17) that the Gospel is a revelation of the δικαιοσύνη θεοῦ (cf. again Rom. iii. 25, 26). St. John here just as emphatically asserts that the idea of the forgiveness of sins involves no derogation from the eternal justice of God. Among the curiosities of interpretation we may notice that of Suarez, who supposes that "faithful" relates to mortal sins, which are forgiven solely by God's free grace, "just" to venial sins, because through penitence and love they *ex condigno* merit His forgiveness.—**to forgive us our sins.** Some commentators, *e.g.*, Haupt and Alford, have held tenaciously to the *telic* force of ἵνα here; but they have been obliged to disguise its form a good deal to make the rendering tolerable. The idea of God being faithful and just, not in Himself, but in order that He might forgive us our sins, could never, it may safely be said, in spite of Haupt's most ingenious and, it may be added, reverent exposition of the passages, have occurred to St. John. Hence, therefore, we must regard ἵνα as having here, as it unquestionably has elsewhere, the force of the Infinitive. (See Winer, "Gr. Gr.," sec. 44, v. Cf. Matt. x. 25; John iv. 34; Luke i. 43.) God is faithful and just, and the result of that faithfulness and justice is that He forgives us our sins and cleanses us from all unrighteous-

---

If the invisible motive be more powerful than visible motives, the fact must display itself in the sphere of the visible. This is the only test of its reality. We could easily deceive ourselves in what is beyond the sphere of our senses—imagine ourselves to be living with God and loving Him when we were but indulging in barren contemplation, unreal ecstasy. Therefore, one result by which we may

ness. If we ask how His faithfulness and justice are evinced by the forgiveness of the sin and the cleansing of the sinner, for the latter we are referred to the thought of the Blood of Christ spoken of above (ver. 7), and for the former, the forgiveness of the sin, to the Propitiation made by Jesus Christ, Himself the Just ($\delta\text{í}\kappa\alpha\iota o\varsigma$). The change of translation in our version obscures the connection of thought most materially.—**to forgive us our sins.** The word here translated "forgive" has many meanings in the LXX. and New Testament, as Pearson's learned note reminds us ("On the Creed," Art. X.) It means, he says, (1) to send forth (Matt. xxvii. 50; Mark xv. 37); (2) to permit (Matt. iii. 15); (3) to leave, desert (Matt. v. 24, viii. 15, xxvi. 56); (4) to omit (Matt. xxiii. 23), and lastly (5) to remit, as in Matt. xviii. 27. It is impossible to avoid feeling that our word remit or forgive does not rise to the full requirements of the word here used. It implies the idea (1) of passing over, that is, of remitting the penalty of sin; (2) of forgiving, that is, of releasing us from the guilt of sin; (3) of setting free, that is, of disentangling us from the consequences of sin; and (4) of dismissing, that is, of purifying us from the contagion of sin. Thus when we speak of the remission of sin, we mean more than its simple forgiveness. We include the idea of restoration to holiness, a complete return to the favour and approval of God.—**and to cleanse us from all unrighteousness.** This clause is the expansion and

---

easily test the reality of our illumination is communion with, *i.e.*, care for, common sympathies and interests with, our neighbours.

II. THE FORGIVENESS OF SIN (cf. Rom. viii. 1). While we are struggling to realise our ideal, to free ourselves from the defilements, "negligences, and ignorances" of our present imperfect condition, we fall into continual transgressions, which are rather sins of infirmity than of deliberate rebellion. These, if our purpose be right with God,

completion of the former. Our sins are pardoned and dismissed. The necessary result is purification of heart and life. How the cleansing is effected we have already seen (ver. 7). Unrighteousness here is obviously the opposite of that attribute of God which has just been mentioned. As δίκαιος means abstractedly just and upright, declining neither to the one side nor the other, so ἀδικία, which corresponds to ἁμαρτία in ver. 8, but presents the idea in a different shape, means, strictly speaking, that which is not right and just, *unequal*, as the word is used in Ezek. xviii. 29.

VER. 10.—**If we say that we have not sinned.** Here the expression is not exactly equivalent to that in ver. 8. "Have" here is simply the sign of the perfect tense. No idea of possession is suggested. But here we find the phrase corresponding rather to the concrete idea of sin put before us in ver. 9 than the abstract condition of sinfulness intended in ver. 8. There sin was a general characteristic of the life of those St. John was addressing; here he would lead us to the thought of the specific acts of sin which have brought about that condition.—**we make him a liar.** We are naturally led to ask, Why this startling increase of vehemence? Two verses back the Apostle simply says that we deceive ourselves, and that we have no part or lot in eternal truth. Four verses back again he says that "we lie, and do not the truth." This may be our misfortune, a state of things in which we are nearly passive. But to make God a liar is an

---

if our will be firmly set towards purification, will be forgiven, though not (see last verse) if we be resolved to "walk in darkness."

III. PURIFICATION FROM SIN. This is, of course, a *gradual* process. But it rests (see Exposition) on the life-giving properties of the blood of Christ, which, communicated to the soul, does not only free it from condemnation in God's sight, but by cleansing the will from the desire to sin, and inspiring it with a bent towards holiness, ends

active insult to His Name. Whence is this? There can be little doubt that the Apostle had in mind (1) the strong statements of God's Word, as collected, for instance, in Rom. iii. 10–18; and (2) no doubt he had moreover in view the whole scheme of redemption, which proceeds upon the assumption of man's sinfulness, and becomes one huge imposture the moment that assumption is removed. All the doctrines of the Christian faith, the Incarnation, the Sacrifice upon the cross, the descent and sanctifying influences of the Holy Spirit, are not merely unnecessary, but false, save upon the supposition of man's sin.—**and his word is not in us.** Most of the commentators here regard the word λόγος as referring, not to the personal Logos, the Son of God, but to the word or doctrine spoken or taught by Him, as in John viii. 31. It may be bold, against so overwhelming a *consensus* as there appears to be on this point, to venture to suggest that while generally the word λόγος means *word* or discourse, except where it is specially applied to the Word of God, yet here the connection with ver. 1 is so near, that we are not entitled altogether to reject the idea that the indwelling of the Eternal Word Himself may have been intended. The strongest argument against it is Haupt's, that as yet we have heard nothing about Christ's indwelling. But if it be not so, the question arises, *what* word is here meant? Ebrard would understand the whole revelation of God, in the Old and New Testament alike. Alford interprets baldly "that

---

by overcoming the sinful desire, and by confirming the will in its submission to the will of God.

VERS. 8, 9, 10.—*The Acknowledgment of Present Sin a Necessity.* The present life is the period of probation. As long as we carry about "this body of death" (Rom. vii. 24) we are liable to the dominion of sin, though in an ever-lessening degree. The conviction of our fault-

which he saith," which (see note on ver. 1) would rather be ῥῆμα than λόγος. "The λόγος means more than mere ῥήματα" (Haupt). He regards it as "the aggregate collective internal unity of the entire Divine announcement, not as to the external words, but to them as far as they are spirit and life." This comes nearest to the spirit of the passage.[1] In a similar way St. Paul speaks of the λόγος τοῦ σταυροῦ (1 Cor. i. 18), the λόγος τῆς καταλλαγῆς (2 Cor. v. 19), and still more emphatically of the λόγος τῆς ἀληθείας (Eph. i. 13; Col. i. 5; cf. James i. 18). The inner meaning of God's whole Revelation, communicated to man, and discerned through the operation of His Spirit, is the λόγος (if we dismiss the idea that it is God the Son Himself) which cannot be in us unless we accept as a necessary condition the doctrine of man's sinfulness.

CH. ii. 1.—**My little children.** This affectionate diminutive is beautifully natural in the mouth of an old man, such as we know St. John must have been when this Epistle was written. It is peculiarly characteristic of him. He puts it but once (John xiii. 33) into the mouth of the Saviour. St. Paul only uses it once (Gal. iv. 19), when he desires to be particularly persuasive, "to change his voice," because he "stands in doubt" of the Galatian Christians. But in this short Epistle St.

---

[1] Professor Westcott interprets of "the Gospel message, which is the crown of all revelation."

---

lessness, and the disposition to pass judgment on others, are the sins that most rouse the anger of the Son of God, as the condemnation He passed on the Pharisees shows. It was no object of His Revelation to produce in us this self-asserting arrogance. A knowledge of our own weakness and liability to sin, a modest estimate of ourselves when comparing ourselves to others, a readiness to remember our own infirmity when dealing with others who sin (Gal. vi. 1), are among the first requisites of Christian perfection. Thus while we gladly recog-

John uses it seven times, and only once is there any doubt (ver. 12) that it refers to *all* whom he is addressing. It is characteristic of the strong impression this mode of address made on the mind of the early Church, that in the touching anecdote recorded by Eusebius ("Hist. Eccl.," iii. 23) of St. John and his young disciple who fell into evil courses, he is represented as saying, "My child ($\tau\acute{\epsilon}\kappa\nu o\nu$), why dost thou fly me, thy father?" The story comes down to us on the authority of Clement of Alexandria, no mean authority. It may very possibly be true. But we may at least say of it *se non è vero è ben trovato;* it is in good keeping with all we know of the Apostle from Holy Writ. And it is this affectionate style of address, as well as his dwelling so much on the love of God, and its consequence, the mutual love of mankind to one another, that has caused us to dwell with peculiar affection on the thought of St. John as "the Apostle of love."—**these things I write unto you, that ye sin not.** Luther, so Braune tells us in his Commentary, says that he is prepared to call that man a theologian who can show the consistency and agreement of this passage. That there is such a close connection the $\tau a\hat{\upsilon}\tau a$ here shows beyond a doubt. "I am writing these things," *i.e.*, what I have written and what I am now about to write, "that ye sin not." St. Augustine regards it as being a warning against expecting to sin with impunity, which some might have taken encouragement

---

nise the goodness of God in purifying us and making us holy, we on the other hand never fail to acknowledge the fact, not only that we have often offended, but that we are still liable to sin, and that the process of purification is as yet only in progress, not finally accomplished.

CH. ii. 1.—*Our Sinfulness is not to be Pleaded as an Excuse for Sin.* The well-known adage, "incidit in Scyllam qui vult vitare Charybdim," is especially true of the Christian life. The moment we

from ch. i. 8—10 to do. Rather it would seem that the Apostle is here pointing out the result to which what he has before written would tend, if rightly understood, namely, as St. Paul puts it, that there is no condemnation to them that are in Christ Jesus, because they walk not after the flesh, but after the Spirit, being made free from the law of sin and death under which they had once groaned, by the law of the Spirit of Life (cf. Rom. vii.–viii. 2). God is light, says St. John, an idea which suggests, not merely intellectual illumination, but perfect moral purity. Fellowship with Him involves such a moral purity on the part of all who attain to it. Yet this moral purity is not *inherent* in him who is admitted to fellowship with God, but is *communicated* to him. And though in the case of each convert it imperatively demands an acknowledgment of former sin, yet the object of the Apostle's message is not that his converts may "continue in sin, that grace may abound." On the contrary, its purpose is that they should cease to sin. Yet since (ch. i. 8) an acknowledgment of present sin is one necessary result of the admission into the brightness of the Divine light, it is necessary to deal with the case of the sins of believers. Thus the doctrine is precisely the same here as in Rom. viii. 1—14. The gradual purifying influences of God's Spirit, diminishing, while as yet they do not destroy, the natural sinfulness of man—the increased sensitiveness to sin, the deepened sense of it, which come

---

shun one pitfall Satan has one ready for us on the other side. We avoid the error of the Pharisee, and meekly and modestly confess our liability to sin. And straightway the enemy seeks to make us contented with that condition, to make it an excuse for our actual shortcomings. We are urged to give up some sins which are a burden to ourselves, a disgrace and stumbling-block to our brethren. We reply that we are not perfect, that we never pretended to be, that no one ever can be, and so excuse ourselves from the effort necessary to attain

from being brought to the light, and from learning to live in it—the need of a daily application to ourselves of the merits of the One Atoning Sacrifice once offered for the sins of men—and the peace and joy which they inherit who feel how they are gradually becoming imbued with the Spirit of their Lord—these are characteristics of Apostolic doctrine, in whatever language it may be expressed. And this would seem to be the connection of ideas in the passage ch. i. 5–ii. 6.

---

to the perfection which is in Christ Jesus. "This is a very dangerous deceit," says the Apostle. "What I am writing to you is intended to lead you to a victory over sin. A low idea of yourself is indeed necessary to true perfection, but was never intended to excuse you from the effort necessary to attain it. My object throughout is to convince you of the truth which I have before taught you, that to claim to be a disciple of Jesus, and not to try in everything to lead the life He did, is a deliberate denial of Him."

IV.

THE FORGIVENESS OF SINS, AND ITS RESULTS.

EXPOSITION.

CH. ii. 1.—We resume our exposition at the point where the Apostle explains that in the Christian Church there is forgiveness for sins actually committed. We have seen (in the Introduction) that the course of the Apostle's argument is, (1) that purity of life and freedom from sin are required of the Christian by his covenant relation to God, and that (2) because, in spite of this, Christians *have* sinned and *do* sin, therefore (3) it is necessary to recognise the fact that there exists a propitiation for the actual sins of those who have already been admitted into fellowship with God, and have therefore been cleansed by the blood of the covenant from all original and past sins. The meaning, perhaps, does not

---

HOMILETICS.

CH. ii. 1.—This verse divides itself into two parts: first, the enunciation of a paradox of faith, and secondly, the proclamation of a propitiation for sin.

First let us consider the paradox, that confession of present sinfulness is necessary in order that we may not sin.

I. PARADOXES ARE COMMON IN THE GOSPEL. Such paradoxes we find in Prov. xxvi. 4, 5, in Gal. vi. 2, 5, in Matt. xii. 30, compared with Luke ix. 50, in Rom. iv. 2 with St. James ii. 20, 21. Hence we

lie on the surface, but the whole argument from ch. i. 5 to the end of ch. ii. 2 lays down the doctrine expressed in the Second Article of the Church of England, namely, that Christ died "to be a sacrifice, not only for original guilt, but for actual sins of men," and this not only for those committed before, but after regeneration.—**that ye sin not.** This is the statement which harmonises the two preceding propositions. The confession of sin is to be a step in the direction of forsaking it. Not yet, it is true, does the Apostle show how this is to be the case, namely, by the tendency of the sense of weakness and sin to lead us to One on whom we rely (1) for forgiveness, and (2) for that change which shall destroy sin in us. The first of these ideas is touched upon in the next two verses. The second is gradually introduced in ch. iii. And thus we have the order which St. Paul follows in the Epistle to the Romans; first the reconciliation after sin committed, and then its destruction in us; first atonement, then sanctification. Eternal truth is full of paradoxes. Like a vast mountain, it has many sides and many points of view. And as we often fail to recognise the outlines of a familiar mountain when seen from a new direction, so God's truth seems to have changed its aspect when regarded from another point of view. Thus nothing could seem at first sight more unintelligible than the

---

may learn a lesson of moderation in theological statement. So vast is God's truth, that it is possible for one portion of it to appear to contradict another, whereas the two sides are but complementary parts of the same truth. What fruitless controversies might have been avoided, what unseemly conflicts might have been escaped, had men but borne this in mind! The Calvinist, who insists on God's foreknowledge and sovereignty, might have remembered that this is not incompatible with the Arminian assertion of His justice and righteousness. The Augustinian doctrine of the necessity of grace would not have been pressed to the exclusion of free will. The necessity of faith

statement, that in order that we should not sin, it is necessary to confess that we have sinned and do sin. Yet nothing is more clear, when viewed in the light of the life, death, and resurrection of Christ. For He has not only made atonement for sin, He has made provision —the only provision possible—that it shall cease to be committed, when the soul, by faith, has attained to perfect union with Him. We shall be able to elucidate this point more fully when we come to ch. iii. 9, and iv. 4, where the force of the original is obscured in our version by the neglect to translate the perfect *as* a perfect. We may, however, add here that the conviction of present sinfulness, deeply felt and steadily acted upon, is not only the best, but the only, earnest of future perfection.—**And if any man sin.** The "and" here is said by Braune to be the "simple copula," and not equivalent to the adversative δέ. Many other commentators have passed it over. But it is obvious from the Hebrew cast of the whole Epistle that here, as in ver. 2, the Apostle uses καί as equivalent to the Hebrew ו, which constantly has an adversative force. Thus the meaning is, "I am writing these things to you, not that ye *may* sin, but that ye may be able to abstain from sin. Yet I would not have you downcast. As I have said, you *do* sin, but you have an Advocate with the Father, who has made

---

to salvation would have been seen not to be irreconcilable with the necessity of works, because their place in the scheme of salvation is not identical, the one being the source, the other the stream. Without the source, there can be no stream; if there be no stream, then the source has run dry. So again in the endless controversy concerning the Sacrament of the Lord's Supper. The reality of the gift need not be denied because its *modus operandi* is disputed. It is not necessary to reduce it to a "bare memorial of a thing absent" because we cannot quite agree about the nature of the presence. We need to beware, lest by insisting too strongly upon one particular aspect of a

propitiation for your sin." Alford, again, would interpret the aorist of the commission of a single act of sin. But, as was stated in the notes on ver. 1, this view of the aorist cannot always be pressed in Alexandrian Greek. Thus Wordsworth's interpretation, *shall have sinned* (or *should* have sinned), is perhaps nearer the mark. It is neither *is sinning*, which would be signified by the present, nor *hath sinned*, which would apply to an act completed in the past, but *should have been committing* acts of sin, and since it answers to the Hebrew imperfect, without any definite note of time, it may include the idea, *should still be committing acts of sin*.[1] Haupt well sums up this passage as follows: "Most supremely must we be on our guard against them (sins of infirmity), for they easily lead to the περιπατεῖν ἐν τῇ σκοτίᾳ. But the consciousness of this danger might very well lead to despair, and therefore the reminder that we have in the Lord Jesus a representative and propitiation, who as such secures the forgiveness of sins."—**we have an Advocate with the Father.** "St. John writes, *if any one . . . we*, in order to bring out the individual character of the offence, and then to show that he is speaking" in what follows, "of the Christian body . . . to which Christ's

[1] Professor Westcott interprets of "the single act" of sin, "into which the believer may be carried against the true tenor of his life."

---

truth, we are practically denying the truth itself. So in the truth taught here. Many have insisted so strongly on the necessity of feeling our sinfulness, that they have practically denied the necessity of sanctification; they have in effect said, "Let us continue in sin, that grace may abound."

II. HOW DOES THE ACKNOWLEDGMENT OF SINFULNESS TEND TO ERADICATE SIN? It is the Apostle's clear meaning here that this is the case. "These things," that is, the truths, that we "have sin" present with us, that we "have sinned" in past time, that we must "confess our sins," are written to us that we *should not* sin. They

promises are assured." The word παράκλητος, as is well known, is translated by two words in Scripture: the first, *Comforter*, in St. John's Gospel, as applied to the Holy Ghost; the second, *Advocate*, here, as applied to Jesus Christ. The word is derived from παρά, *beside*, and κλητός, which in the New Testament is rendered *called*. Thus it means one who is called to our side, to comfort, cheer, or help us, or, as in classical Greek, an advocate or protector. The idea, therefore, of *Comforter* in St. John's Gospel (A. V.) need not be rejected, but only supplemented. The Holy Spirit is not merely a Comforter, but a helper and a sustainer and a protector. And the word *Advocate* here is therefore as far from exhausting the full meaning as the word Comforter. "With the Father" is the same in the Greek as in ch. i. 2 (where see note). And thus we arrive at the full sense of the passage, which is that there is One who stands before the Father, His face ever directed to His throne; One who, as man, needs not to shrink from presenting Himself there, to plead our cause, to obtain for us, not merely the forgiveness—that would be to evacuate the passage of much of its meaning—but to win for us the support, encouragement, help of which we stand in need. We have One who stands by us (παρά), yet looks toward (πρός) the Father, and who, one with us and with Him, can enable

---

could have no effect at all in that direction but for the doctrine which follows, that we have an advocate with the Father, a propitiation for our sins. Thus, then, in connection with this doctrine, the sense of our own sinfulness tends to deliver us from sin, (*a*) *Because we cannot win heaven for ourselves* (Rom. iii. 20, 23, 27, 28, iv. 2, 6, ix. 11, x. 3; Gal. ii. 16; Eph. ii. 9; Tit. iii. 5, &c.). We are thus, by our own sense of sinfulness, driven to seek another, who will deliver us from sin. (*b*) *Because to suppose that we could so win heaven is a total misconception of our position.* We must either, in that case, deny that sin is sin, or be reduced to despair. The first would only be to confuse

us to do all things through His all-powerful aid.—**Jesus Christ the righteous.** There is no article here before the word "righteous," and yet, as Dean Alford has shown, in no other way could we have expressed in English the sense of the Greek, which requires us to give the idea of righteousness, not the Person in whom it was manifested, the prominence. The word "righteous" here signifies the position in which Jesus Christ presents humanity before the Father. In Him not even Eternal Wisdom can detect a single flaw. Hence His fitness to stand before the Father and plead our cause. *We* are not just, but *He* is (we must remember that the word here translated *righteous* is translated *just* in ch. i. 9), and therefore with Him as our representative we need not fear.

VER. 2.—**And he is the propitiation for our sins.** "He" is emphatic—αὐτός, He Himself. The central word in this sentence is ἱλασμός, which occurs only here and in ch. iv. 10. This word is akin, both in its meaning and its application, to St. Paul's ἱλαστήριον (Rom. iii. 25; cf. Heb. ix. 5). Both are derived from ἱλάσκομαι, a word which always in the earlier and generally in the later Greek has the sense of to make the gods propitious or favourably inclined.[1] The word and its compounds are

[1] Professor Westcott's note on the use of these words in the LXX. and N. T. will repay study.

---

right and wrong; to invent theories of obligation, as the Pharisees did, in order to escape from the guilty consciousness of sin. But if the fact of sinfulness were admitted, men might think their case hopeless. They were sinners, and sinners they must remain. So they would go on sinning all their lives, without any attempt to repent and amend. But this, the Apostle says, is not his aim in insisting upon sinfulness. Therefore he tells us that (c) *Sin is not imputed to those who are in covenant with Christ.* Thus the weight of transgression is removed. The past burden of sin at least does not lie on us. If it be possible to cast off sin for the future—upon this point the Apostle does not yet

largely used in the LXX. as the translation both of the Hebrew *caphar*, to cover, and *salach*, to be propitious. So we have it in Luke xviii. 13, literally, "Lord, be propitiated to me the sinner." So in Heb. ii. 17, where the sense is "to make propitiation." It is worthy of notice that in each case where our Lord is spoken of as being a propitiation for sin, He is not spoken of actively as the person who propitiates, but rather in the abstract, as propitiation itself. Thus ἱλαστήριον is the mercy-seat, the place (see Exod. xxv. 22; Levit. xvi. 2, 13; Numb. vii. 89) where God and man meet, where God's special presence resides, and where the incense of devotion and obedience is offered. Jesus Christ is that meeting-point of God's requirements and man's fulfilment. His is the love and mercy of God, and the obedience and devotion of man combined (see also Ps. lxxxv. 10, 11). Here He is spoken of as ἱλασμός, propitiation (not *the* propitiation, as in our version, but propitiation itself). The *manner* in which propitiation is made is not explained; indeed, men have been too anxious to explain it. Our attention is here directed to the *fact*. And we are not so much asked to consider the action of Jesus Christ in propitiating, as the result of that action. Therefore we are taught to rest for our acceptance, not in any particular portion of His mediatorial work, but in Him; "in His

---

enter—we need at least be troubled with no misgivings about the past. "Let the dead past bury its dead." Our business is with the future (Rom. viii. 1; Phil. iii. 13). Freed from an entangling weight of past transgression we can start afresh on our course with the hope of attaining Him, who is our salvation and our reward. And thus we learn, finally, that (*d*) *The way to avoid sin for the future is not to deny that it dwells in us, but to seek to be cleansed from it* (see ch. i. 9). Not the assertion of our own righteousness, but the possession of a righteousness not our own is the mode of escape from sin. Thus, therefore, the first and absolutely essential step towards freedom from

life, death, and resurrection," as John Wesley puts it in his sermon on the *Repentance of believers;* that is to say, in His obedience, in His condemnation of sin in the flesh; in His bearing the wrath of God; in His sufferings as well as His death; in His rising again and passing through the veil of His mortal flesh to offer the perfected sacrifice for ever in heaven (see Heb. viii. 3, 4, ix. 24). He is not merely the High Priest, who offers the sacrifice, nor the victim that is offered, but propitiation itself—the realisation in His own person of all that humanity requires in order to be reconciled to God. This subject will be found more fully discussed in the Homiletic Section, which see.—**and not for our sins only, but for the sins of the whole world.** Nearly every commentator here quotes Bengel: "Quam late patet peccatum, tam late propitiatio." Christ did not come to be a propitiation, as has been stated by President Edwards and others, for "all the sins of some men," but for the sins of all men. "If the salvation of all does not take effect, the fault is not that God will not forgive the sins of any one, but that the unforgiven sinner repels the fatherly heart that moves toward him in mercy" (Haupt). Calvin says, "sub omnibus, reprobos non comprehendit." And *as a fact*, he is correct. Christ is not a propitiation for those who will have no propitiation. But, *as a possibility*, he is

---

sin is not the assertion of innocence, but the confession of guilt. The second part of this verse is concerned with the *means of deliverance*. The first statement is that we have an *Advocate;* the second, that this Advocate is a *propitiation.*

I. WE HAVE AN ADVOCATE. "That ye sin not." "Yet if any man sin." There is no contradiction. The way to holiness is not in ourselves, but in another. The Christian course is not to be run alone. One stands besides us (see note on παράκλητος), to help, to cheer, to console, to plead for us.

II. WITH THE FATHER. A double sense is implied in the preposition

incorrect. When the question arises concerning those who may be comprehended in the propitiation, then we must acknowledge that the whole world is within its scope. None are *necessarily* excluded from its operation. We may invite all men to come and be reconciled to God. A "sufficient sacrifice, oblation, and propitiation" has been made "for the sins of the whole world." A general amnesty has been offered to all offenders. Every one is included, save those who exclude themselves.

VER. 3.—We enter now upon a new line of thought, closely, however, connected with the declaration in ch. i. 5, 6. The Apostle, in this and the next three verses, teaches that the result of this propitiation and reconciliation should be to produce obedience to God's law; thus expanding and enforcing the hint he has thrown out in the words, "Little children, these things I write unto you, that ye sin not."—**And hereby we do know that we know Him.** Attention to the tenses is very important here. While the aorist is usually employed concerning a state of things in progress, the perfect is used for its complete fulfilment. St. John writes here, "And hereby (or 'in this') do we know that we *have known* Him," or, as Lillie has well rendered, "have attained to this knowledge." Thus St. John is not saying that in this life, while we are striving to attain to the knowledge of God,

---

πρός (see note on ch. i. 2). (1) He is eternally with the Father, just as He is with us. He dwells in us, and yet He is ever one in mind and will with Him with whom He pleads. Yet (2) He stands before Him as man pleading our cause. The Head of the Church, the Head of the whole human race who are united to Him by faith, He ever presents Himself at the eternal throne presenting the one sacrifice of His devoted life, consummated and brought to a point, as it were, in His most blessed death.

III. RIGHTEOUS. We are here referred back to ch. i. 9, where the word is translated "just." God is δίκαιος to forgive us our sins because

we shall be able to keep His commandments. What he says is that when we have learned to keep His commandments, we shall have attained to perfect knowledge of Him. "Hereby," here, as in ch. iii. 16, 19, 24, iv. 9, 10, 13, 17 (the phrase ἐν τούτῳ is variously rendered in our version), refers clearly, not to what has gone before, but to what follows. Bishop Wordsworth sees here a reference to the Gnostic heresy. But γνῶσις, or more often ἐπίγνωσις, is a phrase very common with St. Paul, as well as the verb γινώσκω, when no reference to Gnostic heresies can be possible, because they had not yet arisen. And St. John, in his Gospel, tells us how often the words, "to know God," were spoken by Jesus Christ. The phrase, too, is common in the Old Testament. Whether αὐτόν refers to the Father or to Christ is here, as elsewhere, uncertain. But we can hardly separate the two, nor does St. John desire that we should do so. Christ reveals to us the Father. If we know Christ we know the Father. So also we can only know the Father in and through Christ. The question has been supposed to be settled by the use of ἐκεῖνος for αὐτός in ver. 6. But the fact is that another αὐτός is there introduced, namely, the believer.—**if we keep his commandments** (cf. John xiv. 15, 21, 23, xv. 10; also ch. v. 3). If we wish to know whether we have fully attained

---

Jesus was δίκαιος to atone for them. His righteousness was the satisfaction for our unrighteousness, His obedience for our sinfulness. That righteousness, that sinlessness, was the only basis on which He could offer an atonement for our sins. We come next to consider the fact of *propitiation*. And here we will remark rather upon the less than the more obvious aspects of a truth familiar to us all.

I. IT WAS NOT MERELY THE ENDURANCE OF THE PUNISHMENT WE DESERVED TO UNDERGO. Such is the way in which the doctrine is frequently presented to our minds. But such a presentation is inadequate, and in some respects untrue. The problem of satisfaction

to the knowledge of God, the test is a simple one. It is whether we keep God's commandments or not. As long as consciousness of present sin remains, as long as we need the continual application of the propitiation to our souls, so long we may be learning to know God; but we do not yet know Him. When sin has altogether ceased not only to have dominion over us, but to affect us at all, then, and not till then, may we be said to know God. And practically, to each one of us, the result of self-examination (cf. ch. i. 8) will be to teach us that we do not yet "know God," but that we have still much to learn about Him. And thus we shall be ever growing in that which of all Christian graces, except love, is the dearest to Christ, namely, humility. If it be asked in what this knowledge of God consists, we answer, not with Haupt, that it is "to know Him as light," nor yet, with Carpzovius and others, to *love* Him, but that it implies the perception of the fact that He is all goodness and mercy and love, ideas, indeed, which are evidently, as we have seen, included in St. John's idea of light. We should sadly miss the point of the Apostle's exhortation if we failed to perceive that it is not the intellectual, but the moral and spiritual cognition of God that is meant, just as St. Paul tells us that "to know the love of Christ, which passeth knowledge," is to be "filled

---

for sin is a far more complex one than this. It is not denied that He suffered many things to deliver us from suffering them. It is not denied that He bare the burden of our sins. But this was not by the simple substitution of Himself for us, so that He bare that which we otherwise should have borne, and which henceforth we have not to bear. For (1) He has not averted from us the penalty of death, but the truth still holds good, "the soul that sinneth, it shall die." And (2) He did not suffer eternal death—the penalty due to sin—that we might live, for it is our blessed privilege to believe in One who is

unto all the fulness of God" (Eph. iii. 19). The word τηρεῖν should be observed. It is a sign of the Hebrew origin of the writer of this Epistle, for it signifies, literally, to *watch* or *guard*, as well as to keep commandments, and thus is the precise equivalent of the Hebrew *shamar*. And it is a mark of common authorship, that while in the other New Testament authors it occurs but seldom, and then frequently in the stricter sense of *guarding*, it occurs very frequently in St. John's Gospel, Epistle, and Apocalypse, and in each book with the word ἐντολή or λόγος, a connection in which it is not found in any other New Testament author, with the exception of Matt. xix. 17 and 1 Tim. vi. 14. The other authors prefer the similar word, φυλάσσειν, which is sometimes used in classical Greek in this sense. It is further observable that St. Luke, who shows by his style that he was of Gentile education, never uses the word in any other than the strict sense of guarding in prison, save when he is quoting the words of Jews, in connection with the controversy about the necessity of circumcision (Acts xv. 5, 24; xxi. 25). The argument from the use of words may undoubtedly be pressed too far, but it has its value. Yet while it is very freely used to destroy the credit of the New Testament, it is much more seldom used to uphold it. It would be well if those who so confidently

---

"alive for evermore." We proceed, then, reverently to ask in what the propitiation consisted.

II. IT WAS THE OFFERING OF HIS LIFE. The "blood is the life." Thus when He poured out His precious blood for our sakes, He gave His life to God. And thus in the place of our guilty, sin-stained lives, a perfect life, without spot or blemish, was offered to the Father on behalf of mankind.

III. HE DRANK TO THE UTTERMOST THE CUP OF HIS FATHER'S WRATH AGAINST SIN. This He did by being made a curse for us, by enduring all the shame, and scorn, and hatred which the real criminal

tell us that the writer of the Apocalypse was a "narrow-minded Judæo-Christian," and that the writer of the Gospel and Epistles of St. John was an Ephesine Gentile of the second century, would take this striking similarity of style into account, as well as the many alleged divergences, remembering that the argument from similarity is of infinitely more weight than that from divergence. Next, we may observe on the *tense* of τηρεῖν, which, as present, involves the continual, habitual observance of God's commandments. Nor must we, lastly, neglect the word ἐντολή, which has a force of its own. St. John never uses the word νόμος of the Christian rule of obedience (Alford, after Huther). Indeed, in this Epistle the word νόμος never occurs. Instead we have ἐντολή, the idea being that of a charge laid upon us by one whom we ought to obey, a charge which love and duty urge us to fulfil, instead of the old idea of a law enforced by penalties, under which the slightest dereliction of duty constituted us transgressors. In short, he looks on the Christian's duty from the point of view of *personal* rather than *legal* obligation.

VER. 4.—**He that saith I know him.** The construction here is Hebraistic. ὁ λέγων, literally, "the man who is saying"—the Hebrew way of expressing an act taking place at the present moment, the only form, in fact,

---

deserved. This was the cause of the "horror of great darkness that fell on Him," of the cry, "Why hast Thou forsaken Me?" Nor had He only to bear the sense of the Father's wrath, but as our representative, He bowed His head to death, since thus only could He truly be said to represent sinful man. Had He shrunk from this, He would not have been our representative at all.

IV. HE MADE AN ADEQUATE SATISFACTION, ON MAN'S BEHALF, FOR SIN. Though it were impossible for Him, in His own most sacred person, to repent, yet it was possible for Him, as man's representative, Himself true man, to offer to God, on man's behalf, a perfect

which is distinctly present in Hebrew. Thus we learn that the Apostle not only recognised the *possibility* of men saying such things (as in ἐὰν εἴπωμεν, ch. i. 8, 10), but the *fact* that they *did* say such things, that they were saying them then. That here a reference was made to the Gnostic heretics, the foundation of whose system was what they supposed to be knowledge (see 1 Tim. vi. 20, where, however, γνῶσις is unfortunately rendered *science*), can hardly be denied. We need not go further, and suppose, with some (cf. Rev. ii. 6, 14, &c.), that the Apostle had in view some leader of the sect, who was boasting of his knowledge of Christ, but denying the obligation to live as Christ commanded him. See ver. 6. The use of the perfect here, as above, implies perfect knowledge, " He who is saying I have attained to the knowledge of Him."—**and keepeth not his commandments, is a liar, and the truth is not in him** (see note on last verse). Literally, "and in this man truth is not." We may observe how the Apostle deals with greater severity with the offence here than ever before. To say that we have no sin (ch. i. 8) is a proof that the truth is not in us; but the assertion may arise from ignorance. We " deceive ourselves," or " err." To say that we have fellowship with God while we are living in darkness, is a far more serious offence. Common sense and conscience will not

---

μετάνοια, or change of attitude, as regards sin. Man loved sin, he clung to it, he refused to leave it, till Jesus Christ came on earth. When He came, He hated it, abhorred it, cast it from Him, as utterly as did His Father. His mind was one with the Father's as regards sin. And thus, for the first time since Adam's transgression, God and man were at one as regards sin, and the work of the fall was from henceforth undone.

V. HE ACKNOWLEDGED HIS FATHER'S JUSTICE, and thus vindicated the ways of God to man. By dying, He recognised the truth that man deserved to die, and thus rendered it possible for God to be "just,"

let us deceive ourselves in that. We no longer deceive ourselves; we lie. And further, the lie is fixed upon him who does this. Not only he lies, but he is a *liar*. His moral condition is false *ab initio;* he is one who makes it his business to say what he must know to be untrue, and to lead others astray. Hence the inverted form of the sentence, bringing the person into prominence. It is no longer "truth is not in us," but emphatic, "and in that man" (where Germans as well as Greeks would say "this") "truth is not." Again, "in the first chapter we have two kinds of activity, 'to lie,' and to 'do not the truth.' Here we have two states or conditions, to be 'a liar,' and not to partake of the truth" (Haupt).

VER. 5.—**But whoso keepeth his word.** Here the "His" is emphatic, perhaps, as opposed to the doctrine of the ὁ λέγων in the preceding verse. The tense of the word *keep* is the aorist, but its force is somewhat weakened by its being in the conjunctive mood. Still it implies a past condition of long continuance in "His word." Bengel acutely remarks, "*præcepta multa, verbum unum.* His word is the whole body of His commandments." As Haupt remarks, we have here a similar conclusion (after ver. 4) to that in ch. i. 6, 7. But here the thought takes another direction. There we are directed to our common brotherhood, and our common deliverance from a state of

---

and yet "the justifier of him which believeth." Therefore we humbly and thankfully believe that He offered Himself a ransom in our stead, and suffered much in so offering Himself, which we must otherwise have undergone. But it is important to remember that He so delivers us, not by simply enduring what we otherwise should have had to suffer, but by taking us into union with Himself. Thus we are reconciled to God, not only because He suffered *for* us, but because He dwells *in* us. And He delivers us from the extreme penalty of sin, not only by suffering for us, but by freeing us from the dominion of sin, so that, as sanctified by His spirit, we cease to commit it. Justifi-

sin. Here we are directed rather forward, to a condition when we shall have kept God's law, and have attained to perfect knowledge of Him through love.—**in him verily is the love of God perfected.** Rather, "*hath* the love of God *been* perfected." Commentators have learnedly discussed the relations of knowledge and love; but of *true* knowledge and love it must be said with Braune, that "they are intrinsically connected and correlatives." The contrast between the knowledge of this world and love is pointed out by St. Paul in 1 Cor. viii. 1. The intimate connection between true knowledge and love is shown in the second and third verses of that chapter (see also Gal. iv. 9, compared with the context, especially vers. 7, 8; also Rom. xiii. 10). There has also been much discussion on the question whether the love of God to man, or the love of man to God, is here meant, and many great names may be quoted on each side of the question. But surely, as the love of man to God is but the reflex of the tide of God's love to man, as it is but the return to Him of what He has given us (for faith and love are the gifts of God), we must here understand the love of God in its fullest abstract sense, as including all our human reflections of its power in the direction of our heart and affections unto God (see Rom. viii. 39). Thus, then, it will mean the love of God in our heart, displaying itself in every way;

---

cation by imputation, *i.e.*, our being regarded not as what we are in ourselves, but as what we are *in Christ*, is necessary to be believed, (1) Because we need it while we are yet sinners, and because (2) even when, through the power of the Spirit, we have ceased to commit sin, we yet *have* sinned, and therefore in *that* sense, as a fact in our past personal experience, must remain sinners for evermore. But it is to be believed as the first step to sanctification, whereby, our past sins freely forgiven and atoned for, we are henceforth accepted in the beloved, because His righteousness hath been perfected in us, and thus our reconciliation to God hath been perfected also.

love expansive, longing to flow out to others, and manifesting itself in every kind of self-forgetful affection both towards God and all His creatures. This is the quality which the Apostle says "is" (that is, "has been") "perfected in us." By "perfected," is meant that which has attained its end. Thus, since God's will is to regain for Himself the human heart, to make it wholly His, His love has attained its end in us when it has obtained entire possession of us, has driven out all selfish and fleshly desires, and has taught us to fulfil those commandments, the end of which, as St. Paul tells us, "is love out of a pure heart, and a good conscience, and faith unfeigned" (1 Tim. i. 5. See also Eph. iii. 19, above cited, and Col. i. 10–12, iii. 14). So our Lord, in St. John xvii. 3, makes the end and purpose of all life eternal, the knowledge of God and of Himself. This interpretation derives strength from a consideration of the word ἀληθῶς, which (with Ebrard) we must hold to be no mere barren formula of affirmation, but the opposite of "in that man the truth is not" (ver. 5). "The love of God hath been *truly*," not merely in appearance, or in our own opinion, "perfected in us," when we have learned "to keep His word." And here we learn the true test of final acceptance with God, as opposed to false and lying estimates of the signs of dwelling in Him. It is only when we have been enabled to keep His word, that (see next note) we can say that we really

---

VER. 3.—*The test of our knowledge of God is obedience.* Christians have devised other tests of a true conversion. But this is the only test recognised by Jesus Christ. A tree is known by its fruits, He says (Matt. vii. 16-20; cf. John xv. 2, 5, 16; Rom. vii. 4). If, therefore, we want to know whether our conversion is genuine, our faith a saving faith, we only have to ask whether it *is saving* us from the commission of sin, and working in us obedience to God's commandments. All other tests, we learn from ver. 4, are vain.

VER. 5.—*Knowledge and Love.*

live in Him.—*hereby know we that we are in him.* The language of the Apostle is changed once more. He speaks no longer of knowing God, or having fellowship with Him. He penetrates now to the central truth of Christianity, namely, that the Christian who is really such, partakes of the life and being of his Lord. "Hereby know we"—not that we *know* Him, but—"that we are *in* Him." This truth we shall find further unfolded in the remainder of the Epistle, and it is the main truth of Christianity. It was the main object of Christ in coming among us to restore the lost union between God and man, and to increase its fulness and depth. This truth is taught with remarkable clearness and distinctness by St. John in both Gospel and Epistle. We find in the Gospel that the life of Christ is to pass into the believer as the flesh of the Paschal Lamb into the system of those who ate it, and thus to be the means of a mutual indwelling of the believer in Christ (ch. vi.) We find (ch. xv.) that there is to be an identity of life in the Redeemer and His people which bears analogy to the life of the vine transmitted through the branches. The blessed truth is summed up in the pregnant sentence in ch. xvii. 23, "I in them and Thou in Me, that they may have become perfected unto one." In the Epistle we shall find as we proceed the statement reiterated in many various forms, presenting the same truth to us in many various aspects. But our ver-

---

I. KNOWLEDGE IS BUT EXPERIENCE IN LOVE. If we keep His commandments, we know that we know Him. But when we shall have kept His commandments, His love has been perfected in us. Thus, then, to know Him is to love Him, not only because (1) The better we know Him, the more worthy of love we find Him to be, but (2) Because (*a*) all His perfections are summed up in the one word—love; (*b*) all His works are but the manifestations of His love; and (*c*) all His commandments are intended to teach us how to live in His love.

sion has sometimes obscured St. Paul's testimony to the truth. It is clear enough in passages like Rom. viii. 10, 11; 2 Cor. v. 17, xiii. 5; Gal. ii. 20, iii. 28; Eph. ii. 20–22, iii. 17; Col. i. 27, 28, iii. 3, 4, &c. But it is no less clearly expressed in the original in passages like Rom. vi. 23, where the Apostle speaks of life, not *through*, but in Christ, bringing about, not a personal identity, as Pantheism would teach, not an absorption of our individuality into the Divinity, but a unity of mind and will and purpose, a destruction of that opposition which exists between God and man until sin is finally expelled from the soul.

VER. 6.—**He that saith he abideth in him.** Here we have another characteristic of the spiritual life—its *permanence*. In the last verse St. John speaks of our *existing* in Christ. Here he speaks of our *continuing* to exist in Him. Bengel has, as usual, summed up the Apostle's thought in very pregnant language, "cognitio, communio, constantia." This, again, is a doctrine laid down by Christ Himself in very marked language. It is not merely that the life of Christ is to be *given* to us, but it is to be *retained* by us, by a perpetual and conscious exercise of the will. Thus Christ says (St. John xv. 4), "Abide in Me, and I in you;" and again (ch. xv. 9, the word being the same in the Greek), "Continue ye in My love." We may, with Haupt, admit that there is a

---

II. THE KEEPING OF HIS COMMANDMENTS IS THE BEING PERFECTED IN LOVE. All wrong-doing is a violation of the law of love, and comes from desiring our own apparent or immediate well-being at the expense of others, instead of seeking our happiness in theirs. The love of God, as manifested in creation and redemption alike, seeks nought but man's truest well-being. That love is perfected in us, when our will responds exactly to the will of God, and we regard all our fellow-creatures in precisely the same light of eternal love as He does.

VER. 6.—*Our present life is a progress toward that perfection.* The

gradation in the ideas to *know*, to *be in*, and to *abide* in Christ. Yet if we deny that this gradation is the main object of the Apostle here, we do not do so precisely upon Haupt's grounds, but rather because the word μένειν is not here the Apostle's sentiment, but is put into the mouth of another. The main object here would seem to be *progress towards perfection*. The Apostle desires (ver. 1) to guard his readers from sin. Yet, lest they should be discouraged, he reminds them (ver. 2) that there is a propitiation for sin. Then (ver. 3) he points out that the only test of our having grasped the full meaning of that propitiation will be the keeping God's commandments. To imagine that we can know God without keeping His commandments is to be destitute of the truth (ver. 4). By keeping His commandments we are made perfect in the love of God, and when we shall have done so, we shall have reason to know that we have been so perfected (ver. 5). But to return from the future to the present (ver. 6), to be abiding in God now is to steadily pursue the same course as Christ pursued, eschewing all evil, and perfecting our own individual life as Christ perfected humanity (Luke xiii. 32; Heb. ii. 10, v. 9). ὁ λέγων implies that any one who makes a personal profession of union with Christ is bound to follow His example.—**ought.** The word clearly denotes moral responsibility. He owes it to God and to himself; it is a duty incumbent upon him.

---

tense (see exposition) is changed here. From a final, perfected state, we turn to one in progress. Thus, as Christ in His human life took our corrupt humanity, and led it through various stages of growth to its final perfection after His resurrection (we discern this in passages like Luke ii. 52; Heb. ii. 10, v. 9), so the process is continued throughout the human life of each one of us. The spark of Divine life is communicated to us to become, through our care, a fire of love. Here the process is described as a *walk;* a gradual change of place until we come to our journey's end. That is, by steady resistance to the evil

—himself also so to walk. These words are emphatic, and emphasise obligation of ὀφείλει.—**even as he walked** (cf. Eph. v. 2; also John xiii. 14, 15). God (see note on ch. i. 6) cannot be said to *walk*. He remains ever the same. It is only man who advances from one stage of perfection to another. But Jesus Christ, as Man, may be said to do so (cf. Luke ii. 52). The aorist does not (as Bishop Wordsworth, *in loc.*) mean that our Lord's walk was "*one act* of undeviating obedience to God." As before, it relates to a past fact without specifying the time too nearly, differing from the imperfect, because that would imply that the act was being accomplished at some particular time in the past. It would not be right to leave this passage without referring to the omission of οὕτως by some MSS. There seems good reason to believe that it ought to be retained. It is quite unnecessary to the sense, and for this reason many of the best MSS. and Versions omit it. But it is an unmistakable Hebraism, and as such hardly would have been introduced by any transcriber. This is another of the many tokens of Hebrew origin in this Epistle.

---

that dwells within us, by steady obedience to the impulses toward good communicated to us by God's Spirit, we consummate the union with Christ which was begun, so that in the end there is perfect union of will, and soul, and spirit with Him. See Matt. v. 48; Rom. xii. 2; Eph. iv. 13; Phil. iii. 12, Col. i. 28, iv. 12; Heb. xii. 23, xiii. 21; 1 Pet. v. 10.

V.

DARKNESS AND LIGHT.

CH. ii. 7.—We arrive now at a new section of the Epistle. Its connection with what has preceded will best be seen by a recapitulation of what has preceded. In the first section of the Epistle, the Apostle has laid down the twofold truth—(1) that the object of Christ's coming was to make us free from sin, *i.e.*, translate us into a condition in which we no longer commit it; and (2) that in order to this it is necessary (*a*) that we frankly recognise our sinfulness, and (*b*) the fact that a propitiation has been made for it. Then he proceeds to point out (ch. ii. 3), that the proof of our having attained to the knowledge of God is obedience to His laws; that no other criterion of knowledge of Him is in the least degree admissible; that this obedience is the sign that the love of God has been perfected in us, and

---

HOMILETICS.

Ver. 7.—*Christianity no new religion.*
1. Tendencies to exaggerate the distinction between Christianity and former religions. St. Paul has brought out the fact that Christianity has brought a new light into the world (see 2 Tim. i. 10; also 2 Cor. v. 17; Gal. v. 1; Eph. ii. 15, iv. 24; Col. iii. 10; Heb. x. 20). So also in his use of the terms Old and New Covenant. He speaks of newness of life, of the newness of the Spirit, as opposed to the oldness of the letter. This view of the newness of

that God has taken up His abode in us (or perhaps it would be better to put it, that our existence is henceforth a continual living in God). This living a Divine life, he adds, involves conformity to Christ's example. And then he takes a new point of departure, and proclaims a commandment which he asserts to be both old and new. The connection of ver. 7 with what precedes and follows has been variously explained. At first sight the whole construction of the next two verses seems to involve some difficulty. But the main drift of the Apostle's meaning reveals itself after a brief examination, unless we persist in arranging the Apostle's thoughts in a severely logical form. This is precisely the arrangement of which St. John's Gospel and Epistles are least patient. The connection is not so much logical as sympathetic. Very often the thought anticipates its distinct expression. It is, as it were, adumbrated before-hand. Indicated thus slightly at first, it is then repeated, each time in greater distinctness and fulness of meaning, until at last it has been brought before us in all its bearings. Those only, I believe, who have realised this peculiarity of the Apostle's style, have grasped the connection of this passage.

VER. 7.—**Brethren, I write no new commandment unto you.** For *brethren*, the best MSS. and all recent com-

---

the Christian revelation has been caught up and exaggerated by teachers in all ages. The law is "done away"—or rather, as the word should be translated, "made useless," which gives a very different sense—in Christ. Marcion was the first to insist upon this view of Christ's mission. To him the law was not merely useless, but mischievous, and Christianity a religion entirely new. But this was seen to be an absurd misinterpretation of St. Paul's views: and it was felt that, if this view were adopted, it would lead to the conclusion that God had "left Himself without witness" in the world, and the world to itself for ages. Consequently the Church energetically

mentators read *beloved*, a reading which has also been accepted in the Revised Version. There can be no doubt of the correctness of the emendation. The first question the commentators have asked is, *What* is this commandment? The natural reply has been, that of brotherly love. Those who, like Lücke and Ebrard, insist upon the logical sequence of thought, demur to this explanation altogether. How, they say, is it likely that the Apostle should introduce the question of brotherly love in this way? He does not mention it till ver. 10. Is it likely that the commandment can be what he is *going* to say? Is it not absolutely necessary that it should be what he *has* said? Accordingly, we have various explanations of the passage. According to some, it is Christ's whole doctrine which is at once old and new,—"the Word which ye have heard from the beginning." But these last words seem rather to be a further assertion, in St. John's manner (as in vers. 3, 6 of this chapter), of the statement that the commandment of which he speaks is not new. Bullinger, again, interprets thus: In exhorting you to innocency of life, according to the example of Christ (which he supposes to be the commandment), I am giving you no new precept, though to some it may seem so, but simply repeating what you have heard from the beginning

---

repudiated this notion. Yet it has been revived in a modified form since. The mis-translation above mentioned has led to a conviction that the law was abolished, and a similar mis-translation to the idea that "the works of the law" were actual hindrances in the way of salvation. St. Paul has been held to teach that "works" did us more harm than good, and that the less we did to please God the more chance there was of being accepted with Him. This is equally to give "a new commandment" to mankind, and to obscure the fact that Christ's Gospel was the "old commandment which men had from the beginning."

of your adoption of the Christian religion. But the example of Christ can hardly be said to be a "word" or "commandment" (Braune). And can any one imagine that the proposing Christ's example to His disciples to follow, *could* be considered anything new, if we suppose, with Bullinger, that "from the beginning" means from the beginning of the Gospel? The truth is, that the advocates of these interpretations have forgotten two things. First, that, as has been said, no one who attentively reads St. John's writings can suppose them to have been drawn up in logical form; and next, that his habit of continually meditating upon the words of his Divine Master makes those words continually present to his thoughts. And he assumes that those words will be as familiar to his readers as to himself. His Gospel may or may not have been written. But can any one suppose that St. John could have instructed his hearers in the Christian faith, without having repeatedly told them of their Lord's words, "A new commandment I give unto you, that ye love one another" (John xiii. 34)? Or can we suppose that a pious Jew, and a disciple of the Baptist like St. John, could help reflecting that in one sense the commandment was *not* new, but one of the very earliest that had been given to man. It was embodied in the Law, as Christ Himself tells us (Matt. xxii. 39); and of that

---

II. CHRISTIANITY THE EXTENSION, NOT THE REPEAL OF THE LAW. This Christ teaches us (Matt. v. 17, 18; Luke xvi. 16, 17). In fact, the whole of the fifth chapter of St. Matthew conveys this truth. The "good works" of the disciple are to be "seen" (ver. 16). The law is to be kept more perfectly than it had ever yet been (ver. 20). Its precepts were shown to be more searching than had ever been supposed (vers. 21-47). Absolute perfection, and nothing short of it, was to be the Christian's goal. So St. Paul energetically asserts the excellence of the Law (see 1 Tim. i. 5, 8; and yet more emphatically in Rom. vii. 12, 14; and again in Rom. iii. 1, 2, 20, vii. 7). From the

Law not one jot or tittle was to fail (Matt. v. 18). Thus we may easily understand (1) how the natural development of his subject leads St. John to speak of the law of love; and (2) how before he unfolds it as practically new, when taken in all its fulness, he anticipates an objection which had, no doubt, often been made to him before. But we have spoken of this mention of the law of love as "the natural development" of the Apostle's subject. There must therefore be *some* connection between ver. 10 and ver. 6. What is it? It seems so plain, that one wonders how the commentators can have raised so much discussion about it. It is astonishing that men should fail to see the closest and most immediate connection between the example of Christ (ver. 6), and the command to walk in love (vers. 9, 10). Surely they might have remembered, "Walk in love, as Christ also loved us, and gave Himself for us, an offering and sacrifice to God as a sweet-smelling savour" (Eph. v. 2). "God is Love," says St. John. Christ came to manifest God to us. And what was His whole life but one long manifestation of love? How then should it surprise us that St. John should, after mentioning Christ's example, carry his thoughts on at once to the life of love, prefacing his strong exhortation to men to live it, by the declaration that it was a command both old and new? Braune is

---

Old Testament, too, we learn this truth (see Ps. cv. 8, 10, cxi. 7, 8; Isa. lv. 3). And the glory of the Old Covenant is frankly recognised by St. Paul in 2 Cor. iii.

III. CHRISTIANITY THE SUBSTITUTION OF THE SPIRIT FOR THE LETTER. The reconciliation of these two opposite views of the law is to be found in the fact that Christianity altered the mode of working of the law. (*a*) From the beginning it had rested on the two commandments to love God, and one's neighbour (Matt. xxii. 40). This was even a part of natural religion, in that men from the beginning could see that love was better than hate. And so Christianity has

very satisfactory here. He points out how impossible it is to separate the duty of brotherly love from the example of Christ, and regards the former as no more than a clearer definition of the latter. He also cites ch. iii. 11, 23, iv. 7, 21, as instances of the uniform habit of the Apostle to "pass from general precepts to the commandment of love."—**but an old commandment which ye had from the beginning.** The question here is, whether St. John by "from the beginning" means from the beginning of the Gospel, or from the beginning of humanity. The question is best settled by a reference to St. John's usual mode of expression. In ch. i. 1 of the Gospel and of this Epistle (see also ch. ii. 13, 14, iii. 8), "the beginning of the Gospel" would give a very poor and frigid sense. If we reject it there, a consideration of the *usus loquendi* of the writer would induce us to reject it here.[1] Nor is there any reason why we should not reject it. Not only do we find the command given in the Law (Lev. xix. 18), "thou shalt love thy neighbour as thyself," but St. John evidently regards it as implicitly, if not explicitly, given from the earliest times. He states distinctly in ch. iii. 11 (a passage which has been strangely overlooked by expositors), that the "message we had from the beginning" was this com-

[1] In St. John xv. 27, ἀπ' ἀρχῆς signifies from the beginning of Christ's ministry.

---

been held by a whole school of divines (Bishop Butler, for instance) to be a "republication of natural religion" with fresh sanctions. It could not be otherwise, since man was created in the image of God, and until he defaced that Image he must have had tendencies implanted in him to imitate Him in whose Image he was made. And those tendencies remained, though sadly weakened, after man had fallen. Then (*b*) the Law, as we have seen, enshrined those principles of love to God and man. And St. Paul's words, above cited, merely mean that the Law, as an external enactment, had ceased to be of use. (See 2 Cor. iii. 14, where, no doubt, it is the covenant, not the veil, whose

mandment of mutual love; and then immediately goes on to illustrate it by the example of Cain, who sinned at the instance of one "who was a murderer from the beginning" (John viii. 44). It seems hardly possible to understand that St. John could have regarded Cain as responsible for his conduct, if he had not received some precept or internal impulse tending towards brotherly love. "Sin is not reckoned where there is no law," says St. Paul (Rom. v. 13). Thus, then, St. John teaches that the command to mutual love was given to humanity from the very first. Jew and Gentile alike had it. It was written in their very nature, in which the image of God was found, until they chose to deface it by self-seeking and violence. There seems no ground for Haupt's assertion that the Apostle makes any distinction here between himself and those whom he is addressing. We have no right to import such ideas into the text unless the sense absolutely requires it. The sentence is clear enough without any such explanation: "I am writing nothing new to you; I am only writing what you have always been told." It would certainly be a very large assumption to make from such a passage if it occurred in the letters, say, of a clergyman of the present day, that he wished his readers to understand that *he* had never been told anything of the kind. While every word of

---

work is said to be at an end.) We proceed (c) to inquire *how* it is that this commandment can be said to be fulfilled, while thus it is superseded, and virtually useless. And here we find the truth anticipated under the old dispensation. Jeremiah (ch. xxxi. 33) foretells the time when the covenant shall not consist of external enactments, but inward principles. St. Paul (in 1 Cor. iii.) shows how this had actually been fulfilled. The "law of commandments contained in ordinances" (or decrees—δόγματα) has been rendered useless, because for it has been substituted an inward Spirit—the Spirit of Jesus—which enables a man to do, by the promptings of his own regenerate nature, what

Scripture should be carefully weighed, it is quite possible to carry minuteness of exegesis too far.—**The old commandment is the word which ye have heard from the beginning.** The word ἠκούσατε here fixes the meaning of λόγος as the subject of the commandment, not the Personal Word of the Father. Its sense, as we have already explained, means "heard" at some indefinite period in the past. λόγος here signifies not "word" simply, but the subject-matter of a discourse. Here it stands as equivalent to ἐντολή, and implies perhaps much the same as the expression "Word of the Lord," so constantly found in the prophets. The best MSS. and versions omit the second "from the beginning." Accordingly it is not found in the Revised Version. Its omission certainly gives greater force to the expression λόγος. This last word seems here to imply the whole substance of religion, natural as well as revealed. However little it may have been understood, the principle of brotherly love has deep root in the natural promptings of man's heart. It is testified to by the voice of conscience, by the general opinion of mankind, when not blinded by personal motives. It was explicitly taught in the Law. And, as we shall immediately see, it was republished with fresh force in the Gospel. παλαιά hardly seems to

---

had previously been formulated in laws external to him. Thus the commandment remains what it always was, while the clear view of its scope has been indefinitely enlarged, and the power and desire to fulfil it marvellously augmented. Once they were but a vague tendency implanted in us towards a principle inadequately comprehended. Then they assumed the more definite form of prohibitions engraven on stones. Then they were at last recognised as the Word of the living God, ever sounding in men's ears, as it has done from the beginning, if man had but been able to hear it.

VER. 8.—*The commandment new in its form and power.*

I. THE COMMANDMENT NEW IN FORM. As we have seen, at first

square with the view that the beginning of the Gospel is meant above.

VER. 8.—**Again, a new commandment give I unto you.** The word καινός, as Bishop Wordsworth reminds us, means that which has been renewed, as distinguished from νέος, which signifies that which is actually new. Here again the commentators who will have no reference to vers. 9, 10, have gone astray. As they explain the passage, the new commandment is, "the darkness is passing away, and the true light now shineth." How this can be said to be a "commandment" they do not explain, nor does it admit of easy explanation, without straining the force of ἐντολή into *doctrine* rather than commandment. But this, which is bad enough in Greek, is quite inadmissible when we remember that our author was thinking in Hebrew. (See note on ver. 2.) The truth is, that the form in which this "new commandment" is given in John xiii. 34 determines the form of this whole passage. What has been generally supposed to be the new part of the commandment—that which gives it its Christian depth and force—is contained in the words, "as I have loved you." And in this passage we find Christ's example cited in ver. 6, and its necessary results in vers. 9, 10. But this

---

it was but a vague impulse imperfectly felt and obeyed. Then it was formulated (Lev. xix. 18), but had to be expounded by telling men what they should not do, so as at least to enable them to keep it in some degree. Hence it assumed rather a negative than a positive form, by reason of man's incapacity to understand it. But the life of our Lord shed an altogether new light upon it. It became practically a new commandment when men saw it fulfilled for the first time. Then they began to understand something of the "breadth, and length, and depth, and height" of this "love of Christ which passeth knowledge" (Eph. iii. 18, 19). And so for the first time they began to comprehend what God's love was, when they found themselves bidden

thought is expanded in the present passage. The reasons why the command to love one another is a new commandment are given in what follows. Such explanations as Calvin's, that it is in reality old, but is daily renewed by God's inspirations in the soul; or Knapp's, that it is put forth with such energy as to be virtually new—are far from rising to the full height of the Apostle's meaning. Haupt, with deep insight into the hidden conformity of this passage with the last and deepest portion of St. John's Gospel, connects these words, not merely with John xiii. 34, but with the whole narrative from ch. xiii. 1 onward, culminating in the Passion. He sees in the expression, "He loved them unto the end," an expression of the Apostle's conviction that this awful and mysterious portion of our Lord's life was a revelation of Divine love of an altogether unique kind, and intended to lead us, first into an admiration, secondly, into a reproduction, of its spirit. His washing the disciples' feet; His affectionate and most spiritual discourses; the prayer in ch. xvii.; and finally His drinking to the very dregs the cup of sorrow for our sakes, was the placing the command to love one another on a new and hitherto inconceivable basis. Only they who have stood beneath the Cross, who have grasped the full meaning of that consummation of a life of

---

to "love one another, as Christ had loved them." The example was new, and thus the commandment, with this altogether new light upon it, became practically new also. This precept, therefore, was "true in Him and in His disciples." For He only was sinless; He only was capable of the perfection of humanity; He only, by His 'loving His own even unto the end," by the sacrifice of Himself for their sakes, could display to them the inexhaustible nature of true love.

II. THE COMMANDMENT NEW IN POWER. It was in the removing the inability of man to fulfil the commandments of God that the chief

sacrifice, can appreciate the force of the words, "Love one another, *as I have loved you.*"—**which thing is true in him and in you.** The relative pronoun is in the neuter, and therefore does not, except indirectly, mean the commandment. These words have been variously explained. Thus, Erasmus and Bullinger have translated, "what is true in Him, is true in you," which is not very far from the truth. Alford, following De Wette and Neander, explains, "the fact that the commandment is new, is true, both in Him and in you," which seems hardly to rise quite to the level of the Apostle's meaning. Braune's exposition seems to come nearer to the truth: "Brotherly love evidenced in the Christian's walk, is true in Christ the Head, and in the members of the body;" and Haupt, as might have been expected from what has been already said, comes nearer than any, when he says that "the brotherly love now in question as an ἐντολὴ καινή, has been brought into the world only through the example of Christ, and can by us be attained only through fellowship with Him. In truth ὅ ἐστιν ἀληθές is in apposition to ἐντολὴν καινήν. 'I write what is true, in Him and in you.'" That this is very probably the true explanation we shall further see when we come to the next sentence. Meanwhile, let us attempt to expand the Apostle's meaning so far as we have gone. It is true, he says, that the command to

---

blessing of the Gospel lay. "My Spirit shall not always strive with man," God had said (Gen. vi. 3). His fleshly nature was to be allowed to have its full play (ibid.) But now all was reversed. Born of the Spirit of Christ (John iii. 5), man was to be free to walk after His inspirations (Rom. viii. 2). Henceforth, therefore, there was not only an example (see above) to teach him how he ought to walk, but a voice within, crying, "This is the way, walk thou in it;" and a strength coming from union with Christ, which would enable him, in ever-increasing measure, to fulfil it. Thus the fact that the commandment

brotherly love is as old as humanity. Yet taken by the light of the example of Christ (ver. 6), it is practically a new one. Not only has man, from a long course of disobedience, selfishness, and sin, completely lost sight of the truth which, in days of comparative innocence, he was able to discern, but by the sacrifice of Christ the duty of brotherly love has been lifted up into an entirely new atmosphere. Henceforth, it does not merely mean acting kindly to one's brother, treating him as one would treat oneself; it means sacrificing oneself for him; annihilating one's personality on his behalf; living for his sake rather than our own. And this, the Apostle continues, this newness of the commandment, or rather (see above) the obligation to the life which is enjoined in the new commandment, "is true in Him." "Never man *lived* like this Man," might have been said of Him. From His Cross streamed out a new light upon the relation of man to his neighbour. And it is also true "in you," from the time you entered into fellowship with Him—from the time that His Life poured into your soul. From that time the command to lead this new life was transfigured for you also. You can no longer be content with doing no one any harm, with being generally pleasant and agreeable to those with whom you live. You cannot henceforth be content with such a moderate amount of love as the best

---

is new is true, not only in our Lord, but in us, because a new heart and a new spirit has been given to us.

III. REASON WHY THIS IS SO. It is to be found in the Revelation of Christ. He had been the Light from the beginning. But man's sin had caused Him to hide His face, until the fulness of time should come. And then He shone upon mankind. As the dawn enlightens the world around us point by point, until all stands out clear and bright in the light of day, and the darkness flies away like a cloud before the brightness of the day, so the Gospel of Christ illuminates one heart after another, and makes them comprehend what before was

men have heretofore shown to others. No! you must go further. You find yourself inwardly drawn to do more for them, to give yourself up to their service, as Christ did. And there is yet another way, as Haupt reminds us, in which this commandment is a new one. Before Christ's coming, it was a precept outside of us. Now it is a spirit breathed into us (see 2 Cor. iii. throughout; Rom. viii. 2), whereby we do, as by a new nature, the things contained in the law of conscience and of God. We shall find additional illustrations of the community of life between Christ and His members in chaps vi., xv., xvii., of St. John's Gospel. (Also see 2 Cor. xiii. 5; Col. iii. 3, and many similar passages in St. Paul's Epistles).—because **the darkness is past, and the true light now shineth.** The neglect of our version to give the exact force of the tenses has obscured the sense of this passage. The rendering *is past* would imply the perfect tense here in the Greek. In fact we find the present. A vivid force is given to the whole sentence when we translate, "the darkness is passing away, and the true light is now shining." Hence, again, it is that the command is new. A new light has been introduced into the world. The clouds of ignorance and sin are rolling away, as one after another the souls of men are brought under the influence of the Gospel of Christ. The command

---

unknown to them—the fulness of God's love, and the might of His Spirit, which is to transform them from lovers of themselves into men penetrated with the love of God in Christ. So, therefore, lastly, the commandment is new, because when Christ came, then came the Light which first enabled men to discern the will of God.

VERS. 9-11.—*Practical meaning of light and darkness.*

I. FALSE NOTIONS OF RELIGION. There is no word that has been more abused than this word "religion;" and it is abused to this day. The light has shone into the world, and men still love darkness better. They still shut their eyes to the fundamental truth of Christianity, as

is new in its force and scope; new in the illumination that is cast upon it; new in the number of hearts that are brought within its influence. And this interpretation gathers force when we remember what the Apostle means by the true light. "The life was the light of men," he tells us (John i. 4). "That was the true light," he says, "which enlighteneth every man that cometh into the world," or more probably, "which, by coming into the world, enlighteneth every man" (John i. 9). "I am the light of the world," said Jesus Christ (John viii. 12, ix. 5). Thus we see once more how it is the example of Christ, the appearing of Christ, which makes the old commandment new. We see how it becomes new, because it was true in Him, and true in those whose hearts He had enlightened. And the reason why it is true in those whom St. John was addressing, as well as in their Master and his, is given in the words on which we are now commenting. It is true in Him, because of His essential nature. It is true in them, because the darkness is passing away from men, one by one, and the true light—Himself—is gaining an entrance into their hearts. It will be seen how this view strengthens the interpretation we have already placed upon $ἀπ'$ $ἀρχῆς$. If we regard it as referring to the beginning of the Gospel, the difficulty of explaining the meaning of ver. 8

---

revealed here. We will consider some errors on this point before we touch on the truth.

1. *Religion consists in propitiating an angry deity.* Such was the notion of the heathen, such their sacrifices and ceremonies. See the speech of Balak recorded in Micah vi. 6, the passing children through the fire unto Moloch, and the like. Such we find it still in Pagan countries, as the terrible self-tortures of the Indian fakirs, and the human sacrifices in Africa and elsewhere show. And even in some Christian countries the doctrine is still taught, that austerities and penances will conciliate the favour of One who is justly offended at

seems insuperable. Christ was the New Man, the Second Adam. His life is the new life. Consequently the only tenable interpretation of the New Commandment is that which He gave, and illustrated by His Life and Death. And thus it would seem that what is meant is that the command to love is as old as humanity, but that the old commandment is transfigured and made new in the light of the Life of Christ. Before we quit this verse we may notice two words which have been variously interpreted: ἤδη, translated "now" in our version, becomes "already" in the Revised Edition. But this hardly gives the sense of the passage. To an English ear it would suggest a certain amount of surprise that the true light was shining so soon. What it does mean to convey is apparently that the true light not only is, but *has been* for some time shining. The other word is ἀληθινός, which is generally interpreted to mean genuine, as opposed to fictitious; whereas ἀληθής signifies true as opposed to false. This appears to be the true explanation. ἀληθινός is usually applied to things, and not to persons in Scripture. But when it is applied to persons, it is to contrast them with certain pretenders, whose claims will not bear investigation; such appears to be the meaning in ch. vii. 28, and ch. xvii. 3. So here there had been plenty of lights, falsely pretending to be such, in the world. The

---

our transgressions. We have incurred God's wrath, and we have to appease it. And this we must do by inflicting on ourselves the tortures He would otherwise inflict on us.

2. *Religion consists in an intellectual assent to certain propositions.* This is an inheritance from the ancient philosophy, which taught that God was known by argument and inquiry. Through the Gnostics, who placed knowledge instead of faith at the basis of religion, it found its way into the Christian Church. The attempt, justifiable at the outset, to show that there was a Christian philosophy, led to the substitution of intellectual assent to truths demonstrated from Scripture

true light had by this time appeared, and was now shining.

Ver. 9.—**He that saith he is in the light.** (See notes on vers. 4, 6.) Some commentators, *e.g.* Braune here, say that φῶς does not denote Christ, but the "sphere of the Divine life." But the Divine life is that which proceeds from God, and none can come within its "sphere" unless they are in Him. Ebrard, again, says, that the light here meant, is not that which subsists in God Himself, but that which is imparted to man. But where have we any authority to distinguish between them? We must not forget that the Epistle commences with the express "message" that God is Light, and is altogether irreconcilable with darkness. Consequently we shall altogether miss the force of this passage unless we connect it with the fundamental truth which St. John has set himself to explain. We will therefore once more briefly recapitulate the steps of this argument, or rather, perhaps, follow the train of his thoughts; for actual argument there is none. This frequent recapitulation is very necessary in an Epistle like the present, for we are apt, by concentrating our attention on one particular passage, to lose the thread of the Apostle's meditations. Starting then from the statement we have just quoted (ch. i. 5), St. John deduces the conclusion, that if we really have

---

for the subjugation of man's will to God's. Hence comes the widely spread conviction, that anything is better than to be a heretic; the disposition to think lightly of irregularities in life when put in the balance against theological error; just as if any creed whatever, however logically unexceptionable, could be a right one which did not produce conformity to Christ.

3. *Religion consists in a special set of external observances.* This was the Pharisees' error, and it is by no means extinct. The πρῶτον ψεῦδος here—and it is a very common one—is the line of separation drawn between religious and other duties. There is no such separa-

fellowship with God, we shall walk according to that which is His essential nature. This walking in light ensures purification from sin, acknowledgment of sinfulness being one necessary condition of fellowship with God. On the one hand, then, we must own ourselves sinners; on the other, our object must be to be freed from sin. To this end we must first believe that it is no longer imputed to us; that it no longer need sunder us from God; and next, that a power is given to us whereby we can overcome it, and keep God's commandments. Nothing but this can be the token of perfect knowledge of God; this is the true test of His indwelling, even the imitation of Himself. The commandment the Apostle gives is both old and new. Old, because natural morality witnessed to it from the beginning; new, because a new light came into the world in the Person of Jesus Christ. His example shows us that love of the brethren is the true fulfilment of God's commandments; hatred of the brethren, the clearest proof that the light so lately given has not as yet penetrated a man's heart. The threefold repetition of "he that saith" implies that there was a good deal of mere external profession of Christianity in the Apostle's days.—**and hateth his brother.** The first point that has struck the commentators here, is the sharp contrast drawn between love and hate. "*Tertium non datur*," says Haupt, following Bengel

---

tion. All duties are religious duties; and all moral, as distinguished from positive, duties equally binding. And it is not always seen that many so-called "religious" duties fall under the head of "positive" precepts, and are therefore less binding, less truly "religious" than any moral ones. The clear perception of this truth would save men from many errors, and the Christian religion from many scandals. This error branches off into two main channels. The one is an exaggerated attachment to religious observances, which places the keeping of Church rules and Church festivals above truth, or charity, or one's duty to one's neighbour, which attaches undue importance to days

(who says, "Ubi non est amor, odium est, cor enim non est vacuum"). "In the case of brethren, and in relation to them, indifference is impossible." This, however, from a practical point of view, is not the fact. We do *not* always either love or hate our brethren. There is plenty of room for intermediate shades of feeling. Thus Düsterdieck's forcible words, cited with approval by Alford, are eloquent, but utterly removed from the sphere of daily life. To say, as he does, "On the one side is God, on the other the world; here is life, there is death; here love, there hate, *i.e.* murder (ch. iii. 14, ff.); there is no medium,"—is to lead either to hypocrisy, or despair, or that dangerous conventionalism in which men call themselves miserable sinners without the slightest inclination to admit that they have ever done one single thing that is wrong. Other interpreters have therefore softened down the expression μισεῖν into "to love less," "not to care for" (as Bretschneider). This again is to take undue liberties with Holy Writ, both here and in Luke xiv. 26. Haupt is on the right track when he says, "We may speak in common life of inclinations and dislikes; but these are really nothing but stages of love or hatred not yet come to their full development, or into clear consciousness." The truth is that the Apostle sees here but two kingdoms or tendencies, the one of light, and the

---

and times, and ecclesiastical order. The other puts the reading and frequent conversing on Scripture, the use of a certain phraseology, a readiness of thoughts and words in prayer, an avoidance of certain specified vices and amusements, in the place of the devotion of the whole life to God, and the continual striving after higher perfection than one has yet reached.

II. THE TRUE NATURE OF CHRISTIANITY. It is (1) the avoidance of all hate, and (2) the continual practice of love.

1. *The avoidance of hate.* Every angry, or jealous, or unkind thought of others must be driven out. Every selfish impulse must be

other of darkness. In one or other of these directions every man is, at a given time, advancing. Not yet fully under its dominion, but tending to become so, and disengaging himself from its opposite. And as we see habits becoming fixed in men during life, until it becomes impossible for them to shake them off; so the Apostle looks not at the man in his present undeveloped condition, but at the goal to which he is tending. That goal—and here is the Apostle's point—is not indifference, not dislike, but positive hatred. To this, and to nothing else, is he tending, who is a stranger to the spirit of active love. The next question that arises is, What does the Apostle mean by "brother"? To this question there can be but two answers. Either the Apostle means all mankind, or he means the members of the Christian Church. Those who have restrained the words "from the beginning" to the beginning of the Gospel, have seen none but the Christian brotherhood here. Those who have given them a wider scope, feel free here also to take a wider range. But in order to be sure of the Apostle's meaning, we must study more carefully the general drift of the Epistle. Alford has here acutely remarked, that the very fact that the ὁ λέγων is himself outside the sphere of the Christian life, shows that the ἀδελφός cannot be understood of a brother in Christ. True; but the

---

wrestled with, for hate is but selfishness grown to maturity. Hatred is darkness. It blinds the eyes, so that a man cannot see the consequences of what he is doing. He neither sees the temporal consequences—pain to others, unrest, unloveliness, isolation to himself; nor the external consequences—how a man hardens himself in a very bad and cruel thought, until he becomes like to Satan and his angels, and only fit to share their fate.

2. *The continual practice of love.* A true faith must produce love; and a faith which produces love must be, so far as it goes, a true faith. And though intellectual error is an evil, and one which we are bound

speaker is at least, we are led to suppose, in outward communion with the Church. We must, therefore, look further for elucidation of the thought. We find no justification in St. Paul's practice for the wider reference. He appears invariably to use the word in the sense of a member of the Christian Church. But in our Lord's use of the word, we find the wider sense clearly intimated. The Saviour of the world, in His parable of the good Samaritan, has set His seal to the doctrine of the universal brotherhood of humanity. And in passages like Matt. v. 22–24; vii. 3; xviii. 15, 35, we find abundant confirmation of this view. So also, the Hebrew idiom is in its favour. "A man to his brother," or "a woman to her sister," means, "one man or woman to another." And again, if the Apostle had meant to confine the expression to the Christian brotherhood, he would rather have used the expression "the brethren," and thus have run less risk of misinterpretation. And the whole scope and tendency of our Lord's mission was to throw down all middle walls of partition between man and man; to proclaim that "touch" of regenerate "nature" which "makes the whole world kin." We can hardly imagine a disciple of Christ, least of all the beloved disciple, proclaiming the doctrine that he could be "in the light" who carefully restrained his love and sympathies to those who had been

---

to do our best to avoid, yet it is possible to mistake the points on which intellectual error is most dangerous. It is, above all, dangerous in our doctrine about God to forget that He is Love, that He sent His Son to reveal His Nature to us, and His Spirit to produce in us conformity to His image. In the human life of Christ we see (1) the Incarnation of the Divine likeness, and (2) the picture of what human life should be. Our faith, if it be a true faith, will lead us to grasp these truths, and, moreover, to realise the fact that a Divine Spirit is sent forth into the whole world to enable those who will to become thus sons of God. As the life of Christ was the perfection of love; as

brought into the Christian fold. Surely it was just this narrowness of sympathy, this confining love within artificial barriers, which Christ came to remove.—**is in darkness even until now.** Is *in the darkness*, as the Revised Version; though the article (see below, ver. 11) may signify darkness in the abstract. Here we are referred back to ver. 8. There the darkness is said to be passing away. In this verse we hear of those whom the light has not yet reached. And there is a hint, moreover, that they are in the outward fellowship of the Christian Church. Even now, although Christ has been revealed to the world; though these professed believers have come within the influence of that revelation; though they have entered into the Christian fellowship, are partakers of the prayers, the Sacraments, the exhortations, the example of the faithful;—even now their hearts are as dark as that of the heathen who has never heard of Christ.

VER. 10.—**He that loveth his brother abideth in the light.** There is a similarity of thought between here and ch. i. 6, 7. But there the Apostle speaks of *walking*, here of *abiding*, in the light. There, conduct; here, the abiding *condition* which produces conduct, is meant.—**and there is none occasion of stumbling in him.** The word σκάνδαλον is variously rendered in our Version. Sometimes it is *offence*, as in St. Matt. xvi. 23; sometimes *stumbling-block*,

---

the light streamed forth to show us Him who was love; so he who has the light, he whose inward parts the light has penetrated, must show forth in his actions the fact that the light is guiding him, the perfection of that love which the light reveals.

We subjoin two corollaries to these last propositions.

1. *The Gospel is the religion of humanity.* We often hear of the "religion of humanity" in these days. It is simply human reason decking itself out in the borrowed plumes of Christ's Revelation. These philosophers never dreamed of caring for humanity until Christ told them to do so. And now they have caught the idea from Him,

as in 1 Cor. i. 23; and here, *occasion of stumbling*. This last is most in accordance with its derivation, and its use in the LXX. It means what causes one to stumble; and may here mean, either (1) what causes the man himself to stumble; or (2) what causes others to stumble. The commentators, as usual, are divided. But Alford has made out a conclusive case for the former by citing John xi. 10. The words of His Master were ever ringing in St. John's ears. There can be no doubt of his having recalled and applied them here. But this may be thought not so absolutely to exclude the other meaning; and the earnestness with which, in St. Matt. xviii. 7, our Lord warns us against causing offences, might lead us here to number it among the blessed effects of abiding in the light, that the man who so abides does not cause others to stumble also. So Haupt; yet it must be confessed that this interpretation seems a little far-fetched. For the man who stumbles must himself be in darkness, whoever may have been the cause of stumbling to him. And the Apostle's object is clearly here to show that light, and nothing else, preserves a man from stumbling. The form of the expression reminds us of Ps. cxix. 165, where the LXX. has καὶ οὐκ ἔστιν αὐτοῖς σκανδαλον, *i.e.*, God's law is not an offence or stumbling-block to them. Nor can we well help being

---

they cannot carry it out without Him. An acute and impartial writer has lately called the Gospel the "enthusiasm of humanity," and has thus hit off its most essential feature. The exposition above tells us that we must put no limited sense on the word "brother" here. Such a limitation could hardly have occurred to one who had heard the parable of the good Samaritan. Thus, whatever tends to make man happier or better in this world as well as the next, is within the scope of the gospel. Whatever banishes pain, disease, sorrow, want, wretchedness, is part of its remedial agency. Every philanthropic work, every sinner reclaimed, every child trained in the way

reminded here of a similar sentiment in Luke xi. 36 (see also Rom. xiii. 10).

VER. 11.—**But he that hateth his brother is in darkness.** Here again, and throughout the verse, the Revised Version has "*the* darkness." And we are certainly to understand not a mere general idea of some sort of darkness, but that special darkness which consists in separation from God. As our Version renders by *the* light, it is clear that *the* darkness is the only consistent rendering of ἡ σκοτία (see also ver. 8). But the absence of the article in English (see on ver. 9) is calculated to convey the *abstract idea* of light and darkness rather than the idea of any particular *kind* of either. And if the abstract idea of light and darkness just given be the true one, namely, union with and separation from God, the absence of the article throughout, in English, perhaps gives a better sense than its presence. We have here a threefold description of the state of him who hates his brother. He (1) is in darkness; (2) he walketh in darkness; (3) he knows not whither he goes. His state or condition is described by the first (see ver. 9). As Ebrard says, this verse does but repeat the thought of ver. 9 in more distinct terms.—**and walketh in darkness.** This describes the nature of what in Scripture is called his *conversation*—his conduct from day to day. It varies

---

it should go, every scheme for temperance, thrift, self-help, as well as the thousand organisations for mitigating poverty and sickness, are the direct outcome of the religion of Christ. And this, because they flow directly from the example, and are inspired by the Spirit, of Him who first showed mankind that the highest goodness was the most complete sacrifice of self for the sake of others.

2. *We best preach the Gospel when we practise it.* The mediæval missionaries were successful, because their Gospel was at least more loving than the religion it superseded. But they often failed from the want of a better comprehension of their Master's mind. We all

G

from time to time. His circumstances are not always the same. But one thing remains unaltered. Whatever he does, or wherever he goes, or whatever changes may take place in him in other respects, he is in darkness still. That fact no change can ever affect, save the great and vital change of beginning to do the Will of God.—**and knoweth not whither he goeth** (see John xii. 35). Some have interpreted this of hell or perdition. But " we cannot (with Luther) so interpret the passage. It gives a distinctness to the words which is not contained in them" (Ebrard). Haupt thinks that darkness itself is the goal. But there would seem to be great feebleness, or even absurdity in saying, " He is in darkness, he walks in darkness, and he does not know that he is going to darkness." The best plan by far is to leave St. John's words in their suggestive indefiniteness. Darkness, as the next sentence tells us, prevents a man from seeing where he is going. And so with the darkness of which the Apostle is speaking. It keeps a man from seeing what will be the ultimate effect of his actions. Pain, misery, ruin, despair,—all these are inevitable results of sin. Yet it is impossible to make the man see this whose eyes are blinded. Others may see it; they may point out most clearly to the infatuated victim the result of what he is doing. But nothing can make him see it

---

know the story of the heathen, who, with one foot in the font, asked the officiating priest where his forefathers were. On being told they were in hell, he withdrew his foot, and said, "Where my fathers are, there will I be also." Children have been known to weep bitterly at the thought, impressed upon them by those who would convert them to Christianity, that those whom they loved were suffering the pains of eternal fire. A gentler Gospel has more chance of acceptance, but most of all when practice is added to preaching. The Tinnevelly missionaries laboured diligently for many years, but made little progress until the recent famine. But when English liberality fed the

himself. He is contented to go on without thought, utterly heedless of the terrible destiny which he is bringing on himself.—**because that darkness has blinded his eyes.** It may perhaps be needless to point out that the word *that* here is not the demonstrative pronoun. But the revisers, perceiving the ambiguity, have very wisely removed the word altogether. Alford has a note here which gives a very curious sense to the passage. He says, "'blinded,' not 'hath blinded,' because it is no new effect of a state into which he has lately come, but the long past work of a state which is supposed to be gone by, and is not." But, as has already been said, we cannot interpret the aorist as in classical Greek, of a single past act at some special instant of time. Here, perhaps, *hath been blinding* gives the sense best. It is something which has taken place in the past, has continued for some time in the past, but is not absolutely complete. We must not quit the subject without remarking that the whole of this passage is clearly based upon St. John ix., as well as viii. 12, xii. 35, 36.

---

dying, thousands crowded to the baptismal font. "Yours must be the true religion," they exclaimed, "when it teaches you to feed the hungry whom you have never seen." And a touching story is told of some natives of Africa who accepted the faith, because, as they said, "the Arabs enslave us, but you Christian English have set us free." So true is it, that if we wish to bring mankind to the faith of Christ, we must live the life of Christ. Whatever a man's religious profession may be, if he be not warmed by the spirit of love, "he is in darkness even until now."

VI.

THE APPEAL TO THE CHRISTIAN.

CH. ii. 12.—Having laid the foundation broad and deep that love and hate are the practical embodiment of light and darkness, the conditions of being *in* Christ or *out* of Christ, the fulfilment or non-fulfilment of God's commandments, the Apostle, in vers. 12-16 inclusive, makes an earnest appeal to those under his charge to avoid that which constitutes the greatest snare in the believer's path. That snare is the *world*. We shall see hereafter what interpretation is to be placed upon this word. But it seems clear that the introduction here of the exhortation not to love the world, together with the particularly solemn way in which this exhortation is introduced, is connected in the Apostle's mind with the thought that the world is dangerously likely, by its enticements, to

---

HOMILETICS.

CH. ii. 12.—This verse suggests a variety of thoughts, which require, in any homiletic treatment which does not combine the expository element, to be kept distinct.

I. THE RELATION OF PASTOR TO FLOCK. (1) St. John addresses his people as τεκνία (children whom he had begotten) and παιδία (children under his care). So does St. Paul (1 Cor. iv. 15; Gal. iv. 19; 1 Tim. i. 18; Philem. 10). (2) At first sight this would appear to be forbidden by our Lord's words (Matt. xxiii. 9). But in truth there is no contradiction. St. Paul and St. John were careful enough to teach that

draw the believer from the path of duty so plainly put before him.

Our first task is to ascertain the actual form of the exhortation in vers. 12-14. And this is rendered somewhat more difficult by the occurrence of a various reading in ver. 13. It is unnecessary to inform the reader of the Greek Testament that the word translated "write" in our Version is in two different tenses in the original. In the Rec. text, the first four times it occurs it is in the present tense. The last twice it stands in the aorist. But the great majority of editors and MSS. have the present three times consecutively, and then the aorist three times consecutively. And with this reading, which is obviously to be preferred, the two verses arrange themselves in parallel form: first, a general address to St. John's disciples, who are spoken of as τεκνία in the one case and παιδία in the other; next, in each case, an address to the older; and lastly, in each case, to the younger members of the Church. "Whether older and younger in a physical sense must as yet be left undetermined" (Haupt). If, on the contrary, we follow the reading of the Rec. text, we must suppose the word παιδία to refer to actual children. But then it becomes unintelligible why children should be addressed in the

---

they were only ministers, that God was the fountain of all grace (1 Cor. iii. 6; cf. 1 Cor. i. 30, xv. 10; 2 Cor. iii. 5, 6, iv. 5; Gal. iii. 5, unless this verse refers to Christ Himself; Eph. iii. 7; Col. i. 23, 25, &c.) Yet (3) though all that is done be God's work, though ministers be but the channels through which God's blessings flow (see 1 Cor. iii. 7, 8; Eph. iv. 16; Col. ii. 19), the Gospel of Christ, which is intended to promote love, does not forbid, but rather enjoins that we should love those who are made the means whereby God's gifts are imparted to us (Phil. ii. 29, 30; 1 Thess. v. 12, 13; Heb. xiii. 7, 17). And it is a law of nature and grace alike that men love those *to whom* they have been engaged in doing good. (4) Thus, then, it is well-pleasing to

first part of the exhortation and not in the second. Thus on every ground, whether the external evidence of MSS. or the internal necessities of the exegesis of the text, we are driven to reject the Rec. text. The next difficulty that meets us is, why the present is used in the first, and the aorist in the second, triad of exhortations. And here we are met by almost every conceivable variety of interpretation. Thus Ebrard, after rejecting summarily every other hypothesis, very confidently pronounces that γράφω refers to the Epistle, ἔγραψα to the Gospel, to which many, as we have seen, regard the Epistle to be a kind of preface. Braune adopts this view, dismissing, like Ebrard, other interpretations a little too curtly. Luther has avoided the difficulty in characteristic fashion, by adapting his rendering to his theory, translating ὅτι in the first, fifth, and sixth times "that," and in the remainder "for" or "because." But it is obvious that grammar and common sense require ὅτι to have the same meaning throughout, and that here "because" must in each case be that meaning. Lücke thinks that ἔγραψα refers to the preceding, γράφω (I am *now* writing), to the following part of the Epistle. De Wette and Huther, agreeing in this interpretation of ἔγραψα, interprets γράφω of the Epistle as a whole. The interpretation

---

God (a) that those who "labour in the word and doctrine" should take a deep and affectionate interest in all who are placed under their charge, "never ceasing their labour, their care and diligence" in the work of bringing them "to ripeness and perfectness of age in Christ" (Prayer Book, Ordination of Priests); and (b) that those who owe, and feel they owe, to any minister of God either first religious impressions or useful counsel in the way of holiness and salvation, should, without flattery or undue and foolish worship of the man, preserve those affectionate and filial relations which those who receive the treasures of God in Christ naturally owe to those who give them. How (5) we may best instruct those committed to our charge so as to bring them

of Beza, followed in later times by Dusterdieck and, with some slight variation, Haupt, seems to approximate more nearly to the truth. Haupt lays down with his usual clearness that if both γράφω and ἔγραψα refer to the Epistle at all, they must necessarily refer to the whole of it. And he regards the Apostle as meaning by γράφω the work of writing in which he is at present engaged, and by ἔγραψα the Epistle regarded as a finished conception in his mind before beginning it. Beza and Dusterdieck would rather refer the ἔγραψα to the mind, not of the writer, but of the reader, before whom the Epistle would come as a finished work. It seems best, in a question of such nicety, to give the student a choice of interpretations, even at the risk of perplexing him by their variety. But even at the hazard of adding to their number, it would seem reasonable to question whether the force of the Epistolary aorist has been sufficiently weighed in any of these interpretations. And Bishop Wordsworth has called attention to a fact no other interpreter apparently has noticed. It is that whereas, up to this time, the Apostle has used the present exclusively, from ver. 13 he uses exclusively the aorist. This may be seen by comparing ch. i. 14, ii. 1, 7, 8, with ch. ii. 21, 26, and v. 13. The whole scope and drift of the

---

to spiritual maturity will appear best from a consideration of the whole chapters now under review.

II. WHAT SHOULD BE THE RESULTS OF REMISSION OF SIN. We have seen (ch. i. 9) (1) that the words ἀφίημι, ἄφεσις, must not be confined to the simple act of forgiveness, but involve a more complicated process, bound up not with any special portion, but with the *whole* of Christ's mediatorial work. We may observe (2) that the remission of sins does not henceforth involve the impossibility of falling, since the Apostle proceeds immediately afterwards to warn his flock of the danger of being led away by that which is in direct antagonism to God (vers. 15, 16, ch. v. 4; cf. St. James iv. 4; also John xv. 18).

Epistle would henceforth appear to be before St. John's mind, rather than the particular passage with which he is at the moment engaged. It is clear therefore that in the present he regards the act of writing, in the aorist the Epistle as a whole. But whether we should interpret with De Wette or Haupt, or regard the aorist to refer to the fact of writing at all, is a question. If the suggestion now made have any probability, the meaning of the two members of the sentence would be as follows: "The reason why I am writing what I now write is because your sins are forgiven you, and I am desirous that such forgiveness should not be in vain. The reason why I took pen in hand to write this Epistle to you at all is because ye have known the Father, &c., and I am anxious that no surrounding temptations should rob you of that knowledge." That the τεκνία and παιδία refer to the whole body of believers, and not to believers of any particular age or period of religious immaturity, is shown by Haupt, who says, "If actual children had been intended, the Apostle would certainly have arranged the terms in natural order, either advancing from the youngest to the eldest, or taking the inverted line, but to mention the children first, then the fathers, and then again young men, has in it something inharmonious."—**I write unto**

Therefore (3) the result of the remission of sins should be (*a*) a holy watchfulness not to offend again; and this (*b*) by a more careful inquiry into what sin is, and how, by the help of God's Spirit, we may best avoid it. To those entering on life's battle it is of God's mercy that the distinctions between evil and good are usually plain and unmistakable. As we advance in life they grow subtler and more concealed, and more watchfulness than ever is needed in dealing with them. The temptations of the flesh are exchanged for those of the world. We are bound, as life advances, by ties of ever-increasing complexity to our fellow-men, ties of kindred, interest, business, and the like. By the example and persuasions of others, nay, even some-

you, little children. The address here is somewhat less affectionate than in ch. ii. 1 (where see note), where the Apostle has τεκνία μου, thus indicating the special interest he takes in his flock.—**because your sins are forgiven you.** It does not appear at first sight very clear why these exhortations should flow out of the fact that the sins of those addressed have been forgiven (observe the force of the perfect here, as a completed act), or rather *remitted* (see ch. i. 9), nor, it must be confessed, do the commentators throw much light on the subject. Nor does the comparatively modern notion that a full and free remission of sins, once applied in faith to the soul, preserves him who has received it from future reprobation, altogether fall in with the caution so clearly implied in these six verses. It may be therefore not out of place to inquire what the connection of thought is. We have seen that St. John's object in writing (ver. 1) has been to preserve his converts from sin. The thought of the propitiation removes all sense of hopelessness (ver. 2). There is henceforth light on the believer's path, so that he need not go astray. But darkness is still around, though (ver. 8) it is passing away. Dangers and difficulties beset the disciple on all sides. The world with its allurements is very near him,

---

times by their power over us, we are drawn to forget the law of love. And yet such conduct, whatever our religious profession may be, is the result of darkness, not light. The love of the world, in whatever shape it may take possession of us, is the opposite of the love of the Father. Lastly (4), the force of the appeal lies in this, that he whose sins are forgiven has at least no clog of past sin to weigh him down. He may forget those things that are behind. He may forget those sins which, by reason of his faith and repentance, have been washed away in the blood of Christ. He may feel confidence that He who has forgiven his infirmities in the past will forgive them also in the future, provided he still girds himself up to fight the battle of the

and (ch. v. 19) it is plunged in wickedness. Therefore he has need of care, lest he lose the gift of God, even eternal life. His sins have been forgiven him, but it is in order that his hands, once "tied and bound by the chain" of sin, may be untied, and he may thus be enabled to struggle with it unto the end. "I write unto you, little children, because your sins have been forgiven you, that you should not wantonly heap up fresh sins that need forgiveness. There are enemies abroad. Beware of them. Love not the world, neither the things of the world. If any man love the world, fair and enticing as it seems, the love of the Father is not in him." For the form ἀφέωνται, see Winer ("Gr. Gram.," Part II. sec. 14, 4), who regards it as a Doric form of the perfect passive.—**for his name's sake.** For the Hebraism of the name instead of the thing named we may take as an instance Acts iii. 16. The idea was no doubt derived from the practice in early times of worshipping a national deity, with a special name of his own, to which God condescended at Moses' request (Exod. iii. 13). The god each nation worshipped had a separate name (see, for instance, 1 Kings xi. 5), round which every sentiment of gratitude or awe was wont to entwine. To his favour were all successes attributed, while all misfortunes were caused by his wrath. This

---

Lord with unabated energy, and the watchfulness which experience alone can give.

VERS. 12 (*b*), 13, 14.—*Advice to the flock in general.*

I. GROUNDS FOR ENCOURAGEMENT. These are twofold as regards the flock in general, addressed as τεκνία and παιδία.

1. *The consciousness of forgiveness.* St. John here desires to inspire those to whom he is writing with confidence. He has warned them against sin (ver. 1), of the hypocrisy of pretending to be Christ's disciple without endeavouring to do His Will (ver. 4), of the antiquity of the commandment to love and of the new sanctions it has lately received (vers. 7, 8), of the glory of the light and the wretchedness of

we see not only in the Hebrew Scriptures, but it meets us on the Moabite stone, and is also to be found, but to a much slighter extent, in the Egyptian and Babylonish monuments. Thus the Name of God, that which brought His personality home to the individual, is spoken of continually in the devotional language of Israel as synonymous with Himself (see Ps. xx. 1, xxix. 2, cxxxv. 1, &c.) The point is of some importance, moreover, as bearing on the question of authorship. The idea is not a Greek one at all. The use of the expression, "for His name's sake," stamps the author as one well versed in the Hebrew Scriptures (see Ps. cxliii. 11, &c.) It may be well to notice, with Braune, that here the idea is not that of remission of sins through Christ's humanity, but on account of His life and death.

VER. 13.—**I write unto you, fathers.** The $νεανίσκοι$ might possibly be interpreted as neophytes in the faith. But then we should have had in this member of the sentence $πρεσβύτεροι$ or some other word signifying greater knowledge and experience, but hardly, one would think, the word "fathers." Thus we are compelled to conceive rather of the older and more experienced members of the Christian body, who already, it may be, even before their conversion, had learned something from the serious

---

the darkness (9-11). And now he desires to point out that all is in the believer's favour, if he will but believe. His past darkness will not be imputed to him; his past offences will not be cast in his teeth, if he will but believe in the great Propitiation which has been made for sin (ii. 2) and the Paraclete who stands by him and pleads on behalf of his sins. The greatest hindrance to repentance is the consciousness of past transgression. Man cannot believe that his past neglects, his contempt for the Divine Law, his indifference to Him who has made and redeemed him, can possibly be atoned for. Once convince him that this weight of former transgression is removed, and he can begin to advance with confidence on the heavenward path.

responsibilities of life and in the care of their families. By the young men, on the other hand, are meant those who are young, not in faith, but in years, as will appear more clearly below.—**because ye have known him that is from the beginning,** *i.e.* Christ (see ch. i. 1). What it is to know Him we learn from John xvii. 3; 1 Cor. viii. 2, 3; Gal. iv. 9. Life from Him, issuing in love to Him and all whom He has created, is the result of the knowledge which comes by faith. ἀπ' ἀρχῆς here must have the same meaning as in ch. i. 1. St. John writes to the elder members of the Church, the heads of families, those charged with the responsibility of bringing up the younger members of the Church in "the nurture and admonition of the Lord" in order that they may be warned of the snares which the enemy has set for them. For it is difficult to understand the solemnity of this address, unless it is connected both with what goes before and with what follows. With what goes before, because it is necessary that all who profess faith in Christ should know to what practical conclusions they stand pledged. With what follows, because it is equally necessary they should know what disturbing forces there are around, by which they may be "moved away from the hope of the Gospel" (Col. i. 23), and be deprived of that life of love which has been

---

2. *The consciousness of God's Fatherhood.* Another hindrance to the spiritual life is here touched upon. God's name is Jealous (Exod. xx. 5, &c.) He will "by no means clear the guilty" (Exod. xxxiv. 7). He is "of purer eyes than to behold evil" (Hab. i. 13). How then can a sinner dare to approach Him? Such is the idea of man without the Gospel. But those whom St. John addresses are haunted by no such fears. They have "known the Father." They have seen Him in the Person of Jesus Christ. They can thus discern His pity, His love, His tenderness even to the end. They now understand how He can be "just and the justifier of them that believe in Jesus" (Rom. iii. 6). For Jesus has fulfilled His requirements. And they who are

made theirs by the knowledge of God.—**I write unto you, young men, because ye have overcome the wicked one.** This passage also makes it clear that the words "young men" are to be understood literally. Were the neophytes in the faith addressed, we should scarcely have the perfect tense here, nor even the word "overcome" at all. We should rather have had serious admonitions regarding the tremendous reality of the conflict to which they were pledged—exhortations couched in the form of Eph. vi. 10–18; 1 Thess. v. 4–10; 1 Pet. v. 8, 9. See also 1 Tim. iii. 6 for the danger of speaking to one who has but just put on his Christian armour as one who is putting it off. We have to conceive here of a body of Christian young men, who may perchance have been in Christ from their infancy, who at least have been long enough in Him to have approved their fidelity in many a long and weary, but in the end victorious, conflict with the evil one. These young men, sanctified in the Spirit, strong in the knowledge of God which comes through faith in Jesus Christ, have kept youthful lusts at a distance; have preserved their purity in the midst of a society corrupt and self-indulgent to a degree which we in a Christian age and country can scarcely conceive. Yet the aged Apostle, as he looks out upon that corrupt

---

united to Him by faith, are accepted because of His all-holy Life which is given to them. Let them turn their back on the unworthy past; let them give their hearts and lives to Jesus in the present, and they need feel no apprehension for the future.

II. THE EXPERIENCE OF ADVANCED BELIEVERS.

1. St. John speaks next to fathers. He appeals to them (*a*) because of their *influence*, and (*b*) because of their experience.

(*a*) *Because of their influence.* This influence is naturally greatest with their own children, whose early opinions and habits they have power to form. But it is not confined to them. In many relations of life those who advance in years are looked up to for sympathy, help,

society, as he sees the toils of the enemy of souls lying in wait for the believer even in the most innocent pursuits, the most hallowed relations of life, trembles still for those whom he has brought to the knowledge of the Saviour, and bids them beware lest he, whom in his own form they would resist or flee from with horror, should beguile them by presenting himself to them under the cloak of the natural allurements of the world which God has made. It will be undesirable to enter at length into the consideration of the words τὸν πονηρόν here, in its bearing on the controversy as to the rendering of the words in the Lord's Prayer. Here, however, they undoubtedly (as the gender, here unquestionable, elsewhere often doubtful, shews) refer to the devil. Even were the gender doubtful here, St. John could not have congratulated the young men on having obtained a final victory over the evil from which he warns them they are still in danger. But for him to congratulate them on many a decisive victory over an enemy who, though defeated, will be sure to renew the attack, is reasonable enough. This much, however, is clear, that the personality of the author of evil, and his connection with every manifestation of the evil which he brought into being, is as clearly asserted

---

guidance. We may complain that the young are heady, and bent on going their own way; but this is the case only with the minority. Both the wiser and the weaker (who together constitute the majority of the young) feel their need of advice. The wise under all circumstances, the weak, at least in very many cases, when not alienated by want of sympathy, will turn for counsel to those older than themselves. And not only advice, but power rests as a rule rather with the older than with the younger members of society. Thus the influence of the "fathers" is far greater in the community than that of the "young men;" and therefore there is far greater need of its being duly exercised. "Fathers" have also (*b*) experience, especially *spiritual* experience. Not only have they known inward trials, inward wrestlings with the evil one, these are common to old and young alike; but they

here as anywhere else in Holy Writ. For the expression see Matt. xiii. 19, 38; Eph. vi. 16; 2 Thess. iii. 3, &c.

VER. 14.—**I write unto you, little children.** Rather, (see above) *I have written unto you, little ones.* We have here παιδία, not τεκνία. And παῖς has the sense rather of servant than of child, "of subordination rather than of kinsmanship" (Westcott). See Matt. xiv. 2; Acts iv 25; Luke i. 69.—**because ye have known the Father.** We have no longer the fact of the remission of sins as in the former address to the τεκνία, but the result to which it leads, knowledge of the Father. And knowledge of the Father may be distinguished from knowledge of "Him that is from the beginning" if we remember that the former strikes a deeper and tenderer chord than the latter. We know not merely the eternity, but the Fatherhood of God. Thus St. John, as his manner is, with repetition adds confirmation.—**I have written unto you, fathers, because ye have known him that is from the beginning.** It seems difficult to assign any reason for this clause having been repeated unaltered, when the others are repeated but strengthened. Bengel suggests that it is from reverence to the "fathers." But this hardly seems satisfactory, for the "fathers" and "young

---

have also been able to see the issue of these things. They have seen good come out of evil, untold blessings come out of what they have supposed to be the great misfortunes of their lives, temptations even the means of disciplining the soul in holiness, so that they can both counsel and encourage those in trouble. Thus in a double sense they are fathers—in a natural sense as the parents of their own children; and in a spiritual sense as the source, under God, of the spiritual life of many who owe religious impressions or perseverance in the work of grace to their teaching.

III. THE ENCOURAGEMENT TO YOUNG MEN. St. John speaks to young men who have known Christ, and walked in His ways, as already acquainted with the strength that is in Him. Through that strength have they been enabled to "flee youthful lusts." In that

men" alike are the τεκνία and παιδία of the Apostle, whom he addresses as such, before he divides them into classes. We must be content to leave the fact without explanation.—**I have written unto you, young men, because ye are strong, and the word of God abideth in you, and ye have overcome the wicked one.** As the age and authority of the fathers have been appealed to, so is the energy of the young of the flock. Once more the thought is strengthened as well as repeated. Not only does the Apostle speak of the victory over the temptations that "do most easily beset" young men on their entrance into the world, but of the natural vigour with which they are able to encounter them, as well as of the supernatural power with which they are armed for the conflict. The "word of God" here (the Vatican MS. omits τοῦ θεοῦ) probably means the same as in ver. 5, and in John v. 38, x. 35; Rev. i. 9, and elsewhere.

---

strength they may look confidently forward to new victories in years to come. He bids them to be watchful, for new and more hidden temptations are in store for them; but the last thing he thinks of is to chill their spirits with despair. On the contrary, he nerves them to future warfare by their experience of the past. I write to you, not to go forth to your warfare in a spirit of anxiety and trembling, but only of wise caution and foresight. "He who hath begun a good work in you will perform it unto the day of Jesus Christ." The very fact that you have overcome before is a reason why you should overcome again. You have conquered evil within; now you must learn to conquer evil from without. "He that is born of God overcometh" not merely the flesh, but "the world. And this is the victory that overcometh the world, even our faith."

VII.

THE OBJECT OF THE APPEAL—LOVE NOT THE WORLD.

CH. ii. 15.—After the solemn adjuration to all the members of his flock, who are all, old or young, little children, both in age and in opportunities of knowing Christ, compared with the Apostle, he goes on to say what lesson it is he especially desires to emphasise just now. As we have seen, that lesson is, that there is one very great disturbing force close at hand, which may prevent them from realising that life of light, that separation from darkness, which he has been pressing upon them.—**Love not the world.** This is the great snare which may make all belief in Christ useless, if it be not carefully avoided. Our first question then is, What is meant by the term "world" here? It is necessary to remember that two words are thus rendered in our version, αἰών and κόσμος. The first of these, derived from ἀεί and ὤν, and denoting continuance of existence, relates to a course of events of

---

HOMILETICS.

I. THE CHRISTIAN IS BOUND TO RENOUNCE THE WORLD.
1. *What is meant by the world?* (See Exposition.)
2. *In what sense are we to renounce it?* Are we to hate all we see? No, for God made it. Are we to hate our fellow-creatures? No, for

very vast duration. We find it in Matt. xii. 32; xiii. 39; Gal. i. 4; Eph. vi. 12, &c. In the phrase εἰς τὸν αἰῶνα it is translated *for ever*, as in ver. 17. The other word, κόσμος, has a different signification. Connected with κοσμέω, and probably with the Greek κόμη and the Latin *coma*, it has the idea of *order, arrangement*. Thus it refers primarily to the physical universe, which God brought into being, subjected to certain laws, and pronounced "very good." Of this visible order, however, man forms a part. And both the Old Testament and the New tell us how "an enemy" sowed tares in the field, disturbed the good order of God's universe. Henceforth, now that man's whole moral nature is deranged, this visible order is no longer a blessing, but a snare. It has become subjected to another ruler, who is described as ruling over both the present αἰών and the κόσμος (John xii. 31, xiv. 30, xvi. 11; 2 Cor. iv. 4). And it is precisely this double aspect of all around us, God's order at the outset, but perverted by an evil influence, that constitutes the difficulty. There is a compass, but it is out of order; it no longer points true. We have to look up to the heavens to see how far it has been diverted from its proper direction. Many different interpretations of this word κόσμος have been given, as may be seen by a reference to almost any commentary on this passage. Some of them give a different sense to κόσμος in this verse and the two which follow. It is needless to say that this is extremely arbitrary. It is to put man's fancies in the place of God's word. The

---

God "loved them, and gave Himself for them." But we are to take care (*a*) to eschew the evil that is now inextricably intermingled in it, and (*b*) to be watchful over that evil in ourselves which might lead us to set an undue value even on things innocent—such a value, that is, as might lead us to prefer them to God.

notion even of Ebrard and Haupt must be given up here. They regard σκοτία and κόσμος as almost convertible terms. The κόσμος, says the former, is "the world ruined by Adam's fall, so far as it is still the world, and still bears Adam's sinful nature in it;" "σκοτία," says the latter, "is the animating principle, κόσμος the element in which it works." Here we are very near the truth, but we do not seem to have quite reached it. If we take κόσμος in the simple sense in which we have taken it above, as God's order, in which nevertheless an evil principle still works, and even to a certain extent rules, we shall have reached the solution, and have escaped a difficulty which has given infinite trouble to expositors. The difficulty is this: How can we be commanded not to love what God loves? "God so loved the world," we are told, "that he gave His only begotten Son" in order to save it. God *does* love the world, and He intends to save the world, and when He *has* saved it, then we may venture to love it again. But just at present, while we and it are in a transition state, we cannot venture to give our whole heart to it, lest we should by so doing be drawn away from Him who alone is worthy of our love. He, in Christ, is now reconciling the world unto Himself. The mediatorial work is being carried on. When it is completed, then we may love the work as well as the Worker. Until then, the very fact that it is partly His work and partly not demands that we should not give ourselves unreservedly to it, but attach ourselves to Him. The notion that "man and man's world" (Alford, following

---

II. WHY A CHRISTIAN IS BOUND TO RENOUNCE THE WORLD. Because it is corrupt. It is no longer what it was when God made it. It is full of snares and temptations of every kind. So evil has it become that all that is must be destroyed and re-created before man can be safe among things visible.

Düsterdieck) is here meant is too contracted. There is nothing in this world below that may not be a snare to us, for the corrupting principle in the world is in ourselves also, and may pervert the most innocent things around to our hurt.—**neither the things that are in the world.** This might seem a needless repetition; but in truth not one jot or tittle of God's word can be said to fall to the ground. A man cannot renounce the world in general unless he renounces it in particular. On no point have more mistakes been made than in this. One man makes a resolution that he will devote himself to the monastic life, and because he has thereby cut himself off from a great number of pleasures and temptations, he fancies he has renounced the world. Another adopts a particular style of phraseology, gives up certain amusements, devotes himself to certain "religious" works and devotional practices, and because he has thereby separated himself from certain openly ungodly persons, fancies that he has renounced the world. Another is a philanthropist, and because he devotes his life to good works, fancies that he is a perfect Christian, and does not see how much the love of being conspicuous, of being looked up to, of being a leader of others, directs him in his actions. How necessary then the caution here given, that to love any one of the things of this world (see original, $\mu\eta\delta\acute{\epsilon}$, *no nor yet*) better than God is to love the world which God has bid us shun.—**If any man love the world, the love of the Father is not in him.** The best explanation of this passage will be reached by

---

III. WHAT TEMPTATIONS ARE THERE IN THE WORLD? These may be summed up in three heads.

1. *The lust of the flesh*—the incitement proceeding from our corrupt humanity. Every desire implanted in us has its proper object, and proper laws to regulate its action. Man's corruption has altogether

observing the force of the word ἀγαπάω, which, as we have seen, denotes a love of a higher order than is implied in φιλέω. The sort of love here intended is not personal affection merely (φιλία). It implies satisfaction, approbation. It involves something in relation to good of the feeling which St. Paul condemns in Rom. i. 32 in relation to evil, where he regards it as the worst feature of those of whom he is speaking, that they not only commit crimes themselves, but "have pleasure in those that do them." Prof. Cremer puts the matter well in his Lexicon (2nd edition), where he tells us that ἀγαπᾶν is used (1) in all places where the *direction of the will* is the point to be considered, and therefore (2) when an *eligere* or *negligere* takes place. Thus, then, if a man can regard the world in its present condition, or the allurements it offers him, with any degree of satisfaction, he must of necessity be estranged from God. Some MSS. read "God" here; but the reading is rejected by most editors from external and internal evidence alike. It is far more likely that a copyist should have substituted "God" for "Father" than "Father" for "God." It has been asked whether the phrase "the love of the Father" means our love to God or His to us? The love of God to us cannot here be meant, if it be only because He does and can love the world, though we cannot venture to do so. But the love of God *in* us may be meant, which produces in us a reciprocal love to Him, a recognition of His Fatherly kindness, and an irreconcilable opposition to all that He hates. Such

---

destroyed his sense of the harmony of things, his conception of the laws which ought to regulate his desires. He now desires what he ought not to have. He desires even what is lawful beyond the bounds of moderation. Hence the disorder both within and without,—

a love would implant in us an unconquerable aversion to the world, as it now is, and all things in it, when put into competition with Him.

VER. 16.—**For all that is in the world.** Either (1) "all that is in the world" is in apposition to "the lust of the flesh," &c., so that the words refer only to these three sources of evil. Or (2) perhaps the Apostle here means all that is both *in* the world and *of* it, or (3) he may be using the word πᾶν in its usual Hebrew sense of by far the greater part; or (4) he is taking a comprehensive view of the motives of human action in the world of his day, and classes them under the threefold heads, the lust of the flesh, the lust of the eye, and the pride of life. Such is life from a general view of it, such the principles on which men act who live for this world and it alone. —**the lust of the flesh** (ἐπιθυμία). The longing desire after anything; used generally in the N. T. in a bad sense. "Of the flesh," that is, which is prompted by that part of man which we call the flesh. This flesh (σάρξ) is not the body of man (σῶμα), which is God's workmanship, and can be redeemed (Rom. viii. 23; cf. 1 Cor. vi. 19), but the corruptible principle thereof, which was introduced into the world by sin. The lust of the flesh therefore comprises those animal and other passions arising from that part of our nature which is in conflict with the laws impressed upon us in the beginning by God. "The lust of the flesh" signifies inward, as opposed to outward temptations, mentioned under the head "the lust of the eye." To confine the meaning

---

in man's heart, and in the world. And all this proceeds from the present condition of the world, which is no longer as God made it.

2. *The lust of the eyes.* External objects have an exaggerated power over us since man fell. In his normal state his desires would be moderate, rational. Now he desires all he sees that seems pleasant,

here to mere animal passions is to misconceive the Apostle's meaning. *All* irregular desires arising from within are here meant.—**the lust of the eye.** And to these correspond the incitements arising from without, which often stir up the unruly passions within. The lust of the eye, that is, the desire of possession which is aroused in us by seeing any object (see Matt. v. 28), is frequently the cause of bringing the lust of the flesh into action.—**and the pride of life.** Rather, *the boastfulness of our way of living* (see Rom. i. 20; 2 Tim. iii. 2). For there are three words which are translated 'life' in our Version. The first, ζωή, is life in itself: life such as God lives, and such as flows from Him, the eternal life which He promises to His creatures. The second, ψυχή (often translated 'soul,') means the mere animal life of man, breathed into him by God at his creation (Gen. ii. 7), but not involving those higher attributes of perfection which come to him by his possession of a πνεῦμα. The third, βίος, the word used here, relates to our mode of passing life, and the means whereby we sustain it; "table, furniture, equipage, income, rank" (Alford). See Mark xii. 44; Luke viii. 14, 43, xv. 12, 30, xxi. 4; 1 Tim. ii. 2, &c. The boastfulness of life, then, is the spirit that sets value upon such things as these, that prides itself upon rank, wealth, power, education, talent, cleverness, or any other gift that is the source of envy or admiration among the children of this world, and despises those who do not possess them. Such satisfaction have men ever felt, and continue still to feel,

---

and is discontented if he do not obtain it. Hence envy and malice on the one hand, luxury and riot on the other.

3. *The pride of life.* The special guilt of this sin is in the fact that it does not recognise the blessings of life as God's gifts. Taking them, not as a trust, but as an inherent right, it prides itself on them, and

secretly or openly, in the perishing things of this world.—**is not of the Father, but is of the world.** Here, again, we have an apparent truism, but in reality an important truth. There are three principles which rule the world as the Apostle saw it, and which still continue to rule it as we see it, though with a diminished power. These are the corrupt instincts of unregenerate humanity, the tempting baits of pleasure and ambition which stir those instincts, and the disposition to set a value upon external things, to pride ourselves upon having them, to despise and treat contemptuously those who have them not. These principles seem natural and reasonable enough to those who know not Christ, but to those who have known Him it is sufficient to say that these things come not from the Father of Him Who has redeemed us from these corruptible things, but that they are of the essence of that corruption which has seized on the world which God created.

VER. 17.—**And the world passeth away.** Rather, *is passing away* (cf. 2 Cor. iv. 18). The present order of things, which is corrupted, shall be destroyed (see Matt. xxiv. 35; Heb. i. 11; 2 Pet. iii. 7, 10, 12). And there shall be a regeneration (Matt. xix. 28), a restoration of all things (Acts iii. 21), "a new heavens and a new earth wherein dwelleth righteousness" (2 Pet. iii. 13). The words are almost the same, but the thought is somewhat different to that in ver. 8. The passing away of the darkness is a matter of *sight*, the passing away of the world is a matter of *faith*. The Apostle sees as an actual fact the light

---

uses them to humiliate a neighbour. There is no sin more common in social life than this. To desire to set our neighbour down by reason of our wealth or position, the desire to eclipse by vainglorious display, either of wealth or knowledge, the greed for power and the anxiety to display it when we have it, the use of all we

of Christ entering one heart after another, and dispelling the darkness there. He also beholds in faith the world hastening to its destruction, and reads the truth in the mutability of all earthly things.—**and the lust thereof.** 'Thereof' is bracketed by Westcott and Hort, with manifest advantage to the clearness of the thought. The αὐτοῦ may easily have been added, from the idea that it was wanted to the completeness of the sentence. But the Apostle's idea was no doubt that lust itself was at least as transient as the world which gave rise to it. Here, no doubt, there is a nearer and a further fulfilment of the Apostle's words. All earthly desires are fleeting. Some pass away with fruition; some are replaced by others as we grow older, and our tastes alter; all vanish, as far as we are concerned, when we bid farewell to this world. Hence we may gather how all these earthly lusts will disappear with the world that gives them being. But one thing is unchangeable, and that is the will of God.—**but he that doeth the will of God abideth for ever.** The nature and completeness of the union between the believer and Christ is not yet explained. It is more clearly pointed out as the Epistle goes on. But here we learn that if we desire to escape the sentence of death which is pronounced upon all things here below, our wills must be one with the unchangeable will of God. We do not yet learn how this is to be, how that "God hath given to us eternal life, and that this life is in His Son" (ch. v. 11). To this great truth the various parts of this Epistle lead up. A hint is given us in ver. 5 of

---

have to aggrandise ourselves and depreciate others, this is what St. John means by the boastfulness—the empty strut, conceit, swagger—of life.

IV. THE REASON WHY WE SHOULD RENOUNCE THE WORLD. Because it cannot last. It is hurrying to the end prepared for all

this chapter that the believer *is* united with God. And here we learn that if we are to be partakers of His life, there must be a complete subjugation of our wills to His. Our affections must not be set upon the perishable things of the world we see, but upon the doing His will Who is invisible to the eyes of sense, and can be discerned by the eyes of faith alone.

---

things visible. If we cast in our lot with it, we too shall pass away with it. If we choose a higher lot, there may be temporary inconvenience, but there will be eternal gain (1 Pet. v. 10).

VIII.

THE WORK OF ANTICHRIST.

CH. ii. 18.—After the solemn appeal to his "little children," the fathers and young men of the flock, to avoid the temptations which surrounded them and threatened to engulf them once more in the darkness which the revelation of God in Jesus Christ was removing, the Apostle proceeds to enforce his exhortation from a different point of view. This enticing world was rendered yet more enticing by a spirit that dwelt within it. The "last times" so often spoken of were at hand, and the Antichrist who had been foretold had already his forerunner in the world, corrupting the faith of many.—**Little children, it is the last time.** More literally the *last hour*, as Wiclif, the Rhemish, and the Revised Version translate. Our translation here, as in so many other places, follows Tyndale. The literal translation emphasises the fact that the Apostle, like all his brethren,

---

HOMILETICS.

CH. ii. 18, 19.—*Characteristics of the last time.*
I. IT IS THE LAST TIME. This expression has two meanings in Holy Scripture. It means the last age of this present world, and next, the life to come which is to succeed it. (1.) This last would appear to be its meaning in 1 Pet. i. 5, when compared with the preceding verse. Of course the "last time," when used strictly, refers to this new order of things, the "times of restitution of all things" (Acts iii. 21), the

believed the coming of the Lord to be nigh. "He at once intensifies and sharpens the usual phrase ἔσχαται ἡμέραι into ἐσχάτη ὥρα, and we are at once penetrated by the feeling that he beholds this last preparatory fraction as hastening to its end, and the final castastrophe as impending" (Haupt). *How* near he regarded it as being we need not ask. He must have well remembered the words, "of that day and that hour knoweth no man, no, nor the angels of heaven, neither the Son, but the Father." And though the selection of the word ὥρα instead of ἡμέραι implies a notion of nearness, yet on the other hand the absence of the article clearly signifies that the nearness was an indefinite nearness—that the termination of the "last hour" was in no man's power to fix. (We may compare "the last day" in John vi. 39, 40, 44—made definite by the article, and clearly signifying the day of judgment.) What is meant by the last hour there can be little doubt. The idea was familiar to the writers of the Old Testament. The *Acharith hayamim* (the *aftertime*), variously translated in our Version (see Gen. xlix. 1; Numb. xxiv. 14; Deut. iv. 30, xxxi. 29; Isa. ii. 2; Dan. x. 14; Micah iv. 1, &c.), is rendered frequently in the LXX. by such expressions as ἐν ἐσχάταις ἡμέραις and the like. The Talmudic expression, which may no doubt be traced back to times anterior to that in which the Apostle wrote, spoke of this time as the

---

"regeneration" (Matt. xix. 28), when the "new heavens and new earth, wherein dwelleth righteousness" (2 Pet. iii. 13; cf. Isa. li. 16, lxv. 17, lxvi. 22; Rev. xxi. 1), shall have appeared, when the "former things shall have passed away" (Rev. xxi. 4), and "all things are become new" (2 Cor. v. 17; Rev. xxi. 5). But (2.) it usually refers to the last age of the present order of things. The history of the world, regarded from the order of God's dispensations, is divided into four parts. First, the antediluvian world, when mankind were given up to

coming era ('olam habba). This era had now arrived (see also Acts ii. 17; 1 Pet. i. 20). What its duration was to be no one could tell. This only men knew, that it was the *last*, and therefore a time for serious thought. Moreover, the Christian Church had already had serious warnings concerning those times. St. Paul had spoken of them[1] in language sufficiently solemn in the two first Epistles he had written (see 1 Thess. iv. 16, v. 4; 2 Thess. ii. 1–12). He had repeated his warning in 1 Tim. iv. 1; 2 Tim. iii. 1. St. Peter too had spoken of the great day as coming "as a thief in the night" (2 Pet. iii. 10), and of men living in the "last days" in thoughtless indifference to its near approach (2 Pet. iii. 3, 4; cf. Jude 18). Nor should we forget that the Apocalypse had then been written, if we would enter fully into the spirit of the exhortation, "Little children, it is the last hour." Bengel's explanation may be noticed as a curiosity, that the words mean the last days of St. John's own life.—**and as ye have heard that Antichrist shall come.** Here again our translation is due to Tyndale. Wiclif, the Rhemish, and the Revised Version render

---

[1] Haupt expresses a doubt whether the Epistles to the Thessalonians had as yet reached Asia Minor. But St. Paul had been dead nearly thirty years. He was well known to the Church at Ephesus. Is it likely that his earliest Epistles would have been unknown to Churches in which he had lived and taught, and which he had addressed in some of his most striking Epistles? See also below, on Antichrist.

---

their own devices, and finally perished in one common ruin. Next, the patriarchal period, when men as a rule were left to themselves, but a spark of Divine light glimmered in a single family. Next, what may be termed the educational or preparatory period, when God's chosen people lived under the training of the law, and other nations were trained under the inferior but by no means useless method of speculation and philosophy. And then, the final period, in which man-

literally *cometh*, *i.e.* is to come. "The future," says Braune, "is implied in the idea of coming; the present indicates the certainty of the event." Wordsworth refers for this construction to Matt. ii. 4. The aorist ἠκούσατε refers to some indefinite period of past time, and is well rendered by our perfect here. Daniel had spoken of an Antichrist (ch. viii.); St. Paul had spoken yet more distinctly (2 Thess. ii. 8) of a "lawless one" who should set himself deliberately and distinctly, not only against Jesus Christ, but against the God whom Jesus Christ had revealed. This passage, as we have just contended, could hardly have been unknown to the believers at Ephesus. And the phrase "*ye* have heard" may not unfairly be pressed to mean something more than could be found in the Jewish Scriptures. St. John himself, no doubt, had spoken of adversaries of God in the Apocalypse, and these, no doubt, are included. But inasmuch as he speaks, and that very mystically, of *two* beasts embodying this spirit of resistance to the truth (Rev. xiii.), we cannot help seeing that it is of something more definite that he is speaking here. The ἄνομος of St. Paul, mentioned frequently no doubt in the oral as well as written teaching of the Apostles, is the idea present to the mind of St. John. The received text here has the article before ἀντίχριστος. Wordsworth and Alford reject it. Haupt does not seem to have observed

---

kind enjoyed the full revelation of God's purpose in Jesus Christ. On this last period we may remark—

1. *That it has disappointed expectation.* The Apostles looked for an immediate end of the world. Nor was it surprising that they should have done so. The hideous and revolting wickedness of the age, the persecution of the elect, the huge antichristian tyranny of the Roman Empire, seemed to fulfil exactly the predictions of Christ. There have been other periods which have struck men's imaginations with an awe

the various reading. As it is not found in ℵ and B, we shall naturally expect to find it absent from Westcott and Hort's text. There can be little doubt that it should be omitted. St. John's object here is to direct attention rather to the spirit than to the person of Antichrist. " As ye have heard that an Antichrist is to come, so I warn you that practically you may meet him already."— **Antichrist.** Two explanations have been given of this word—(1) *instead of* Christ, (2) *against* Christ. The supporters of the first opinion would see in the word one of the false Christs whom Jesus prophesied should come before His second advent. Those who advocate the second see rather in Antichrist the impersonation in bodily form of the adversary who resists Christ. The majority of commentators prefer the latter, and it unquestionably falls in with the view of Antichrist put before us in the Second Epistle to the Thessalonians. It will hardly be expected that here we should enter fully into a question of so great complexity and difficulty as the nature and coming of Antichrist. Some salient points, however, of his character as revealed in Holy Writ may here be noted. (1.) St. John does not distinctly speak of a personal Antichrist, though, as Haupt remarks (after Calvin, Neander, and others), his teaching does not exclude the possibility of the coming of such a being. The word only occurs here, in ver. 22, in ch. iv. 3, and

---

of His immediate coming. At the time when the Western Roman Empire broke up, the hordes of barbarians who overran the empire, their unbridled lust and pitiless ferocity, the unscrupulous tyranny of their leaders, seemed again to answer to our Lord's description. Once more, when the tenth century drew near its close, men imagined that the cup of iniquity was full, and that the world would soon come to an end, a conviction which shaped itself into the lines of St. Bernard of Morlaix—

in his second Epistle, ver. 7. (2.) He seems to regard it (Ebrard) as an embodiment of the principle of σκοτία, or opposition to light, of which he has before spoken. (3.) The special form which this opposition to light takes in all time is worthy of special note. It consists in *the separation between Jesus and Christ* (ver. 22), the denial (ch. iv. 3 ; 2 John 7) that Jesus is *come in the flesh*. (4.) St. John seems to distinguish between the *spirit* of Antichrist and his personal revelation. Of the latter he says nothing, of the former he says much. And this is probably because he would have us understand, after St. Paul, that the mystery of iniquity is already in active operation (ἤδη ἐνεργεῖται, 2 Thess. ii. 7), but that in every age there are certain antagonistic influences at work, which prevent the combination in one man of all the evil influences working against the Divine Person and purposes. Thus there are many antichristian influences in the world, and many people inspired by them, who are all more or less embodiments of that great principle of evil which is destined one day to find a personal representative on earth—one, that is, who, without a direct incarnation of the spirit of evil, which would hardly be permitted, will lend himself to carry out that evil spirit's purposes in all their entirety. Thus the view which has regarded as Antichrist either the Popes or the Roman Catholic Church

---

"The world is very evil,
The times are waxing late."

Again, in the sixteenth century, the Papal party imagined that they saw the end of the world in the rush of independent thought, not always unmingled with scepticism, which overwhelmed the barriers erected by authority, and seemed to many likely to sweep away truth in the flood of licence. Later still, those who regarded the Papacy as the

from its position as a worldly institution, designed to win temporal authority, has some foundation in the facts of the case, insomuch as facts clearly show that this authority, as practically exercised in the working of the Roman Catholic Church, is not that of Christ, but frequently issues in a direct defiance of His precepts, and thus is in open opposition to Him. But as Antichrist is to be one man, he cannot, of course, be the Popes in general. Nor can he be the Roman Catholic Church, for no man can worship the beast, or receive his mark on forehead or hand, without drinking of "the wine of the wrath of God" (Rev. xiv. 10). We cannot say this of every member of the Roman Catholic communion. We are therefore driven to look for the revelation of Antichrist as still to come.[1] In what direction we are to look for it we may discover from what has already been said. The denial that Jesus has come in the flesh, the separation between Jesus and Christ, is the sign of Antichrist. That is, the denial of the truth that in Jesus Christ we have God incarnate in the flesh; the assertion that God has *not* revealed His will to us, that He remains ever "unknown and unknowable," and that Jesus Christ was

[1] Bishop Wordsworth regards the Man of Sin in 2 Thess. to be distinct from Antichrist. The former he sees in the Church of Rome; the latter in the "open, impious denial of the Father and of the Son." Most commentators, however, identify the two.

---

true Antichrist, observing the signs of its decay, have seen in the growing weakness and final destruction of the temporal power the sign that the end is approaching. But "the end is not yet." Many a principle has yet to be worked out; a new conflict is at hand under new conditions. The Gospel has still to be preached throughout the whole world. Like all other prophecies, this of Antichrist (see "Davison on Prophecy") has a nearer and a further fulfilment. The Neronian era, or downfall of the Roman Empire, is the nearer one.

I

a simple Galilean peasant of pure morals and extraordinary abilities, who contrived to persuade His disciples that He had Divine powers, and that He had come to make known God's will to mankind. This is the direction in which we are to look for manifestation of the Antichristian spirit. This manifestation has lately taken a new direction, which may very possibly be the last one. The Positivist philosophy consists in a denial of God and a deification of man. "God is man, and man is God," it cries, in a strange travesty of the Christian creed. On this principle it is proposed to found a Church. That Church is to have one object of worship, the spirit of humanity. It is to have a ritual, involving the worship of famous men, but above all of the "spirit of man." The goal is the perfection of humanity through the progress of science, the spread of knowledge, the intellectual and material advancement of mankind. And with the immense material resources at the command of mankind, and the increasing distaste of Christians for the appeal to force, such a principle might easily develop into a tyranny of a most formidable kind. There are not wanting signs of a possible outbreak in the direction of Nihilism—the negation, that is, of all that men have hitherto held to be truth. Such a power would combine in itself all the Antichristian elements which have existed in the world before its time. It would display

---

But as regards the final one, it is still true that "of that day and that hour knoweth no man."

2. *Yet it is always at hand.* Antichrist is ever "ready to be revealed." And it may be said that he is more ready now than ever. The least thoughtful among us must see what a vast yet silent revolution is passing over us. The ends of the earth are brought together by steam and electricity. Ideas flash with lightning rapidity to the ends of the earth. Movements arise and are brought to their comple-

the cynical contempt for human life and liberty, for the rights of conscience, the sacredness of the family, which have distinguished the Roman hierarchy, with the greed for gain and conquest, the disregard of one's own word, of treaty obligations, of the claims of right and justice, which have characterised Antichristian rulers and conquerors, as well as the disregard of morality, of law, of everything but force, which animated the fierce soldiery who have in past times been let loose upon the world. Its vehement hostility to Christianity might impel it to "wear out the saints of the Most High." But its reign would be short. Perhaps the "thousand two hundred and ninety days"—the "time, times and a half" of Dan. xii. 7, 11,—are to be understood literally, and we are to expect a brief reign of force, coupled with a denial of God and a contempt of all His laws, as that "great tribulation" which must herald the coming of Jesus Christ, and the destruction by the breath of His mouth of all who oppose Him. Braune reminds us that we must reject all those interpretations of Antichrist which regard him as a "solitary historical personage" in days already past. Thus the Greek Fathers, and after them Luther, and Calvin, explain the passages of Ebion, or Cerinthus, or other heretics. So Grotius applies it to Barcochba, the false Messiah who perished in Hadrian's time; Calovius to Mohammed; Luther, again, not very

---

tion in a generation which once would have required centuries for their development. The whole world is fermenting with new ideas and the new application of old ones. Evil men have a new and fearful power of working their evil deeds. The secrets of Nature have been explored, and men can now do evil upon a gigantic scale. And the restraints of force are being slowly and surely removed. There is an impatience of control, a prejudice against punishments, against interference with personal liberty, which sets men more free than ever

consistently, to the Pope; and the Roman Catholic expositors to Luther. Dr. Von Döllinger, in his "First Age of the Church," Appendix I., regards the whole passage in 2 Thess. concerning the Man of Sin as referring to the then Roman Emperor, and the mention of the temple must mean, in his opinion, the then existing temple at Jerusalem. But he does not exclude altogether a belief in a final apostasy and an appearance of Antichrist before the last judgment.—**even now there are many Antichrists.** That St. John is here referring to the Gnostic heresies there can be no doubt. The disciples of Simon Magus and Nicolaus, who taught all kinds of strange travesties of the Gospel; the Ebionites, who many of them reduced Jesus to a mere man; the Cerinthians, who taught that the Æon Christ descended upon Jesus at His baptism, and left Him before His passion, were all manifestations of the Antichristian spirit, as were also the later Gnostic heresies which as yet had not appeared. The philosophical tendencies of that age, which supposed matter to be essentially evil, and a union between the material and the Divine to be absolutely impossible, were striking at the two main doctrines of Christianity, the sovereignty of God and the regeneration of man. They taught that there was a whole region which lay outside the power of God, and that in this region was comprised an integral portion of

---

before to work their will whether for good or evil. It is therefore quite possible that the present age may see an outbreak of wickedness more formidable than any that has yet been experienced.

II. THERE ARE MANY ANTICHRISTS IN THE WORLD. This is as true as ever. But our space will not permit us to enlarge on the truth. We will briefly enumerate them. (1) Disrespect to authority. (2) Impatience of restraint. (3) Unchecked licence of speech and thought, even on the most sacred subjects. (4) Contempt for moral considera-

human nature. Thus the redemption and sanctification of the body, the possibility of a pure and innocent life in accordance with the natural laws of the world, was rendered an impossibility, and a man must either become unnatural or immoral. To these two tendencies Christianity was irreconcilably opposed. And it set in opposition to them the one harmonising, reconciling, atoning principle, "*Jesus Christ come in the flesh.*"— **whereby we know that it is the last time.** Because Jesus Christ had foretold that false Christs and false prophets should arise, who should deceive, if it were possible, even the very elect (Matt. xxiv. 24). And His Apostles had re-echoed the warning (see passage cited in p. 125). One of the signs of the "last days" would be the number of false doctrines and evil men to be found. Among the most necessary duties of the elect were watchfulness, that they might not be beguiled by teaching which was inconsistent with that of their Master, and steadfastness, whereby they might persevere to the end in spite of opposition of every kind.

VER. 19.—**They went out from us.** The "many Antichrists" mentioned in the last verse are obviously referred to here. And one point to be noted in the character of Antichrist is that it involves *rejection of Christ*. Had these teachers not gone out from the Christian Church, they would not have been Antichrists.

---

tions (in some quarters). (5) Disbelief in revelation, and even in the existence of God. (6) Schemes of public plunder, advocated by Socialists and Communists in opposition to the Christian theory, which recognises a man's right to his own, though he is encouraged to share it with others. (7) Nihilism, the belief in nothing—the denial of religion, morals, property, honour, temperance, the family—the absolute reversal of all that has been hitherto held sacred among mankind. This, and nothing else than this, is the Nihilistic platform,

The particular circumstance which aggravated their guilt was, that they had had the opportunity of knowing Christ and had flung it away. The heathen world at large was not Antichristian. The opportunity of knowing Christ had not as yet been given it. But a special guilt must clearly have attached to those who had joined the Christian Church, had taken part in its worship, had tasted of its spirit of unselfish brotherhood, had enjoyed the privilege of its inner spiritual teaching, had feasted on the Body and Blood of the Incarnate God, and had then gone forth and "denied the Lord that had bought them" (2 Pet. ii. 1). Somewhat of the same feeling may be discerned in Acts xx. 30, where St. Paul evidently feels it a great aggravation of the offence of the false teachers of whom he speaks that they would arise "out of your own selves." It was the very spirit of Judas which such men shared, to whom Christ Himself had applied the words of the Psalmist, "he that hath eaten bread with me hath lifted up his heel against me" (John xiii. 18). Some discussion has arisen on the question whether, with the Vulgate, we should render *prodierunt*, which is equivalent to "they originated with us," or simply *exierunt*, i.e. "they went forth," which is the rendering of all the chief English versions, even those which, like that of Wiclif and the Rhemish Version, might be supposed to be most under the influence of the Vulgate.

---

as put forward openly by its advocates. The Christian has still, as ever, but one weapon to encounter these adversaries with. It is that placed in our hands by St. John, "Jesus Christ come in the flesh."

III. ONE SPECIAL CHARACTERISTIC OF ANTICHRIST IS THE REJECTION OF CHRIST. "They went out from us." The Antichrist must arise from among Christians. And in Christian nations there are many who deliberately reject Christ. This rejection may be (1) speculative, (2) practical. And each one of these ultimately leads up

THE WORK OF ANTICHRIST. 135

As Alford reminds us, we must take the ἐξ of the verb in a slightly different sense to the preposition that follows. The former means simply local separation, the latter unity of origin: "they went away from among us because their present principles are in no sense derived from us." We must not forget that these words have a special historical sense. Early Christian history tells us of several of these Antichristian teachers. Simon Magus (see note on last verse), as we might have imagined from his utterly unspiritual conception of Christ's kingdom, was one of those who had "no root." When he found that only persecution and suffering, instead of worldly success, was the lot of the disciples of Christ, he speedily separated himself from among them, and became one of their chief opponents, borrowing as many of their ideas as suited him, and combining the grossest impostures with a life of open immorality. The Nicolaitans again (Rev. ii. 6, 15), whether they were the disciples of Nicolaus the deacon, as some say, or not, were among these apostates from the Christian Church; for the similarity of the Greek Nicolaus to the Hebrew Balaam (lord of the people) suggests a connection between the passage just cited and 2 Pet. ii. 16 and Jude 11, while the allusion to Balaam would lose its point if there were no abuse of spiritual gifts. St. John's horror of Cerinthus, too, as displayed

---

to the other. There are those who profess to reject Christ, but to hold fast to the morality which He first brought to light. These have let go the anchor; and though at present they may seem to remain safely where they were, they are sure at the first stress of weather to be driven ashore. There are those, again, who professedly believe the doctrines of Christianity, but who positively refuse to be guided in their conduct by Christ's precepts. These must ultimately be driven to deny the doctrines which have no real hold on their consciences.

in the well-known and well-authenticated story of his refusing to remain a moment in the bath with such a heretic, lest the roof should fall on their heads, would seem to indicate that he also had had the opportunity of knowing Christ and had rejected Him. The earliest accounts of this heretic, however, do not say that he ever joined the Christian Church, but they agree in imputing to him a denial of the truth that "Jesus Christ is come in the flesh." He taught that the union between Jesus and the Æon Christ was merely temporary; that it began at the baptism of Jesus and ended before His crucifixion. It is generally supposed that St. John's teaching in the Gospel and Epistle is more especially directed against his heresy than against any other. Rather, however, we may suppose that it was directed against the general tendency towards Gnosticism which was *in the air*, so to speak. All the Gnostics, in one way or other, made a distinction between Jesus and Christ. They could not conceive of an union between spirit and matter. They could not grasp the idea of a purification *of* the flesh. All that they could imagine Christ doing was purifying us *from* the flesh. And thus two radically false tendencies, which are still to be found in men's minds, diverged on either side from the eternal truth as revealed in God's Word: the one regarding all that was connected with the flesh as sinful, and thus confounding innocent and guilty

---

And both must end in the rejection of Christ. Thus is Antichrist ever "ready to be revealed" in the persons of those who "will not have this man to reign over them."

IV. THE LAST TIMES ARE TIMES OF TESTING. "They went out from us" because "they were not of us." Time and circumstances have tested the reality of their belief. To this testing process every man's Christianity must be submitted. It is a law of this disordered world that wherever the truth is proclaimed it will be resisted. As Hübner puts it, "where God builds a temple Satan is sure to build a

enjoyments in one common condemnation; the other regarding all that was connected with the flesh as utterly indifferent, and so teaching that no amount of fleshly indulgence, however sinful, could touch the calm and pure intellectual or spiritual life, which lay in a sphere of its own entirely apart from the world of sense. These tendencies existed in St. John's time. They blazed up into sudden and dangerous activity a few years afterwards. They still smoulder unsuspected in many regions of the Christian consciousness. We may observe, in passing, how they are condemned by a single word in the Church Catechism, which calls the Christian to renounce only "the *sinful* lusts of the flesh," thus explaining the somewhat indefinite word "carnal," which meets us in the Baptismal service.—**but they were not of us.** This phrase has already been explained; but we may add a very pertinent illustration which Alford quotes from St. Augustine's treatise on St. John's Epistle. That Father compares these spurious Christians to certain corrupt humours, which, though they are in the body, are not only no part of its proper constitution, but are opposed to it. Hence they are expelled by the action of the various functions of the body. This serves still further to manifest their incompatibility with the body which refuses to retain them. And the reason why these persons did not remain in the Christian Church is because they had not expelled

---

chapel by the side of it." So the Scriptures invariably represent this life as a time of testing (see Matt. xiii. 20; 1 Cor. iii. 13; James i. 2, 3, 12; 1 Pet. i. 7, iv. 12, 13, &c.) And so when any new form of resistance to God's truth arises among us, we can easily see in whom that truth has taken firm root, and in whom it has not. There may be a good deal of outward profession of religion; but though outwardly reckoned in the Church, those could never be really of it whom the first breath of temptation carries away.

V. SEPARATION FROM THE CHURCH SHOWS PREVIOUS ALIENATION

these evil humours from their own hearts. So says St. Augustine. "Qui se in melius commutat, in corpore membrum est; qui autem in malitia permanet, humor malus est."—**for if they had been of us, they would no doubt have continued with us.** On this passage, among others, has the Predestinarian system been built up. But it does not touch the question either way. Alford has well remarked here how the attempt of the Vulgate and the English Version (here following Tyndale) to translate ἄν has sometimes altered the sense of the passage in which that particle occurs. The words "no doubt" are not in the original, and are omitted in the Revised Version. If ἄν be translated at all, the Rhemish "surely" is the best way of rendering. But it is simply the particle expressing uncertainty, which appears in every hypothetical sentence, and has no proper equivalent in English. The meaning of the passage is simple enough. It contains no deep theological principle of the indefectibility of grace, nor can such be legitimately deduced from it. There is no assertion of a general theological principle; what is said refers solely to the persons here spoken of. We may not unreasonably, however, go so far as to draw the inference from this special statement that the Apostle regarded it as a very unlikely thing—a thing practically impossible—that any one who had ever properly realised by faith

---

OF SPIRIT. To avoid misinterpretation, it may be well to state that the word Church here is used in its widest sense, of the whole body of baptized believers who are manifesting their present acceptance of their Lord by participation in the Lord's Supper, which He has ordained specially to be a means of confessing Him before men. And separation from the Church is regarded as involving nothing short of a denial of Christ as Lord. No mere separation *between* those who confess Christ is meant, but the actual refusal to acknowledge Him. And here it may be observed—

the intimate personal union between a believer and his Lord would ever draw back from that union. But there is no definite assertion, either that no combination of unfavourable circumstances could render such backsliding possible, or that there were no rudimentary stages of Christian faith short of that vivid realisation of the personal presence of Christ in the heart which constitutes the true blessedness of the mature Christian, and with which it is most improbable that he would allow himself to part. See, for the distinction between the immature and mature Christian, such passages as 1 Cor. iii. 1; 2 Cor. v. 16; Heb. v. 12-14; 1 Pet. ii. 2, 3. The difference between the spiritual and the carnal Christian, between the νήπιος and the τέλειος, is distinctly marked in such passages. Both, in a sense, are in Christ; both are partakers of the privileges of the Christian life. But in the latter the new life is far more deeply "rooted and grounded" than in the former, and consequently it is far more difficult for such to be "moved away from the hope of the Gospel." The νήπιοι, though to a certain degree "in grace," can hardly be said to be "of us" in the sense in which St. John uses the words. "Of us" would seem to imply something more than a mere rudimentary reception of the life of Christ. Rather it is the being "rooted and grounded in love," Eph. iii. 17. Alford has a long note here on the

---

1. *That the passage does not involve Predestinarian doctrine.* For there is no assertion of the doctrine that "once in Christ, always in Christ." What is said is, not that these persons never were "of us," but that whether they ever were or not, their departure proved that they had ceased to be so. It is quite possible to suppose that a gradual deterioration may have taken place, a gradual decay of love and faith, until the once sincere believer has become a mere external professor, and only needs the stimulus of outward circumstances to sever himself altogether from the company of the faithful.

Predestinarian question, and Düsterdieck a far longer one.[1]—**but they went out, that they might be made manifest that they were not all of us.** The first question that occurs here is, How is the blank in the original to be filled up? A glance at the Authorised Version will show us that the words "they went out" are no part of the original, but are supplied to fill up the meaning. The Revised Version supplies the same words as the Authorised Version. Many of the early English translators leave the passage as it stands in the Greek. Tyndale fills up with "it fortuned." The Geneva Bible has "this cometh to pass." The turn of phrase is characteristic of St. John (see John i. 4, ix. 3, xiii. 18, xiv. 31, xv. 25). It would give a very good sense if in all these passages we could translate "and so it comes to pass that." But the grammarians are almost unanimous against such a rendering. The question is of course debatable whether St. John uses Greek particles in their strict grammatical sense. In the same way some learned Hebraists have denied that לְמַעַן is always used in the sense of *in order that*, and Ps. li. 6 and Amos ii. 7 are cited in support of this view. Here, however, the telic sense of ἵνα suits the passage very well. We must supply some words such as

---

[1] "The fact of separation revealed the imperfection of their fellowship. The words will not admit of any theoretical deductions. The test of experience is laid down as final."—Westcott.

---

2. *That watchfulness is a necessary characteristic of the spiritual life.* We have here before us the example of those who have apparently been members of the Christian Church, enjoying all the privileges of membership. And yet their fellowship with Christ was no real fellowship. A sudden blast of vain doctrine, and they cease to be members of Him altogether. Had they really believed in Him, they would not have denied Him. What more necessary, then, than to inquire carefully whether our profession of Christ be a real profession, or whether we be deceiving ourselves. If we believe in

the Authorised Version supplies. The Syriac supplies "this they did;" Calvin "this God did." But the conclusion is just the same whatever words we add. It all happened in order that the true character of these persons might be known. And this is not unreasonable. It was God's will that their character should be manifested in this way, as a warning to Christians to remember the words "all are not Israel that are of Israel," nor all Abraham's true seed who are lineally descended of him (John viii. 39; Rom. ii. 28, ix. 7; Gal. iii. 7, 29). There might be "spots in their feasts of charity" (or love-feasts, as the Revised Version translates) of whom it was their duty to beware. And the secession of these persons from their midst was Divinely ordered, in order to make those who remained more careful in their scrutiny of their own lives and conduct. That some such idea was in the Apostle's mind will hardly be doubtful to the reader of such passages as Rev. ii. 2, 14, 20. The modern commentators have taken infinite trouble to justify the rendering "they were not all of us;" and, as it appears, in vain. It is quite impossible that any of such persons could have been "of us" in the Apostle's meaning of the words. And therefore Grotius' translation, so contemptuously rejected by most modern commentators, "that none of them were of us," is, we may venture to believe, the true one. There is a third

---

Him, it must be as One who can sanctify our mortal flesh, can "mortify and kill all vices in us," and who not only *can* do so, but *is doing it*. Is this our condition? "What I say unto you I say unto all, Watch."

3. *There are many, externally members of the Christian Church, who never attain to a real saving knowledge of Christ.* To be vitally in union with Christ, we need (1) God's election to spiritual privileges, and (2) our acceptance of that election. If, by virtue of our admission into the Christian Church, we become entitled to all the blessings of

rendering suggested which is at least admissible, and it is the one adopted by most modern commentators, "that not all (who are among us) are of us." But had this been the Apostle's meaning, he would surely have expressed himself more precisely to that effect. The fact is that sufficient allowance has not been made for the Hebraistic idiom of the Apostle. Thus in Exod. xii. 16 the literal rendering of the original is "all work shall not be done," and the construction is so common as to defy all attempts to enumerate the passages in which it appears in the Old Testament. We have instances of the same construction in Matt. xxiv. 22; Mark xiii. 20; Luke i. 37; Rom. iii. 20; Rev. xxi. 27. It is true that Alford endeavours to escape from the force of such passages by declaring that the word "all" is emphatic in each of them. But this is not the case with 1 Cor. i. 29 (where the use of μή instead of οὐ does not affect the question, since the construction of the Hebrew לֹא and אַל are precisely alike with כֹּל). Where οὐ and πᾶς come *together* it is admitted that the proper translation is "not all," but here they are separated by a verb. And not only in the present verse, but in vers. 21, 23, we have a similar construction. "No lie is of the truth" (ver. 21); and again, "No one who denieth the Son hath the Father" (ver. 23), where, though we have οὐδέ instead of οὐ, the Apostle means to include not some, but all,

---

spiritual union with Christ which it is His will that all members of His Church should receive, it needs an act of faith on our part in order to appropriate these blessings, and make them actually, as they have hitherto been virtually, ours. God does not repeat the proffer; it remains ever in force, but it becomes efficacious only when we stretch forth our hands to make it our own. The lives of many in the Christian Church show only too plainly that in their case this appropriation of God's proffers of grace has not been made. These

within the scope of his meaning. Thus then it seems far more probable that the rendering of Wiclif, Tyndale, and Cranmer, as well as the Peshito, in which "all" is omitted, comes nearer to the sense than that of our Version, or the proposed modern emendation. It is not that *some* of the seceders were not imbued with the true spirit of Christianity; it is not that a general allegation is made that not all Christians must be regarded as genuine ones, but that *none* of those who had abandoned the Christian Church had ever really known what its true principles were. This rendering at least makes the connection of the next verse more clear. If it be true that what the Apostle meant was to lay down the principle that many professing Christians were not real Christians, the question irresistibly forces itself upon us, who were the ὑμεῖς of vers. 20, 21? And to that question it is impossible to find any answer. Translate οὐ πάντες *none*, and the sense is clear.[1] Those who were so ready to leave us were all mere surface believers, who "had no root." But ye who remain steadfast to your principles, who have not followed them in their desertion of the Lord, "we are persuaded better things of you."

[1] "When the πᾶς is separated by the verb from the οὐ, the negation, according to the usage of the New Testament, is always universal (all . . . not) and not partial (not all)."—Westcott.

---

are they who, morally or doctrinally, are ready at any moment to break loose from the restraints of Christianity. Hence the sad scandals of shameful lives or open apostasy from Christ. The object of all faithful teaching should be to urge men to exchange this mere formal lip-profession into that inward union with Christ which displays itself in a character and course of conduct modelled on His. Those only who possess that union can be said to be "of" the true assembly of believers. Those who have it not are sure, sooner or later, to "make it manifest that none of them were of us."

IX.

THE EFFECTS OF BELIEF IN THE TRUTH.

CH. ii. 20.—**But ye have an unction from the Holy One.** There can be no doubt that the unction here has some reference to *Christ* and *Antichrist*. The disciples of the Anointed partake of His unction, of which those who reject Him are utterly destitute. But (1) what is the connection between this verse and the foregoing, and (2) what is meant by the unction ? As regards (1) we may remark that the καί of the original has become *but* in our Version. This adversative sense causes great surprise to Alford (and to Haupt, who supposes that because δέ is not used there is no immediate connection with what precedes), who, as has frequently before been remarked, has no clear apprehension of the strong Heb-

---

HOMILETICS.

VER. 20.—*The unction from the Holy One.*

I. THE UNCTION IS THE GIFT OF THE HOLY GHOST. (See Exposition.)

II. THAT UNCTION IS PROMISED TO EVERY BELIEVER (John iii. 5, 6; Acts ii. 38, viii. 15, xix. 2 ; 2 Cor. i. 22, v. 5 ; Eph. i. 13, 14, iv. 30; also Rom. viii. 15 ; 1 Cor. ii. 12, xii. 13 ; Gal. iii. 2, 3, &c.)

III. IT IS IMPARTED TO US THROUGH VARIOUS CHANNELS. There is no disposition to insist upon what is matter of controversy. Those, therefore, who are not disposed to agree with what is set down under this head can pass it over. But a large number of Christians in the Church of England accept it as truth.

raistic element in the Greek of this Epistle. That ὑμεῖς (emphatic) is in opposition to the seceders of the last verse can hardly be doubtful. And if so, any one acquainted with the various shades of meaning of Vau copulative in Hebrew would not fail to render the καί here by "but;" not with any strong disjunctive force, but simply as marking the antithesis between the true and false believers. As regards (2) we have to remember that the word here used does not mean the *act of anointing*, as the rendering of the same word *anointing* in ver. 27 would lead us to suppose, but the fact of having been *anointed*. The ointment is the Holy Ghost Himself, who comes ἀπὸ τοῦ ἁγίου (see Acts x. 38). Düsterdieck refers us here to the various ways in which Christ Himself is anointed and imparts the Holy Ghost to those who believe on Him (see John i. 33, iii. 34. Also Acts ii. 33; 2 Cor. iii. 17, 18; Gal. iv. 6; Eph. iii. 16; Phil. i. 19; and Rom. viii. 9, 14). We may observe that unction is closely connected with the gift of the Holy Spirit in such passages as 1 Sam. x. 1, 6, 10; xvi. 13. What effect this unction has upon the position of Christians is not difficult to understand. Since it served to brighten and beautify men's countenances (Ps.

---

1. *Baptism is a channel whereby the "unction" is conveyed.* This is supposed to be, if not proved, at least indicated, by such texts as John iii. 5; Acts ii. 38; 1 Cor. xii. 13; Tit. iii. 5, 6 (especially in the Greek). It should be explained here that it is not supposed (1) that the unction thus conveyed cannot be withdrawn, or (2) that it is effectual until the faith of the believer comes into co-operation with the will of God (see notes on last verse, III. 3).

2. *Confirmation is a means of fresh and fuller unction.* This doctrine is supposed to be conveyed by Acts viii. 17, 18, xix. 6, by comparison with 1 Tim. iv. 14; 2 Tim. i. 6.

3. *The Holy Communion renews this unction.* If it be true that he who comes in faith to this sacrament is fed with the spiritual food of the Body and Blood of Christ (John vi.), it is also true that

K

civ. 15; cf. also Ps. xlv. 7; Heb. i. 9), ointment became the symbol of consecration to a particular office. The priests were set apart by anointing to their sacred calling (see again Exod. xxx. 22-33; also xxix. 7; also Levit. vi. 22, viii. 12, xxi. 10, 12). Prophets were anointed (1 Kings xix. 16). Kings, moreover, were, and are still anointed. And He who bears the title of the Anointed united in Himself all these three offices, and imparts in their measure this threefold character to all who are united to Him by the Spirit. Two of these three characteristics of the believer are mentioned in 1 Pet. ii. 9, and Rev. i. 6. It is the third, the gift of supernatural knowledge, which is more particularly indicated here. Again we may remark that oil had a threefold use in the ancient world. It was used (1) to soften the skin, which might be burnt up by the heat, and to ward off the stings of insects. It might (2) be used as food, or at least in the preparation of food, whence we find it frequently mentioned with corn and wine in the Scriptures (as in Neh. x. 39, xiii. 5, 12; Numb. xviii. 12; Deut. vii. 13, &c.) It was also used (3) to give light. In all these capacities it was used in the worship of the sanctuary (see Exod. xxx. 22, xxxvii. 29; also

---

the Spirit of God is the means whereby this union is effected (ver. 63). It is the Spirit who enriches us with all the spiritual blessings which come from union with Christ. The "unction" is the Spirit and Being of the Anointed. (Whether 1 Cor. xii. 13 is to be referred to this or to the last head depends upon whether we render ἐποτίσθημεν "were made to drink" or "were watered.")

4. *The ministry of the word imparts this unction.* This we learn from passages such as Gal. iii. 2; Acts x. 44; 1 Cor. ii. 4, 13, iii. 2; 2 Cor. iii. 3, 6, 8, 9, and perhaps Gal. iii. 5, &c.

5. *None of these means are efficacious apart from the union of the soul with Christ.* See Acts ii. 42, iv. 29, vi. 4, ix. 15; 1 Cor. x. 16 (where blessing is an act of worship); Eph. vi. 18, 19; Col. iv. 3, 4; 2 Thess. iii. 1.

xxv. 6, xxvii. 20; Levit. ii. 1, 2, vi. 15). The unction of those who were called upon to "offer up spiritual sacrifices, acceptable to God through Jesus Christ," might partake of all these characteristics. By the "Holy One" may either be meant the Father, the "Holy One of Israel," who is the ultimate source of "every good and every perfect gift"; or it may be Christ, who is thus spoken of in Acts iii. 14 (cf. James v. 6, and 1 John ii. 1 and Rev. iii. 7). See also Mark i. 24; Luke iv. 34, and the reading of the best MSS. in John vi. 69. Practically it makes no difference whether we interpret of the source or the stream, since the latter is the only channel through which the living waters of holiness, flowing down from the Author and Giver of all good things, can reach us. One of the gifts of the Holy Spirit is knowledge (John xiv. 26, xvi. 13), and this is the gift which is spoken of here.—**and ye know all things.** Here many of the later editors, including Westcott and Hort, read "ye all know" ($\pi άντες$ for $\pi άντα$). Westcott and Hort also (with the Codex Vaticanus) omit καί. Thus in their edition the words run, "and *ye*" (emphatic) "have an ointment from the Holy One—ye all know." The MSS. reputed the best are divided on the point.

IV. THE GIFT IS INWARD.

1. *It is not merely outward.* (See Exposition.) The modern sacerdotal theory, which reaches its highest development in the Church of Rome, would tell you that each lay person should resort to his priest, and the priest to the bishop, and so on till we reach the infallible Head of the Church. It would have been impossible, had any such theory been present to the mind of the Apostle, that he should have neglected such an obvious course as to point out such an authority, as a means of escaping the snares of heresy. The absence of any such advice is a pretty clear proof that no such infallible authority was known to him.

2. *The outward is not altogether excluded.* The Apostle says "ye," and not "each one of you." He does not regard each of us as standing

The Alexandrian supports the Received Text, the Sinaitic and Vatican the emendation. It may be questioned whether πάντα was not rejected because (in spite of John xiv. 26, xvi. 13, which probably did not occur to the transcriber) it seemed to assert too much of the knowledge of the believer. And πάντες may have commended itself to him from the πάντες in the last verse. It may be questioned too whether internal considerations are not against πάντες. To predicate knowledge of these things of every individual believer would seem to contradict what the Apostle had just said concerning the possibility of there being those *in* the Christian Church who were not *of* it. Whereas if we understand οἴδατε potentially, as of a Divine power existing in the Christian Church, which if properly used would lead every member of the Christian Church, not perhaps to the solution of every problem which might be submitted to his intellect, but to the full understanding of everything practically necessary to his salvation, we shall be giving a rational explanation of the passage. "You need not be led away by these Antichristian doctrines which surround you on every side. You have been anointed with the Holy Ghost, and in Him you will find the explanation of every

---

alone, but as parts of a great whole. There are some who would, in their denial of the infallibility of the Pope, take refuge in the infallibility of the individual Christian, as though any one of us could sum up in himself all the graces and perfections of the Christian character. No one who has grasped the foundation of all Christian virtue, humility, would think of pretending thus to stand alone. When we are in difficulty we must take counsel with God and our brethren, in accordance with the precept, "if anything be revealed to another that sitteth by, let the first hold his peace" (1 Cor. xiv. 30). Nor would any one who seeks true enlightenment despise the voice of the "Apostles and elders" of the Christian Church. The Ultramontane theologians, it is true, pretend that the Pope only delivers his sentence as the mouthpiece of Christendom. But any one who possesses the least particle of fairness

difficulty that may assail you." It will be observed how entirely this passage negatives the idea of any external authority to settle disputed points of doctrine or of morals. Such an authority is not even hinted at. The true refuge from all the vexed questions of life is a full faith in the "unction from the Holy One," that Holy Spirit who will "make it plain" to all who will trust in Him. Nothing could be more utterly alien to the spirit of this passage than the explanation of the Jesuit commentator Estius, who expounds it as follows: "Ye have bishops and presbyters, by whose care and whose anxious thought for your Church you are sufficiently instructed in the things which relate to the truth of Christian doctrine." The interpretation of the passage which has been given derives additional support from ver. 27. There the unction is said to place him who receives it in a position to dispense with all teaching, and to teach him "concerning all things." It is clear that only an inner illumination could be spoken of in this way.

VER. 21.—**I have not written unto you because ye know not the truth, but because ye know it.** For "I have not written" see the note on ver. 14. The connection of

---

can see what a caricature of full and free Christian discussion a Roman Catholic Council is. And here the Apostle speaks not of the recourse to official authority, but of the gift with which the Church as a whole is endowed.

3. *The final decision comes from within.* The ultimate court of appeal for each one of us is his own conscience. We seek what illumination we can from our brethren, who have the same promises as ourselves, we weigh them, we lay them before God in prayer, we wait for the answer, and then we may fearlessly act upon it. And thus, eventually, we "need not that any one should teach us," for we have the inward conviction that what we have learned is true. Not that at any particular moment of our lives we actually "know all things;" but we have sufficient light for our present needs, and we may rest secure that in the end we shall be guided "into all the truth." It must be remem-

this with the preceding is as follows: "I have said that ye know all things, in virtue of the gift of the Holy Spirit. But this knowledge is virtual, not actual. It requires to be put into operation. Without this power of knowing all things, inherent in you as Christians, my Epistle would have been useless. It is the consciousness that I am appealing to a faculty within you which needs only to be stirred up, which has induced me to write this Epistle. Use this faculty of spiritual insight, and my object in writing, which was simply to quicken in you the action of gifts which you already possess, will not have been frustrated. The snares of Antichristian teaching will have been spread before you in vain."—**and that no lie is of the truth.** There are two ways of translating this part of the verse. The first is to take the ὅτι here as depending, like the former ὅτι, upon ἔγραψα, and translating it "because." The second is to take ὅτι as depending on οἴδατε, and to translate "that," as our own Version does. The Revisers prefer the former rendering, which gives this clause as one of the Apostle's reasons for writing, "I write unto you because no lie is of the truth." All the chief ancient English versions, except of Wiclif, agree with the Authorised

---

bered that we are speaking here, not of the ministry of reconciliation, but of the deciding of controversies.

V. THE UNCTION CONSECRATES US TO BE—

1. *Prophets.* We may each one of us be inspired to declare the will of God to others (though we may not be commissioned to declare it publicly) if we seek the inspiration.

2. *Priests*, "offering spiritual sacrifices" to God through Jesus Christ, through (*a*) prayer, (*b*) praise, (*c*) obedience, (*d*) devotion of ourselves to God.

3. *Kings* (Rev. v. 10, xx. 6, xxii. 5), who bear rule first over themselves, and then over others who are as yet babes in Christ; but, observe, not by force and authority, but by the hidden influence of purity and love.

VI. THE OINTMENT IS FRAGRANT (Exod. xxx. 22-33).

Version, and so do the great majority of the expositors. As Haupt remarks, "the καὶ ὅτι adjoins, *as is fully acknowledged by expositors,* the matter of the following clause as a second and co-ordinate element in the knowledge of the truth." He refers as an illustration to ch. i. 5. There may seem to be something in Alford's defence of the former rendering, that it removes a little of the apparent truism contained in the sentence; though we must not forget that the whole Epistle seems full of truisms to those who do not penetrate beneath the surface. He adds, "The two facts, the one, their knowing the truth, the other, that no lie is of the truth, are concurrent reasons for the Apostle's writing, viz. that he may set plainly before them what the lie is, that they may at once discern their entire alienation from it." But it may be remarked, on the other hand, that this would imply that they did *not* know the truth as St. John had just declared they did. Thus the two reasons for writing would be mutually self-destructive. On the whole, therefore, the Authorised Version is to be preferred, and St. John is here only preparing the way, as his custom is, for the introduction of a new point. "You know the truth. You know that

---

1. With the fragrance of sacrifice to God (2 Cor. ii. 15, 16; Phil iv. 18).
2. With the fragrance of a holy life.

VER. 21.—I. THERE IS AN INNER INSTINCT IN A CHRISTIAN WHICH RESPONDS TO THE TRUTH. Hence (1) *the value of the Christian ministry.* Human efforts for the sanctification of believers will not be in vain. The treasure is committed to earthen vessels, but the human is the channel of the Divine. And human hearts are so fashioned as to respond to human efforts. There is something to work on. Somewhere in each heart there is, however hidden or defaced, the image of God. If wilfulness and pride be set aside you may reach it after all. We should never despair of any soul. And here (2) is *the test of the Christian ministry.* If there be *no* response to our efforts, if all be dead, dull, indifferent, if we influence none, reach the hearts

no lie can possibly be of the truth. But the Antichristian spirit is essentially a lie, since it denies the Person and twofold nature of Him who has revealed Himself as ' the Truth.' "[1]

[1] Professor Westcott inclines to the view adopted by Alford. Haupt, though he regards the clause as a co-ordinate one, regards it as depending on οἴδατε. It is not, according to his view, that one ὅτι is co-ordinate with the other, but that this clause introduces a co-ordinate element *in the knowledge of the truth.*

---

of none, there must be something wrong with the message. We are building "wood, hay, stubble" instead of gold, silver, and precious stones.

II. IT RESTS WITH EACH INDIVIDUAL WHETHER HE WILL OBEY THAT INNER INSTINCT OR NOT. For *general* failure the teacher is responsible; for *individual* failure not so. Even Jesus Christ Himself did but sharpen some men's antagonism to truth. Of St. Paul it is written that some believed the things which he said, and some believed not. There is a tremendous and awful power of self-determination resident in each man which decides his future. And equally tremendous and awful is the responsibility of using that power.

X.

REJECTION AND ACCEPTANCE OF GOD'S REVELATION.

CH. ii. 22.—**Who is a liar but he that denieth that Jesus is the Christ?** We have here a statement very similar to one in ch. iv. 3. At first sight it would seem that the Apostle is but repeating there in other words what he has said here. This is not precisely the case. There the statement is in connection with St. John's doctrine of the Holy Spirit. Here it refers to the spiritual condition of the believer. Here he deals with opposing principles; there he refers these principles to their source, the Divine Spirit, and the spirit of Anti-

---

HOMILETICS.

VERS. 22-24.—*The antagonism between truth and falsehood.* In ver. 21 the radical antagonism between truth and falsehood is pointed out. At first sight the words appear mere repetition, and as such (see Exposition of ver. 21) their purport has been misunderstood. But the reason why they have been added can only be understood by referring to the drift of the whole section. We have on one side God, on the other the world; on the one side Jesus, the Christ—God's Anointed One, on the other Antichrist; on the one side truth, on the other lie. An active effort (see vers. 18, 19, 26) is being made to pervert the truth, and by this means to draw away believers from the faith. And the Apostle strives on the one hand to comfort and strengthen the Christians of his day by pointing out the unchangeableness of the will

christ. This verse carries forward the statement, so carefully led up to in the last verse. Ye know the truth. Ye know that no lie is of the truth. But I proceed to warn you that there are those who teach lies, and would fain persuade you that they are truth. These are they who deny that Jesus is the Christ. Some discussion has been raised on the form "the liar;" "the Antichrist," which is the correct translation, and is given by the Revised Version, though all the earlier English versions, without exception, have neglected to give the force of the article. Some have thought that Antichrist was signified (just as the devil is called the liar κατ' ἐξοχήν, in John viii. 44). Others have supposed some particular false teacher to be aimed at. Rather the article refers back to the idea of the last verse. "No lie is of the truth. And who is guilty of a lie (Bengel), but (εἰ μή, if is not) the man who denies that Jesus is the Christ?" The words had of course an immediate significance. Cerinthus, as well as other heretics, made a separation between Jesus and Christ. Yet on the identity between Jesus and Christ depended the whole scheme of redemption. If Jesus were a mere man, and Christ a Divine Being

---

of God, which designs their salvation through the sanctifying influences of His Spirit (1 Thess. iv. 8, v. 9), and on the other to warn them by reminding them of the weak and variable human will, which renders them so easy a prey to the deceitful utterances of the spirit of evil which is in the world. Thus, then, he points out to them that there is but One Truth; that all error comes from the spirit opposed to God; that all error is fatal in its tendencies and ultimate results; and that all error springs from one root, the denial of the Messiahship and Sonship of Christ. Apply this to the present day. There is evidently error enough in the world. Let us consider it under two aspects: (1) its deadly nature, (2) its connection with a denial that Jesus is the Christ, the Eternal Son of the Eternal Father.

I. ALL ERROR IS DEADLY. This is one of the doctrines most energetically denied in our times. The most favourite doctrine of the day

temporarily united to Him, the redemption of man became an impossibility. This is the immediate reference of these words. But there is of course a sense in which they are always true. To deny that Jesus is the Anointed of God is in effect to deny that He is the Eternal Son of God; and this denial of His Eternal Sonship is in effect the denial of all revelation and redemption.—**he is Antichrist, that denieth the Father and the Son.** Observe how the Apostle's language increases in sternness and strength, as he points out more clearly the necessary consequences of a denial of Christ. It seems probable that the effect of the Antichristian spirit (as in ch. iv. 3), rather than the personal Antichrist, is here referred to (see also ver. 18). Every man who denies the Messiahship of Christ is himself Antichrist, so far as that denial is concerned (see notes on ver. 18). For, as we have seen, he strikes at the root of all revealed truth. And, as Ebrard proceeds to remark, he implicitly teaches all lies, since all false doctrine has either assumed the form of teaching that Jesus is not the Christ, or that Christ is not Jesus, but a general idea of salvation, realised not in the Person of a God-Man, but in humanity collectively. The one

---

is that it does not matter what a man believes, as well as that a man is not responsible for his belief. Since Pope's time the couplet has been an embodiment of popular belief,—

> "For modes of faith, let graceless zealots fight;
> He can't be wrong, whose life is in the right."

Now (1) *this doctrine is opposed to Scripture.* Nothing is more clearly laid down there than *that faith alone can save.* And this faith must be a *right* faith. It were a ludicrous absurdity to say that a wrong faith can save a man. All faith, so far as it is saving in its nature, must be a *right* faith. Either, then, a right faith is necessary, or no faith at all is. For this truth see John iii. 15, 16, vi. 40, xi. 25, &c.; Acts xx. 21; Rom. i. 17, iii. 30; Gal. v. 6; 2 Thess. ii. 13; Heb. xi. 6, &c.

denies the incapacity of man to save himself, the real seriousness and awfulness of sin; the other takes away the only real hope of redemption, which consists in appropriating by faith the holiness of the one only Perfect Man. Only, as Haupt reminds us, no mere theoretical or intellectual acknowledgment or denial is here intended. The whole scope of the Epistle precludes such a supposition. The acknowledgment or denial must be taken as a basis of action. And thus the acknowledgment that Jesus is the Christ, the Son of God, is the only permanent basis upon which the regenerating process in man can take place, just as on the other hand the denial of the only restorative and life-giving power vouchsafed to us must end ultimately in utter wickedness and alienation from God.

VER. 23.—**Whosoever denieth the Son, the same hath not the Father.** This verse explains the former. How is it that to deny Christ is to deny, not only the Son, but the Father also? Because "no man knoweth the Father, but the Son, and he to whom the Son will reveal Him" (Matt. xi. 27; Luke x. 22; cf. John i. 18, xiv. 9). To

---

2. *A wrong faith must necessarily produce a wrong practice.* We may see this in the affairs of this world. Any man who labours under a mistake of any kind must suffer in consequence. If a man takes a wrong road, under the impression it is the right one, he must find out, confess, abandon his mistake, or he can never get to his journey's end. If a man does not understand his orders, or his business, inconvenience and even ruin is the result, unless he finds out his mistake in time. In a thousand ways we find error is the parent of mischief and misery. And so, if we misconceive God, we, and the world in general, must suffer countless ills in consequence.

3. *Tendencies do not always produce their full results.* The reason why the world is not utterly ruined is because error has been but partial. A wrong faith on some points has been in some degree compensated for by a right faith on others. Faith, so far as it is right, has saved the individual and society from the results which wrong faith

deny that Jesus is the Christ, is to deny his Eternal Sonship. To deny the Eternal Sonship is to deny the Father also. For we only know the Father through the Son. The denial of the Son therefore leaves us, in regard to the Essence and Nature of the Father, at the mercy of every blast of vain doctrine. And worse; for since we have rejected the teaching of the only One Who can tell us what He is, we must of necessity believe Him to be what He is not. And since He is the source of all moral perfection, and we have proved ourselves not only unable but unwilling to recognise moral excellence when we see it, there remains for us nothing but a gradual declension from all that is good, a gradual separation from all that is Divine, and from all that is wise, tender, and loving, such as the idea of the Father contains within itself. So Haupt: "If no man hath ever seen God or can see Him, but He is declared only by His only-begotten Son, it follows that he of necessity loses the knowledge of the Father, who rejects the way in which alone it is to be found. If Christ as the $\mathrm{\mathring{a}\pi a\acute{\upsilon}\gamma a\sigma\mu a}$ of the Father is equally with the Father the truth,

---

has produced, and is producing. A good many erroneous beliefs, be it remembered, are a mixture of truth and error. Thus superstition mingles belief in God with wrong conceptions of His nature, and thus it leads to mixed results.

4. *It is a matter of importance to believe the truth.* All the misery and distress in the world is due to wrong beliefs. Some men believe that God will not punish sin. That leads to the belief that we may sin with impunity. Some believe that there is no life beyond the grave. That tends directly to despair; to take away the motive for good. Some take a view of God incompatible with His justice. That leads directly to confusion between right and wrong. Some regard Him in a way irreconcilable with a belief in His love. That leads either to superstition or recklessness. Some men reject His revelation in Christ. That leaves the world without a standard of right and wrong. Some believe in the doctrines of Christianity, but

it follows that he who has not the One has not the Other, else would he at once have and not have the truth." It is remarkable to see how Socinian interpreters, like Socinus himself and Grotius, strive to evacuate the word "hath" of its force. They would explain it, "hath not a right opinion of God," "knoweth not God's will towards the human race." Their great difficulty is to evade the force of the truth that by Jesus Christ alone, by the communication of His Divine Humanity, do we attain to fellowship with the Father. St. John is leading up to this truth all through this Epistle. At the end (ch. v. 11–13), he at length declares it in all its fulness, even as his Master had declared it in the words he records in his Gospel (ch. iii. 15, 16, iv. 14, vi. 27, 47, 57, &c.) Even commentators like Düsterdieck water down the force of this passage by saying that without the Son, the Father cannot be "perceived, believed on, loved." So hard does it appear to be to grasp the truth that the Apostle is speaking of a communication through Christ of the Divine Life.—**but he that acknowledgeth the Son hath the Father also.** This passage is in italics in our Version,

---

not in its practice. That leads to hypocrisy and practical disbelief in revelation. Yet the belief of all men, while on earth, is imperfect. It is the imperfection of the saints which gives half its vitality to sin. Hence the importance of believing implicitly God's Revelation (1) in His Word, (2) in His works. For this cf. Rom. i. 16, 17, 20.

5. *How is a right faith to be attained?* Here (*a*) comes in the Roman Church with her favourite proposition that some external authority is necessary in order that we may be able to decide which of the many conflicting sects holds the right view of the truth. But she is put out of court by two considerations; first, that she confines her articles of belief to the theological, rather than the moral doctrines of the Gospel; and second, that she stands condemned by the precept of our Lord—"by their fruits ye shall know them." The fruits of faith (and they are many) in the Roman Church do not usually display themselves in those in authority, nor are they any results of her

not because it was interpolated by the writers, but because it was absent from several of their copies. All the best MSS. have it, as well as the Vulgate. The confession (this is the literal meaning of the word translated "acknowledgeth") here referred to is primarily of course outward (cf. Rom. x. 10). But of course the confession meant is a sincere, not a hypocritical confession. Hence the Authorised Version gives the real sense of the original. He who acknowledges the Son; that is, who confesses the Son to be the true revelation of the Father, and acts upon his confession, he has the Father as well as the Son (cf. John xiv. 23, xvii. 21, 23). Before we leave this verse the "three steps of the argument" (Düsterdieck) are to be noted. (1) The denial of Christ is a lie, and even breathes the spirit of Antichrist himself. (2) It is a denial of God's own Son. And since He, the Father, manifests Himself by the Son, and Him alone, (3) to deny the Son is to deprive ourselves of the Father. Similarly, to confess the Son is to receive the Divine life of the Father. For to confess the Son is to realise what He is, namely, the imparter of the Divine light and life, the medium

---

despotic system. They are produced rather *in spite of*, than in consequence of, that system. They result from the amount of truth which is preserved within her pale. But her system of authority has, during its sway, sanctioned every kind of cruelty, perfidy, and murder —the very opposite of the morality of Christ. It has resulted in the substitution among the majority of a dull acquiescence for a living faith. And where it has had due play, it has ended in the revolt of the mass of the population from the faith, the Name, and the example of Christ. That there must be something wrong about a system that produces these results is tolerably clear. What, then, (*b*) is the means whereby a right faith is to be attained? In answer to this we must (a) dismiss the idea that any man, while in the flesh, can possibly attain to infallible certainty on all points whatsoever. For (β) our condition here is progressive. Enough knowledge is given us to guide our actions by. The revelation of God in Christ is clear enough to

whereby all that is in the Father is given to the world. And he who acknowledges this, opens his soul to all the fulness of Divine Being which is given to the Son.

VER. 24.—**Let that therefore abide in you which ye have heard from the beginning.** On "from the beginning" see ver. 7. Here, however, as Alford remarks, the ἠκούσατε restricts the meaning of "from the beginning," just as the ἦν of ch. i. 1 extends it indefinitely. Here it no doubt does mean from the beginning of the Gospel, as in ver. 7 it *might*, but probably does not mean, and as in vers. 13 and 14 it clearly does not mean. The Authorised Version does not give the emphatic force of ὑμεῖς, which is correctly translated in the Revised Version "as for you." The Apostle desires to mark the contrast between the true disciples of Christ and they who follow after Antichrist. It must be remembered that the object of the whole section, from ver. 15 especially, is to mark this contrast, to remind the flock (1) of the advantages and privileges they possess as members of the Christian Church, and (2) of the dangers which threaten them from

---

enable us to ascertain His will for ourselves, by diligence and prayer. The general consent of Christians on the main points of the Christian faith, as displayed in the Christian creeds, is hardly likely to be wrong. And those points are clearly enough laid down for us in Scripture. If we meet with people who do not believe them, we shall find that they do not accept the teaching of Scripture. Nor is this, as some say, faith in a Book. The only ground on which we accept the Scriptures is that they tell us what was the teaching of Christ—rudimentary in the Old Covenant, authoritative and final in the New. Let us read Scripture with humility, teachableness, and prayer, and we shall not long be in doubt either what Christ would have us believe about Him or do by His indwelling, though we may be quite unable to lay down a complete system of theology for the instruction of mankind in general. The further consideration of this subject will be found under the next head.

without. If they will but be true to themselves, the Apostle implies, they are safe. "No one," save themselves, "can pluck them out of the Father's hand" (John x. 28, 29). The οὖν has been rejected by most editors. It is certainly omitted in the best MSS. and versions. But it is a particle most characteristic of St. John (take for instance a single page at random, it occurs in ch. xii. 50 of the Gospel, in ch. xiii. 6, 12, 13; and again in ch. xiii. 24, 25, 26, 27, 29, 31). And when we see that the following letters are **OHKOTΣ**, it is by no means impossible that it was originally omitted by inadvertence. It is, however, equally probable that it was added to lessen the abruptness of the transition. The word μενέτω is a reminiscence of St. John xv. As is the case there, so here, the force of the passage is much impaired in the A. V. by the use of "abide," "continue," and "remain" as the translations of one Greek word. Haupt has reminded us how exactly the form of the exhortation here corresponds to that in John xv. 7. The disciples are told (for various readings, see below) that if they take care to keep what they have been taught, they

---

II. ALL ERROR IS BASED UPON THE DENIAL THAT JESUS IS THE CHRIST.

1. *Revelation is necessary.* For otherwise we are left on all points, whether relating (1) to the unseen world, (2) to man's future, (3) to man's conduct, to the teaching of man. And men have arrived at agreement on no single point. They do not know (1) whether there be a God, (2) whether man is immortal or not, (3) in what the foundation of morals consists.

2. *The only revelation is that made by Jesus Christ.* Briefly, every other religion professing to be a revelation from God has broken down—notably the last, that of Mohammed.

3. *The essential feature of revelation is that it was made by one Anointed, i.e., commissioned to declare God's will.* Thus we are forbidden, on any point on which God's will is clearly declared, to question it. To deny Jesus to be the Christ is to deny all authority to His

shall abide in the Son and in the Father. To believe what Jesus teaches is to acknowledge Him to be the pouring forth of every good thing that comes from the Father. And to accept this truth is equivalent to receiving the abundance of good gifts which the Father has to give, the fulness of life that dwells in Him. Haupt further discusses the reversed order in which the thoughts occur here to that in which they are presented to us elsewhere. Sometimes the abiding in God comes first, and the abiding in His word afterwards. In one sense this is the true order. No man can come to God of himself. The presence of God in the heart is necessary before the first faint stirrings of the spiritual nature can be discerned (see John vi. 44). On the other hand, the order in which the thoughts are presented here is equally true from the point of view of Christ's redemptive work. Here it is "God in Christ, reconciling the world unto Himself," "putting the word of reconciliation into His ministers," and thereby, when those words are received, implanting that regenerating power in the heart which

---

teaching. He has announced himself to be the Only Begotten Son of the Father. When He speaks, therefore, all men must hear. *All that He means by what He says we may not expect to know in this world.* Enough to "save ourselves from this untoward generation" we *can* know, and we need no more at present.

4. *How, then, do unbelievers in Christ lead moral and admirable lives?* They can do so, only so far as they believe what Christ tells them. If they believe that to be right which Christ says is right, they are, so far, believers in Christ. A belief in a correct standard of duty, and in a power which enables us to perform it, is a belief in God, in much that God has revealed, and in His Holy Spirit sent from Him. A belief in the dignity and perfectibility of humanity is, so far as it goes, a belief in a power which has regenerated, and will save mankind. And no doubt such beliefs as these are better than the most implicit acquiescence in the Athanasian Creed, the Creed of

produces conformity to God's will, the result of the Divine indwelling. We may further observe with Ebrard that the doctrine does not remain *with* us, as many in these days seem to imagine, but *in* us. It is a seed sown in the heart springing up into everlasting life.—**If that which ye have heard from the beginning shall remain in you, ye also shall continue in the Son, and in the Father.** The word abide (see above) should be retained here throughout. And the use of the aorist here requires us to translate "shall have abode," *i.e.* at the day of Christ's coming. We ought not to pass over the closeness of the union between the believer and God here indicated. That union with the Son involves union with the Father we have already seen. But the inward and hearty acceptance of the facts of the unseen world as revealed to us by Christ, produces, as its natural fruit, a participation of the Divine life. The Socinian attenuation of this blessed truth may serve to give point to our realisation of it. It is not, as Grotius interprets, to enjoy to a very high degree the favour and friendship of God. It is not

---

Pope Pius the Ninth, or the Westminster Confession, when coupled with the distinct refusal to follow Christ's Example. But it is none the less true that "not one jot nor tittle of the Law shall fail;" not one jot or tittle of Christ's teaching can be allowed to fall to the ground without eventually producing evil results of greater or less consequence.

5. *Continuance in the Son and in the Father the only possible means of salvation.* The denial of this truth leads directly to the destruction of all moral principle whatever (see above, head 1). The moral lives of unbelievers are due to their acceptance of the moral principles of their age. These moral principles are Christian principles. But Christian moral law without its Law-giver is a superstructure without a foundation. And a superstructure without a foundation cannot stand long (Luke vi. 48; 1 Cor. iii. 11; Eph. ii. 20, &c.) Denial of revelation, then, is ultimately denial of all truth. And it also cuts away the only power that can enable us to "do the truth." Thus

merely to revel in the possession of God's good gifts. No; what God gives to the believer is Himself. "Because I live, ye shall live also," said the Saviour. "In that day ye shall know that I am in My Father, and ye in Me, and I in you" (John xiv. 20).

---

continuance in the Son and in the Father is the only means whereby (1) error, the source of all evil, can be gradually dispelled, and (2) truth, the source of all holiness and goodness, enabled to take full possession of the heart.

XI.

THE BLESSING OF ABIDING IN THE TRUTH.

CH. ii. 25.—**And this is the promise that he hath promised us, even eternal life.** Familiar as the word ἐπαγγελία is to us in the New Testament, it only occurs once in St. John's writings. This fact has been noticed by the commentators. But the fact shows that too much stress must not be laid on the absence or presence of certain words as a proof of genuineness or the reverse. We use words when we want them, or as the course of our argument dictates. They may be entirely absent from many of our writings, and may appear in the most natural way when circumstances require. The truth is that arguments about style require the finest tact, the most delicate appreciation of likenesses and differences. It is a coarse and clumsy way of treating a question of this kind to say, "Here is a word which we do not find

---

HOMILETICS.

VER. 25.—*The Life Eternal.*
I. THE RESULT OF DENYING THE TRUTH. We sum up in ver. 25 the teaching of the previous verses. In them we learn that to deny that Jesus is the Christ is to lose Himself, and to lose Him is to lose the Father. Thus we learn that the only way to abide in Christ is to believe what He has told us. The acceptance of the revelation He has brought is an indispensable condition of salvation. And this

elsewhere in this writer, therefore the book, or the passage, cannot be genuine." No one has impugned the authenticity of this particular passage on these grounds. But in the discussions on the genuineness of other writings of the New Testament a great deal has been built in this way upon a very slender foundation. The promise of life eternal mentioned here is found in many places in Scripture. (See Matt. xix. 29, xxv. 46; Mark x. 30; Luke x. 25, 28; John iii. 16, vi. 47, 54, &c., xi. 25, 26.) The mention of this promise is the climax to which vers. 23 and 24 lead up. To have the Father through the Son, to abide in the Son, and through Him, in the Father, is to realise the promise which God has given us in His Son, even eternal life. St. John recurs to this doctrine towards the close of the Epistle, and asserts it in even fuller terms, ch. v. 11, 12. We next come to a summary of the present section, concluding St. John's remarks on the dangers which beset the Christian, and repeating, more emphatically and earnestly than ever, the advantages which the χρίσμα of the Holy Spirit confers on Christians. If they employ that blessed gift as they should, it leads them to abide in God, and thus to secure the promise of eternal life.

VER. 26.—**These things have I written unto you concerning them that seduce you.** Rather *deceive* you. Our translators have here followed the Rhemish Version, and

---

acceptance must embrace the whole man. It must not be an intellectual assent merely, but it must include the will, affections, desires. Without such a faith there can be no salvation. Either the intellectual or the practical denial of Jesus as the Christ, the Anointed One of God, is ultimately fatal to our whole complex being.

II. THE RESULT OF ACCEPTANCE OF THE TRUTH. Three steps are here placed before us. If we accept God's revelation in Christ (*a*) we abide in the Son; (*b*) in the Father; (*c*) we have eternal life. That is to say, we participate in the common life of Father and Son; we are

departed from the rendering of Tyndale, Cranmer, and the Geneva Version, which render here "deceive you." The Revised Version has "lead you astray." The word does mean "*cause to wander*," but it seems strange that here our revisers should not have restored Tyndale and Cranmer's rendering when they have adopted it in chapter i. 8, and in 2 John 7, as well as in 2 Tim. iii. 13, and elsewhere. This is especially noteworthy, as one of their canons has been to render, wherever possible, the same Greek by the same English word. This passage plainly points out the object of the foregoing section, namely, to set before the Christian community the dangers that beset it. In fact, this verse is intended as a conclusion to this portion of the Epistle, as ver. 28 opens the second portion (see below). As was said in the introduction, the Epistle is divided into two chief portions: (1) God is Light; (2) God is Righteousness. Fitly, therefore, does the first part end with a reference to that unction from the Holy One which teaches all things to God's people, and leads them to abide in the life which comes from Him. The Revised Version agrees with our own in rendering ἔγραψα "have I written." Perhaps the most strictly accurate translation, according to the *usus loquendi* of the New Testament in regard to the aorist, is "have I been writing," and this also keeps the fact that the Epistle is not yet finished before the reader. But "have I written"

---

made partakers of the Divine nature (θείας κοινωνοὶ φύσεως; 2 Peter i. 4). To such a high privilege are the sons of God, through faith, advanced, that they not only abide in God, but partake of the very life that dwells in Him. Such is the "promise" of which St. John speaks, identical, as we see, with the "exceeding great and precious promises" of St. Peter (2 Peter i. 4). Such promises we find in John xiv. 19; xvii. 2, 3.

VERS. 26, 27.—*Them that seduce you.* This verse is for all time. They that seduce, or rather, deceive us will never cease until the

conveys the sense fairly enough. The present tense of πλανώντων shows that the seductions of the false teachers are a present danger, "those who *are deceiving* you." Their influence for evil did not cease when they left the Church. It needs continual watchfulness to guard one's self from their suggestions of error.

Ver. 27.—**But the anointing which ye have received.** *Received*, not, as A. V., "have received." The word *anointing* is translated *unction* above, ver. 20. And the ὑμεῖς is emphatic. "And as for you." See above, ver. 20. Nor is there any "but" in the original. We owe its introduction to the Geneva Version. The Rhemish is strictly accurate here. The "but," perhaps, a little obscures the sense, though only a little. The Apostle is giving here, as we have seen, a brief summary of the section, with a special reference to the practical duty it involves—that of abiding in God.—**of him abideth in you.** Rather, *from Him*. From whom? The αὐτοῦ here refers to the same Person as the αὐτός in ver. 25, and is therefore Christ, cf. ver. 20, as well as the promises of the Holy Spirit in chapters xiv., xv., xvi. of St. John's Gospel.—**and ye need not that any man teach you.** It will be observed that these words, like those in ver. 20, are addressed to the community. They were *potentially* true, of course, of every member of it. But they were not *actually* true of each individual Christian, otherwise there would have been no need to

---

eternal flames of God's wrath have consumed ungodliness. Their seductions are divided into two classes—deceits from without, and deceits from within.

I. Deceits from without. The spirit of Antichrist was in the world when St. John wrote. It has never ceased to work since. "Evil men and seducers" still abound, "deceiving and being deceived." And perhaps the "deceived" are more dangerous, because more unconscious in their error, than the "deceivers."

1. *Intellectual error.* This has been largely dealt with in the notes

caution them. The fact is, that the spiritual gifts vouchsafed to the members of the Christian Church are conditional, like all other gifts, upon a proper use of them. There is no warrant here for the presumption of the fanatic, who imagines that because an idea has taken strong possession of his soul, he is entitled to believe that he has been led into all the truth. There is no support to the arrogant notion entertained by some that we have no need of any other man's assistance to understand "all mysteries and all knowledge." The fact is, that here, as in many other points, the Gospel presents to us a paradox like the two sides of Gospel teaching, as regards faith and works, contained respectively in the writings of St. Paul and St. James. We each of us *have* sufficient enlightenment to be able to attain to the knowledge of the truth, and yet humility forbids us to imagine that we can attain to that knowledge without the help of our neighbours. Each of us serves as a "supplying joint" (see Eph. iv. 16) to his brother in the things of God. It was "the foolishness of the preaching" which spread the faith in Christ throughout the earth. The ministrations of fallible men keep the torch of truth burning throughout the world. Each man *could*, if necessary, attain to all truth by himself, by virtue of the inward enlightenment of God's Spirit; but inasmuch as God has ordained that mutual dependence is the law

---

to the preceding verses, so that there remains the less to be said here. But we may observe that this error is abroad in various forms. *All* error is to be traced to the denial that Jesus is the Christ, *i.e.*, as He Himself defines it, "He whom God hath sanctified and sent into the world." It matters not, therefore, whether it be the belief of the humanitarian, who regards Christ as only a man pre-eminent among men, though teaching the truth of God, or of those who go farther, and reject His message; all who fail to see in Jesus Christ the only begotten Son of the Father sent into the world to reveal His sacred

of humanity, it is by no means likely that he *would*. The paradox is evident in St. John's own words. They "have no need that any man teach them." And yet he *does* teach them. And that because however much, theoretically, each man possesses in himself the capacity of independently arriving at truth, he practically, as long as he is encompassed with the infirmity of mortal flesh, will need the assistance of his brethren to exhort, quicken, warn him in his task. And thus St. John writes "ye," and not "each one of you." Knit together in the Spirit, sharing in the common life that comes from Christ, the Christian community may rest secure from all deceits of the enemy, and may ever, as need requires, draw truth from the fountain of truth. If this picture has not been realised, if Christians have drifted away from the truth as it is in Jesus, if they have "taught for doctrines the commandments of men," if superstition and self-assertion, despotism and anarchy have rent the body of Christ in a thousand pieces, it is not Christ's fault. The unction of the Holy One was always there, but men would not avail themselves of it. Human reason, human authority, have taken the place of prayerful dependence upon God. And not till men have learned to set aside their own fancies, and to draw inspiration from God's Spirit alone, will the time come when these words shall once more be true. — **but as the same anointing teacheth you.** The

---

truth, well-pleasing to the Father by reason of His perfect obedience, satisfying the Father's righteous requirements by His sacrifice of Himself, giving life to the world by the power of His glorified humanity, have gone astray from Him, have admitted the first germs of error, which, if not burned up and destroyed by the fire of God's truth, will "choke the word" in their hearts, so that it first "becometh unfruitful," and finally destroys them in whom it has rooted itself. This is true of all kinds of error, whether (as in some) it assume the form of naked and outrageous blasphemy, and fiendish hatred of God's

anointing, referring, however, not to the process, but to its results (see above, ver. 20), is the Spirit of Christ, cf. St. John xiv. 16, xv. 26, xvi. 7–15. The best MSS. and the later editors accept here αὐτοῦ for αὐτό, "*His* anointing" (or unction) for "the same." This reading will be found adopted in the Revised Version. It makes very little difference here, but it affects somewhat the interpretation of the latter part of the verse.—**and is truth, and is no lie.** The following words have been taken in two different ways. (1.) Some have supposed that the sentence is to be broken up into two members. The first begins with "as the same anointing," and ends with "is no lie;" the second with "and even as," ending with "abide in Him." The sense would then be as follows: "As the same (or *His*) anointing teacheth you of all things, it is also truth and no lie. And as it has taught you, ye shall abide (or 'abide') in Him." The objection to this rendering is, that it presents to us a complete *non sequitur*. It does not in the least follow that because the anointing teacheth us of all things, it is truth and not a lie. Though many commentators of note, with Luther at their head, adopt this rendering, we can hardly consent thus to reduce St. John's words to an absurdity. (2.) The other interpretation, which is that adopted by all the English Versions (except the Rhemish, which is here baldly literal, and therefore hardly intelligible), is rational

---

truth such as we have sometimes seen displaying itself even in a court of justice; or whether it assume the more delicate form of refined ridicule and perversion of Christian doctrine; whether it deny (with some) a future life, or (with other so-called philosophers) the freedom of the will, or (with others again) it deny the power of God to work miracles—the order and subordination of all laws to the source of all law, the will of God, exercised, as it is ever exercised, for the good of His creation.

2. *Moral error.* "All error is deadly." Moral error is as deadly

and coherent. "Ye have the anointing, it abideth in you. As it supplies all your needs, as it is true, and not false, then follow its leading, and, as it teaches you to do, abide in Christ." The translation "truth," is grammatically, though not spiritually, misleading. All the chief early English translations have the accurate rendering "true," and the Revised Version has returned to it. The strong desire of our translators to produce a version which should be elegant and readable is the only reason for the change here. Grammatically, it has been said, the rendering is misleading. For the Apostle's statement is that the anointing is *true*, not that it is *truth*. But inasmuch as the anointing is the gift of the Holy Spirit, and He is the Spirit of Truth (John xiv. 17, xv. 26, xvi. 13), nay even, is Divine Truth itself, there is no real error here, nor difficulty, save upon the surface. If we ask why the Apostle finds it necessary to repeat his statement in other words, to strengthen it by adding "and is no lie," we may find the answer partly (1) by the form of the statement here, and partly (2) by referring back to vers. 21, 22. The unction, says the Apostle, (1) is a *true* unction. But this may merely mean subjectively true. It may signify that the unction is a real process, admitting those who have received it to a share in the threefold office of their Lord, namely, the prophetic, priestly, and kingly office. But the Apostle

---

as intellectual, nay, even more directly deadly. And now, as ever, there be those who "call evil good and good evil." There be those now, as ever, who seduce the young by their lying words. The young Christian is in as much need as ever of the caution, "My son, if sinners entice thee, consent thou not;" of the warning against those who cry, "Cast in thy lot among us; let us all have one purse." Luxury and self-indulgence are the crying sins of this age, and they are incompatible with devotion to Christ. More than ever before habits of extravagant expenditure, of dissipation of time in amuse-

adds, "and is no lie." That is to say, the essential character of the anointing is the imparting of Truth. The Spirit is a Spirit of Truth. He communicates Truth to all on whom He is poured out. Not only is the unction a real pledge of having received sanctifying influence from on high, but it contains the special gift with which the Apostle is at present concerned, namely, the gift which enables a man to cast aside all the deceits of Antichrist, to resist all the seductions of false teachers. And a reference to vers. 21, 22, shows us (2) that the words "and is no lie" were introduced to *warn* men against these seductions. The spirit of Antichrist is in the world, and it breathes no mere harmless set of opinions or speculations, which men may amuse themselves with, may take up or lay down without injury to themselves. They are in total antagonism to God and Truth. If dallied with, they eat into the soul as doth a canker. They are absolutely destructive of the life of God in the soul. And so, if the Apostle here again subjoins the words "is no lie," it is because he would again warn his readers that the doctrine of Jesus, come in the flesh, is one in which no compromise is possible. Deceit there is everywhere in the world around. It lies in wait on every side. But here, at least, no deceit is possible. Here is a safe resting-place for the soul. Jesus Christ came to reveal the Truth, and He Himself

---

ments which do not profit, are prevalent among us, and the result is a relaxation of moral fibre, an incapacity for serious thought or earnest devotion to a purpose. Men make haste to be rich, and care not how. They squander their riches in such a way as to increase the distress their πλεονεξία has caused. Self-indulgence leads to vice, and vice produces misery. Hence the terrible juxtaposition in our civilisation, in the closest vicinity, of the extremes of magnificence and misery, wealth and destitution. Nor can the unremitting efforts of the toiler in Christ's name overtake the evil which man's selfishness is daily

is the Truth. Upon the ointment of His Spirit, poured out upon your head, and running down even to the skirts of your clothing, you may depend for protection against all the wiles of the devil.—**and even as it hath taught you, ye shall abide in him.** Perhaps the force of καὶ καθώς is best given by omitting the "and" of our version, and translating καὶ by *even*. As His anointing (in the sense not of the process, but of the process as accomplished— the *results* of the anointing oil) is teaching you concerning everything, and is truth, and is not a lie,—well, then, "even as it hath taught you, abide ye in Him." The substitution of "He" for "it" as the nominative to the verb ἐδίδαξε (Alford), can hardly be defended. If τὸ αὐτοῦ χρῖσμα is the nominative to διδάσκει in the former part of the sentence, it must also be the nominative to ἐδίδαξε here, otherwise we introduce another idea into the sentence, for whose introduction the Apostle gives no warrant. It is the Spirit Who teaches,—the Spirit "Whose name is as ointment poured forth" (Cant. i. 3),— "poured forth" from the day of Pentecost (see Acts ii. 33, in the original) even unto the end of the world. The rendering μένετε for μενεῖτε, that of all the best MSS. and versions, is adopted by our revisers; but the imperative rendering, which gives by no means a bad sense, is relegated to the margin. On the whole, their

---

augmenting. "The love of money is the root of all evil," says the Apostle, and the men deride his saying and declare it to be the root of all good. Not until the spirit of Jesus has enslaved mankind to the "law of the spirit of life;" not until God, and not self, is acknowledged to be the object for which men live, shall we be free from the need of warning against "them that deceive you."

II. DECEITS FROM WITHIN. The devil is ever busy within the soul in making "the worse appear to be the better reason." He is skilled in putting the enticements of appetite in their most attractive light. He provides us with fine names to call our sins by. Extravagance is

rendering is preferable. This clause then corresponds to that above, "the unction ye received from Him abideth in you." The drift of the passage then is as follows :—" I have written this to you concerning those who are leading you astray. But as far as you are concerned, the unction you have received abides in you. Therefore you need no teaching. You have only to listen on all points to the true and infallible guide you have within, and then you abide in Him whose unction it is, according to His teaching." If we ask who "in Him" refers to, the now accepted reading αὐτοῦ for αὐτό before χρῖσμα assists us to see that our abiding in Christ, and through Him in the Father, is meant. This conclusion is established by a comparison of ver. 28 with 24. And the Apostle has clearly once more John xv. 1–10 in his mind, a discourse which, having once heard, he was never likely to forget.

To this conclusion, then, the Apostle leads us in the first part of his Epistle. You have been called to unspeakable blessings (ch. i. 1–7). But you are encompassed on all sides by dangers. First and foremost there is your own sinfulness (i. 8, ii. 1), though for that God has provided a remedy (ii. 2–6). Then there is an evil world, lying in darkness, in the midst of which your lot is cast (ii. 7–19). Against this, too, God has

---

liberality and freehandedness; sinful indulgence is manly enjoyment; revelry and riot are companionableness and good fellowship; waste of time is necessary amusement and sociability; *dilettante* selfishness is a taste for literature and the arts, culture, refinement, love of the beautiful; unbelief is free and independent thought, originality, freedom from bigotry and superstition; greed of gain is an honourable ambition, development of material resources, commercial activity and the like; indifference is a laudable impartiality, the holding the balance even between conflicting opinions. And thus evil becomes good and good evil, "unstable souls" are "beguiled." There are

forearmed you (ii. 20–25). Therefore cling fast to the one safeguard against all that may lead you astray. His Divine guidance, vouchsafed in your hearts, is that safeguard. You may dwell in peace, because you abide in Him.

"mockers" who "walk after their own ungodly lusts." "Sensual" (or rather, "natural," *i.e.* unregenerate,—see 1 Cor. ii., iii. in the original), "having not the Spirit," they "separate themselves" from the true congregation of the faithful. One only is able to "keep us from falling," and to "present us faultless before the presence of God's glory, with exceeding joy," even He who has anointed us with His Holy Spirit. We can be safe only if we "abide in Him." "In him is Life, and the Life is the Light of men." Believe in Him, and you shall abide in Him. Abide in Him, and none of these "seducing spirits" shall be able to "pluck you out of His hand."

XII.

THE RIGHTEOUSNESS OF CHRIST TO BE MANIFESTED IN US.

CH. ii. 28.—We now commence the second portion of the Epistle. Some commentators would begin this portion at verse 29. But it is more in accordance with St. John's manner to begin a new portion with the repetition of the last idea of the old. No one who has not devoted some time to the study of St. John's writings can fully understand the wonderful coherence, as well as depth of the thought, in this portion of the Epistle. Under the apparent artlessness and simplicity there lies an immense profundity and closeness, not of reasoning, but of meditative interdependence. At first sight much

---

HOMILETICS.

CH. ii. 28.—*Abiding in Christ the source of boldness in our Christian course.* In the former portion of the Epistle, abiding in Christ is regarded as the means whereby we may resist the temptations of the age and society in which we live. Here it is put before us as the ground of our boldness or "assurance," as it is sometimes called.

I. THE NATURE OF CHRISTIAN BOLDNESS. The Christian scheme is full of paradoxes. Indeed, as we have frequently had reason to observe, it is the nature of truth to be so. And one of the most prolific sources of error is the firm grasp we are apt to take of some particular truth, to the entire exclusion of the complementary truth with which its existence is bound up, but which we, in our heat and haste, imagine

appears mere repetition, and much has no visible connection with what has gone before. But the more we study either Epistle or Gospel, the more we perceive the deep, inner unity of each. Every thought arises out of that which has preceded it. Every thought has some inner relation to all that has gone before. And it is only when we have pondered upon the passage verse by verse, that the full majesty of the meaning dawns upon us. To the superficial observer the language may appear, as it did to John Stuart Mill, "poor stuff," manufactured by the yard out of Philo. To the careful and reverent student it is the inspired teaching of one whose face beams with the light reflected from above. Here, then, as Haupt points out, we can see the new section of the Epistle arising naturally out of the old. And we may remark in passing that Haupt here and in the next few verses seems to surpass himself. Nowhere does his profound study of the Epistle, and his clear insight into the Apostle's meaning, appear to greater advantage than in his exposition of this portion of the Epistle. He points out how not only the ideas of being begotten of God, and of doing righteousness, which we find in ver. 29, are continually introduced in the remainder of the Epistle,

---

to be its contradictory. This is the case with our present subject. Humility and confidence are alike characteristics of the Christian life —distrust of ourselves, confidence in God. But it is difficult to be truly humble without being in danger of distrusting God, or undervaluing what "He has done for our soul." It is, on the other hand, difficult to feel implicit confidence in God, absolute certainty that He will complete the good work that He has begun in us, that He will free us from sin, and work out in us the perfection of Jesus Christ, and yet to prevent this confidence from gliding into presumption. It is always possible for Christian reliance on God to degenerate into Pharisaic pride, the more especially as our faith is faith in a Saviour from sin, and our experience, if it is what it ought to be, is that He *has* saved us from sin, and that He has enabled us to grow in wisdom, holiness,

but that the leading thoughts of ver. 28 also continually recur. Thus, for instance, we find the idea of manifestation in this verse recurring in ch. iii. 3–8; the idea of boldness, in ch. iii. 21, iv. 17, v. 14; and in the second of these passages, as here, it is connected with Christ's coming. That coming is also referred to more or less clearly (see exposition there) in ch. iii. 2. And he remarks, in addition, that "all the ideas, with the exception of the μένετε, with which he begins, are new ones," and that it "would be a startling close of a discussion which should introduce a new series of ideas, instead of summing up the old ones;" and, it may be added, very much unlike St. John's manner. While the καὶ νῦν, as he further points out, is used here, as it is in ch. xvii. 5 of the Gospel, of bringing in some new idea on the basis of the former ones. Further, the idea of the first part of the Gospel is the antagonism of light and darkness, of Christ and Antichrist; of the second, righteousness, or, as St. Paul would call it, sanctification, flowing from the new birth or begetting, man has received from God through Jesus Christ. In accordance with this, ver. 28 looks to the future rather than to past or present. Thus three considerations lead us to begin the

---

and knowledge of His Will. And one of the most common reproaches against Christians, a reproach not always undeserved, is that they are Pharisaic in their self-satisfaction, that they pride themselves on their freedom from sins to which other men are prone. It may be well, therefore, to point out the essential distinctions between Pharisaism and Christian confidence.

1. *The Christian's trust is in God, not in himself.* He does not attribute his good deeds to his own merits, but to an indwelling Spirit. He does not regard the renewed life he possesses as anything of his own, but as a "life hid with Christ in God." He acknowledges with shame that whenever he lived or acted for himself, the result was sin. He feels that it is the same with other men; that when they would live for themselves, think for themselves, act for themselves,

second portion of the Epistle here: (1) That it is in accordance with St. John's manner to begin a new section from the standpoint of the former; (2) that the words καὶ νῦν emphasise the fact that he is doing so; and (3) that the idea in ver. 28, its commencement excepted, are introduced for the first time, and belong, not to what precedes, but to what follows.—**And now, little children, abide in him.** This repetition, in the shape of a command, of what in the last verse stands as the assertion of a fact, is in St. John's manner. See ch. i. 10, and ii. 1, ch. iv. 16, 21. It is as though he said, you are *able* to abide in God. It is His Will and purpose concerning you. Take care that it is the *fact*. For this remaining firm in Christ, which was to keep them steadfast against the assaults of Antichrist and of the powers of darkness, was to be the starting-point of a new departure in the Christian life. Not only was evil to be resisted; not only was the Christian to turn his face from the darkness that was passing away, and allow it to be irradiated by the light from heaven which was now revealed, but this abiding in Christ was to lead to development and growth in righteousness, to the putting on His likeness from Whom all righteousness proceeds, to the

---

they fall into every kind of error and crime, and that it is only when they realise how, with other men, they are possessors of a common life, flowing to them *from* the Father, *through* the Son, and *by* the Spirit, that they can possibly do anything that is good. Thus his impulse is not towards separation (the meaning of the word Pharisee), but towards union. He longs to make all men possessors of this common life. The more he possesses it himself, the more he yearns to impart it to other men. So far from being puffed up with pride, or alienated by his virtues from those who possess them not, he becomes ever more and more convinced (1) of the power of God, (2) that "He hath made of one blood all nations that dwell upon the earth," and 3) that the same Spirit that has been mighty to the pulling down the strongholds of sin in his own heart, can do the same great work in the

preparing for the manifestation of that Presence before which all that is base and wrong and wicked must vanish away.—*that, when he shall appear, we may have confidence.* Before we proceed to explain this passage we must correct the translation. For ὅταν the best MSS. have ἐάν, and the literal translation of φανερωθῇ is "shall be manifested." "Appear" is the rendering of the early English Versions, but the Revised Version has "if He shall be manifested." It is easy to see how ἐάν would be corrected to ὅταν, but not so easy to see how ἐάν could have been introduced. If it be the correct reading it must refer to the uncertainty of the moment of Christ's coming. For "of that day and that hour knoweth no man." Therefore we must interpret with Alford, "In case of His second coming taking place." It is to be remembered, however, that the rule which selects the more difficult reading may be pressed too far, and that ὅταν may be traced as far back as the Vulgate and Syriac Versions. The word translated "confidence" again is not πεποίθησις or ὑπόστασις, but παρρησία or boldness of speech. The Authorised Version here departs from Tyndale, who (with Cranmer and the Geneva Version) has "*that we may be bold*" and follows

---

heart of every other man, if he will but open that heart to its gracious influences.

2. *The Christian compares himself not with other men, but with himself and with Christ.* (a) He compares himself with himself (it is very doubtful whether the true reading in 2 Cor. x. 12 is not that which makes St. Paul praise, not blame, such self-comparison), not with other men. He looks back on his past life, and remembers with shame the stains of sin which he allowed to rest on his soul before he knew Christ as he does now. He knows that if he had been left to himself he would still have been such as he once was. And so he gives the glory, not to himself, but to God, the more so as he reflects how His Spirit can do equal works of grace in every other man's heart, as soon as that heart is given to God. (b) He compares himself with

the Rheims (Roman Catholic) Version, the Revised Version returning to the more correct translation (may have boldness). Haupt draws out the inner meaning of this passage very ably. He points out how, while the other writers of the New Testament speak of Christ's coming as an ἀποκάλυψις or unveiling, St. John here speaks of it as a φανέρωσις or manifestation. He somewhat exaggerates, however, the contrast between the two expressions; ἀποκάλυψις, he says, invariably designates a revelation which has taken place in an extraordinary way, through a direct interposition of God, and therefore as a perfectly new development, whereas a φανέρωσις is in all cases a "making visible of potencies long working secretly." But an ἀποκάλυψις is necessarily a drawing back the veil from something already existing—a communication to man of a hidden purpose of God already formed, if not already in operation. Still, it may be conceded that the word φανερόω lays more stress than ἀνακαλύπτω on the present existence of the thing to be manifested. And thus the coming of Jesus Christ is set before us as simply the bringing to light of an existing fact. He is ever present with His Church (Matt. xxviii. 20). His manifestation brings that fact to light. The

---

Christ, and finds nothing but shame and humiliation in the comparison of his weakness and imperfection with the glorious holiness of the Lamb of God. Nor does he dwell simply on the sinlessness of Jesus. This negative view is too common. But the instructed Christian does not forget to dwell on the *active* side of the holiness of Christ, and to meditate on the streams of strength, and pardon, and forgiveness, and enabling power which pour forth inexhaustibly from Him, as from a well of life, and which every true believer is bound to minister to his brethren.

3. *The boldness consists in a belief in the Fatherhood of God.* It is this which gives the Christian confidence. It is not a mere belief that he will be saved in the end, whatever other men may be. It is not merely a belief that an atonement has been made for his sins. It is

Apostle even regards the Resurrection as a thing present (John v. 25, xi. 25). And here we may observe on a remarkable confirmation of the genuineness of St. John's narrative. Hymenæus and Philetus (2 Tim. ii. 18) said that the *resurrection was past already.* It is easy enough to see whence they obtained their doctrine. It was a perversion of these words of our Lord, which, though not yet recorded by St. John, were doubtless current in the Church. The Apostle therefore describes by ἐὰν φανερωθῇ that day in which the Lord, who abideth with His people always, will make His Presence apparent at once and for ever to all eyes. The word παρρησία means originally *freedom of speech,* and hence it comes to mean that frame of mind which begets free speech, **boldness,** absence of all fear. So we find it used in passages like Eph. iii. 12 ; Heb. x. 19. Here it refers to the calm and tranquil frame of mind which he who is and feels that he is united to Christ by faith, will be able to preserve when the final judgment is at hand ; not relying on himself, but on Him Who has destroyed the power of sin within him.—**and not be ashamed before him at his coming.** Literally, these words mean "not be ashamed from Him," *i.e.*, not shrink back abashed before His

---

the certainty that all slavish fear may be put aside, that God loves to hear and grant our supplications ; that His "heart's desire" for us all is "that we should be saved from sin and every other evil, that we should dwell for ever in that unclouded happiness which only perfect sinlessness can give." His boldness has nothing to do with self. On the contrary, it forgets self altogether in the contemplation of a Father's universal love.

II. WHAT GROUND HAVE WE FOR THIS BOLDNESS? Our boldness to approach to the throne of grace is due to the reconciliation or atonement which has been made between God and man by the life and death of Jesus Christ. In the faith of that reconciling work we can approach God as our Father, confident that the "handwriting that is against us" has been blotted out. See Eph. iii. 12 ; 1 Tim. iii. 13 ;

Presence. The word translated Presence is *Parousia*, which may almost be denominated the technical word by which the Apostles of Christ are wont to express His coming and its results. Among those results is the one graphically and tersely referred to here, but which is elsewhere spoken of in Scripture in language of a more definite character. "Then shall they begin to say unto the mountains, Fall on us, and unto the hills, Cover us" (Luke xxiii. 30; cf. Isaiah ii. 19; Hos. x. 8). There is a connection here with the thoughts so prominent in the former part of the Epistle. These words express the attitude of the children of darkness and Antichrist at the coming of the Son of God, as contrasted with that of the children of light.

VER. 29.—**If ye know that he is righteous.** We have first to consider what is the connection of this verse with the preceding. St. John has just advised his "children" to abide in Christ, that they might appear with joy and not with grief, at His appearing. He now again knits the second part of the Epistle with the first. "In the first part" the fellowship between God and man "comes into consideration as an internal habit; in the second it is rather its confirmation in works" (Haupt). And as

---

Heb. iii. 6, iv. 16, x. 35. In the first of these passages it is connected with the ready access we have to God through Jesus Christ. See also iii. 21, iv. 17, v. 14 of this Epistle. We must not forget that the leading idea of this boldness is *freedom of speech*, and that it has nothing to do with the other words translated "bold," "boldness," in our version, derived from τολμάω and θαρρέω.

III. THIS BOLDNESS IS HERE CONNECTED WITH OUR ABIDING IN CHRIST. We must remember that the atonement spoken of in the last head is not a mere blotting out of the memory of our transgressions. Beyond and above this, it brings about union with Christ through the Spirit, the indwelling of God in the soul. Not only is God not angry with us; not only is He willing to listen to us, but He dwells in us and we in Him. It is obvious that this consideration infinitely streng-

he commences the second part with the conclusion to which he had brought us in the first—the necessity of abiding in Christ—so now he points out once more the reason why he has taught us so to abide, because God is righteous (ch. i. 9, ii. 2), and there can be no righteousness apart from Him. It is to the acquirement of this Divine Righteousness that he exhorts us, and he takes care, before doing so, to lead us to seek its root not in ourselves, but in God. The next question that arises is, who is meant by "He"? Both God Himself, and Jesus Christ, His Son, have been declared to be righteous in the texts just cited. We may therefore interpret this passage of either, so far as the predicating of righteousness is concerned. But as Haupt reminds us, the latter part of the verse settles the question. We are "born (or begotten) of Him." Now we are never said to be born of Jesus Christ, but through Him to be born of God. Hence it is the essential righteousness of the Eternal Father that is spoken of here, as the reason why all His children should be righteous. The righteousness of the Son is derived from His Father and manifested to us. But it is the actual source of all righteousness whatever to which the Apostle now refers. "As the nature of

---

thens as well as justifies the belief in freedom of access and address to God.

IV. THIS BOLDNESS WILL ANIMATE US IN THE DAY OF JUDGMENT. The feeling of the natural man at the thought of the coming of Christ is well expressed by Malachi:—"Who shall abide the day of His coming, and who shall stand when He appeareth?" (Mal. iii. 2). The Apostle here encourages us by the thought that the day at which all mankind else shall tremble, will not disturb in the slightest the confidence of the Christian. "*Comfort* (or *encourage*) one another" with the thought of His coming, says St. Paul (1 Thess. iv. 18). And St. John here points out the indwelling of God in the Christian soul gives it a confidence which even the great and terrible Day of Judgment will not shake. The more we unite ourselves to Christ by

God is Righteousness, so must this same righteousness be the token of sonship in relation to Him; the children must bear the father's stamp upon them" (Haupt).—**ye know that every one which doeth righteousness is born of him.** As a specimen of the frigid and unmeaning expositions which have been wont to pass current as exegesis of an author so difficult as St. John, we may instance Ebrard's comment here. He says, "The exhortation 'Abide in Him' is changed (ver. 29) into the *more general* exhortation to ποιεῖν τὴν δικαιοσύνην." There is no such meaningless change. There is not even an exhortation to do righteousness. Even if there had been it would be an exhortation to what it is the object of the whole Christian scheme to effect. And the exhortation would derive its whole force from the fact that every believer is united to Christ and must maintain that union unimpaired. So that a specific exhortation would not have been changed into a general one, but an effect have been derived from its cause. But in reality the Apostle is pointing to the doing of righteousness as a proof of the inward union of the believer with Him Who is Righteousness itself. "Abide in Him," he says, "as I have bidden

---

faith, the more thoroughly we conform ourselves to the pattern of His life (the natural and necessary result of true faith), the more ardently we shall long for the day of His manifestation, the more utterly will all dread or fear of Him be banished from our minds.

VER. 29.—*The test of the new birth.* The connection of thought between this and the last verse has been drawn out in the exposition. It may be well here, before expanding the idea of this verse, to summarise it briefly once more. The abiding in Christ is the ground of our calm expectation of the Day of Judgment. This calmness in the expectation of what others dread is strengthened by the thought that we have received a new birth from God. And the proof of our having received that new birth is the doing righteousness. If we can conscientiously feel that we *are* doing righteousness, our claim to be born of God is established. We know (see notes on ch. i. 9, ii. 1) that He

you, and I will give you a fresh reason for doing so. When He comes you will meet Him with boldness, and not with trembling like the children of darkness. You know that He is righteous, because I have told you so, and because your own hearts bear witness to the truth of what I said. And if you know this, if you know that He is the sole fount of every good and righteous action, you know moreover that every one who has conquered temptation and sin, and has learned to do His Will, must have received the precious gift of a new birth from Him. See (ch. iii. 1) what love it is on God's part, that He permits us to be called His children." There is a doubt whether γινώσκετε is to be regarded as indicative or imperative. But the question does not much affect the sense. The former is preferable. Some editors, again, read καί after ὅτι. The two favourite MSS. of modern critics, the Sinaitic and the Vatican, are divided here. But the omission or insertion of the particle does not affect the sense appreciably. The Apostle's meaning here is a practical one. It is equivalent to his Master's "By their fruits ye shall know them." What he would convey to us is (1) that God is the source of all righteous-

---

is righteous. And had we not been born of Him, we could not have done that of which He is the only source.

I. WHAT IS THE NEW BIRTH? The word used by St. John to express this process means either *birth* or *begetting*. Hence it refers to the *first starting-point* or *origin* of life, as distinct from its further development. It means the implanting of the first germ of the renewed humanity of Christ in the heart. It is the commencement of a process which is destined eventually to revolutionise the whole man, to change not only his relations to God, not only the point of view from which he looks upon God and God upon him, but that which was formerly corrupt and tending to destruction, into the image of its Lord and Saviour. Sometimes Scripture views this process in its origin (as in John iii. 3, 5), sometimes in its progress (as in the famous 7th chapter

ness, and (2) that every man who does righteousness must needs have been born of God. And thus the evidence of a life conformed to God's Will is the only evidence of the reality of our regeneration, the only unmistakable proof of our dwelling in God and God in us. And just precisely in proportion to the extent to which we act on the eternal principles of truth and justice is the process of our regeneration complete. Our whole life here is, if we be true believers in Christ, one long "travail in birth until Christ be fully formed in us." So Haupt: "In the preceding passage the παρρησία, in the Day of Judgment, was made dependent upon the μένειν ἐν τῷ θεῷ; here it is said further how it is that this παρρησία comes into effect,—that is, it operates thus, that he who continueth in God, and therefore is born of God, becomes firmly assured of this his fellowship with God, through his ποιεῖν τὴν δικαιοσύνην." And Alford: "When, therefore, a man doeth righteousness, γινώσκομεν, we apprehend, we collect from our previous knowledge of these truths, that the source of his righteousness is God: that, in consequence, he has acquired by new birth from God that righteousness which he had not by nature. We

---

of the Romans), sometimes in its completion, as in this Epistle, where St. John always refers to it in the perfect tense.

II. WHAT IS THE SIGN OF THE NEW BIRTH? Invariably, in Scripture the evidence that a man is born again is to be looked for in his *conduct*. This fundamental principle is laid down by our Lord in His first discourse (Matt. vii. 16). It is laid down alike by St. Paul, St. Peter, and St. James (see Gal. v. 6, 22; Rom. viii. 5, 14; 2 Cor. iii. 18; Eph. iv. 24; 2 Thess. ii. 13, 14, &c.; 1 Peter i. 21-23, ii. 1, 2, 9, 11-15, 21, &c.; James ii. 22). And here we have the following principles laid down. The Christian abides in God. God is righteous. Hence every one who "doeth righteousness" can discern that he has been born of God. But the objection may be raised, Who is there that doeth righteousness? "There is none righteous, no, not one." Therefore there is none that is born of God. In one sense this is true.

CHRIST TO BE MANIFESTED IN US. 189

argue from his ποιεῖν τὴν δικαιοσύνην to his γεγεννῆσθαι ἐκ θεοῦ." We may add that when a man has attained to that state described in ch. iii. 9, when his sinful habits are broken off, when sin is slain within him, then the process of birth is complete, then he is perfect in Christ Jesus. This is implied here, and by the use of the perfect tense in every case where this word occurs in this Epistle, save ch. v. 18 (if indeed that applies to the believer at all—see note there). See iii. 9, iv. 7, v. 1, 4, 18. It may be remarked, before quitting this subject, that St. John's meaning has been strangely misapprehended or attenuated by various classes of commentators. Thus the Socinian writers, as Alford reminds us, have read his meaning backwards, making the doing righteousness the condition of our becoming a child of God, instead of the proof that we have become such;— while the mediæval expositors have lost the fulness of St. John's meaning in the fictions of so-called dogmatic theology, and speak of works of infused righteousness, which are given with grace, and which admit the man to a sort of participation with the Divine essence, expositions which are not so much incorrect as incomplete, exchang-

---

That is the sense in which the Apostle speaks in ch. iii. 9. No one can lay claim to this impeccability in this life. St. John must be referring to the time when the regenerating principle has completed its working; when the union of the believer with Christ has been perfected. But on the other hand, Christ's redeeming work would have been an absolute failure unless His children should do at least *some* righteousness here. As in one sense there is no one who "doeth righteousness," that is, uniformly and invariably, so in another there is not a single soul united to Christ by faith who does not "do righteousness" frequently and continually. And the more advanced in the Christian life he is, the more accurately does the phrase "doing righteousness" express his life as a whole. Any one single act done simply because it is right is an evidence, if not of faith in its fulness, at least of a measure of faith in God (see Homiletics on vers. 22-24 of this

ing the warmth and breadth of Christian doctrine for a kind of hard scientific precision, substituting a system of narrow technical definitions for the infinite mystery of God's dealings, which pass beyond the boundaries of human knowledge.

---

chapter, pp. 153–164). The germs of the Divine life are there, even in the case when the actual entering into covenant with Christ has not quickened them into full vitality, and placed before the soul the full measure of God's requirements. If, then, you feel that in any sense you are "doing righteousness;" if, that is, you find any motive directing your actions above that of your own interest, any standard of right and wrong by which you desire to act which is based, not upon the shifting passions, desires, opinions of men, but upon some eternal standard outside and above the visible and the tangible, the signs of the new birth are there. You have only to go on doing that Will which has been revealed to you, and you shall "know of the doctrine." You shall steadily make your way out of darkness to the Eternal Light.

XIII.

THE PRIVILEGES OF THE CHRISTIAN.

CH. iii. 1.—**Behold, what manner of love the Father hath bestowed upon us, that we should be called the children of God.** This verse, as we have seen, is intimately connected with the last, and arises out of it, as is St. John's wont. "You may know," he says, "that any man who doeth righteousness has been born of God. Think what a great privilege and blessing it is to be so born." The word ποταπός (more properly ποδαπός) signifies originally "of what country." Hence it is here correctly translated "what manner," instead of (as is preferred by some expositors) "how great." "St. John exhorts his hearers to ponder not the greatness, but the kind and nature of the love God has bestowed upon us" (Ebrard). But, he adds, we need not go so far as Calvin and import the

---

HOMILETICS.

CH. iii. 1.—*God is our Father and we His children.*

I. GOD IS OUR FATHER. This doctrine (*a*) was unknown to the world of St. John's day, save to the Jews, and misunderstood even by them. The Gentile belief, originally a belief in a bright, glorious, resplendent being, of which the sun was the type, had degenerated sadly in the Apostolic times. The pages of the early Fathers teem with denunciations of the monstrous, absurd, and immoral fables then current respecting the gods—fables which would justify any crime,

idea of *desert*—"how undeserved a love." It is the quality of the love to which our attention is asked. This thought may include the greatness, fulness, freeness of the love, because these ideas are parts of its character, a character unfolded in succeeding passages of the Epistle, notably in ver. 16; iv. 8-10, 16, 19. And the special feature in its character on which stress is here laid is the fact that God has made us His children. It is a thought which would strike those to whom the Epistle was addressed far more than it does us, to whom the idea has been familiar from infancy. The idea of the affectionate relations of father and child being used to describe the relations of God to man was a new one to all nations of the world at that day, save the Jews. If the heathen held themselves to be "God's offspring" (Acts xvii. 28), it was a cold and distant relation that was thus implied. His offspring by creation they undoubtedly were. But of the near and tender relation between God and His creatures described, for instance, in Psalm ciii., "Like as a father pitieth his children, so the Lord pitieth those that fear Him," the Greeks and Romans knew nothing. Hence the reference to the quality of God's love from this point of view would meet with a hearty response from those who had just learned what it was. The next point that invites our attention is

---

however horrible, and had little to do with either purity or love. Plutarch has some striking observations on the slavish, superstitious fear of hostile powers unseen, which reduced many a life in his time to abject wretchedness. The Jews, again, if they theoretically believed in God as their Father, had practically brought down their belief to a mere justification of their right to stand aloof from, and to despise other nations. And (*b*) it cannot be said that Christians have risen to the full conceptions of what is involved in the idea of God as a Father. The idea that He is "far from every one of us," which St. Paul felt it necessary to repudiate (Acts xvii. 27), that He needs all kinds of

the word δέδωκεν. The Alexandrian MS. reads ἔδωκεν. But, as Ebrard remarks, the other reading is not only better authenticated, but is more internally appropriate. It is a "good and *perfect* gift" which God has given us in this love. We next have to remark on the word δέδωκεν itself. God has given us love of a certain kind. Some expositors here, again, have been tempted to water down the passage; ἀγάπη becomes with them "the gift of charity," "a benefit," "an evidence" or "proof of God's love." No; God gives us His Love itself, as Luther's warm heart perceives, "Usus est Joannes singulari verborum pondere: *non dicit* dedisse nobis Deum *donum aliquod*, sed *ipsam caritatem et fontem omnium bonorum, cor ipsum*, idque non pro operibus, aut studiis nostris, sed gratuito." And next, observe the words, "the Father." The emphasis of this word also is apt to escape us from our very familiarity with it. The word, I say, not, alas! the idea. The idea of the Fatherhood of God is with some as much obscured as ever. But that is the idea St. John would make prominent here. God is "the Father." Not the stern, wrathful, inexorable Judge Who is extreme to mark what is done amiss, Who exacts relentlessly the very last farthing, Who needed a Being of inexhaustible love to arise and turn His wrath away; but *the Father*—the Being whose loving heart ever yearned towards His

---

expedients to propitiate Him, that His wrath is stronger than His love, that He is "extreme to mark what is done amiss," still lingers in many a heart. And therefore (c) we need to lay greater stress, in our preaching, on the truth that the gentleness, tenderness, and sympathy of Christ is but the revelation of a Father's heart; that the Death upon the Cross is nothing more than a Father's Will translated into action, that everything that the fullest, freest, most expansive ideas of love in its widest sense can suggest, is expressed in those words, "God so loved the world, that He gave His only begotten Son, that whosoever believeth in Him should not perish, but have everlasting life."

creatures, Who ever intended their restoration to the fulness of His favour, and Who manifested His purpose and His heart towards the world in the Person of His "beloved Son, in Whom He was well pleased." He it was, Who had given such tender love to mankind, as to number them among His own children. Our next inquiry is into the meaning of the word ἵνα here. Are we to press the strict meaning of the word, and to explain the passage thus: that God gave this love to us *in order that* we might become His children? Or are we to regard this becoming His children as simply the *result* of the love that He has shown? We have already more than once observed that the strict sense of ἵνα cannot always be pressed in the New Testament. And therefore we must decide from the context in each particular passage what interpretation to put on it. Here the more natural interpretation would certainly be the latter. It is the fact that we are the children of God which indicates the manner of love that God has bestowed upon us, rather than the love is bestowed upon us in order that we should become His children. "The great majority of commentators, ancient and modern, assume, correctly, that the clause with ἵνα serves to specify *wherein* this δεδωκέναι ἀγάπην consists" (Ebrard). He would supply ἐν τῷ βούλεσθαι, &c., before ἵνα. Instead of calling upon us to remark on the *nature* of God's love,

---

II. WE ARE GOD'S CHILDREN. It would be impossible to enumerate the various consequences which flow from this thesis. Suffice it to notice two, *obedience* and *affection*. With regard to the first, it must be remarked that it is nothing if not complete. There is no man who is not jeopardising his Sonship if he does not set himself to do his Father's will in *everything*. Any one who is content deliberately to disobey God on any one point, is doing his best to sever the connection between his Father and himself. A man is a "debtor to do the whole law." If he "offend in one point, he is guilty of all." And they

we should have rather expected, if the telic sense of ἵνα is to be pressed, the sentence to run thus: Behold, my brethren, the reason why the Father has bestowed His love upon us! It is that we might become His children. With regard to the expression τέκνα θεοῦ, Haupt points out the special love involved in the expression. He is disposed to exaggerate the difference of thought between St. John and the other writers of the New Testament here. He insists that St. Paul lays greater stress upon the return to the original nature of man in his references to the new creation (Gal. vi. 15), the ἀνακαίνωσις (Rom. xii. 2; Col. iii. 10, and elsewhere), rather than upon a new creation from God; that he speaks more strongly of adoption (υἱοθεσία) than of the actual sonship on which St. John insists. There is much less difference than Haupt supposes. The ἀνακαίνωσις of St. Paul means rather a return to the original plan of humanity existing in the Mind of God, than to any concrete embodiment of that plan in the person of Adam; and if he speaks of the process of reconciliation as an "adoption," there is no mistake about the reality of the Divine Sonship which he supposes to have come about thereby (Rom. viii. 14, 16; Gal. iv. 6). When Haupt says that St. Paul regards the Sonship of the Christian as the result of "renewal or re-impartation of the original gift of the Spirit, whereas St. John never fixes his eyes upon the mere outpouring and

---

therefore are much to blame who make their assurance of Sonship rest upon something which took place in their past lives, instead of upon their loyal and dutiful obedience to their Father in the present. While as regards the second, *affection*, it points out the claim our Father has upon our *heart*. Not only ought we to *say* we love Him, but there ought to be no difficulty in *doing* what we say. Whether we look at the world of nature or of revelation, we have evidence sufficient of His love. We ought therefore to pay Him a *willing* and not a *grudging* obedience. We ought not to look upon our service as a tribute harshly exacted by

help of grace, but always on the communication of God's own Divine Nature," he forgets for the moment that the impartation of the Spirit *is* the communication of God's own Divine Nature. Theology, at least in the West, has preferred too much to dwell on "the mere outpouring and help of grace," rather than on the gift of the Divine Nature itself. But it cannot claim St. Paul as an abettor of this natural tendency of the human heart to put God further off than He really is. Regeneration and renewal by the Holy Ghost are a communication to us of the Divine Nature (as St. Peter expressly says—2 Peter i. 4; and St. Paul, almost as clearly, Rom. vi. 23, in the original); grace is simply the favour and goodness of God in giving us this precious gift of life in Him. It is not merely, as Haupt says, that St. Paul teaches that for Christ's sake God gives us the *rights* of children, while St. John regards us as receiving through Christ the *nature* of children, but that both alike regard the faith which rests upon the Divine power to transform us into the Divine image (2 Cor. iii. 18), as the means whereby we are, in point of fact, united to God, by virtue of which union we are not simply *regarded as* God's children, but have actually become so; and that, with each of them equally, the reconciliation between God and man is not merely a process carried on between God and Christ *on our behalf*, but one which, beginning with Christ, is

---

a hard taskmaster, but as the offering of an affectionate heart to One who has a thousand claims upon that affection. We ought not only to take a pleasure in serving Him, but in worshipping Him, in public or in private. His Word, His Day, His Praise, the privilege of addressing Him in prayer, all ought to be inexpressibly dear to us. And any sacrifice of our own wills which He may desire of us, in order to carry out His wise purposes for the good of all mankind, ought to be cheerfully rendered, not as if to One who took a pleasure in seeing His creatures unhappy, but as to one who knows that only by the

actually carried on in each one of His members by the bringing every act and thought into submission to the Divine law. Our next point is the word κληθῶμεν. The commentators here have been very anxious to repel any idea that this was any mere empty title. Unnecessarily anxious, perhaps it may be added. Few of them seem to have connected the word with the well-known expressions of St. Paul, κλῆσις, ἐκκλησία, with which every one St. John was addressing must have been familiar, as well as the Hebrew קהל (one of the most common words to denote the congregation), and the constant reference to God's calling in the Old Testament. The best MSS. and the Revised Version add here "And such we are." Erasmus, it is true, regarded these words as spurious, and the Vulgate misinterpreted them (et simus). The words might, of course, have been added by those who felt the difficulty which the word κληθῶμεν has occasioned to expositors. But all the best MSS. and Versions contain them. Cranmer inserts them "and be in dede." Haupt, on the other hand, rejects them from internal evidence as an early gloss. They make but very little difference to the sense, though they certainly emphasise it. For we are told in the next verse that we are (ἐσμεν) the children of God. And besides, "God's gifts and calling are without repentance" (Rom. xi. 29). God's calling is a *real* calling. If He calls us to be His children, we

---

crucifixion of all unrenewed affections and passions can we arrive at the glorious liberty of the children of God.

III. THE FULNESS AND FREENESS OF THIS LOVE. God has "given it us," we read. "He has given us His heart itself, the very fountain of love and of all goods," as Luther says. There is no arbitrary selection of this or that person. There is no stint in its overflowing abundance. "God will have all men to be saved and come to the knowledge of the truth." Full and free salvation from all evil and sin and misery is offered to every one who will embrace it. All the fulness

scarcely need to be told that we are such. If such express information be needed, it can only be by reason of our weakness, not of His changeableness. Still, this is no argument against the genuineness of the words καὶ ἐσμεν. St. John does not elsewhere use the words καλέω, κλῆσις, and he would naturally desire that no one should mistake his meaning here. St. Augustine has seen that "hic non est discrimen inter dici et esse," and Calvin remarks that "in his titulus esse non potest." But even with the rest of the New and Old Testament before them, expositors have launched into profitless discussions on the possible meanings of the expression κληθῶμεν, and whether it could or could not be equivalent to ἐσμεν. It is therefore far more likely than not that an inspired writer like St. John would take care from the first to avoid all misunderstanding, and explain carefully to those whom he addressed that they were not only called, but actually *were*, the children of God. Another reason may have weighed with him. The very closeness and affectionateness of the relation thus affirmed between God and man may have been a reason why people should fail to apprehend it. Indeed, the history of the last eighteen centuries shows us that it has been so. There was therefore the more need that the Apostle should emphasise the closeness of the relation, and

---

of God is to be ours, according to our capacity for receiving it. "Every good and perfect gift" (James i. 17), not only is His to give, but it "cometh down from the Father of the lights," upon all who dispose their hearts for the reception of such gifts. The gift of being a child of God involves likeness to our Father. And so St. John says (ver. 3), "When He shall be manifested we shall be like Him," Who is the εἰκών of His Father, the beaming forth of His glory, and the χαρακτήρ of His substance (Col. i. 15; Heb. i. 3).

IV. THE WORLD KNOWETH US NOT, AS IT KNEW HIM NOT. It knew not God, for it neglected the revelation of Himself that He had

remind those to whom he wrote that the words "children of God" were no mere *title*, but the expression of a *fact*, a fact which was to colour all their thoughts and actions, to banish superstitious fear, and to fill them with a thought of ever-present love, which should sustain them in all the trials and distresses of the world. That this last thought was in the Apostle's mind is shown by what follows.—**for this cause the world knoweth us not, because it knew him not.** Here Tyndale, Cranmer, and the Geneva Version read "you" for us, a very common various reading in the New Testament. But as St. John has taken care in the former part of this verse to include himself in his mention of the privileges of Christians, it appears probable that he would do so here. And the authority for the reading of the Authorised (which is also that of the Revised) Version is very considerable. We have here a touch of that sadness which must affect every good man when he looks upward to the ideal of life displayed to him by God, and then outward to the degree in which that ideal is comprehended and realised by man. The Baptist felt it (John iii. 32); St. John himself felt it (John i. 5, 10); our blessed Lord Himself frequently expresses the feeling (Matt. xxiii. 37; Luke xiii. 34, xix. 42, 44; John v. 42, 43). And all who have laboured in His cause have at one time or

---

made from the beginning (Rom. i. 21, 22). Even in the centre of the intellectual life of the civilised world, it confessed its ignorance (Acts xvii. 23). And so when the last and most perfect revelation of Him was made in the Person of His Son, it not only did not recognise Him, but displayed the fiercest hostility against Him, even unto death. It treated God as the vilest criminal, so far were its perceptions blinded by sin. His disciples cannot expect any other treatment. They ought not to complain if their actions are misconstrued or their motives misrepresented. They must not be surprised if men fail to understand them, if their "life" is regarded by "fools" as "madness," and their

another felt the weight of this burden. St. John desired to comfort those whom he addressed in the manifold cares and troubles of their lives by the thought of their heavenly calling and its reality. "You are encompassed about with hatred and opposition, but be of good cheer, there is One whose child you are, and He will not forsake you. The world is still in darkness, but ye are the children of light. The very fact that you are such will bring hostility upon you. 'The disciple is not above his Master.' They persecuted Him and put Him to death, and you cannot expect that it will be otherwise with you. Remember His words, 'If they have persecuted Me, they will also persecute you' (John xvi. 20). Therefore comfort yourselves with the thought Whose children you are. It is this, no doubt, that brings upon you the troubles you endure. But from that very fact also, remember, you can derive your consolation." There is some difficulty in deciding to whom the word αὐτόν refers—whether to the Father or to Christ. But no doubt the indefiniteness was in the mind of the Apostle. They knew neither the Father nor the Son, neither the Revealed nor the Revealer (ch. ii. 22, 23). "Ye neither know Me nor my Father; if ye had known Me, ye should have known my Father also" (John viii. 19). If this be so, how can you be surprised that you are living

---

"end" believed "to be without honour" (Wisdom of Solomon v. 4). The wonder would be if it were otherwise. The children of this world live for immediate gratification. Their conscience is "the experience of the tribe," the public opinion of the hour. Their desire is the gratification of their passions, the satisfaction of their appetite for riches and honours, their ambition the approbation of their fellow-men. What have they in common with men who set themselves against the "vox populi" in matters of the gravest importance ; who put a curb upon their passions ; who despise riches, and set no store by honours, and regard the approbation of their fellow-men as a snare?

in a world which misunderstands and misrepresents your conduct and principles of action? They know not the Father; they do not receive the Revelation of Him which the Son came to bring; how should they know you, who have been begotten as His children by His Spirit?

How can they expect that men shall understand their zeal for the spread of God's kingdom, their interest in religious and charitable works, their regard for the honour of God, their reverence for His Word, their zeal for His worship and His House? Must they not feel daily that between themselves and those who live for this world there is "a great gulf fixed;" the only difference between this world and the next being that here one can pass at will from one side to the other? If we are disposed to complain that we are misunderstood and calumniated in this life, let us remember that on the entrance to God's kingdom stand inscribed the words, "Perfect through suffering;" and over the doorway is upreared the Cross of Jesus Christ. "For even hereunto were ye called, because Christ also suffered for us, leaving us an example, that ye should follow His steps" (1 Pet. ii. 21).

XIV.

THE FUTURE OF THE CHILDREN OF GOD.

CH. iii. 2.—**Beloved.** Once again, as in ch. ii. 7, do we find this affectionate expression, and once again we may call attention to it as introducing quite a new style of address into the world. We are familiar with the φιλία or personal affection of a philosopher towards his pupils, in the case of Socrates, as depicted by Plato. We see warm affection breaking through the stern rebukes of the Jewish prophets. But nothing like this habit of love of the brethren, *as such*, had ever been introduced into the world until Christ came.—**now are we the children of God.** St. John repeats himself once more here, and once more with the intention of taking a new departure. The assertion in the last verse that we are the children of God looks backward to the former section, and regards the fact as explaining the hostile relations between the Christian and the world. This time it looks forward to the future of the Christian in the next world, for which (ver. 3) we are bidden to prepare. St. John

---

HOMILETICS.

CH. iii. 2.—*The Vision of the Future.*
I. AT PRESENT WE CANNOT CONCEIVE WHAT IS IN STORE FOR US. There is a "glory to be revealed in us" (Rom. viii. 18). What that glory is, the Spirit will reveal (1 Cor. ii. 10). For He searcheth the

emphasises the fact which he has just stated (ver. 1) in order that it may be the starting-point of a new career. We *are* the children of God. What this will lead to we do not at present exactly know. Yet we know that it must lead to a likeness to our Master.—**and it doth not yet appear what we shall be.** There are two difficulties here, (1) the tense, (2) the nominative to be supplied before ἐφανερώθη. Dean Alford (1) would translate *it was never yet manifested.* Professor Westcott regards the aorist as "pointing back to some definite occasion on which the revelation might have been expected." Yet if the view we have previously expressed of the aorist be correct, and that it is frequently used as the equivalent of the Hebrew imperfect, it may relate to indefinite past time. It may therefore be rendered by *hath not been manifested.* For our *hath been* is by no means a definite perfect, like the Hebrew and Greek perfect. See note on ch. ii. 18. *Hath not been manifested* simply means that such a manifestation has never taken place at *any* period in the past, not that the manifestation has never been finally completed, which would be "*is* not yet manifested." In regard to (2) we should naturally be inclined to supply the same nominative to the verb in both clauses. But the context forbids it. There can be little doubt that here we should supply *it*, and in the next clause *He*. Therefore we must translate with R. V. *it is not yet* (or rather *it hath not yet been*) *made manifest.*—**what we shall be.** That is to say, we are at present conscious of a close and intimate re-

---

deep things of God. But He makes these known, not to our intellects, as we are tempted to suppose, but to our hearts. He brings us into contact with the mysteries of Divine holiness and love. And He disposes our minds to love these things and to desire to conform ourselves to them. But while as yet on the threshold of the Christian life how shall we understand what is involved in likeness to God?

lation to God. But to what results that blessed condition shall lead has not yet been made clear to us. As it hath been written, "Eye hath not seen, nor ear heard, neither have entered into the heart of man, the things that God hath prepared for them that love Him" (1 Cor. ii. 9). This does not mean, as some have supposed, to indicate that sonship to God will hereafter become something different in *kind* to what it is now. But it obviously involves what in the very nature of things is necessary, that it will hereafter be very different in *degree*. Sinlessness cannot be predicated of us in our present condition. Yet sinlessness is the goal to which we are advancing. And not only this, but other indescribable glories await us. Who can tell what it will be to "know even as we are known" (1 Cor. xiii. 12)—to see no longer "in a mirror, darkly," but "face to face,"—to gaze with unveiled face upon the vision of the Lord (2 Cor. iii. 18)? —**but we know.** This phrase is very common in this Epistle. See ch. ii. 3, 5, iii. 14, 16, v. 15, 18, 19, 20. And οἴδατε occurs just as often. See ch. ii. 20, &c.—**that when he shall appear.** Some have translated here, *when it shall appear*, so as to supply the same subject as in the former part of the verse. So Tyndale and Cranmer. The Geneva returns to the older rendering of Wiclif, *he*, and is followed by the Rhemish Version. The translation *it* does not give a bad sense. "It does not yet appear what we shall be, but we know that if it *does* appear, it will involve our likeness to Him." But all these versions

---

How shall we, at the first glimmer of the dawn, be able to imagine what the prospect will be when the sun is risen in its fulness? How shall we, who have but just begun the task of self-crucifixion, be able to comprehend the joy he feels who is in heart and spirit one with God? That subjugation of the will must begin here. Through what processes it may pass as we "soar through worlds unknown" we

mistranslate ἐάν *when*. "*If* He shall appear" is, however, without much doubt the true rendering. It gives a much better sense, whether we regard the context or the theology of the passage. For in ch. ii. 28 we have the same words, referring unquestionably to Christ. This gives a strong reason for supposing they must have the same reference here. And the appearing of Christ—His *Parousia*, is according to all Christian teaching the moment when our perfection will be accomplished. See 1 Cor. i. 7, xv. 23; 2 Cor. iv. 14; 1 Thess. iii. 14, v. 23; 2 Thess. ii. 8; Tit. ii. 13, 14; Jude 24. The explanation of ἐὰν φανερωθῇ has been given under ch. ii. 28. There seems in it some under-current of conviction that the final manifestation of Christ might occur at any time. "If He should be manifested *at any moment*" seems the idea present to the mind of the Apostle. He is certain to come. But if He were to come, we know that we should be made—and remain (ἐσόμεθα)—like Him. Or it may be (see below) that ἐὰν φανερωθῇ is the explanation of οἴδαμεν.—we shall be like him. It has been asked whether αὐτῷ here refers to God or Christ. We may reply, as elsewhere, to God through, or rather *in* Christ. The next question that is asked is, Do we become like God *in order* to see Him, or *because* we see Him? We unhesitatingly decide in favour of the latter. It is from looking unto Jesus that we are able to approach Him, by gazing on His perfections that we insensibly reflect them. This is indicated by Ps. xvii.

---

cannot tell. Suffice it to remember that it is a work, and one of gradual advance to perfection—so gradual, that we must at present be quite unable to conceive what it will be when it is complete. "It is not yet manifested what we shall be."

II. YET WE KNOW IT MUST ISSUE IN LIKENESS TO HIM. The process, crucifixion of self, the end, likeness to the Crucified. And if

15, which, literally translated is, "In righteousness (*i.e.* by a holy life in accordance with the Divine teaching—the true way of gazing on God) I shall gaze on Thy presence: I shall be satisfied by waking in Thy likeness." And the thought is worked out more fully in the magnificent passage in 2 Cor. iii. 18, where the believer is represented as at once gazing on and reflecting the Image of Christ, and being transformed by the Divine Spirit from one stage of glory to another, until the perfection of Him on Whom He gazes is mirrored back to Him. The same idea is presented to us in Rom. viii. 29, where we are bidden to be "conformed (συμμόρφους—of the same form with) the Image of the Son of God." See also Rom. xii. 2; Phil. iii. 10. In John xvii. 24, the idea comes before us in another light. The disciples are one day to be with Christ, that they may behold His glory. The thought is more nearly approached still in ver. 22 of the same chapter, where the glory Christ has is said to have been given to His disciples. The idea of likeness to Christ is also brought before us in other passages, as in Phil. iii. 21; Rom. vi. 5. And the same doctrine is yet more emphatically taught in 1 Cor. xv. 28, where it would seem that each one of us is to be brought into so great likeness to Christ that we shall each be able to see God for ourselves, and not, as at present, through the medium of the Divine Manhood of Christ. ἐσόμεθα, as we have already intimated, means being, not becoming. That is to say, we are now invited to contemplate, not the

---

likeness to the Crucified, then likeness to the Father who sent Him. For the crucifixion is, as it were, the refraction, through an impure medium, of the Love of God. The Crucifixion of Jesus is simply Divine love in contact with an evil world. It is love burning to extinguish pain, eager to take it on itself, to shift it off the shoulders that are staggering under its burden. It is more than sympathy, it is

process, but the result. This explains further why St. John says that we are *now* the τέκνα θεοῦ, and that we are some day to be something more. The words τέκνα θεοῦ denote "a relative and transitory designation" (Haupt), while St. Paul's υἱοὶ θεοῦ denotes a "position of privilege" (Westcott). In this particular phrase it is St. John who is looking at our present position, and in the use of υἱός St. Paul is regarding the ultimate result. But St. John does not stop short at this phrase. He would lead us first to look at "the community of nature with the prospect of development" (Westcott). But he goes on to point out to what the development ultimately leads. From our rudimentary union with Christ here we grow into a final likeness to Him.—**for we shall see him as he is.** This gives the reason for the last statement. And thus we have a statement precisely parallel to 2 Cor. iii. 18, only in language simpler, less figurative and striking. It is the Vision of God in Christ that produces the likeness to God (see above). It is by "looking unto Him" Who is at once "the author and perfecter of our faith" that we finally reach the goal (Heb. xii. 2). Cf. Job xix. 26 (where "from my flesh," the literal rendering, at least as naturally suggests the point of view *from* which a thing is seen as the idea of separation). The idea of "seeing God," is a Hebrew as well as a Gentile idea. See Gen. xxxii. 30; Numb. xiv. 14; Job xlii. 5; Ps. xvii. 15; Isa. vi. 5, xxxviii. 11. But the heathen philosophers

---

Sacrifice. It is vehement hatred of sin, because it is unloving. But sin can only be destroyed through love, and love is the sacrifice of self. We can only learn love by contemplating the Sacrifice of Christ. As Moses lifted up the serpent in the wilderness and they who looked towards it were made whole, so must our eyes be fixed on the great Exemplar of perfect love. And thus it comes to pass that when God

considered the vision of God to be an intellectual, while the Hebrew Psalmists and prophets regarded it as a spiritual process. Our Lord shows us that it involves moral considerations, when He says (Matt. v. 8) that the pure in heart shall see God. And that this idea was present to St. John's mind when he wrote these words is clear from ver. 3. This, therefore, is the point at which the Apostle is aiming, the progressive purification and co-ordinate sanctification of the Christian by virtue of His participation in Christ's nature. This is clear from ver. 3 and what follows, especially ver. 5. And from what goes before also. There must be a separation between us and the world. The world must not know us, any more than it knew Him. A relation has begun to exist in us which must lead to consequences we are at present unable to imagine. But we know that if God *be* manifested it can only be to those who are like Him, because we shall see Him in His actual Divine Nature. But before we can do this, we must ourselves have in us the power to see that Divine Nature. That is, we must have been purified from all which renders it impossible for us to discern it. Dean Alford thinks that even in the glorified body this will be impossible. "Beyond the keenest search of the created eye there will be glory and perfection baffling it and dazzling it." But the teaching of 1 Cor. xv. 27, 28, seems to imply the contrary. Perhaps, however, both views are right. Intellectually, it may be we shall never be able to comprehend

---

is manifested, we shall be like Him. For it is only to those who are like Him in mind and will that He can be manifested. No others could see Him, though He were before their eyes. It is only those who have attained to likeness to—union with—Him, who can "see Him as He is."

God, even though we have eternity in which to accomplish the task. Spiritually and morally, however, we may be said to "see God as He is" when no alienation of the will prevents us from uniting ourselves to Him, when no taint of self prevents us from being one with Eternal Love.

XV.

PURITY BY ABIDING IN CHRIST.

Ch. iii. 3.—We will, before proceeding, recall the thread of the argument. The second part of the Epistle, beginning at ch. ii. ver. 28, is intended to enforce the truth that he who abides in God must do righteousness. The Apostle has begun by urging his disciples to abide in God, that they may not be ashamed at His appearing. He bids them next (ver. 29) recognise the two facts, that God is righteous, and that every one who acts righteously must have received the initial impulse from God. He next (iii. 1) breaks out into an apostrophe on the love which has granted this new and higher life, and remarks on the opposition which it creates between the believer and the world that knows not God. This higher life (ver. 2) is ours at present, but only in its rudimentary stages. We do not know to what heights of blessedness it will lead us, but we know this much, at least, that it involves likeness to

---

HOMILETICS.

Ch. iii. 3.—I. *The Christian's hope.*
1. HOPE ONE GREAT FEATURE OF THE CHRISTIAN LIFE. St. Paul (in 1 Cor. xiii.) lays down three great principles of Christian life, Faith, Hope, and Charity, or rather Love. Faith is the source of all Christian life, Hope the animating principle, Love the practical result. That hope *is* a leading feature of the Christian religion need hardly be

God, a likeness which proceeds from the perfect vision of His glory. And the hope which this belief implants in us leads us to seek this likeness now (ver. 3). To refuse (ver. 4) to do this is to reject God. Sin is nothing else but the rejection of God, the more so as His Son (ver. 5) came solely in order to take it away. He took it away (*a*) by conquering it, and (*b*) by granting (ver. 6) to those who by faith abide in Him a share in His victory over it. Those who have not yet obtained this victory cannot as yet be truly said to know or see Him. Next (ver. 7) comes a passage intended to drive home the lesson of the preceding. He only who lives righteously has fellowship with Christ. He who indulges himself in sin belongs to God's enemy.

VER. 3.—**And every man that hath this hope in him.** The hope is of course the hope of "seeing God as He is." "The Apostle's aim in inserting here the reference to the future consummation in the other world becomes obvious in the third verse. His eschatology is altogether practical. To this estate of glory we attain only through intermediate stages; it is not reached through any act of Divine despotic power, but a way is definitely marked out. If the goal is likeness to Christ, it is of the utmost importance to have that goal always and steadily and practically in view" (Haupt). It is worth noticing that for "*in* Him" (*i.e.* in God, not in ourselves) we ought to have "upon Him" ("set on Him," Revised Version). All

---

demonstrated. It is constantly appealed to by the writers of the Old and New Testaments. It may suffice to cite such passages as Psalm xxxix. 7; Jer. xvii. 7 in the one, and Rom. viii. 24, xv. 4, 13; Eph. iv. 4; 1 Thess. v. 8; Tit. ii. 13; 1 Pet. i. 3 in the other. But this rootprinciple of Christianity has been deliberately challenged of late. We are told that this hope of eternal life to which Christianity appeals is a selfish principle. A well-known writer of fiction (George Eliot) has lately, in a volume of Essays, given vivid expression to this belief. It

the old English versions countenance the ambiguity here. Here, however, it specially refers to the hope of seeing God hereafter. Whether we regard "Him" as referring to the Father or the Son will depend upon the view we take of the reference in the preceding verses. It is difficult to decide, but there seems no sufficient reason for refusing to carry back the sense to ver. 1, where the Father is expressly mentioned. It is true that the interpretation we shall give of the latter part of this verse tends the opposite way. But all depends upon whether ἐκεῖνος can be taken in opposition to αὐτός, or whether they must refer to the same person. See this discussed below.—**purifieth himself.** Here the old versions give various renderings, testifying to the want of clearness of perception of the precise meaning of Scripture words. Thus, Wiclif has "makith him silf holi;" Tyndale "pourgeth him silfe;" the Rhemish "sanctifieth himself." Our Version is the first to hit on the right word: "purifieth himself." The word is used in the LXX. of ceremonial purification. So also in the New Testament, as John xi. 55; Acts xxi. 24, 26, xxiv. 18. But, strictly speaking, it means the absence of moral taint. The use in the LXX. is somewhat alien from the original meaning, which means freedom from anything that defiles. ἁγνός is that which is pure in itself, καθαρός, rather that which is made so. καθαρίζειν, strictly speaking, would be used of the *process* of purification, ἁγνίζειν of the *state* of purity,

---

is a nobler motive, she says, to refrain from injuring another because you feel a repugnance to harm a fellow-creature, than because you seek for a reward, or fear of punishment in another world. Abstractly it may be so. The point is not worth arguing. The English are a practical people, and have no taste for abstract disquisition. The practical fact remains, notwithstanding, that hope has been the spring of all the noblest deeds which have benefited humanity. The hope of glory, of fame, of respect, of happiness—what would even this life

inherent or produced. This is quite in keeping with this particular passage, where the result, not the process of purification, is clearly meant. And so also the word ἁγνός does not refer to the process of purification, but indicates one in whom the condition—spotlessness, stainlessness—is to be found. It is unfortunate that in English we have but one word to express the two ideas (the A. V. has "clean" sometimes for καθαρός). But ἁγνός and its derivatives will be found in such passages as 2 Cor. vii. 11, xi. 2; Phil. i. 16, iv. 8; 1 Tim. iv. 12, v. 22; James iii. 17; 1 Peter iii. 2. In all these cases it conveys the idea of "irreproachable." ἁγνός is connected with ἅγιος, with the same idea of separation, but without the idea of special consecration, special setting apart from all profane and common things, that is involved in the latter word. We next ask what the Apostle means by the expression "purifieth *himself.*" No man can purify himself. "Apart from Me," says our Lord (John xv. 5), "ye can do nothing." "The blood of Jesus" (ch. i. 7) and it alone "cleanseth us from all sin." Yet there is no contradiction. We must "work out our own salvation," because it is "God that worketh in us." The words refer to the conscious effort which the believer is ever making to bring himself into conformity with those holy influences which are ever at work in his soul. We may look in vain for many direct assertions of the truth that effort is necessary in the

---

be without them? Would that eminent author tell us, were she still among us, that no hope of success or fame animated her when she sat down to write her famous works? Would she—would any one—write unless there were hope that some one would read, admire, it may be, profit? Strike out the hope from a child's life, a young man's or young woman's, and what is there but a stifling, oppressive sense of despair? Would any one be so cruel as to wish to rob the young of that abounding hope of love, of happiness, perhaps of usefulness, which

Christian course. But to those who penetrate beneath the surface of Scripture such a truth is seen to underlie many passages, where it eludes the superficial observer. The believer must set himself to use the helps tendered to him. As Ebrard says, he must "set all his powers towards the attainment of this object (sinlessness); his constant position must be that of one who is in the act of repelling and putting away his sin." In fine, man has his part to do in the work of salvation as well as God. God's part is to provide all the means whereby man's salvation can be effected; man's part is to dispose himself to receive them. In this sense only, in the sense of displaying willingness to receive and to use the blessed gift of salvation through Christ, can man be said to "purify himself." Cf. Phil. ii. 12; 1 Tim. vi. 12; and such passages as 2 Cor. xiii. 11 (in the Revised Version); Gal. vi. 8, 9; Eph. iv. 3, vi. 12, 13, &c.; in which the work of salvation is regarded as man's. See also ch. v. 21.—**even as he is pure.** "ἐκεῖνος is Christ, according to the constant use of that word in juxtaposition with αὐτός in the writings of St. John; cf. ch. ii. 16. While the context required us to apply αὐτός to God, ἐκεῖνος may and must be applied to Christ, as the more remote subject" (Braune). Alford thinks that ἐκεῖνος here applies to the Father, "in whom essentially abides this perfection of purity." But, as Haupt reminds us, ἁγνός is never used of God, though ἅγιος is. ἁγνός is only

---

spreads out so smiling a landscape before them? And if hope be the animating principle of action in this life, why should it not be so when it is over? Go to the dying man or woman, and say, "My friend, you have had your day, soon you will die, and cease to be;" and see what a blank of hopelessness falls on the victim of so dreary a creed. But tell them that God is good, that life is eternal, that hope is deathless, and see how the eyes will brighten, the depressed energies rally.

used of that which can be conceived of as possibly impure, and it therefore may be used of the manhood of Christ, which in itself was after "the likeness of sinful flesh," and capable of temptation. Christ could not sin, but His manhood, conceived of apart from Himself, was liable to sin. And hence the term ἁγνός, used of one who has preserved Himself free from stain in a world of temptation, can be used of Him as man, though it would be inapplicable to Him as God. "For His present glory He reached, according to Scripture, only through His absolute obedience, in virtue of His overcoming all temptations, and most entirely submitting Himself to the obedience of the Father's will" (Haupt). Two further points may be noticed: (1) that Christ is said to be pure, not to have purified Himself (Plummer), because we have to "cleanse ourselves from all filthiness of the flesh and spirit," the very shadow of which filthiness never rested on Him; (2) that the words "even as He is pure" involve not comparison, but relation. Our purity is not merely *like* Christ's, it is *derived* from Christ's, because the renewed life of the Gospel is (ch. ii. 29) the being begotten of God.

VER. 4.—**Whosoever committeth sin transgresseth also the law.** Here again the desire of our translators to produce an elegant translation has somewhat obscured the peculiarities of St. John's style. In ver. 3 we have πᾶς ὁ, translated "every man that." Here it is trans-

---

No creed can permanently influence the human mind, that does not rest on the hope of immortality.

2. THAT HOPE IS THE HOPE OF THE LORD'S APPEARING. Rewards and punishments are the rule of God's dealings with us in this life. They are, therefore, not unlikely to be the rule of His dealings with us in another. Here, again, we have fact against speculation. What God does now, He is likely to do hereafter. When He comes He will

lated "whosoever." In ver. 6 again, we have "whosoever," and also in ver. 9. Thus the antithesis between ver. 3 and ver. 4 is obscured. Then again, while in ch. ii. 29 we have "*doeth* righteousness," we have here "*committeth* sin." And lastly, τὴν ἀνομίαν ποιεῖ is translated *transgresseth also the law*, after the Geneva Version, instead of *doeth lawlessness*, the literal translation. We should translate, therefore, *Every man that doeth sin, doeth lawlessness*, if we want to preserve the antithesis complete. The question next arises, What is St. John's meaning here? At first sight the passage in English appears a mere truism. And as such the superficial reader at once sets it down. But in fact it puts before us a most essential truth. ἁμαρτία is literally a *missing of the mark*, and might suggest therefore the idea rather of infirmity than guilt. St. John points out that this excuse, if caught at, cannot be admitted. Just as the sin offering for ignorance was regarded as involving guilt (Lev. v. 17–19), so he who does sin does *unlaw*. That is to say, he more or less deliberately and consciously violates the decree of God. We must continue to bear in mind St. John's purpose, to show the "exceeding sinfulness of sin," its incompatibility with the Christian's calling, and the need, therefore, of the utmost resolution and watchfulness on his part to root it out. Sin will condemn us at Christ's coming. That coming is of One clothed with all purity, Whom we must be like, if we

---

reward those who have diligently served Him. See Matt. xx. 1-16; xxiv., &c. And thus it is that we look for His appearing, who shall reward us according to our works, Tit. ii. 13; Rom. ii. 6; Rev. xxii. 12, &c. "Christ in us" is described by St. Paul as the "hope of glory" (Col. i. 27), because He will share with us (John xvii. 22) the glory which the Father hath given to His Son (ver. 24).

II. *The Christian's hope an incentive to purity.*

The hope of glory of which the Scriptures speak, is not only a hope

are to reign with Him in glory. Such a hope inspires every one who possesses it to strive after that likeness. He who does not so strive, is not merely missing something which he might have attained, he is deliberately setting himself in opposition to the Coming One, and rendering himself unfit, not only to reign with Him, but even to behold Him.—**for sin is the transgression of the law.** Better, *and sin is lawlessness.* There is no "for." The "and" simply carries on the thought. "Lawlessness" is the only single word which will translate ἀνομία. It is, perhaps, somewhat too strong. ἀνομία is that condition of mind which sets itself in opposition to law. And what we are told here is that all sin amounts to a deliberate setting our wills against God's. ἀνομία is not merely a being without law; it is a setting ourselves against law. But this setting oneself against law is, of course, confined to the single act of sin. It does not apply to the whole condition of the man. It does not represent him as in a state of entire rebellion against God. But so far as the one act of sin is concerned, it is an act of lawlessness. But St. John evidently contemplates sinfulness as a possible, and even a certain characteristic of those who had given themselves to Christ (ch. i. 8).

This passage has caused great perplexity to Roman Catholic commentators (Estius, for instance), who have regarded it as referring in the main to mortal sin, though

---

of pardon, based upon a belief in Christ's Sacrifice on the Cross—it is a hope based upon our identity of purpose with that Sacrifice, inwrought in us by a living Lord who dwells in us. Therefore we strive to cultivate the mind of Jesus regarding sin, evidenced by His Death on the cross. That is, we strive to hate it, to root it out, to separate ourselves in every way from it. By His Spirit that dwells in us, we "purify ourselves," until we reach that purity which He has rendered possible for man. Every lust, every evil appetite, everything

venial sin is no doubt in the same category until it is repented of. The true view is no doubt that of Haupt, who gives a very admirable exposition of this passage. "It is only too common to establish distinctions and gradations among individual sins. As to the countless little failures and defects in common life, no man indeed who is filled with the spirit of Christ will justify these, or even hold them as indifferent; but have we, in relation to them, a pressing consciousness of the actual transgression of law? Do we look at the manifold discords of our life, and its deviations from the line of the Christian ideal, as positive sins, every one of which immediately and certainly separates us from God, and can be expiated or abolished only by deep repentance, and a distinct act of forgiveness. Most assuredly in multitudes of cases it is not so; such things are thought of as imperfections, but do not press on the consciousness as ἀνομία. Now St. John declares here that this current view of the matter as entertained by us is *not the truth*." This exposition may seem to be contrary to ch. v. 17. But it is only so in appearance. The idea there is that there are sins, which, whatever their actual guilt, do not so entirely separate him who commits them from God, that prayer for him who commits them must necessarily fail to come within the terms of the advice given in ch. v. 16. See note there. The fact is that every sin has a direct tendency to separate him who commits it from

---

that opposes itself to the laws and commandments of God, must be steadily resisted, until Christ be fully formed in us, and we cease to have even the desire to transgress the Divine will.

Ver. 4.—*What is sin?*

I. Sin is a missing the mark. It is a failing to arrive at that high purpose which God has prepared for us. It is a falling short of the true glory and dignity of humanity. It is a wandering from the orbit in which we were formed to revolve. And as in the natural

God. But when he who commits it is in that spiritual condition that he is inclined to repent and seek forgiveness, he is one for whom prayer may be offered with a full security that it will be answered, since he has not resolved to resist the will of God.

Our last question here will be, Against what law does the sinner offend? "Not the law of Moses, because St. John furnishes no instance of the word νομός, standing absolutely, being applied to the Mosaic law. It is true that in two passages (John vii. 49, xii. 34) it stands absolutely and as the definition of the Old Testament Canon; but it must be observed that this is put into the mouth of the Pharisees only; and elsewhere there is the invariable addition ὁ νόμος ὑμῶν, ὁ νόμος Μωϋσέως, and the like" (Haupt). What is meant is clearly the Divine Moral Law, laid down from the beginning for man's guidance, discernible by conscience (see Rom. i. 19, 20), the law by the transgression of which man fell, and involved his descendants in his ruin.

VER. 5.—**And ye know that he was manifested to take away our sins.** We now take another step in the comprehension of the irreconcilable opposition between sin and God. We have seen that to commit the slightest sin, of any kind, is to involve ourselves in a direct breach of God's law. We now go further; we find it in open opposition to the purpose for which Jesus Christ came into the world. ἐκεῖνος here again refers to Jesus Christ,

---

world the failure to fulfil the law imposed upon us would lead to the most fearful results (see an eloquent passage in Hooker's first book) so the terrible results of our aberration are visible in the sorrows and sufferings of our kind.

II. SIN IS A DELIBERATE SETTING OURSELVES AGAINST GOD. This is clear if we ask *what* mark it is we miss. The νόμος—the law imposed upon us by God. Now *every* sin, of whatever kind, partakes of this character. The smallest deviation from the track may in the end

"God manifest in the flesh." But what is the meaning of ἄρῃ? We naturally are referred to the remarkable declaration of the Baptist in John i. 29,—a declaration which seems to have made an ineffaceable impression upon his disciple; so much so that it has been conjectured that one of those who heard it was St. John himself. He is, moreover, supposed to have been the disciple to whom, with St. Andrew, that declaration was repeated the next day. From that day forth this announcement became the centre and core of his religious consciousness. Jesus Christ came to take away sin. Not merely to bear sin; still less to do no more than bear sin's punishment, but to remove it utterly and altogether from the world. So says St. Matthew i. 21, "He shall save His people from their sins." So he repeats, when (viii. 17) he applies the prophecy "He took our infirmities and bare our sicknesses" to the *removal* of them. αἴρω no doubt means to *bear* or *lift up*. But it means to bear or lift up in order to remove. It is a question whether we should read τὰς ἁμαρτίας ἡμῶν here, with the Rec. Text. It is supported by the Codex Sinaiticus, but rejected by the Vatican and Alexandrian MSS. If we omit it, we must read "to take away sins," *i.e.*, *all* sins, of every kind. It must be confessed that this gives a far better sense. St. John is enlarging upon the incompatibility of sin with the Christian character. "Sin is defiance of God's commands," he says, and more than

---

produce the most serious results. Thus, in Gen. iii., man's first transgression is most agreeably to the facts of human life represented as a slight one, (not, however, the eating of an *apple*, as has been so strangely supposed). It could not have been otherwise. But once committed, it *must* lead mankind farther and farther from God, and could only be repaired by supernatural means.

III. THEREFORE THE LEAST SIN IS MORTAL IN ITS TENDENCY. We may not, with mediæval and Roman divines, make any distinction

that, it is just the very thing Jesus Christ came to remove. He (ἐκεῖνος) was manifested to take away sins. The Revisers omit *our*, and so does Professor Westcott. This was the object of His coming. How, then, can we imagine it possible to be a genuine disciple of His, and rest contented in a state of rebellion against Him? And we may observe the word "manifested." Professor Westcott has pointed out that Christ's Incarnation is described in four different ways in Scripture. In regard to the Father, it is a Mission. In regard to the Son Himself, it is a Coming. In regard to form it is in "Flesh" (or might we not say it is assuming flesh?). In regard to man, it is a Manifestation. So St. John says in ch. i. 2, and he uses precisely the same phrase in this chapter (ver. 2) in regard (though it *may* refer to Christ) to the future of our own being. See also vers. 5, 8. Nor is the expression confined to St. John. St. Paul uses it in 1 Tim. iii. 16. And it is the object of the whole prologue of St. John's Gospel to inculcate this truth. The effect of the coming of Jesus was the making clear and evident, to those who chose to see it, the whole character and purpose of God in relation to man. In a human form, and therefore in a manner intelligible to human capacities, the life and death of Jesus made it plain what was the will of God concerning us. That will is explained in a few words, that sin should be taken away.—**And in him is no sin.** The

---

between venial and mortal sin. *All* sin is venial if repented. *All* sin is mortal if unrepented. And this because all sin is an evident, and since Christ came, preventible departure from the course marked out by God for us to walk in. Thus, then, the proper attitude of the Christian is irreconcilable hatred to all sin, and to attain this condition should be his one object and aim. This will be more clearly seen by the considerations which follow.

VERS. 5, 6.—*Christ's object is to destroy sin.*

inner connection of thought here will elude no one who has reflected on the doctrine of salvation through Christ. He came to take away sin by uniting us in heart and spirit with Himself. In Him was no shadow of sin. The result of the union with Him, which is accomplished by faith, is the driving out, expelling, annihilation of every sinful desire and thought. St. John's language is very emphatic. "Sin in Him *has no existence;*" (οὐκ ἔστι) there is no such thing, it cannot be conceived of in connection with Him. And only such a sinless nature could impart holiness to us. Only a power utterly antagonistic to the poison which is destroying us can drive that poison out. As St. Augustine well says, "Si esset in illi peccatum, auferendum est illi, non ipse auferret." But since there is no sin in Him, and since He imparts Himself to every believing soul, He is capable of taking away the sin of the world.

VER. 6.—**Whosoever abideth in him, sinneth not.** Here, again, the literal translation is "every one who," as in verses 3 and 4, and the passage is an instance of that cumulative repetition so characteristic of St. John. The connection of this verse with that which precedes is sufficiently obvious, if the drift of the whole passage be borne in mind. St. John's object is one with that of his Master. He desires that sin should be taken away. He sees it to be a terrible fact, not only in the world in general, but "even among them that are regenerate."

I. CHRIST CAME TO TAKE AWAY SIN. See Isa. liii. 5, 6, 11 (where the word translated *bear*, may also mean *take away*); Matt. i. 21; Heb. i. 3, ix. 26; Rev. i. 5. And the words "crucified with Christ" imply the death of sin. See also Rom. vi. 2, 4, 11, &c. Christ's object was not merely to enable the Father to pardon sin, but to destroy it. Not merely its "guilt and power," but it. Sin was the means of all this disorder in God's fair world. That disorder can never cease till sin and sinful appetite for ever cease to be.

His object is to teach the Christian that he must not rest content with this state of things. He must neither "continue in sin that grace may abound," nor sit down in an attitude of comfortable apathy, declaring that man is compassed with infirmity and that "what cannot be cured must be endured." He desires to stir up the Christians of his day to a holy and perpetual warfare against sin. The defiled and sin-stained cannot endure His presence. All who have hope to behold that Presence betake themselves at once, with their Redeemer's unfailing aid, to the task of continual and earnest self-purification. With His aid, because He came to take away sin. Sinless Himself, He expels (this sense—see note on ch. i. 9—is surely contained in the word ἀφίημι, generally translated *remit* or *forgive*) sin from those in whom He dwells. This sentence has been toned down by various interpreters. It means to "persist in sin" (Luther); "to allow sin to reign in him" (Hunnius); "to be wicked" (Capellus); and by Roman Catholic interpreters generally, "does not commit mortal sin." Alford very ably and energetically repudiates these explanations. According to him sin and the life of God "are incompatible, and in so far as a man is found in the one, he is thereby separated from the other. . . . If the child of God falls into sin, it is an act against Nature, deadly to life, hardly endured, and bringing bitter repentance. It is as the taking of a poison, which, if it be not corrected by an antidote, will

---

II. How Christ came to destroy sin. We have seen (see notes) that Christ came to destroy sin by giving Himself, in whom is no sin, to us. When we are fully united to Him by faith, sin is destroyed. The object of our probation here is to effect this union, by giving up ourselves to the promptings of His Spirit; by surrendering our wills to His purifying power, until the last traces of sinful appetite are destroyed.

III. Sinlessness the goal of our lives. The believer's desire

sap the very springs of life." Mr. Plummer explains the passage by the internal contradiction of which every one is conscious, and cites Rom. vii. 20, and Gal. ii. 20, as illustrations of it. "If what I would not, that I do; it is no more I that do it, but sin that dwelleth in me;" and "Yet not I, but Christ liveth in me." But St. John's point of view is somewhat different from that of St. Paul. The *fact* of the contradiction is as evident to him as to St. Paul. But here, as in previous passages (*e.g.*, ch. ii. 4), he fixes his gaze beyond it. In the passages just cited St. Paul's practical mind is occupied with the struggle. The more meditative St. John passes on to the *issue of the struggle*. It is to the tendencies at work that he invites our attention. The result of the knowledge of Christ is the destruction of sin. To *abide* in Christ, that is, not merely to be united to Him for the moment, but to remain in that union to the end, must infallibly issue in the overthrow of every sinful appetite. The question, then, for each Christian is, To what goal is your life leading you? Is sin being combated and rooted out? Is your mind growing into union with Him who knew no sin, and was manifested to the world that we might cease to know it? Is the work of sanctification going on in your heart? Because, if it is, the tendency must be manifest. The whole bent of your life must be towards holiness. If you are to *abide* in Him; if you are not to be "cast forth as a branch and be burned" (John xv. 6),

---

is to "win Christ and be found in Him," possessing a righteousness due to no virtue indwelling in ourselves, no effort of our own, but simply to that union with Christ which faith achieves, producing a righteousness which is not our own, but Christ's (Phil. iii. 8, 9); which is derived from that one perfect life which is the only possible source of all human perfection. "In Him," and in Him alone, "is no sin." In sinlessness alone can happiness be found. But sinlessness is out of man's power, save it proceed from our inward and vital union with

you must be approaching daily nearer that state which he proceeds to describe.—**whosoever sinneth hath not seen him, neither known him.** Our chief discussion here is the force of the perfect tense in the verbs "seen" and "known." It is not disputed that in classical Greek the perfect ἔγνωκα may have a present signification. But what is frequently forgotten is that the author of this Epistle is a Jew of Palestine; that his tenses are to be interpreted by the genius of the Hebrew, not of the Greek language; that the Hebrew perfect has far more decidedly the sense of completed action than the Greek; and that thus the meaning of St. John is, that in the man who is still committing sin (ἁμαρτάνων) the perfect vision and knowledge of God is as yet unattained. On the difference between *seeing* and *knowing* it may suffice to observe that the first is objective, the second subjective, and that in the spiritual life the former must always precede the latter. We "know God, or rather are known by God" says St. Paul (Gal. iv. 9). "Then shall I know, even as also I am known" (1 Cor. xiii. 12). We see the truth of God as revealed by Him to us in the Person and Work of Jesus Christ; and then we proceed to realise it in our own consciousness, and display it in our actions. In every case it is the revelation of God to the heart which produces such experimental proof as we call knowledge. The vision of God first to the soul; then the perception of that vision, and its translation into that consciousness of fact which is the basis of all life

---

Christ. Hence toward that union should all our thoughts be directed. That it may be more complete every day, should be our one effort and prayer. Perfect peace can never be ours till it be effected. Not till we are wholly united to Him—till we actually *abide* in Him—can sin cease to be.

IV. OUR PRESENT SINS AN INCENTIVE TO SPIRITUAL PROGRESS. They are a proof that the condition of abiding in Christ is not yet reached. Our daily falls are a proof, not that we know nothing of

and action. When this vision of God is perfectly comprehended, and perfectly inwrought into the texture of our being, then sin is at an end. God has at length appeared to us, and we have "seen Him as He is." As long as sin remains in us, it is a proof that in us this perfect apprehension of Him does not yet exist. And it never will exist for us unless we lead a life of conscious effort, of earnest co-operation with the Spirit of God, directed to the extirpation of everything which tends to hinder its arrival.

Christ, that not even the most distant vision of His glory has ever dawned upon us, that we are still in that "outer darkness where is wailing and gnashing of teeth;" but that we are still very far from that *completeness* of union with Him which should be our hope and aim. They are to be warnings to us; sources of dissatisfaction and uneasiness, prompting us to more vigorous effort toward the way of holiness; admonitions to seek an increase of faith, to press on to a more vital union with the Saviour. It is clear that so long as we sin we have not fully "seen Christ," nor "known Him." Let us "press toward the mark for the prize of the high calling of God in Christ Jesus." Let us strive in everything for the exchange of the state in which we "know in part," for that in which we "know even as we are known" (1 Cor. xiii. 12).

XVI.

TRUE HOLINESS.

CH. iii. 7.—**Little children, let no man deceive you.** The Apostle goes on to emphasise his exhortation to live righteously by a warning against those who would teach men to do otherwise. The words are always applicable. There is always a tendency to rest upon some sort of *opus operatum*, either "*of* man" or "*on* man," as Haupt most strikingly remarks, and so to escape the necessity of believing in that continued conscious co-operation of the human will with the Holy Spirit, that continued struggle after the settled habit of self-mastery, in which, if we are to believe Bishop Butler, the perfection of man will in all probability be found to consist. And so, on the one hand, comes the error of those who would teach man that he can of himself come up to the standard of

---

HOMILETICS.

CH. iii. 7, 8.—*The necessity of holiness.*

I. THE GREAT MISTAKE. "Little children, let no man deceive you." The fundamental error into which men have fallen from the first, and still fall, is the divorce of religion (so called) from holiness. In early days men first believed the body beyond redemption, and so they held that sensual sin could not defile it any further than it was already defiled, and was powerless to touch the spirit. Then came the period, a long one, when a "right faith," as it was called, though

God's law, and who invariably end by bringing the law down to the level of man's capacities, instead of educating man to the level of the law's requirements; and, on the other, the error of those who would lead men to depend upon some past fact in their spiritual history, and so to escape the continued effort necessary to bring the gift of God implanted in them to perfection; or, as Haupt admirably puts it, are so " content with the consciousness that they stand in some special relation to the Lord," that they " come to regard sin as an unavoidable evil which is not so very hurtful as might be thought." It would, therefore, be a mistake to confine the scope of the Apostle's words, as some commentators do, to the heretics of his own day, rather than to apply them to tendencies inherent in the heart of man. Nevertheless, there is, no doubt, an immediate reference in his words. The earliest of the Gnostic heresies, the Syrian, were Antinomian in their tendency (see above, p. 137). They aimed at the *separation* of flesh and spirit, not at the purification of the former through the latter. And so they taught that if only the soul were exercised in philosophical contemplation, it mattered little what deeds were done in the body. Against so monstrous and polluting an error St. John might well raise an earnest voice. "Little children, let no man deceive you " (or

---

what was meant was correct speculative theories, took the place of conformity to the spirit of Jesus Christ. Is the danger past now? Is there no fear that men in these days will substitute something else for the need of entire sanctification of man's whole nature? By no means. Men still substitute some notion of their own for the "truth as it is in Jesus." They suppose still, sometimes, that (*a*) an orthodox faith is the be all and end all of religion. They may differ among themselves as to what constitutes this orthodox faith. With some it is what are called "clear views of the Atonement." With others it is concerned with correct conceptions of the Trinity, the Catholic Church,

" lead you astray" as the Revised Version translates). "He, and only he, who doeth righteousness maintains his connection with God. Every one who doeth otherwise is God's enemy."—**he that doeth righteousness is righteous, even as he is righteous.** We have already remarked (on ver. 6) that while St. Paul has in his eye the struggle of mankind with sin, St. John keeps before him the issue of the struggle. Not that he ignores the absolute necessity of a struggle. This is involved in the words "purifieth himself" (so Ebrard, very acutely) in ver. 4. The process of self-purification cannot be effected without a struggle. The present tense here, though of course it is possible to treat tenses in *too* technical and pedantic a way, may not unnaturally be interpreted of continued, habitual action. "He who is in the habit of acting righteously," and no one else, can be described as "righteous." This passage, like many others, has been the fierce battle-ground of contending schools in reference to the question of justification. It would seem necessary, before attempting to understand it, to sweep away all the technicalities of the schoolmen about grace *de congruo* and *de condigno*, about *fides inchoata* and *fides formata*, about righteousness imputed and righteousness infused, and recur to the simple language of Scripture, which speaks of faith as bringing us into union with the

---

and the doctrine of the Sacraments. With others, again, it consists in accepting without question the dogmas of the Church of Rome. A man who adopts what by each of those parties is regarded as sound orthodox opinions, may fail egregiously in temper and charity; he may display the greatest unlikeness in his life to the spirit of Christ, nay, he may even set at nought the most ordinary principles of morality (as when, not many years ago, the Pope presented the rose, his token of appreciation of the virtues of the "most Catholic" sovereign, to a woman whose whole life was a scandal to her sex). But he has the root of the matter in him; he may safely (for practi-

perfect humanity of the Son of God, through the operation of the eternal Spirit. This union effects, first, purification, and finally, purity; so that he who has lived in the realisation of it becomes at length righteous, even as He is righteous; in other words, consummates and completes his union with Him Who is the source of all righteousness, and destroys in the end all that tendency to stray from the paths of His commandments with which each man was born into the world. Some discussion has been raised on the point whether "He" here means God or Christ. Perhaps some of those who have discussed this point have forgotten for the moment that Christ is God. The Apostle is contemplating rather the Unity of Essence than the distinction of Person; Christ is spoken of as δίκαιος in ch. ii. 2. But He is this because He is the Word of the Eternal Father, partaking in every respect of the life which flows from Him.

VER. 8.—**He that committeth sin is of the devil**, or rather, with the Revised Version, *doeth* sin, just as we have "doeth righteousness" in ver. 6. The Authorised Version obscures the antithesis between "doing righteousness" and "doing sin." The first thing to be noted here is the assertion of *the personal existence of the devil*. We may compare it with the words of our Lord Himself in St. John viii. 44, on which words, no doubt, the

---

cally it comes to this, however much it may be theoretically asserted to be otherwise) neglect that holiness "without which no man can see the Lord." Or (*b*) the conception of salvation, not as a work in man, but as what Haupt has called "an *opus operatum* ON man," may be held to relieve a man from the necessity of that effort, that watchfulness at every moment, which is necessary to all who would realise the life of Christ in their own. He has been "converted," he has been "saved," and so *of course* his life, whatever it is, must be a holy one. If the evidence of facts seems to imply that he is as yet very far from having attained full fellowship with Christ, "so much the worse for

present passage is founded. The words ἐκ τοῦ διαβόλου and ὁ διάβολος ἁμαρτάνει ἀπ' ἀρχῆς, are incompatible with the idea of an impersonal principle. We have then to inquire in what sense the words "is of the devil" (ἐκ denoting the source from which anything proceeds) are used. And here the great divine, Origen, whose comprehensive and far-seeing intellect is now beginning to receive a tardy recognition, comes to our assistance by observing that while he who sins is said to *be* of the devil, he is nowhere said to have been *born* or *begotten* of the devil. Therefore the words apply, not to the origin of the man's *being*, but of his *present condition*. It is, as Bengel says, a "corruptio," not a "generatio," that he owes to the devil. *How* that present condition of man is connected with the devil, is shown in what follows.—**for the devil sinneth from the beginning.** Here our first difficulty is with the words ἀπ' ἀρχῆς. They occur, as we have seen, in ch. i. 1. *There* we referred them to the origin of the Word before all time. If we so interpret them there, why not here also? Because, as Haupt reminds us, we must fix the meaning of the words by the context. See also note on ch. ii. 24. Of course it may be contended that these words assert the eternity of the author of evil—that they fix on St. John the responsibility of asserting the Gnostic

---

the facts." Either these faults of his are *not* sins, *cannot* be sins, since he is saved, redeemed, justified, sanctified once for all by Christ's blood, or if they *are* sins, they do not do him so much harm after all. They are necessary infirmities which will be put off when the mortal flesh is put off. They are not the work of the devil, to be struggled with, wrestled with, mastered by the might of prayer. They do not tend to make him who commits them "of the devil." Once again, "Little children, let no man deceive you. He that doeth sin is of the devil."

II. ONLY HE THAT DOETH RIGHTEOUSNESS IS RIGHTEOUS. This

dualism. The words *may* have that meaning. That they *must* have such a meaning is more than can be proved. They are, in reality, identical with the words in John viii. 44. But then, the devil could hardly be a manslayer before man existed. And, therefore, here we may fairly contend that the interpretation of the language is to be found in the context, and that "the devil sinneth from the beginning" means no more than that the devil is sinning now, and has been sinning ever since he first began to sin (or we may take the words to mean since *man* began to sin). To sin, we must remember, means here to err from the right path, to swerve from the proper law of one's being. And so the whole passage must necessarily refer to a created being, who has rebelled against the law imposed upon him, as all creatures can do who are capable of moral choice. ἁμαρτία cannot be predicated of one who is himself the eternal source of all opposition to what is good. Sin, then, disobedience to the law of God, is the act of a created being who has set himself in opposition to the Will of the Creator. And all sin, we are here told, is the work of that one being. "This is a great mystery," we may say, in the words of St. Paul. Few, indeed, are the glimpses we are permitted to catch of the secrets of the world unseen. But thus much we are told, that all

---

would seem the most obvious truism, but for the tendency to substitute the imputation of righteousness for the sanctification of the man. If there be not visibly in us the work of Jesus Christ, uprooting in us all evil desires, and leading us into all holiness, then, whatever our opinion of ourselves, we are not justified, we are not sanctified. If we are to become righteous, it can only be by the work of the Divine Spirit within, cleansing us from all corruption, and implanting in us the nature of Him Who is righteousness itself.

III. HE THAT DOETH SIN IS OF THE DEVIL. Observe, this is true of *all* sin, of every kind. We cannot explain away God's Word. We

sin took its rise in the act of one mighty being who resisted the Will of God. "He who first falls from God," says Haupt, "places himself, in virtue of this apostasy, over against God." It seems to have been the effect of the first deliberate departure of any of God's creatures from the path assigned to it, that it set the whole universe in disorder. As the slightest aberration, in however slight a degree, of a single star in the firmament from its appointed orbit, would, were it possible, involve in the end the whole universe in the most disastrous consequences, so the departure of one single being from the moral order cannot fail to bring about results utterly incommensurate with the first transgression, considered by itself. Hence the reasonableness of the narrative in Gen. iii. And the physical universe, when interrogated in regard to this fact, bears witness to the truth of revelation. We see signs of disorder, of suffering, long before man began to be. And so science and revelation alike, in reference to the origin of sin, carry us back to a period in an indefinitely distant past, and, what is most material to our present subject, a period long anterior to the creation of man. Science and revelation alike bear witness to the fact that man's sin is due to an influence outside him. They bear their concurrent testimony to the truth, " he that committeth

---

cannot make classes of sins, some of which are, and some of which are not, at variance with the elements of our spiritual life. The "sin unto death" is sin indulged. The "sin not unto death" is sin resisted. But until the very last vestige of evil habit is eradicated from our soul, we are still "of the devil" so far as we continue to commit sin.

VER. 8.—*The existence and personality of the devil.*

I. THE DEVIL IS A CREATURE (see Exposition). Most dangerous is the language of Braune, in a note on this passage, who accepts, without protest, Strauss' monstrous doctrine that the personality of God is

sin is of the devil." Thus, then, in every action of life, every man is subject to evil influences from without. Solicitations to evil proceed from powers of whose existence he cannot but be aware, even though he may be very slightly acquainted with their nature. Influences toward good, on the other hand, are plentifully poured forth from the source of all good, tending to purify his life. If he yield to the one he becomes one who habitually commits sin, and the source of his inspirations is the author of all evil. If he submit himself to the other, he becomes one who is habitually in the practice of righteousness, until at last he reflects the Nature of Him Who is the Author of all good.—**For this purpose the Son of Man was manifested, that he might destroy the works of the devil.** Ebrard refers, for the use of the word λύειν here, to John ii. 19, in the sense of destroy (cf. 2 Peter iii. 10–12); v. 18, vii. 23, x. 35, and Eph. ii. 14. The original idea is that of resolving into its constituent elements, and thus the destruction of an organic whole. But it is applied in various ways in the passages above mentioned, to the body (and this strictly), to the Sabbath, to the Law of Moses, to a wall of partition. It is also applied in Acts xxvii. 41 to the destruction of a ship. It may be unreasonable to attempt to fix the meaning of the word too closely. Yet it may perhaps be that some-

---

inconceivable without the personality of the devil. This, however much it be disavowed, is the old Gnostic dualism revived. Once admit it—once regard the kingdom of evil as a moral necessity, once suppose that the idea of a personal God requires the idea of the personality of an anti-god, and you destroy the whole Christian scheme. For the Christian scheme depends upon the fact that God is stronger than the devil, that good is more powerful than evil, that we have only to surrender ourselves to the influence of the life-giving power, to be cleansed from sin. But if the evil power be the necessary correlative of the good, then the two powers are on an equality, and one is

thing is meant where one word is preferred to another. The idea here seems to be to bring to nought *by loosing the chain of connection*. Satan's energy is divorced from the material on which it was wont to work, namely, the thoughts and purposes of man. And man, freed from this fatal foreign influence, is restored to the natural working of the law of his being imposed by God. This result is achieved, as we have before seen, by the *manifestation* of the Son of God, that is to say, by the making known His character and purpose to man, from whom that character and purpose were previously hidden. The destruction of the works of the devil answers to the "taking away of sins" mentioned in ver. 5; and cannot therefore be understood, as we there said, of mere forgiveness, but must be interpreted of deliverance from a yoke, of freedom to follow the impulses of the spirit of holiness. Dean Alford asks if we are to regard sin and sorrow and death as the works of the devil, and rightly replies that though in a way they may be regarded as his work, they are not the sort of works which are here contemplated, but rather the Apostle would have us understand acts of deliberate rebellion against God. The truth is that suffering and death are, strictly speaking, not the works of the devil at all, but only the *results* of his work. They are God's witness against the transgression of His Law,

---

no stronger than the other. Then sin becomes not a fault, but a misfortune, and man can plead the over-mastering power of temptation as an excuse. Nay, if evil be a necessary complement of good, then evil men are necessary as a foil to good ones, and it may be impossible for a man to "recover himself out of the snare of the devil." Grant the subordination of the devil, and evil has no necessary existence *in itself*. It is but that transgression of the true law of their being which is inseparable, it is true, from the existence of beings who are endowed with the power of choice; but which dis-

just as physical pain is at once a warning against the transgression of natural law, and the punishment for having transgressed it. Before we go on to contemplate the new idea suggested to us in the next verse, it will be well to notice how far the last two verses have advanced the reader beyond the point to which ver. 6 has carried him. St. John's method of advancing step by step, while to the careless reader he seems to be but repeating himself, is a feature of his Epistle too often overlooked. In ver. 6 we are told that he who is in the habitual commission of sin is an utter stranger to God. But this is not all. He is not merely a stranger to God. He is linked by the closest of ties to the author of all evil. Nay, his being, such as it at present is, may be said to be derived from that mysterious personality whose work it is the sole object of the Son of God's appearance here on earth to thwart and bring to nought. Not only, therefore, is the man who sins a stranger to God, but he has placed himself in an attitude of the most uncompromising hostility to Him; he is leagued, body and soul, with the source of all opposition to the Divine Will.

VER. 9.—**Whosoever is born** [or *begotten*, as the Revised Version] **of God doth not commit sin.** Here again the whole difficulty of the passage vanishes if the tense be

---

appears when the soul has formed the habit of invariably choosing the good.

II. SIN EXISTED BEFORE MAN. We have seen (in Exposition, p. 233) that pain, suffering, and death were clearly in existence before man steps on the scene. Resistance to God's law, then, was clearly in existence before man was created. Accordingly, our inspired historian represents to us man from the very moment of his creation, exposed to that malign influence. And the secret history of every heart is sufficient to show that man's corruption is not sufficient to explain all his aberrations from the path of duty. He is exposed to temptations *from without*. The spirit-world—that with which the highest part of

borne in mind. The birth, or begetting, spoken of here, is regarded as a completed process. This life, it is to be remembered, is the whole, or at least an important part, of the process itself. The birth from God which forms so prominent a feature of St. John's teaching, is the result of the abiding in God mentioned in ver. 6. When a man has abode in God, when he has steadily resisted every effort of the antagonistic principle to sever him from the Divine life, such a man may be said to have been born of God. Henceforth, for such a man, sin is an impossibility. He "doth not commit it" or rather *do* it (see above). That is to say (for this is the force of the present here), he is in a condition in which sin is not committed. Nay, further, "he cannot sin," (that is, he can no longer err from the way) "because he *has been* born of God." We are not, with some commentators, to regard this passage as the antithesis to "he that committeth sin is of the devil," because this is itself the antithesis to the "he that doeth righteousness is righteous" of ver. 7. It is rather the summing up of the whole thought, after the law of synthetic parallelism so familiar to students of Hebrew psalmody. The climax of the whole section is reached in the words, "He cannot sin, because he is born of God."—**for his seed remaineth in him.** This, we must

---

his nature has to do, is itself disordered, and solicitations to sin assail him in the spirit as well as in the mind and flesh.

III. THE DEVIL IS A PERSON. So (*a*) Scripture teaches from the beginning to the end. It is needless to multiply texts. Next (*b*) the temptations from without are no workings of an abstract principle. They display the subtlety and energy of a perverted spirit. The attitude that spirit has assumed of opposition to God develops a restless activity in bringing others into that attitude of resistance. And we must remember that while we know much of the world of sense, we know little of the attributes of spirit. The means of communication between spirit and spirit are an enigma to us. All we know is that they are

not fail to observe, is the Apostle's explanation of the statement he had just made. He who has been born of God is not in the habit of committing sin *because* His seed remaineth in him, or rather, with the Revised Version, (which keeps to the same word in rendering μένει) *abideth* in him. *Whose* seed? is the first question. The answer can hardly be doubtful. *God's* seed. God's seed abideth in the man who has thus attained to victory over evil. But what is this seed? It is strange that commentators like Dean Alford should be so under the influence of preconceived notions as not merely to overlook, but deliberately to reject the interpretation which alone falls in with the spirit of the passage. To interpret the passage of the spoken word, as in the well-known parable of the sower, is to evacuate it of all its force. The word σπέρμα must of course be taken in connection with the word γεγεννημένος. It refers to a process of Divine generation, analogous in some way to the processes of generation of all things here below. In this last a spark of Divine life is mysteriously communicated to, and connected with matter, and thus is formed a living, sentient being. We have, as Professor Westcott reminds us, σπέρμα, not τὸ σπέρμα. Our attention is not directed to the particular case, but to the general rule, and perhaps we

---

not limited by the necessities of our corporeal life. We are not without some instances of the fact of spirit communicating with spirit, between persons locally separated by distances which would make all ordinary communications impossible. How then shall we wonder that pure spirits, entirely unconnected with matter, should possess capacities which transcend our utmost powers to conceive?

VER. 9.—*The new birth.*

1. ITS STAGES. (*a*) It has a *beginning.* Whosoever is "born of water and the spirit" has started upon the new life. He possesses now the *power* to resist sin, and "mortify (or *kill*) the deeds of the body." The "water" of purification refers to the radical taint of an

may also be reminded of the *variety* of God's gifts. "All flesh is not the same flesh" (1 Cor. xv. 39). There are many different forms of life. *All* life is the product of the word of God. And of this abundance He gives a special gift to man. From Him a new and higher life-principle is imparted to us, capable of rising to higher things than the natural man, however true it be that he himself derives his being from God, could ever have attained. Latin theology from the beginning has displayed a tendency to interpolate a *tertium quid* between man and God, to interpose something, be it grace, faith, the word spoken in the heart, or anything whatever that man's intellect may have devised, in the place of the actual creation of man anew through the Spirit of the New Man, Jesus Christ our Lord. This tendency has been too strong for most commentators. And so they forbid us to see here the Divine regeneration of the soul, following precisely the law of generation of things here below; the gift of a seed of life, which by its nature attracts to itself all things calculated to nourish and to develop that life, and the resulting advance of the man who possesses such a life to the destined goal, his true perfection. "Whosoever has been born of God commits sin no longer, because a germ of Divine life, God-implanted, abides in him." "It unfolds

---

evil *bent* or direction of the mind. There is something that needs washing away. (*b*) It has a *course*. The life thus given is nourished. There is a power to seize on, and to assimilate the elements necessary to sustain life that subsist around. The "means of grace," the circumstances of our lives, the example and warning we derive from observation of our fellows, all these may be so used as to strengthen our spiritual vitality, to carry on the growth and increase of the power which is given us. (*c*) It has a *completion*. But that completion has never yet been attained within the course of this present life. Sufficient for us while here if we are pressing steadily onward toward the goal. For that goal is nothing short of the standard set up before

a continuous energy" (Haupt). It "has its perfect work."
And it "abides in him." It has not been lost by carelessness or wilful resistance. It has been preserved by
a living faith. And it is no power external to the man.
It works by no "law of commandments contained in
ordinances." It works, not from without, but from within,
producing by its Divine energy that separation from all
error and corruption, that conformity to all that is holy
and God-like, which results in the final triumph over
every evil appetite, in the dedication of the whole man,
body, soul, and spirit, to the service of God.—**and he
cannot sin, because he is born of God.** The doctrine of this
passage is clear. The perfect γέννησις takes place when
the seed of life is fully developed. But there is a period
of preparation, in which the seed is developing. The
perfect birth is only effected when the seed first implanted
abides. *Then* the condition of sin is no longer possible.
This is the climax, as we have said, to which the whole
passage leads up. The next verse points the moral before
introducing a new subject, namely, the fact that the
absence of sin necessarily involves the presence of love,
or, in other words, that " love is the fulfilling of the law."
We are there told that "by their fruits we shall know"
the children of God from the children of the devil; that

---

us in the first discourse that Jesus ever uttered, "Be ye perfect, as your Father in heaven is perfect."

II. ITS METHOD. It consists in the implanting of a Divine seed of life within the soul. This seed is to be brought to maturity by the processes above mentioned. But if they be neglected, the seed will *die*. Only he in whom the seed *abideth* can be said to have been born of God. And no seed can abide unless all evil influences be steadily resisted. While it remains a germ it is capable of being destroyed by such influences. But let it once take vigorous root, and it will by degrees overcome those noxious growths, while as to itself it "increaseth with the increase of God."

there are certain obvious signs by which we may discern God's servants from His enemies. But the point to which the Apostle has been leading us in this section is the final and assured victory which he who is born of God obtains over evil. And he points the moral on the side of resistance to sin rather than on that of the attainment of holiness. And this because they are in a world of evil, because they are encompassed with evil on every side, and because, therefore, it is more practical to set before them the way in which they are to free themselves from that all-pervading power, than to amuse them with dreams of ideal purity and righteousness which, as yet, they are unable to understand.

III. ITS RESULT. Entire freedom from sin. "He cannot sin, because he has been born of God." If we will but undergo the trouble of the process, the end is assured. The process is steady resistance to all that is evil, steady cultivation of every habit and desire that is felt to be good. He who will give himself to this task, trusting to the power of the Spirit within, will find, to his own surprise very often, that temptations once powerful have lost their charm, that evil, once seductive, has ceased to attract; that the life of self-mortification and self-control to which Christ has invited us is ever more and more alluring, until it is seen that the voice is by no means a delusive one that bids us hope for perfect union with God.

XVII.

LOVE THE SIGN OF THE BELIEVER.

CH. iii. 10.—*In this the children of God are manifest and the children of the devil.* The Apostle here, as we have before remarked, takes a new departure, though, as usual, the new thought is intimately connected with the old. As before (chaps. i. 5, ii. 10, 11) he had directed the attention of those whom he addressed to the essential antagonism between light and darkness, so he now points to this antagonism, manifested visibly in the consequent antagonism between the children of the light and the children of the darkness, between the children of God and the children of the devil, as displayed in their conduct (see below).

HOMILETICS.

CH. iii. 10.—*The Church and the world.*

I. RELIGIOUS TENDENCIES CONSIDERED IN THEIR RESULTS. St. John, as we have said before, has the issues of the struggle between light and darkness continually before him, while St. Paul has frequently the struggle itself. Each point of view has its advantages. The latter displays that sympathy with mankind as it is, which is a necessary element in dealing with souls. But the former has this advantage, that it brings out clearly the object at which Christ's Gospel aims. That object is nothing less than the endeavour to disentangle each soul from the tyranny of evil habits, and to translate it

The words "in this" do not simply refer to what goes before, as Braune asserts, nor to what goes after, as Ebrard will have it. They refer both to what precedes and what follows. The children of God and the children of the devil are manifest by their lives. He who hath been born of God doth not commit sin; whereas he who is of the devil is necessarily unrighteous. So Dean Alford interprets, "ἐν τούτῳ at the same time looks backward and forward; backward, for the children of God have been already designated by the absence of sin (ver. 9); forward, for the children of the devil are designated below by the presence of sin in the second half of the verse." Not that any one is in this life completely the child either of God or of the devil. For "there is no moment in the Christian's life when he is purely ἐκ τοῦ θεοῦ; as, also, by parity, no moment when he is ἐκ τοῦ διαβόλου" (Haupt). Yet so far as we possess the will to become what at present we are not, so far as we are renewing day by day our covenant with God, with the attitude of self-surrender which it involves, we are at least, for the sake of, and by virtue of our union with, the Great Head of the Church, Whose life throbs in our members, regarded as what at present we are not, but as what we are not

---

into the condition of likeness to Christ in His sinlessness, into the "glorious liberty of the children of God." It is a vast assistance to us to have this goal constantly in view. It clears our minds when perplexed by practical difficulties to ask ourselves, Will this or that course of conduct lead most certainly to the great result? St. John does not leave us in ignorance what that result is. It is repeated over and over again, in various forms, in the present chapter. Purification, freedom from sin, a condition of absolute sinlessness; these are the steps by which he has led us to the climax, a life of unchanging love. St. John does not tell us that this blessed condition of existence is ever reached in this life. But it clears our spiritual vision very effectually if we recognise it as the goal to which our efforts are tend-

only hoping, but daily tending to become. This is what is meant by "justification" in the Pauline sense. In this sense only can St. John say, in consonance with the facts, "We have passed from death unto life" (ver. 14). "She hath done what she could," as Haupt says, is a maxim which applies to our condition, and the will to do more is accepted, "in the beloved" in the place, as yet, of the deed. But there is no encouragement here to stand still. Unless the will is resolved to press forward, and to do at some future time what is not at present in our power, there is nothing for God to accept. We are not "the children of God," but "the children of the devil." The necessary mark of the true believer is the "pressing on toward the goal unto the prize of the high calling of God in Christ Jesus" (Phil. iii. 14). The question has been asked, How can we be said to be the children of the devil here in the same sense that we are said to be the children of God, or, if this be not the case, what distinction can we make between the two expressions? The explanation is the same here as in ver. 8. ἐκ τοῦ διαβόλου there does not mean that the devil is in any strict sense our creator, but that our present mode of life is due to his influence. We quoted Origen's

---

ing. In the purpose, at least, the children of God and the children of the devil are manifest enough, whatever they may be in the process.

II. RELIGIOUS TENDENCIES CONSIDERED IN REFERENCE TO THEIR AIM. But this distinction is not confined to the result. It exists, if not quite so definitely, yet quite definitely enough, in this present world, to divide men into two great classes. Even in this life the children of God and the children of the devil are manifest. If we stand in the street and two men pass by us at the same time, we can tell the direction in which a man is going by the way in which his face is turned and his steps directed. Just so can we distinguish between the children of God and the children of the devil by the main

remark on ver. 8, that though we are said to *be* of the devil, we are never said to be "born" or "begotten" of him. Both the great Father of the Church and we ourselves were guilty of an apparent inadvertence, for the phrase here certainly, at first sight, appears to involve the idea of birth or begetting. Yet, in fact, no such meaning is really involved. The expression "children of" (or "sons of," the Hebrew being the same) is a very common Hebraism, involving likeness to, being under the influence of any habit or quality. Thus we read of "sons of Belial" (Deut. xiii. 13); sons "of perdition" (John xvii. 12); of "a curse" (2 Peter ii. 14); of "wrath" (Eph. ii. 3), and the like. Consequently, in reality, the term τέκνα τοῦ διαβόλου involves a less close relation between the unbeliever and the devil than the ἐκ τοῦ διαβόλου of ver. 8. And if we proceed to ask with Haupt, what right we have to attach a sense of closer relationship in the case of the τέκνα τοῦ θεοῦ, the reply is that we should *not* be entitled to do so from this passage alone. Taken by itself, it does but mean that we conform ourselves to God's precepts. It is from other passages that we learn the close and intimate relationship of the believer to his Lord, which invests the term "chil-

---

object of their lives. It it not difficult to discern, among many errors and weaknesses, the motive power by which a man's actions are as a rule directed. If "his face be as though he would go up to Jerusalem," the Samaritans can see it plainly enough to arouse their animosity. In other words, "in this the children of God are manifest and the children of the devil." And as life goes on, the difference becomes daily more manifest. As the cares and sorrows, the temptations and pleasures of life, reach their vanishing point with him who is going to leave it, the child of God fixes his gaze ever more intently upon what is to come, and has an ever-lessening regard for those things which once had power to tempt him to forget God. But the child of the evil one has nothing but regret for a past which is slipping

dren of God" with a deeper meaning than any language of a similar kind applied to any other being. The language here, in ver. 8, and in John viii. 44, applied to the relations between the sinner and the devil, means (see note on ver. 8) that the present condition of the sinner is due to his having submitted to the influence of the first of God's creatures who strayed from His ways, and became thus the tempter of all others. It has been asked, to *whom* are the children of God and the children of the devil manifested? Those who answer "to God" have missed the sense of the passage. St. John, after having dwelt on the character of the new life in itself, wishes now to point out the visible evidences of this life in the conduct of believers. See next note.—**whosoever doeth not righteousness is not of God, neither he that loveth not his brother.** Cf. Rom. xiii. 8, 10, and Gal. v. 14, and remark on the absolute identity of the teaching of the two Apostles in spite of the difference of their minds. The thought here is the same as that of ver. 7, only turned in the opposite direction. *There* it has reference to the *source* of the life, here to its stream. Here we are invited to see the Divine life manifesting itself by its effects. We learn to distinguish in those around us the

---

away from him for ever, and, strange as it seems, clings the more tenaciously to the vanities he has always loved, in proportion as the time comes daily nearer when he must part with them for ever.

III. THE DISTINCTION BETWEEN THE CHILD OF GOD AND THE CHILD OF THE DEVIL. Briefly, it is this: the child of the devil seeks his own advantage; the child of God leaves his own advantage entirely out of sight. Yet by forgetting it, he secures it. The only way for any man to be happy is to take care that all men are happy. And thus, by caring for the happiness of others, we secure our own. The devil himself fell from his high dignity by thinking of his own rights and privileges; of what was due *to* him, rather than what was due *from* him. And so do his children fall. So "whosoever doeth not

children of God and the children of the devil. "I will give you a test," he says, in effect, "whereby you can tell whether this life of which I have spoken be in you or in others or not. And it is a very simple one. Do you love your brother, or do you not?" The truth is that the last clause of this verse explains the last but one. What is meant by he that doeth righteousness? It is he that loveth his brother. The two things are identical. "Love is the fulfilling of the law." Whatever is loving, that and nothing else is right. If you are in doubt what doing righteousness in any given case really means, do what is best and kindest and most for your brother's welfare, and you have solved the problem. The καί which connects the two clauses has occasioned difficulty to some interpreters. But it is a simple Hebraism. It brings in no new idea. It does but repeat the former thought in a new way. And thus, by the most natural and least arbitrary connection of thought, does the Apostle bring in the dominant idea of the present section (vers. 10–18), *love as a practical principle distinguishing the Christian from other men*. The last question suggested by this verse is, what is meant by the word "brother"? Many commentators have been led astray here. The

---

righteousness (*i.e.* that which is just and fair to others) is not of God, neither he that loveth not his brother."

VERS. 12, 13.—*The antagonism between the children of God and the children of the devil.*

I. THEIR AIMS ARE IRRECONCILABLE. The one seeks his own benefit at the expense of other people, the other seeks other people's at the expense of his own. Such a vast practical divergence must necessarily bring men into conflict: and it does so in a thousand ways. (*a*) There are those who devote themselves to religious objects, to collecting money for the spread of Christianity at home and abroad. On the other hand, there are those to whom such appeals are irksome, odious, insupportable. (*b*) There are efforts for educating, helping,

ἀδελφός has been held to refer to the members of the Christian community, because the relation of the believer to the unbeliever is not one of love, but hate. But is this quite so clear? The world hates the children of God, it is true. But were the children of God to hate the world in return? On the contrary, is not the precept given, " Love your enemies, bless them that curse you, do good to them that hate you " (Luke vi. 27)? Ebrard has grasped the meaning of the passage in his reference to Luke x. 29–36. "The requirement to love our brother," he nobly says, "is pre-supposed to be of universal application." The principle here is that of the universal brotherhood of man. If the question be asked, Who is my brother? the reply is, Every one. And the decisive test whether a man is doing righteousness or not is the presence or absence in him of love to all mankind. Those who are as yet untouched by the life of Christ are actuated by hate, and it is a special feature of their case that they hate most those who are striving after a worthier ideal than their own (ver. 13). But the possession of the Divine life is evidenced in one way, and in that alone. The man who has it is full of love to all who have been created in the Divine image. See note on ch. ii. 10.

---

raising the ignorant and degraded. And there are those whose selfishness revolts at the work, who would fain keep those down who are down already, that they may retain their power, their superiority over them. How many are loud in their indignation that the "lower classes" should enjoy luxuries, comforts, leisure, of which they would be extremely enraged if it were proposed to deprive themselves. (c) There are schemes on the part of the charitable and Christian to prevent the "haves" from using their power to oppress and injure the "have nots." We deny the right of the possessor of property to wring the last farthing out of an ignorant and degraded tenant by housing him in a way in which it is impossible for him to do other than become more ignorant and degraded still; of the ship-owner to send his

VER. 11.—**For this is the message that ye heard from the beginning, that we should love one another.** For *message* the older versions have *tidings*. Most commentators would make the demonstrative pronoun a predicate, and the sentence would then run " for the message . . . is this, that we," &c., which makes the passage a little more emphatic. "From the beginning," here obviously means, as in ch. ii. 24, from the beginning of the Gospel. This doctrine was practically preached in the Sermon on the Mount. It was distinctly formulated in the last discourse of Jesus before His crucifixion (John xiii. 34, 35, xv. 12, 13). Cf. ch. ii. 7. The reason why we have ἀγγελία here and ἐντολή there, is because there the Apostle has been speaking of keeping God's commandments (ii. 3–5), while here he is speaking of the purport of the commission he himself has received, and which it is his duty to execute. The "for" with which the passage commences, gives the reason for the assertion in the last verse. What the Apostle there says on the duty of Christian love, is what Christians have been from the very first instructed to make known. We cannot, with Braune, regard ἵνα here as "denoting the *purpose* and *work to be done*, and not only the *substance* or *contents* of the ἀγγελία." The

---

brother men to sea in unseaworthy ships, while he himself by insuring heavily is secure from all loss; of the capitalist to make use of his capital so as to secure a monopoly of business for himself; of the impure to use his money so as to secure a constant supply of what he wants for the gratification of his desires, at whatever cost in the degradation and suffering of others. But to endeavour to prevent such crimes rouses the indignation of the selfish and wicked. And such indignation is often displayed in no measured terms, and would, did not Christian society step in to prevent it, proceed to actual violence. (*d*) We contend that a due recognition of God, of His day, of public worship, of the brotherhood of Christians, of the duty of private prayer and of a diligent study of God's Word, are the necessary

instances in the New Testament are far too numerous where we must admit that the original definite sense of purpose has dwindled into the less definite meaning of result. Christians did not hear the message *in order* that they might love one another. Still less can we say that the message assumed this form in order that Christians should love one another. The command to love one another was the *message itself*. It is not denied that ἵνα has constantly this sense of purpose. But there are quite sufficient exceptions to make it unnecessary to strain the sentence to bring it in. And this we should do, if we rendered " and the message which ye heard from the beginning, *is this, in order that* ye should love one another." But the ἵνα may certainly serve subtly to indicate a purpose and aim, if not directly to assert it. That is to say, the message is intended to produce a purpose in our lives. Lastly, what is meant by " we " and " one another " here? Many have striven to confine it to the Christian society here, and, no doubt, the first and most obvious realisation of the precept was within the bounds of the Christian Church. But that Church was intended to embrace the whole world. It was prophesied that " the earth shall be full of the knowledge of the Lord,

---

means of keeping alive the spirit of religion in our midst. Yet there are those who deny and despise these "means of grace," who will not attend the house of God, who treat Sunday like any other day, who think they can read and pray at home, and so on, and who mock at those who think otherwise. There are plenty of ways still in which the man of the world and the man of God come into collision.

II. AS IS SHOWN IN THE CASE OF CAIN AND ABEL. (1) The tendency of religion is to make men prosperous even in this life, as is shown in the cases of Cain and Abel; of irreligion to make them wretched, and hence to make the latter jealous of the former. Yet this tendency is checked in two ways in a highly organised society. (*a*) A man may either be shortsightedly or longsightedly selfish. He may either squander his means directly he has them, or he may care-

as the waters cover the sea" (Isa. xi. 9). It was God's will that "all men should be saved and come to the knowledge of the truth" (1 Tim. ii. 4). Therefore, it was proclaimed from the beginning of the Gospel that all men should love one another.

VER. 12.—**Not as Cain, who was of that wicked one, and slew his brother.** Revised Version, *Not as Cain was of the evil one and slew his brother.* There is no *that* in the original, as the italics of the Authorised Version indicate, nor need it be supplied. "*Evil one*" is better than "wicked one." But we cannot leave the sentence without something to supply the *hiatus*. Neither, as Winer warns us, can we, with a host of commentators, supply ὦμεν or ποιῶμεν, for that would require μή and not οὐ. The most natural course would be to supply ἐσμεν, and the relative pronoun after Cain. "We are not as Cain, who was of the evil one." The first murder has always imprinted itself very strongly upon the human imagination. And St. John, doubtless, uses it here as the best illustration of the tendencies of evil, even as his Master, in the Sermon on the Mount, taught that the actual breach of the sixth commandment took place when we began to be angry without a cause (Matt. v. 22). The

---

fully arrange his actions so as to enjoy prosperity and power in years to come. These two classes are equally alien to the mind of God. Nevertheless they are often more opposed to one another than to the children of the kingdom. The spendthrift hates the calculating man of prudence; the prudent man despises the worthless spendthrift. The man of God sees little difference between them, save that since there is another world, the man of calculating prudence may some day be the worse off of the two. (*b*) The more misery there is in the world by sin, the more the Christian is drawn to cast away all his comforts in order to relieve it. In a primitive condition of society, if there were misery, it was not organised misery, so to speak, and it was directly traceable to a man's own misconduct. In civilised society the sins of the fathers are more heavily visited on the children than in a less

Commentators have, naturally enough, referred to the Rabbinic fable that Cain was not Adam's child, as Abel was, but the child of the evil one. But the fable is most likely later than the Apostle's time, and may even have been derived from his teaching here, diverted into a Rabbinic channel, and put forth in a Rabbinic form. But St. John, like Christian writers in general, is speaking of spiritual influence, not of natural generation. The word σφάττω has attracted attention; first, because it only occurs elsewhere in Scripture in the Book of the Revelation (v. 6, &c.), a fact denoting common authorship; and next, because in the Revelation it is used of the slaying of a victim. The word certainly denotes a more deliberate act of violence or cruelty than our word *slay*, and is more nearly equivalent to the kindred and stronger word *slaughter*.—**And wherefore slew he him?** The question gives liveliness and point to the argument. "I ask you to observe this as an illustration of my principle, that there is a manifest difference between the children of God and the children of the devil; existing, first in the motive, and then displayed in act. There is an essential difference, as I have said, between the two classes of men, and you can see for yourselves what it is."

---

highly developed life. The degradation of the children is deeper and more difficult to remedy. And consequently the sacrifices entailed on those who, like their Master, would sympathise with and suffer for others, are greater and more continuous than they could have been at the dawn of human existence. Thus prosperity is now as likely, or even more likely, to be the lot of the wicked than of the righteous. (2) Yet the principle that the man who loves evil hates and would destroy, if he could, the man who does good still holds. For, (*a*) there is the conflict of wills referred to under the former head ; (*b*) there is the jar and fret of 'an utter absence of sympathy, and (*c*) there is the voice of conscience perpetually condemning the selfish man. (3) This tendency must not be supposed not to exist because in modern society it is under restraint. The man who once, like Cain, would

—Because his own thoughts were evil, and his brother's righteous. The essential antagonism between good and evil, the Apostle would point out, is the cause of Cain's deed. Abel's holy and blameless life was a rebuke to Cain. A selfish, unloving life is hatred in disguise. And the disguise is sometimes stripped off, and love of self stands revealed as hate of our brother. Those who cannot, or will not, become the tools of our purposes, must be put out of the way. And as righteousness includes justice, and justice a sense of duty, we can easily see how the evil man learns to hate the good man, and is a murderer in will, if not in act. Dean Alford speaks here of a difficulty raised by those who see no reference made in the narrative in Genesis to this "ethical difference." Like many other difficulties which have been raised, it does not amount to much. For surely the only ground of the acceptance or non-acceptance of the offering must have been the ethical condition of those who made it. Nor have those who have read the narrative in Genesis pondered sufficiently the way in which the regard God paid to the one, and not to the other, was manifested. Our mind is so penetrated with the idea of the miraculous in those times, that we in-

---

have slaughtered his brother, now tries to undermine his influence, to thwart his action, to combat his opinions. He cannot kill him, but he does his best in various ways to render him powerless.

III. THEREFORE IT IS NO WONDER IF THE WORLD HATES US.

1. *What is meant by hate?* Rich and cultivated society in our time avoids violent passions. They disturb its repose. The polite man of the world does not hate, he scorns. He does not kill, he avoids, or if he cannot avoid, he is cynical, contemptuous, amused, stolidly indifferent. He does not openly oppose, he simply refuses to move. Passive resistance is often more difficult to overcome than active opposition. A man who questions your accuracy, ridicules your enthusiasm, points out coolly your exaggerations, insinuates suspicion as to the purity of your motives, may be a more formidable enemy

sensibly suppose that the pleasure and displeasure of God related to a single offering, and was displayed by some visible miracle. Like Lord Byron, we picture to ourselves a whirlwind blowing down the one altar, and scattering the fruits, while the smoke of the other ascends gently and peacefully to heaven. But is it not far more likely that Abel's life, spent in prayer and self-control, and prudence and foresight, was growing daily more prosperous; while Cain, indulging his lusts, squandering the good things that God had given him, felt the continual pressure of hunger and poverty? He was as scrupulous as Abel, no doubt, in offering to God the tribute of external worship. And he could not understand why God dealt so hardly with him, so gently with his brother. Dark and malignant passions boiled tumultuously in his breast, and, at last, in a frenzy of passion and jealousy, he slew the brother whom he had learned to hate. And so were the Apostle's words exemplified, "because his works were evil, and his brother's righteous."

VER. 13.—**Marvel not, my brethren, if the world hate you.** It would seem as if the sub-section ended here. St. John would say, "This antagonism between the chil-

---

than the most passionate antagonist. Therefore hate, in these days, has become dislike, or cool, critical analysis. But it would become hate again, if the tone of society changed. And there are circles where hate flourishes, where the man who takes Christ for his Lord is as actively hated as ever.

2. *What do we mean by the world?* The "world" here and the "children of the devil" are convertible terms. Therefore the world means those who are bent on pleasing self and no others. But there are those who imagine that to have incurred the dislike of other people is a sure sign that they are disciples of Jesus. But this does not follow. They may have excited opposition by intemperance of language, by excess of self-will, by one-sided and unreasonable views, by trying to coerce others instead of to persuade them. The hatred

dren of God and the children of the devil is an universal one. As it was in the days of Abel, so it is now. *You must not be surprised if you find in the world—that which was once God's order, but has so sadly ceased to be such—the same evil passions as of old. And as the absence of love is the characteristic of the unregenerate man, so he will display that characteristic even in his dealings with those who have nothing but love in return for his hate."* How true this was, the history of Christianity shows only too plainly. And it is shown still, whenever duty compels us to denounce the crimes of wicked and selfish men. It is perhaps because our Christianity is often of a feeble and nerveless type, because we tamely acquiesce in wrong-doing, which long prescription seems to excuse, that we feel so little of it. But let any man boldly raise his voice to condemn iniquity in any rank of life, and he will soon learn what hate is. We may observe, moreover, that the Apostle does not, as the Authorised Version would lead us to suppose, regard this hatred of the world as a hypothetical possibility. He regards it as a fact. "Marvel not, if the world *hates* (Revised Version, *hateth*) you." If you find it to be a fact, do not be surprised. It is but the

---

of the world of which St. John speaks must be incurred by our adherence to duty, not by our departure from it. Therefore before we congratulate ourselves upon being disliked let us first make sure *why* we are disliked.

3. *Does the world hate the good man?* This question is immensely complicated by the fact that there is no sharp line of demarcation between the Church and the world in these times. Society is strongly permeated by Christian principles. Even heathens are not wholly corrupt. And thus the good man, notwithstanding all his imperfections, will, in the course of time, win the respect of all right-thinking and of many wrong-thinking men. Still, the rule holds good. Bad men do not like good men. They do not like to be shamed by the contrast between such men and themselves. This dislike sharpens

result of a truth too manifest to escape notice. There is an essential incompatibility between a righteous and an unrighteous man. They must come into collision if they attempt to act together. But while the righteous man tries to reconcile as much as possible his love for his unrighteous brother with his love to other people, the unrighteous man feels no love at all. And indifference which quiesces in contempt, so long as men's paths in life lie separate, becomes hate, when they are brought together, and the righteous man refuses to have either part or lot in deeds of evil.

---

into something more when the two come into collision on any matter. A man is sure to bring more or less odium upon himself if he steadfastly adheres to what he thinks right, whatever other men may say. Especially is this the case in public matters when a man, from conscientious motives, separates himself from those with whom he was wont to act. However much Christianity may have deadened the animosity between man and man, every true Christian has passed through periods of life when he was forced to draw comfort from the words, "Marvel not if the world hate you."

XVIII.

PASSING FROM DEATH UNTO LIFE.

CH. iii. 14.—**We know that we have passed from death unto life, because we love the brethren.** The thought of this section, which is also the leading thought of the whole Epistle, namely, brotherly love, is advanced another stage in this verse. We have been taught (i. 6) the necessity of walking in the light and not in the darkness; (ii. 4) the necessity of keeping God's commandments; (ii. 10) that the abiding in the light implies the love of one's brother; (ii. 15) that we must not love the world; (ii. 29) that every one who doeth righteousness has been born of God; (iii. 10) that whosoever doeth not righteousness, and loveth not his brother, is not of God. Now we are called upon to regard the love of the

---

HOMILETICS.

VER. 14.—*The test of true conversion.*

I. THE CONTRAST BETWEEN THE CHURCH AND THE WORLD. The foundation of the first is love, of the second, hate. And this because the guiding principle of the latter is self, of the former crucifixion of self. To seek one's own well-being at the cost of the well-being of another is the very essence of hate, and must at length manifest itself as hate if it be consistently carried out. It is a mistake to confine the definition of hate to that violence of passion which is aroused in selfish men when any one crosses their path. Hate is the opposite, or absence, of love, and that man is at least as full of hate who calmly and without passion sacrifices his neighbour to his own

brethren, if it exist in any heart, as a sign that he who so loves has passed from a condition of death to a condition of life. In the last two verses the contrast and even the antipathy between the child of God and the child of the devil is exemplified in Cain. And then, as his manner is, the Apostle alternates between the two thoughts, marking the contrast between the two kinds of life ever more and more fully. The new life is here presented to us more distinctly than it has yet been presented, as a state of deliverance from a condition in which the rest of the world still lies (see this thought yet more emphasised in ver. 19). Nor should we fail to notice that the figure is changed. We have had light and darkness set before us as the emblems of these two conditions. Now they are represented to us under the emblems of life and death. The contrast is drawn between life, which involves love, and death, which is the necessary result of the absence of love. This contrast is marked by the ἡμεῖς, which is emphatic. "*We* know that we have passed from death to life, because we love the brethren;" but he that loveth not, whether he know it or not, is still in the condition from which we have been freed. The having passed from a condition of

---

interest, as the man of most uncontrolled temper. But the Christian has the ideal of his Master's life before him. And in that life no thought of separating His own happiness from that of others was allowed to enter. Thus the Christian Church and the world were two societies acting upon principles utterly antagonistic. The maxim of the heathen world was "Love thyself." The Christian Church, on the contrary, said, "Deny thyself;" "have no self." "Devote thy whole life to the welfare of thy fellow-men." In the present day the lines of demarcation are far less distinctly drawn than they were. Many partially act on one principle and partially on the other. Still, society is divided into two great classes, those who make their own interest the sole measure of their duty, and those who, to a greater or less degree, acknowledge their obligation to consider others.

death unto one of life, which is by Jesus Christ Himself (John v. 24), attributed to faith in Him, is here regarded as evidenced by love. In other words, "faith worketh by love" (Gal. v. 6). And those who are on the lookout for similarities between the teaching of St. Paul and St. John will find them in such passages as 1 Cor. vi. 11; Rom. viii. 2, 6 (see Revised Version), 10; Col. iii. 3, &c. Observe next, "we have passed." Not a single act, which entirely negatives all idea of continued effort on our part, but a practical result of conduct. We know that this change has taken place in us, because now, instead of opposing ourselves to the life of love, we have submitted to it. By steadily resisting all the assaults of the deadly principle we have remained in the position in which we now find ourselves, that of manifesting in our lives the Divine life, which is a life of love. Again, the preposition here is ἐκ, not ἀπό. It is change of state, not of place. But how can this change be predicated of us in our present imperfect condition? We see that it is unhesitatingly predicated by St. John of those of whom he is speaking. And yet it is equally clear that he regards their future as very far from finally decided. See ii. 1, 15, 24, 26, 28, iii. 7, 18, and many

---

II. THE TEST OF TRUE RELIGION IS LOVE TO OTHERS. We can only know the heavenly life from its fruits. It comes from above, from God, with whom no hate is known, save of hate itself. And if this be its source, its character, it must give evidence of its presence by conduct in keeping with it. In other words, it must be a life of love. And until love is the watchword of our lives, until we are untiring in our labours for our brethren, we cannot say "we have passed from death unto life." We may be *passing* from one to the other. We may be slaying the evil desires that have so much power over us. But as long as one single unkind or unloving thought is harboured against a single being who bears the Image of God, our transition from the one state to the other cannot be said to be achieved.

other passages involving the same conclusion. The answer is, as before, that the Apostle regards the *direction in which we are moving*. There is no one, it is to be hoped, entirely devoid of love, entirely ruled by the passion of self-interest in this life. Neither is there any one who is as much penetrated with love as he ought to be. Nevertheless, if we desire to grow in love, and are so growing, we may venture to claim this promise for ourselves. If our conscience tells us that this is not the case, then we cannot appropriate it. See vers. 20, 21. "The brethren" is regarded by many commentators as referring to the Christian Church. And there is no doubt that it does primarily refer to Christians, as in Acts xi. 29, xii. 17, xv. 1, 1 Cor. viii. 12, &c. But inasmuch as love to all mankind is the principle of the Gospel, we may believe that there is a secondary and subordinate reference to the whole human race.—**He that loveth not his brother abideth in death.** The words "his brother" are without authority here. It is the absence of love from the heart that killeth, or rather that retains the man in his previous state of spiritual death. "Death" here is of course not to be construed quite literally. It means "dead in trespasses and sins." For according to

---

III. A LIFE OF HATE IS AN ABIDING IN DEATH. For it is death to be without God, and he who hates, or, which is the same thing, he who does not love, is without God. We never, in this life, see any monster so utterly lost to all humanity as to be utterly without love. But we see men tending to be such. And in another world the tendency may develop into this essentially devilish condition. For it is the characteristic of the devil to be without love. And it may be that eternal death is no other than a condition from which all love is banished. As long as a spark of love remains in the spirit this eternal death is not reached. On the other hand, it is only by the active exercise of love that we can escape that condition. The world of St. John's day, which "lay in wickedness," was only too near this terrible condition. Only the Spirit of God and of love, which then began to

this passage, the whole world, with the exception of those who have been rescued in Jesus Christ, and translated into the life of love, abideth in death. But this cannot mean absolute cessation of existence. A lower life even unregenerate man has. But to the higher life of the Spirit and of love, he is an utter stranger. As "faith without works is dead," so an unloving heart is dead also.

VER. 15.—**Whosoever hateth his brother is a murderer.** The authority for this statement is Matt. v. 21–26, where the real breach of the sixth commandment is shown to consist in a spirit of animosity and hate. "Man looks," we are told, "on the outward appearance, but God on the heart" (1 Sam. xvi. 7). It may not seem so to us, but the truth is that every one who wishes ill, nay, we may even go so far as to say does not wish well, to his neighbour, has really a mind to destroy him. Outward circumstances may hinder that mind from being carried into effect. And they may, moreover, blind us to the real state of our heart. But the truth remains, that every man whom we do not love we should kill were all the outward restraints of society removed. "This is a hard saying; who can hear it?" Nevertheless, it is written "for our admonition, in the

---

brood on the face of the dark waters, could deliver it from stiffening in the true death of the soul.

VER. 15.—*The principle of self in its results.*

I. THE UNLOVING MAN IS REALLY A MURDERER. As we have seen, it is St. John's custom to view the life of the soul in the light of the end towards which it is travelling. Here, like his Master, he points out that all absence of love is nothing less than murder. The man who loves himself better than others will not shrink from destroying them when they cross his path. For nothing but a spirit of love and mercy and pity would restrain him. See Homiletic notes on ver. 12.

II. EVEN THE UNENLIGHTENED CONSCIENCE CAN DISCERN THE GUILT OF MURDER. "*Ye know* that no murderer hath eternal life

Word of God.—**and ye know that no murderer hath eternal life abiding in him.**" "Once more," as in ver. 14, says Mr. Plummer, "the Apostle appeals to the Christian consciousness." This time, however, it is not a matter of experience, gained by investigation and trouble. It is obvious upon the face of it. The human conscience condemns this crime. It did so instinctively at the moment of the first murder. It was the voice of conscience that cried "What hast thou done? The voice of thy brother's blood crieth unto Me from the ground" (Gen. iv. 10). No doctrine is here laid down as to the possibility of the future forgiveness of a murderer, for it would of course equally involve the impossibility of improvement or forgiveness for any one who had ever indulged hate, or even who had at any time failed to love. This is obvious from a glance at the whole verse. All therefore that is meant is that it is obvious that no murderer is in possession of so inestimable a blessing as eternal life at a time when he is capable of such a deed. "The whole phrase," says Professor Westcott, " is unique. Elsewhere 'the word' (ii. 14, John v. 38, comp. xv. 7), the 'unction' (ii. 27), the 'seed of God' (iii. 9), the 'love of God' (iii. 17), the 'truth' (2 John 2), are said to

---

abiding in him." When principles are pushed to their results, we can see what their tendency is. Behold then the results of failing to love! They are plain enough. In the abstract, humanity condemns them, though in the particular case numberless excuses enable us to blind our eyes. But if the absence of love be really nothing short of murder, we need no further exhortation to show us its guilt.

VER. 16.—*The only possible alternative to the murderous spirit.*

I. THERE IS NO MIDDLE COURSE BETWEEN THE SPIRIT OF CHRIST AND THE SPIRIT OF MURDER. For "herein" and in nothing else, have we received a pattern of love, in the Life and Death of Jesus Christ. This is the only alternative to hate. St. John here again fixes our glance on results. The spirit of hate leads directly to our taking another's life for the attainment of our own objects. The

'abide' in the believer and also God (ver. 24, iv. 12, 13, 15f.) and Christ (John vi. 56, xv. 5). Even to the last man has not 'life' in himself. This is the Divine prerogative alone." And yet, if God and Christ abide in us, then eternal life, which is God's prerogative, must dwell in us also. For the form of the phrase "no murderer hath," see note on ii. 21.

VER. 16.—**Hereby perceive we the love of God.** Rather, *herein have we known love*. The words "of God" are wrongly supplied in our version, which here "collects the errors of other versions," as Mr. Plummer says. Wiclif and the Rhemish translate literally, ἐγνώκαμεν, we have known. They translate ἀγάπη by *charity*, and, following the Vulgate here, add the words "of God" which are not in the original. Tyndale has substituted the present for the perfect, "perceive we love," and Cranmer has followed him. The Geneva translates more correctly "hereby" (where Wiclif and the Rhemish have "in this," or "in this thing") "perceive we love." But "perceive" is not the right rendering. γινώσκω refers rather to the knowledge gained by experience than by intuition. This last is expressed by οἶδα. Thus the true translation gives us a far deeper and

---

spirit of love leads as directly to the surrendering our own life for others' sake. And these two are the only possible issues for human life. We must in our daily conduct, as in the principles on which it is based, be tending to one result or the other. If we desire to love, we know no other pattern of love than Jesus Christ. If we will not acknowledge His life as our guide, we must "abide in death."

II. CHRIST OUR EXAMPLE. If our belief in the Satisfaction of Christ be a saving faith, it must produce in us likeness to Him. For the Cross was only a satisfaction to God's Justice in that it was a manifestation of love. The fall of man consisted in the knowledge of evil instead of good. But all evil, being contrary to the Will of God, must consist in absence of love—in caring for oneself instead of for others. Hence it was that murder was so speedy a result of the fall,

more striking sentiment than the A. V. In the act of Jesus in laying down His life the world first had the opportunity of recognising what love is. Up to that time, so far had they strayed from the path of true righteousness, that they could form no conception of it. Neither can we now, save as evidenced by the sacrifice of Jesus on the cross for our redemption.—**because he laid down his life for us.** We have before discussed the meaning of ἐκεῖνος. Here, though neither God nor Jesus Christ is mentioned, there can be no doubt who is meant. The reference can only be to the Man Christ Jesus. The words "of God," it will be remembered, are not in the original, but are introduced in the A. V. Therefore also they cannot be adduced, as they might incautiously be adduced, as a proof of the Divinity of Christ. ὅτι had better be translated "that." The word ἔθηκε has been noticed as remarkable. It is only found in this sense, with ψυχή, in St. John's Gospel and Epistles, and we are so familiar through our translation with the expression to "lay down a life," that we do not always stop to consider its meaning. Haupt interprets it here as *staking* one's life. But it is better to interpret it in the sense of *laying aside*, cf. John x. 17, 18.—**and we ought to lay**

---

being the natural result of want of love. If, then, the work of the fall were to be undone; if God's Justice were to be satisfied by a perfect obedience, that obedience must be the manifestation of Love in its fullest and amplest measure. There must be the most complete reversal of the principle that self-interest is the natural guide of conduct. And therefore the willingness to lay down even life itself was necessary to that obedience. And inasmuch as Christ came to take away sin, the likeness of this His Love must be reproduced in all whom He has saved. No one can have received the Atonement unless he is washed, purified, permeated by the Blood of the one Sacrifice, so that he, too, is ready to give up all to secure blessings for others beside himself. When the Spirit of Christ controls every deed, word, and thought, then are we in truth saved by His Blood.

down our lives for the brethren. This passage alone would be sufficient to prove that our Lord's death is not to be regarded simply as substituted for the death of all other men. On the contrary, it is the expression of a principle the Saviour introduced into human life, the type to which all of us should be ready to conform. Not that the death of any other, from what motive soever undergone, can be to the world what His was. But from this one Death, considered as the representative Death of mankind, our whole human life should take its colour. Submission to God's law, love to all our brethren, the desire to remove evil from the race by cheerfully bearing its consequences ourselves; in these, when they are inwrought into the texture of our being, we find the proof that the atonement has taken place in us. We have "put off the old man, which is corrupt after the deceitful lusts, and have put on the new man, which after God is created in righteousness and true holiness." And the term "lay down," applied to us, would imply a "taking again;" the gift of a restored and revivified $\psi v \chi \acute{\eta}$, inspired and exalted by the Spirit which comes from God. Here, again, as in ver. 14, it seems a mistake to confine the term "the brethren" to Christians

---

but then we shall be as He is. He laid down His life for us, and we are equally ready to lay ours down when our brother's need requires it.

VERS. 17, 18.—*The practical realisation of love.*

I. THERE IS A TENDENCY AMONG MEN TO ADMIRE GREAT PRINCIPLES, AND TO NEGLECT TO CARRY THEM OUT. This abstract admiration for Christianity, which is content to praise its spirit, and to forget to act on that which it praises, is common in every age. People hear a good sermon, and speak well of it, and their lives, though condemned by it, remain unaltered. People speak of the high morality of the Bible, and refuse to carry it out. They speak enthusiastically of the "beautiful Litany" of the Church of England, which prays so touchingly for those in need or distress, but they will do nothing to relieve the needs for which it prays. And so it is possible

alone. If He, our example, laid down His life for the whole world (for His enemies, Rom. v. 10), we ought to circumscribe our willingness to lay life aside within no narrower limits. And His Apostles and missionaries in every age have been willing to give themselves up, even for those to whom they have been compelled to say "the more I love you, the less I be loved."

VER. 17.—**But whoso hath this world's goods**, or, "and he who happens to have worldly goods," which seems to give the force of ἄν best. βίος (see ch. ii. 16) signifies that which sustains life, and hence property, goods of any kind. The translation is Tyndall's. The Revised has "goods," Wiclif "catel," and the Rhemish "substance." Professor Westcott has an admirable note here. "St. John turns from considering the greatness of our obligation to notice the ordinary character of failure. By the transition he suggests that there is a danger in indulging ourselves in lofty views which lie out of the way of common experience. We may, therefore, try ourselves by a more homely test." Ebrard has remarks of a similar kind. And they are much needed wherever sentimental meditations about dying with Christ, and the beauty of self-sacrifice and self-surrender, are apt to

---

to be lost in ecstatic admiration of the Love which was consummated, as far as human perceptions go, upon the Cross, and to express the warmest approval of the principle that we should "go and do likewise," and yet to forget that this principle, if true, must not be confined to one heroic act, to the performance of which we never may be called, but must govern all the details of our daily life.

II. OUR RELIGION, IF TRUE, MUST BE REAL. A religion of mere external profession is worth nothing. It is a religion of "word and tongue," not of "work and truth." Here observe that *truth* is coupled with *work*. The former pre-supposes the latter. A religion which does no work for God and man is a false religion, however unexceptionable its sentiments may be. No mere abstract admiration for the Christian Creed, for the beauty of holiness, for the Life of Christ, for

take the place of the fact. Some of us are in the third heaven with saints and angels on Sundays—somewhat below the level of ordinary kind-hearted folk during the week.—**and seeth his brother have need.** Revised Version, *and beholdeth his brother in need.* The word θεωρέω is a favourite one with St. John. It always seems to imply a kind of sight in which the intellect is concerned. Perhaps *perceive* is the best English equivalent. But our word *see* is quite adequate to the occasion. It is used of intellectual as well as physical perception. Therefore we may venture to think "beholdeth" a change somewhat for the worse. For χρείαν ἔχειν in the sense of being in need see also ii. 27.—**and shutteth up his bowels of compassion from him.** The words "of compassion" are not in the original, and are only added to explain it. The older versions substitute "compassion" for the more literal translation. The Rhemish has "bowels" simply. The expression is a Hebraism, and occurs only here in St. John's writings, though it is not uncommon in the New Testament. Instances of "bowels" in the sense of the seat of the affections occur constantly in the Old Testament. See, for example, Genesis xliii. 30. The nearest equivalent in modern English would

---

the principle of self-sacrifice, will avail in God's sight. No mere enunciation of moral sentiments, no, not even the belief in the efficacy of Christ's Sacrifice to save souls, will be of any avail unless there be in us the spirit of that Sacrifice, a spirit which can only be present when there is real, hearty work for God's cause, which is man's cause also.

III. AND IT MUST DISPLAY ITSELF IN SMALL THINGS AS IN GREAT. It is the characteristic of love that it wearies itself to find out opportunities of showing itself. It is ready to die for a brother. But inasmuch as to live this fleshly life is often "more expedient" (or rather "profitable") for that brother, it "dies daily" for him. That is, it daily gives up something for his sake. Whatever he "has need" of, that it is willing, if it can, to give. And this is the only

be "steeleth his heart against him." It seems as if a certain effort were implied here; as if the Christian, when refusing to help a brother in need, not only did violence to the principles of Christianity, but even to the promptings of his own nature. This much seems implied by "shutting up his compassion from" his brother.—**how dwelleth the love of God in him?** Better "abideth," to keep to the word we have used all along. "Dwelleth," moreover, weakens the meaning which the preceding words convey, that the Christian must exercise a certain force upon himself to act against his better feelings, must, in fact, "grieve the Spirit of God." "How doth the love of God abide in him?" (Revised Version), gives the idea of a love which once possessed him, but is now in danger of ceasing to do so. "The love of God" means God's love, shed forth into our hearts, and manifested thence by our actions.

Ver. 18.—**My little children, let us not love in word, neither in tongue, but in deed and in truth.** This form of address is always used when the Apostle wishes to address his flock with peculiar solemnity, and especially when he desires to warn them against some error. See chaps. ii. 1, iii. 7, v. 21. With these

---

true manifestation of love. He or she who dreams of deeds of heroic self-sacrifice, and is daily neglecting opportunities of self-sacrifice which are not heroic, will fail when the opportunity offers at last, or be among those who "give their bodies to be burned, yet have not love." The little kindnesses of ordinary life which require a constant readiness to give up our own will and pleasure to serve others, these are the threads which when woven together make up the life of Christ in the soul. It is not all who can devote themselves to some great work of charity. But all can minister, in one way or another, to the needs of those around them. Those needs are of various kinds, physical, mental, spiritual. Only they who are striving to the best of their power to minister to such needs, can be said to have the love of Christ abiding in them.

words he closes this sub-section, opening the next, as his manner is, with the idea with which he has closed the former. That idea here is *truth*. We should read "the tongue" here for "tongue." And $\H{\epsilon}\rho\gamma\wp$ is usually translated "work." But the sense is plain enough, that our Christian membership is to be no barren lip-service, but to be the devotion of the heart, shown forth in the life. What is the doom of those who make professions they do not attempt to carry out in practice, is seen in the miracle of the barren fig-tree.

XIX.

CHRISTIAN ASSURANCE.

CH. iii. 19.—**And hereby we know that we are of the truth.** The "and" is doubtful here, the ancient MSS. and versions being about equally divided. "We know," according to the best supported reading, should be "we shall know." "Hereby," as in vers. 10, 16, should be "herein," or "in this." So that the whole passage should run thus, "[And] in this we shall know that we are of the truth." "In this" refers here clearly to what goes before. If we love in deed and in truth, we shall know that we are of the truth. For "of the truth," see note on ver. 8. It means deriving the whole tone and character and substance of our lives from the truth.—**and shall assure our hearts before him.** For the various interpretations of this most perplexing passage see below. The rendering of the Authorised Version and the Revised

---

HOMILETICS.

VER. 19.—*The doctrine of Christian assurance.*

I. THE DESIRE FOR ASSURANCE. The most natural question, and the most necessary question, for every Christian soul, is, Am I in a state of acceptance with Christ? Yet, vital as it is, it is to be feared that there are not many who ask it. A vast number are content to go on from day to day, hearing the Word, and partly acting upon, and partly rejecting, the doctrine of Christ; halting between two opinions; content to be "lukewarm, and neither cold or hot" (Rev. iii. 16).

Version here seems preferable to any other. The meaning assigned to πείσομεν, "satisfy," "set at rest," seems supported by Matt. xxviii. 14. Somewhat of the same idea appears in Acts xii. 20. And if it be objected that πείθω followed by an accusative and ὅτι, elsewhere means to "persuade a person that" something is the case, we must remember (1) that the word does not occur elsewhere in St. John's writings, and (2) that he evidently thought in Hebrew, though he wrote in Greek. Hence a correct idiomatic use of the word πείθω can hardly be safely assumed as a matter of course in his writings. Whether we should read "heart" or "hearts" here is uncertain. Both are well supported, but the former is most in keeping with the context. "Before Him" means in this life, not, as some have supposed, at the great day of judgment.

VER. 20.—**For if our heart condemn us, God is greater than our heart and knoweth all things.** The Authorised Version cuts the Gordian knot here by omitting to translate the second ὅτι in this passage, the cause of all our perplexity. The Rec. text does not reject it, though it is absent from some MSS. Bishop Wordsworth's interpretation, which has been strangely overlooked by recent commentators, seems to be by far the best that has been propounded of this difficult passage. He renders, "be-

---

Some excuse may be made for them by reason of the fact that there are so many different explanations given by various teachers, and most of them propounded with the utmost confidence as the true and necessary doctrine of Christ. But variety of teaching, though it may excuse, cannot justify indifference. The matter is one of life and death, and cannot be safely neglected. If men had one spark of reality in them, they would search the Scriptures, to see whether the things they are told be so or not. If they neglect to do so, the blame is theirs.

II. VARIOUS THEORIES OF ASSURANCE. With some it is (a) assur-

cause, if our heart condemn us, [it is] because God is greater than our heart, and knoweth all things." In other words, conscience is the voice of God. If it accuse us, we know that we are not "of the truth." Only when our heart acquits us have we the παρρησία which is the Christian's privilege. In what follows we have proceeded on the principle that all interpretations, however grammatically permissible or even necessary, which imply that God overrules the verdict of the individual conscience, must be set aside, as conflicting with the whole tenor of the Apostle's teaching. This appears to be a moral necessity to which all grammatical niceties must bow. Throughout the whole Epistle St. John has appealed to the verdict of conscience on our conduct as settling the question whether we are of God or not. "If we say that we have fellowship with Him, and walk in darkness, we lie, and do not the truth." "In this we know that we know Him, if we keep His commandments. He that saith I know Him, and keepeth not His commandments, is a liar, and truth is not in him; but whoso keepeth His Word, in him verily hath the love of God been perfected. *In this we know that we are in Him.*" Cf. also chaps. ii. 9–11; iii. 7, 8, 10, 14 and 17. It seems impossible, in the face of these reiterated declarations, to suppose for a

---

ance of final salvation. An inward voice assures the man that his final deliverance is secure, that his sins are washed away by the blood of Christ, that Christ's Righteousness is his by faith, that the handwriting which was against him is blotted out, and that all he has to do henceforth is to walk in this blessed assurance, and he shall finally be partaker of "the inheritance of the saints in light." But without denying that this blessed sense of pardon and peace with God is a necessary element of the redeemed life, we may doubt whether something more is not wanting. Nowhere in Scripture is it definitely laid down that a sense of present and future forgiveness is *all* a man need

moment that the Apostle here could contradict himself and say that if our heart accused us of breaches of the law of love, we might rest satisfied that God, who knew us better than we knew ourselves, would set aside the verdict of our conscience, and assure us that in spite of those breaches of the law, we were nevertheless in fellowship with Him. Especially does it seem impossible when St. John has just told us that it is by loving, "not in word nor in tongue, but in deed and in truth" (ver. 18) that we are to "know that we are of the truth," and to feel confidence that we are in the right way (ver. 19). It is not that there is not a truth in the view we reject, taken by itself. The will, it has been contended in these pages, is accepted, for the present at least, in the place of the deed, the daily effort after better things as the earnest of future victory. But this view is designedly kept out of sight by the Apostle, save in chaps. i. 7 to ii. 2. He continually keeps the end, perfection in love, in view, and strives with all his might to discourage the slightest falling short of it. Not only to hate one's brother (ver. 15) but even to deny him our compassion in the minor ills of life, is to fail of having the love of God in us (ver. 17). Love in word and in tongue is worse than useless (ver. 18). Only by love in deed and in truth can we know that we are of the truth, and

---

possess in order to secure the eternal inheritance. Nor do we find that it is laid down as impossible that a man should ever fall from a condition of acceptance into one of reprobation. And, therefore, we have others teaching (*b*) that assurance means *assurance of present salvation*. It is possible to fall from grace given. But the comfortable assurance of acceptance with God at the present moment is sufficient proof that we possess it. We only need to guard the precious deposit, to live in a continual sense of Divine favour and forgiveness, to accept the blessed truth that we are justified by the merits and blood of the Redeemer, to cling to Him as our only Saviour, to

can assure (or persuade) ourselves that we are in Him. If our heart accuse us of not loving in deed and in truth, we may be sure that God knows it better than we ourselves; nay, we know it *because* He knew it first. If we desire to have boldness in the day of judgment, let us be careful to have "a conscience void of offence against God and man" (cf. also Rom. ii. 15, 16). Again, it is a question whether the Apostle would speak of our heart as "condemning" (or "accusing," since the word used refers to the verdict of conscience) us, if its witness were to the effect that, in spite of numerous falls through weakness, the main purpose and effort of our lives was to serve God. It is at least hardly conceivable, if such a limited form of accusation were meant, that some words should not have been added to show the restricted sense in which this self-accusation was spoken of. "If our heart accuse us of occasional falls, yet in consideration of the steadfast purpose of our whole lives, we may believe that God will overlook our transgressions." The weighty authority against this interpretation, including most of the best later commentators, as Haupt, Dr. Westcott, and Mr. Plummer is frankly acknowledged. I would, however, ask the student to ponder the words of Dean Alford, "the ἐὰν καταγινώσκῃ and the ἐὰν μὴ καταγινώσκῃ are *plainly and necessarily opposed*, both in hypothesis and in result."

---

depend upon Him for grace here and glory hereafter, and we shall remain to the end His faithful servants, and shall enter into the joy of our Lord. This, too, is true as far as it goes. The only question is whether Holy Writ anywhere gives us ground for believing that our sense of acceptance with God depends on any opinion we may entertain regarding our own condition, and not rather on certain obvious facts which of themselves bear testimony to the truth that we are in very truth reconciled to God.

III. THE TRUE TEST OF ASSURANCE. (*a.*) *Meaning of assurance in Scripture.* This word, on which so much has been built, only occurs

Once more, the Apostle tells us that we have boldness (παρρησία) toward God when our heart does not accuse us. Is it not a fair inference from his words that we cannot possess that παρρησία, which (chaps. ii. 28, iv. 17, v. 14) is one of the characteristics of the Christian life (cf. also Eph. iii. 12 and 1 Tim. iii. 13), when our heart does accuse us? Moreover, Mr. Plummer notices the "progress by means of opposites" so peculiar to this Epistle, as in chaps. i. 9, 10, ii. 10, 11, iii. 7, 8, iv. 2, 3. But if we make both these "opposites" refer to πείσομεν, and to denote different grounds for satisfaction with our own condition, we have in fact no "opposites" at all, but only different phases of the same condition. But the Apostle's manner compels us to regard these two sentences, like all the others, as in direct opposition. The heart that condemns is contrasted with the heart that does not condemn. A brief summary of the various interpretations of the passage is here appended. They depend upon two considerations; (1.) the proper rendering of πείσομεν, which may be construed with either of the two ὅτι's that follow, or be taken absolutely, as in the Authorised Version and Revised Version; (2.) the rendering of ὅτι in each case, which may either be a conjunction or a relative pronoun, and may also either be translated "because" or "that." We have thus the

---

seven times in all, in the English Bible. Add to this the fact that the verb *assure* only occurs in the present passage, and the particle *assured*, three times, and we have at least ground for the assertion that the "doctrine of assurance" has been given a prominence in some modern theology to which, whether it be entitled to it or not, it does not receive in Holy Writ. Add again (1) that here it is πείθω (persuade) which is translated "assure," and that the word "assurance" is usually the translation of the Greek πληροφορία, implying a full persuasion of some truth, and (2) that assurance is described by Isaiah as "the *effect of righteousness.*" It is, moreover, used in con-

following alternative renderings: (1.) *We persuade our heart* (or *hearts*) *that if our hearts condemn us, we persuade them, I say, that God is greater than our heart.* (2.) *We persuade ourselves in whatever* (ὅτι being taken as a pronoun) *our heart condemn us, that,* &c. (The objection to this is that this is a somewhat strained rendering of ὅτι and gives two accusatives to πείσομεν.) (3.) *We persuade our heart . . . because if our heart condemn us, because, I say, God is greater,* &c. (4.) *We persuade our hearts in whatever our heart condemn us, because,* &c. (5.) *In whatever our heart condemn us, we persuade our heart that God is greater,* &c. (These two renderings also put a forced construction on ὅτι.) (6.) *We quiet our heart, because, if our heart condemn us, because, I say, God is greater,* &c. (7.) *We quiet our heart, whereinsoever our heart accuse us* (would ἡ καρδία not have been repeated were this the true rendering?), *because God is greater,* &c. This is the rendering of Dr. Westcott and the Revised Version. An 8th rendering is still possible. *We quiet our heart, on whatever point our heart may accuse us, by the thought that,* &c. The 9th rendering has been given above; " We shall assure our hearts before Him. Because if our heart condemn us it is because God is greater than our heart and knoweth all things." It is when our heart does *not* condemn us that we can have boldness in the sight of God. The words,

---

nection with *understanding* (Col. ii. 2), hope (Heb. vi. 11), and faith (x. 22). And in 1 Thess. i. 5 the Gospel is said to have come "in much assurance." In none of these cases is the word used of the assurance of the final salvation of the individual, but simply of the firm conviction and persuasion of the certainty of the things revealed.

(*b.*) *What is meant by acceptance?* The being "in Christ." We are accepted not "on account of," but "in," the "beloved One." We are asked to "examine ourselves" and "prove (or rather *test*) ourselves," whether we are "in the faith." And this is further explained by the words, "Know ye not that Jesus Christ is in you,

"God is greater than our heart and knoweth all things" seem to corroborate slightly the view taken above. For καταγινώσκω must be taken in the sense of knowing something against oneself. The proposition that God knows all things may not unnaturally be taken to imply that whatever we know God knows also. Had St. John intended to oppose God's knowledge to ours, he must surely have used some word signifying acquittal, much as he says in ch. ii. 1, "If any man sin, we have a Paraclete with the Father, Jesus Christ the Righteous One, and He is the propitiation for our sins."

VER. 21.—**Beloved.** The earnestness of this commencement would seem still further to indicate the opposition between this verse and the last. It is introduced like the words "little children," to mark an appeal of special solemnity. "Beloved, let not this be the case with us. Let us seek to avoid the curse of an accusing conscience. Thus, and thus only, can we secure boldness before God."—**if our heart condemn us not, then have we confidence toward God.** For παρρησία, see ch. ii. 28. The idea here is not, however, as in chaps. ii. 28 and iv. 17, of boldness in the day of judgment, but as in ch. v. 14, Rom. v. 1, and elsewhere, of *present* confidence. We may believe that a man's heart may tell him that as regards his aims and principles, his object is

---

except ye be ἀδόκιμοι (*i.e.*, men who have not stood the test)!" But they who are in Christ must display some proof of His presence within. He cannot be in any heart in which no signs of His presence appear. Consequently the only true token of assurance is *holiness*. The sense of pardon, of forgiveness, of peace is necessary to start with. We can make no progress in God's favour until we know that we are reconciled to Him. But that sense of His favour is a delusive one, unless we display the fact of reconciliation in a *reconciled life*. There is indeed "no condemnation to them that are in Christ Jesus." But we must finish the text. They that are in Christ Jesus "walk not

to do the will of God. But his failures cannot but make him uneasy, as showing that at present, at least, he cannot feel so full a confidence as he could wish. So far as his heart *does* condemn him, so far his heart must fail him. And thus the passage becomes a fresh incentive to loving, "not in word and in tongue, but in deed and in truth." "Towards God," implies the attitude of the believer, looking towards God, and walking towards Him, while the attitude of the unbeliever is spoken of as turning away from God. Before leaving this verse, we ought to remark on St. John's use of καρδία. It is used as equivalent to St. Paul's συνείδησις, a word which does not occur in St. John, save in the doubtful passage in ch. viii. of his Gospel. St. John uses it in the sense in which the Hebrew word for heart is used, not, as in ordinary English, as indicating the seat of the affections, but of the moral discernment. And this sense has passed over into English theological terminology.

VER. 22.—**And whatsoever we ask, we receive of him.** Literally, *from* Him. Observe the presents, as indicating the continuity of the condition spoken of. It is the normal condition of the believer to receive what he asks, unless he asks amiss, Matt. vii. 7, 8; John xiv, 13, xvi. 23, 24. This is only one instance among many of the way in which St. John's mind is saturated with his

---

after the flesh, but after the Spirit, because the law of the Spirit of life hath made them free from the law of sin and of death" (Rom. viii. 1, 2). And thus we can lay down no theory that the sense of reconciliation, pardon, and peace *will* produce the likeness of the Son of God. We want the evidence of the fact that it *has* produced it. Otherwise it was no true sense of pardon and reconciliation, no true peace. "In this we shall know (see Exposition) that we are of the truth. . . . If our heart condemn us not, we have confidence towards God." "In this we know that He abideth in us, from our possession of (ἐκ) the Spirit that He hath given us."

Master's teaching. Haupt connects this verse with the former by saying that the idea of boldness in speech is contained in the word παρρησία, and that the having our prayers answered is at once a cause and a consequence of this παρρησία. See also ch. v. 14, 15.—**because we keep his commandments, and do those things that are pleasing in his sight.** This verse may either indicate the ground on which our petitions are granted, *i.e.*, our doing what God commands may assure us that we shall receive what we ask, or it may explain to us the means whereby we receive it. In point of fact both these views are included. Not that our obeying God's commands gives us any merit in His sight, so that we might demand as a right that He should grant our requests, but that the condition of obedience is an essential pre-requisite for our reception of God's blessings. A disobedient spirit dams up, turns back, the flood of Divine favour ever flowing towards us. We raise up by disobedience a barrier which shuts out every Divine blessing. Obedience, on the contrary, the setting our hearts to follow the impulses of the Holy Spirit, also opens our heart to all the blessings He has to give. And, besides, he who sets himself to do what God pleases will also ask what He wills. And if he asks what God wills, he may be sure his petitions will be granted. The Roman Catholic

---

VERS. 20, 21.—*The witness of conscience.*

I. THAT WITNESS MAY BE TRUSTED. To that witness St. Paul never failed to appeal. He evidently regarded its verdict as decisive. See Rom. ix. 1 ; 2 Cor. i. 12, iv. 2 ; 1 Tim. i, 5, 19, iii. 9 ; 2 Tim. i. 3; cf. Heb. x. 2, 22. Even when it is mistaken, its verdict is to be accepted, as long as that verdict is given. See Rom. xiv. 23 ; 1 Cor viii. 12, x. 28, 29.

II. CONSCIENCE IS THE VOICE OF GOD'S HOLY SPIRIT. So we learn from Rom. ix. 1. It may sometimes be ill-formed and over-scrupulous, by reason of our infirmity. But that is no fault in the

expositors here characteristically make a distinction between *precepts* and *evangelical counsels*. There is this much soundness in their interpretation, that to do what is pleasing in God's sight involves a higher standard of spiritual excellence than to obey a precept directly delivered. Where the mistake in this kind of distinction lies is in supposing that we are not all equally bound to strive after the higher grace, to seek to find out what God loves, as well as to do simply what He commands. See also next note.

VER. 23.—**And this is his commandment, that we should believe on the name of his Son Jesus Christ.** The expression here is remarkable. In fact, it occurs nowhere else. Instead of πιστεύειν εἰς τὸ ὄνομα we have πιστεύειν τῷ ὀνόματι. The one expression conveys the idea of approach towards, rest upon, the name of Christ. The other suggests a notion equally familiar to the Christian, that is, trusting *to* Christ, looking to Him as the source of every good. Here we have the *first mention of faith* in this Epistle. From henceforth the idea is frequently introduced. It is frequently supposed that St. John is the Apostle of love and St. Paul of faith. The very converse of this might as readily be asserted. From John i. 12, and iii. 15 onward, we can see that faith in Jesus Christ is as much the foundation of the Christian life

---

voice itself, but only of the medium, our own corruption, through which it reaches us. But whatever it is, if faithfully followed, it leads to the perfect light. If resisted, such resistance issues in darkness. See Eph. iv. 21, 1 Thess. v. 19.

III. WHETHER IT ACCUSE OR ACQUIT, WE MUST HEAR IT. Cf. Rom. ii. 15. Here we are told (*a*) that if our heart condemn us, there is One above who cannot fail to see what we see ourselves, because He has shown it to us. If we feel that we have come short of the law of love, we know that we have come short, just so far, of Him whose law it is, and by whose abiding we have learned it. Only when our

with St. John as it is with St. Paul, while love (unfortunately translated *charity* very often in St. Paul's Epistles) is absent from no single one of his writings, and is the subject of a panegyric in 1 Cor. xiii. which throws into the shade even St. John's emphatic declarations of the necessity of love. Faith in Christ's name, of course, is faith in Himself, "in his self-manifestation" (Haupt) "as the Son of God and the Saviour of the world." And we learn here that the one indispensable condition of doing God's will is to believe His Son. Men are now laying down other principles to ensure excellence. They declare that they can be as moral, as self-sacrificing, as thoroughly admirable in every relation of life, without Christ as with Him. But there is always something lacking in lives like these. Admirable as they are in many ways (and their excellence, little as the truth is recognised, is due to faith, such as that faith is) they are on a lower level than the lives of Christian men. Saintliness, holiness, are words that cannot be used of such lives. The sense of a divine consecration is absent. Here, as elsewhere, it is true that "the first man is of the earth, earthy; the second man is the Lord from heaven." But before we can rise to the true level of human excellence, we must bring ourselves to the foot of the Cross, and there, in adoring love, look up for in-

---

heart acquits us of any breaches of that law, can we have confidence towards God. When, as is most frequently the case, our heart tells us that we have tried to keep that law, but in many instances we have failed, we must realise the truth that in Christ is all forgiveness, all love, all strength, "all the fulness of the Godhead bodily." And we must set ourselves once again to fulfil that law more thoroughly. And then we have forgiveness, and once more we venture to feel "confidence towards God."

VER. 22.—"*Whatsoever we ask, we receive of him.*"
The special idea here is the strength to fulfil the law which He has

spiration to the absolute surrender of His whole being to God's will, which made the death of Christ the propitiation for the sins of the whole world. There is a question whether we should read πιστεύωμεν or πιστεύσωμεν here. Both are well supported, but the former is more likely to have been a correction than the latter a mistake. A copyist, seeing ἀγαπῶμεν in the latter part of the verse, might have supposed that the former verb ought to correspond to it. Yet πιστεύωμεν, it must be confessed, yields the best sense. Faith, like love, ought to be an abiding principle of the spiritual life (1 Cor. xiii. 13). But if we read the aorist here, we are led rather to the initial resolution of the soul, which gave its direction to the whole future life. Ebrard well remarks here, "St. John sums up the multitude of the ἐντολαί in the unity of the one ἐντολή. Of the legalist character stamped upon the Romish theology and Church he knows nothing. Even the 'believing in Christ' and 'loving one another,' are not to him two commandments but only one; because where there is genuine and living faith, there must be love, as certainly as with the sun there must be light." We will lastly ask how this believing Christ can be said to be His commandment? The answer will be found in John iii. 16, vi. 29, 35, 38, xi. 25, 26.—**and love one another, as he gave us commandment.** Rather, *according as*.

---

set before us. It is, however, true that the general includes the special.

I. WHATEVER WE ASK ACCORDING TO GOD'S WILL, WILL BE GIVEN US. See Matt. vii. 7, xxi. 22; Luke xviii. 1; John xiv. 13, 14, xv. 7, 16, xvi. 23, 34.

II. THIS PROMISE IS CONFINED TO HIS TRUE DISCIPLES. It is addressed to those who "believe in Him," John xiv. 12; to His "friends," xv. 15. And this is implied in the Sermon on the Mount, which is addressed to those who were ready to become His disciples.

III. WHO ARE HIS TRUE DISCIPLES? Those whose heart "con-

Faith, says St. Paul, worketh (or is put in action—ἐνεργεῖ) by love. The two commandments are inseparable. For belief in Christ is no mere abstract opinion concerning His Godhead. Neither is it any persuasion that our future salvation is secured. Nor is it even an intellectual and moral acceptance of the perfect satisfaction made to the Father for our sins upon the Cross. It is faith *in Him*. It is reliance on Him as the source of all goodness and holiness. It is confidence that He will free us from all the power of sin, and re-create us in the image of Himself. It is the putting ourselves *en rapport* with His Nature and the influences ever proceeding from Him. Thus a life of love is the necessary result of belief in Him Who is love and Who is necessarily in conflict with every unloving deed, word or thought. The Apostle postpones the further consideration of faith to ch. v. He has before this led us to Christ, the *object* of faith. What he here presses upon us is the public confession (ὁμολογία) of Christ. And (see next verse) he lays stress on the inward and spiritual origin of this ὁμολογία. It is not until this correspondence between the inner motive and its outward expression is sufficiently insisted upon, that he recurs to faith as the link of connection between the individual and the spiritual forces that encompass him. It is here that St. John first definitely

---

demns them not" (see last verse). Those who "do what He commands them" (John xv. 14, 15, cf. Matt. xii. 50). Those who "walk not after the flesh but after the Spirit." Those over whom sin has not dominion (Rom. vi. 14). Those who keep His commandment, and do those things that are pleasing in His sight. This finally and irrevocably. Initially and increasingly those who, "forgetting the things that are behind, and reaching forth unto the things that are before, press toward the mark for the prize of the high calling that is in Christ Jesus" (Phil. iii. 13, 14).

explains what he means by the "new commandment" in ch. ii. 8. We might there have inferred his meaning from the context. Here it is clearly stated. See notes on ch. ii. 7, 8.

VER. 24.—**And he that keepeth his commandments dwelleth in him and he in him.** For "dwelleth" we should once more render "abideth." See note on ch. ii. 3. St. John here would impress on us the true indication of our being in Christ. The keeping God's commandments is not the *cause*, it is the result and external manifestation of the fact of Christ's indwelling. (It may be remarked in passing that the word *indwelling* has come to be used from the Authorised Version in this and other passages; but, though not unscriptural—see Rom. viii. 9, 11; 1 Cor. iii. 16—it does not, at first sight, express the exact idea of μένει, which signifies *abiding, remaining*, rather than dwelling, and involves the idea, not merely of inhabitation, but of the closest and most permanent union. But it is true, nevertheless, that the word indwelling has come in many minds to have the meaning which has just been indicated.) If the question be asked whether the Father or the Son be here meant by αὐτός, we may refer the inquirer to ch. v. 20, and more especially to ch. ii. 23, 24.—**and hereby we know that he abideth in us, by the Spirit that he hath given us.** Literally,

---

VER. 24—*Another test of acceptance. The possession of the gift of the Spirit.*

This and the preceding verse carry on the same line of thought as in ii. 3, 10, iii. 14, 19. The homiletic notes to be found on those pages will suggest a similar line of treatment here. But one or two additional points suggest themselves.

I. THE SPIRIT THUS GIVEN IS THE SPIRIT OF CHRIST. So He is called in Rom. viii. 9; Gal. iv. 6; Phil. i. 19; 1 Pet. i. 11. Not as receiving His being originally from Christ. The Father is the source of *all* life, created or Divine. But as *partaking* of the being of Christ

in this, not *hereby*. See ch. ii. 3, 5, iii. 10, 16, 19. It may not be amiss to notice that there are here four signs of the presence of the new life in the heart: (1) obedience, (2) the doing of righteousness, (3) the loving in deed and not in word only, (4) the possession of the Spirit. The fifth ἐν τούτῳ (in ch. iii. 16) relates not to the signs of the presence of the new life in us, but to the life of Christ as the manifestation of love. ἐκ τοῦ Πνεύματος implies that the Spirit is the source of the knowledge. Dr. Westcott remarks that neither in St. John's Epistles nor in the Apocalypse does St. John apply the epithet "holy" to the Spirit. 1 John v. 7 is, of course, not genuine. See notes there. The expression, though it is to be found, is by no means common in St. John's Gospel. This may be regarded as a slight indication of the common authorship of the three books. ἔδωκεν should not be translated "hath given," but "gave" us. The Apostle refers to the moment when each one of us entered into fellowship with God, and into covenant with His Son, *i.e.*, in all ordinary cases, our baptism (see John iii. 5). St. John here, as his manner is (see notes on chaps. ii. 28, 29, iii. 10, 19), prepares for a new section of the Epistle. In connection with our Lord's declaration in John xiv. 15, the new idea which he here introduces is the gift of the Spirit, which is expanded in the next chapter. Thus we

---

(John xvi. 14), as given or sent by Christ (John xv. 26, xx. 22; Acts ii. 33). See also John iii. 34. We cannot say here with certainty whether the Spirit be called the Spirit of God or of Christ. But as we have before stated the doctrine of the inseparable unity between the Father and the Son, there can be little doubt that the Spirit is here regarded as the Spirit of both. How could it be otherwise? The Son is the revelation of the Father. The Divine Spirit must, therefore, be the Spirit both of the Father and of the Son.

II. HIS WORK IS TO BRING ABOUT IN US THE LIKENESS TO GOD. See Rom. viii. 1-30, where the work of the Spirit is shown to lead up

have the whole scheme of salvation before us; the Father loving us, and sending His Son to be a propitiation for our sins; the Son making satisfaction for sin, fulfilling all righteousness, pleading our cause, and coming to abide in our hearts; the Spirit sent forth from Him to be the power and influence which transforms us from the likeness of sin into the likeness of the Saviour; faith as the disposition of our hearts which brings us within the sphere of the Saviour's influence; obedience the test of fellowship with Him; love the result of His close and enduring union with us. This is the good tidings Christ came from heaven to proclaim. This is the Gospel which is, or should be, preached in His name to all the world.

---

to our being conformed to the image of Jesus Christ, 2 Cor. iii. 18; Eph. iv. 21-24 (with which compare Titus iii. 5, 6, as well as John iii. 5; also John vi. 63). He not only gives life, but *is life*. Rom. viii. 2, 10 (cf. John. xi. 25, xiv. 6); 1 Cor. ii. 11, 12; Eph. ii. 22; 2 Thess. ii. 13. And the practical test whereby we know that Jesus Christ abideth in us is the presence of His Spirit in the heart. A tree is known by its fruits. So is the Christian in whose heart Christ abides, by the fruits of the Spirit (Gal. v. 22, 23).

XX.

SPIRITUAL INFLUENCE.

CH. iv. 1.—As we have seen (iii. 24), St. John, as usual, at the end of one section of his Epistle, brings in the leading thought of the next. The dominant idea of the present section (vers. 1–14) is *spiritual influence*, either Divine or antichristian. As before we have had the antagonism between light and darkness, the duty of obedience, the antagonism between the world and the Church, the need of righteousness, the fact that all righteousness is summed up in love, so here we are told of the *enabling power* by which alone we can do what God's revelation in Christ requires—the Spirit of God. The deep inner agreement between St. Paul and St. John has not unfrequently been pointed out in these pages. Another remarkable instance occurs here. As

---

HOMILETICS.

VER. 1.—*The duty of testing the spirits.*
I. THE FAITH OF THE CHRISTIAN RESTS UPON INWARD CONVICTION, NOT ON ANY LIVING OUTWARD AUTHORITY.
 1. *Scripture proof of this.* (*a.*) We are commanded by more than one Apostle to test the doctrines delivered to us. See 1 Thess. v. 21. Also 1 Cor. ii. 10, 14, 15, and x. 15. (*b.*) The foundation of our faith is declared to be such. John vi. 45, xiv. 26, xvi. 13; Eph. ii. 18, iv. 21; 1. Thess. iv. 9; Heb. viii. 10, 11; 1 John ii. 27. Also Rom. xiv. 6; Col. ii. 2; 1 Thess. i. 5.
 2. *The occasions on which the Apostles spoke with authority of their*

St. Paul places in the forefront of his most elaborately doctrinal Epistle the fact that the Gospel is the "power of God unto salvation" (Rom. i. 16), so St. John here leads us to the source of that inner strength (see especially ver. 4) whereby we are enabled to do that which God seeks from us.

VER. 1.—**Beloved, believe not every spirit.** We may observe here the tenderness of the true Christian mind. When the Apostles of Christ desire specially to enforce upon those committed to their charge any particular truth, their language assumes a peculiar gentleness; ἀδελφοί, ἀγαπητοί, and the like, are the expressions that fall naturally from their lips. We have grown used to them. But they must have had a strange charm for those to whom they were altogether new. See chaps. ii. 7, iii. 2, 21, and ver. 11. The word here gives point to the affectionate urgency with which St. John would warn the brotherhood not to trust implicitly to every utterance which may seem to be of spiritual origin, but to remember that there are spiritual utterances which come from God, and spiritual utterances which come from God's adversary, and that it is the duty of all to test such utterances, so as to know whence they are. It will be observed that we have spoken here of spiritual *utterances*. It is in that sense that the word πνεῦμα in this passage,

---

own had to do with minor matters. The Gospel they had to deliver was intrusted to them from above. See 1 Cor. ix. 16; Gal. i. 8, 9. Over that they had no power. It was God's message. They could neither add to it nor subtract from it. See also Eph. iii. 2, 3; Col. i. 25; 1 Tim. i. 11. But St. Paul does speak of his authority in the *application* of the principles of the Gospel, as in 1 Cor. v. 3, vii. 12, 25, 40, xiv. 37, and 2 Cor. x. 8, &c.

3. *The external authority of the faith is that it was "once for all delivered to the saints"* (Jude 3). There is but one faith. And it is what "we have heard from the beginning" (ch. ii. 24). It is the same for all time. Its value for us depends on the fact that Christ taught

SPIRITUAL INFLUENCE. 289

whether in the singular or plural, is to be understood. We know, from 1 Cor. xiv., that spiritual manifestations were common in the Apostolic Church, and that the prophets were supposed to speak under spiritual influence (observe in this connection the collocation of prophecy and spiritual agency or influence in 1 Cor. xii. 10, xiv. 32, 37; and 1 Pet. i. 10–12). What the Apostle here means then is (and the expression ψευδοπροφῆται confirms this view) that every person speaking under spiritual influence is not, therefore, to be believed. There are false revelations as well as true ones (and the number of these magical pretenders in the early ages of Christianity from Simon Magus downwards was very great), and he would have men understand that there exist certain objective tests whereby the true and false revelations may be distinguished. What those tests were, the Apostle tells us in ver. 2.—**but try the spirits, whether they are of God.** The Revised Version here goes back to the rendering of all the chief early English translators from Wiclif downwards, and translates *prove*. But the Authorised Version has hit upon quite as good a word. The modern English *test* is perhaps nearest to the original. It is remarkable that even the Jesuit commentator Estius is compelled to admit that this duty of testing the truth of doctrine is not to be confined to those who are

---

it. But it is for the conscience of man to respond to what is thus received.

II. YET OUTWARD AUTHORITY HAS ITS OWN FUNCTION IN THE CHURCH OF GOD. What that function is may be deduced from the preceding head. It deals, not with the truths of Christianity itself, but with rules and ordinances, which touch, not the essence of the Church's life, but its details. Thus, when any authority claims to define doctrines, we are bound to test its decisions by the Scriptures. In Gal. i. 8, 9 (above cited), we learn that no new revelation can be made. The original revelation may be explained where necessary, as at the Council of Nicæa. But it cannot be added to. And while, on the

T

commissioned to teach, but that it extends to the whole body of the faithful. With this passage we may compare St. Paul's teaching in 1 Cor. xii. 10 (above cited), and also how in his very first Epistle he urges upon believers just newly fledged the duty (1) of paying attention to spiritual utterances, (2) of holding them in due reverence, and (3) of *testing* them (1 Thess. v. 19-21). Mr. Plummer has remarked on the large number of different English words by which δοκιμάζειν is translated in the Authorised Version, a variety which tends to obscure the homogeneous character of New Testament teaching. —**because many false prophets are gone out into the world.** With this we may compare chapter xi. of the recently discovered "Doctrine of the Twelve Apostles," where several tests are given whereby the false prophet may be distinguished from the true one. Among them are a mercenary spirit and inconsistency of life. The word translated "gone out" has caused some little difficulty. It is not ἐληλύθασιν but ἐξεληλύθασιν—"gone out *from*." From what? Not "from us," as in ch. ii. 19, but from Antichrist, who is mentioned in ver. 3. As we shall see presently, St. John traces all the "spirits" that are in

---

one hand, the conscience of the individual, when opposed to the general conviction, is likely to be wrong, it cannot be assumed of necessity that it is so. Too many instances exist in the history of the Church of *Athanasius contra mundum*,—of some man of extraordinary spiritual insight discerning the importance of some truth which other men have been incapable of recognising, to allow us to admit as a safe principle that we must all, in every case, bow to the voice either of authority or of the majority. To be in a minority should teach us caution. But it does not bind us to absolute submission. We must "try the spirits," and though we must approach every question in a spirit of humility (this, too, is a "spirit" in reference to which we must "try" ourselves), yet we are bound to believe nothing which does not approve itself to our conscience as true.

III. THE TRUE LIMITS OF OUTWARD AUTHORITY. We find this question fully discussed in Hooker's "Ecclesiastical Polity," and espe-

the world to two sources, the "spirit of truth and the spirit of error" (ver. 6), *i.e.*, God and the evil one. The words "into the world" imply the *variety* of their action. This was true of the Apostolic age, when the spirit of error assumed various forms. And it is true still. Error is hydra-headed. It takes shapes the most various and diverse. But the truth is one, because He in whom it inheres is One.

VER. 2.—**Hereby know ye the Spirit of God.** Literally *in this*. The words are very characteristic of this Epistle, from ch. ii. 3 onward. In the English and Greek alike the form of the sentence is ambiguous. It is impossible to say positively whether "know ye" is indicative or imperative. The first gives the best sense, and agrees with the Apostle's *usus loquendi* elsewhere (see chaps. ii. 5, iii. 10, &c.) Nor does the fact that the person is changed here to the second give any just ground why we should contend for the imperative sense here. The next words fall in better with the indicative than the imperative rendering, though they are compatible with either.—**Every spirit that confesseth that Jesus Christ is come in the flesh is of God.** It is to be observed that

---

cially its general principles laid down in Book I. Every society must have its rules. And these rules are binding upon its members. So are the rules laid down by authority in the Church, unless they are clearly contrary to the first principles of Christianity. Even here we must "try the spirits." Our conscience must be satisfied that there is nothing wrong in principle in these rules. But we must not, as is often done, mistake our self-will for our conscience. And if the inconsistency of rules with first principles be not clearly shown, we must not set ourselves against them.

IV. BY WHAT TEST ARE WE TO TRY THE SPIRITS? One test only is given here—the confession of Jesus Christ come in flesh; in other words, the doctrine, or rather truth, or fact, of the Incarnation. But as this is not the whole Gospel, we are bound to extend it to the whole Gospel, *i.e.*, the message delivered with one mouth by the Apostles of Christ, enshrined in the creeds and contained in the sacred Scriptures.

the Christian life has two sides, the inward and the outward. Of the first *faith* is the essential characteristic, of the latter *confession*. The first determines the relation of man to God, the latter his relation to his fellow-men. And the Christian life of necessity passes from the inward to the outward, from the vital union of the soul with God to external brotherhood with those who are similarly united to Him. Thus ὁμολογία—public confession of discipleship of Christ—is the necessary consequence of a genuine faith. Therefore St. John in this Epistle lays stress on it (see ch. ii. 23, and ver. 15 of this chapter). St. Paul does not often mention it, though we have it in Rom. x. 9, 10. It occurs several times in the Epistle to the Hebrews. But it depends on the emphatic words of our Lord in Matt. x. 32 (cf. Luke xii. 8), which are reflected in this Epistle. The confession lies at the root of the Christian sacraments, and is involved in the very idea of a visible Church. Next we have to consider how the words Ἰησοῦν Χριστὸν ἐν σαρκὶ ἐληλυθότα are to be taken. They may be taken in three ways: (1) confesseth "that Jesus is Christ come in flesh," or (2) "that Jesus Christ," the man known to men

---

V. THERE ARE MANY ERRORS ABROAD. St. John warns the Christians of his day against error. The warning is equally necessary now. It needs not to specify instances. But it may be remarked that they fall under four heads: (1) traditional corruptions of the faith, whether in a Roman or a Protestant direction; (2) new revelations, such as Swedenborgianism, Irvingism, or Mormonism; (3) neglect or exaggeration of portions of revealed truth, such as has often led to the formation of sects; and (4) denial of all revelation, as in the various forms of infidelity.

VERS. 2, 3.—*The spirit of Antichrist.*

We have already referred to one aspect of this subject in our notes on chapter ii. There the special point singled out for notice was that Antichrist means the rejection of Christ. We proceed to notice other characteristics of Antichrist brought before us in this passage. We notice:—

by name as Jesus, and acknowledged by them as Christ, "has actually come in flesh" (so Authorised Version and Revised Version), or (3) confesseth "Jesus Christ come in flesh," connecting the whole phrase with the confession. Professor Westcott is, on the whole, in favour of (3). But it is possible, considering that the whole point of every one of the Gnostic sects consisted in the denial of the possibility of God's uniting Himself to a material body, and that one sect after another insisted upon making a distinction between the Aeon Christ and the man Jesus, that St. John here desires (1) to point out that Jesus and Christ are one inseparable Person, and (2) that this Person has actually appeared in fleshly shape. Cf. St. Paul's phrase in Col. ii. 9, where he definitely asserts that the whole Pleroma, *i.e.*, the whole circle of Divine powers and attributes, were manifested in Jesus Christ *in bodily form*. If this view be correct, the second of the two interpretations, which, as we have seen, has the sanction of our Revisers, is to be preferred. As Ebrard remarks, the interpretation "come *unto* (or *into*) flesh," which some have suggested, is inadmissible, were it only on the ground that St. John thought in Hebrew, and

---

I. THE RELATION BETWEEN ANTICHRIST AND THE MAN OF SIN. Antichrist, we are told (1) rejects Christ, (2) denies the Father and the Son, (3) denies that Jesus Christ has come in flesh. The man of sin (1) assumes to himself Divine honours (2 Thess. ii. 4), (2) denies the claim of any other being than himself to be Divine, (3) sets himself against the law of God (ὁ ἄνομος). Whether these two descriptions can be reconciled in every respect is not perfectly certain. But there appears no absolutely conclusive reason why they should not apply to the same person. For to assume Divine honours is to deny Christ, and to deny Him is to deny the Father who sent Him; and denial of Him involves rejection of His law.

II. THE SIGNS OF THE ANTICHRISTIAN TENDENCY. If, as seems at least highly probable, Antichrist and the man of sin are to be regarded as one and the same person, we have the almost Divine honours paid to the Pope as one sign of the antichristian tendency.

that in Hebrew the prepositions signifying *in* and *unto* are not interchangeable. This, then, was the test of all spiritual revelations. They must accept as a starting-point the fact of the Incarnation; the fact that Jesus Christ was *one Person*, and that this Person had manifested the Godhead to the world in our mortal flesh. To deny this, is to deny the fundamental verity of the Gospel. There could be no redemption for humanity until God had sanctified and perfected our mortal flesh by taking it into union with Himself. Nor are we able even to conceive of Him aright, save through His image, namely, perfect man. We may compare St. Paul's language in 1 Cor. xii. 3. But it is much less definite. We should not fail to observe the perfect. Christ *has* come. This is an "abiding fact" (Westcott). He not merely came once to the world and left it again, but He abides in it still, by His Spirit. And by flesh is meant simply the material of which our bodies are composed. The Gnostics denied that the Deity could be united to matter, which they believed to be essentially alien to the Divinity. And so they denied the perfect manhood of the Son of God. The Apostle asserts, on the contrary, that

---

"Every pope," says the late Bishop of Lincoln, "on his election is carried into the principal church at Rome, his cathedral, St. Peter's. He is there lifted up by the cardinals, and is placed on the high altar. When there placed, and sitting in the church of God, on the altar of God, he is *adored* by them *kneeling* before him, and kissing his feet." This act, the Bishop further says, is expressly called "the adoration." He has lately (1870) been credited with personal infallibility, so that, at least when he speaks as the mouthpiece of the Church, his utterances demand the assent of the faithful, whether they be utterly contrary to the whole historical development of Christianity or not.[1] This,

[1] Roman controversialists will declare that it is impossible that the Pope could decree anything contrary to the historical development of Christianity. But this is little to the purpose, because it is a pure assumption. And some of the Infallibilists were rejoiced at the Vatican decrees, because they enabled them to set all historical inquiry aside.

He condescended to be "born of the flesh," that we through Him might be "born of the Spirit" (John iii. 5, 6).

VER. 3.—**And every spirit that confesseth not that Jesus Christ is come in the flesh is not of God.** First of all, we may remark that the true reading here is *confesseth not Jesus is not of God.* The rest has evidently been added, as is so often the case in the later MSS., to make this passage agree with the last. This had, in the present case, already been done when the Codex Sinaiticus was written. But, as Mr. Plummer remarks, St. John's antitheses are seldom verbally complete. See chaps. i. 5, 6, 7, 8, 10, ii. 10, &c. Some very ancient Fathers read here ὃ λύει for ὃ μὴ ὁμολογεῖ. It is easy to see whence this reading originated. The teaching of St. John in ver. 2, as opposed to the Gnostic sects, is that Jesus Christ "is not two, but one Christ." Some early Father, Irenæus, most probably, in contending with the Gnostics, has paraphrased the passage, and substituted ὃ λύει for ὃ μὴ ὁμολογεῖ. We find the words in Irenæus' treatise against the Gnostic heretics. And it seems almost certain that, catching the drift of the Apostle's thought, he has substituted the one phrase for the other, and that hence the reading has been

---

too, almost amounts to a Divine prerogative. So also we find in Gratian's *Decretum* (a collection of canons for the Roman Church) the following:—" Satis evidenter ostenditur a sæculari potestate nec ligari prorsus nec solvi posse Pontificem, *quem* constat a pio Principe Constantino *Deum appellatum*, nec posse Deum ab hominibus judicari manifestum est" (Dist. 96, 97). But this, after all, is but the exhibition of a tendency. Christ is not, as yet, denied. Nor is his Incarnation denied. The full revelation of Antichrist will be one in which the autocratic tendency and the creature worship of the Roman Church will be supplemented by the rejection of Christ. For other signs, therefore, of that readiness to be revealed which we read of in 2 Thess. ii. 7, we must look to the opposite quarter. Not Agnosticism, for Antichrist claims for himself Divine honours. But rather, perhaps, in the direction of Positivism. Extremes meet, and a development of Romanism which ends in rejecting Christ, might coalesce with a creed which

introduced by some copyist into the text. But it is clear that it is a gloss, not the real text of the Epistle. Not to confess Christ as come in flesh *is* to dissolve Him, to divide Him into two. And in this way it comes to pass that Tertullian and Origen (in the Latin translation, however, be it observed, of his works), following Irenæus, have so paraphrased the words. But, with the single exception of the Vulgate (which Wiclif follows in his translation *fordoith*), not only *no Greek MS.*, but no version, and no Greek Father, has this reading, with the single exception of Socrates, the ecclesiastical historian, who charges Nestorius with being wilfully ignorant that it was the reading of the older copies, and affirms that the text had been tampered with for doctrinal purposes. Though the words " come in flesh " are not found in the text, they must of course be mentally supplied. To deny His indissoluble union in one Person with the Godhead is to deny Jesus Himself. If He were not God manifest in the flesh He was a crucified man and nothing more. He was no longer the Jesus whom the Apostles preached and on whom the disciples believed. Professor Westcott com-

---

desired some embodiment of the ideal of humanity, the only thing, we are told by some writers of our own age, which is really Divine.[1]

The restraints of civil society are no doubt the forces which hinder the development of such a power. But it is abundantly clear that it can still be said of the spirit of Antichrist, " even now already is it in the world."

VER. 4.—*The ground of the Christian's confidence.*

We have already spoken of the nature of Christian assurance. It needs not, therefore, that we go over that ground again. What is here

[1] This is the teaching of the advocates of Positivism, a creed of which Mr. Frederick Harrison is the prophet, and Mr. Swinburne the poet. In " Songs before Sunrise," by the latter, we read,

" But God, if a God there be, is the substance of men that is man."

And again,

" Glory to man in the highest, for man is the master of things."

But if we pursue our researches into Mr. Swinburne's poems, we shall find far better ground for the assertion that he is, very often, their slave. And we shall perchance be convinced that there is such a thing as " shame to man in the lowest " depths of moral degradation.

pares this passage with ch. iii. 10, and remarks that "the confession of the Incarnation embodied in the life must produce the effort after righteousness which finds its absolute spiritual support in the belief in the Incarnation." Nor is this all. Without the belief in the Incarnation, it would be impossible to "do righteousness." For the power to "do righteousness" comes to sinful man only through the fact that it *has been done;* that man has fulfilled the will of God. And until each man makes this truth his own by faith, until by faith he unites himself to Him by whom it has been done, the task remains for him an impossibility.—**and this is that spirit of antichrist, whereof ye have heard that it should come.** Most of the commentators supply "spirit of" here. But Dr. Westcott and Bishop Wordsworth, more correctly, would have the rendering more general, "this is the temper," or "tendency," or "character" of Antichrist. "The many spirits, the many forces, which reveal his action" (Westcott). That "it" and not "he," as the earlier translators render, is correct, appears from the neuter ὅ.—**and even now already is it in the world.** Better as Revised Version:

---

meant by confidence is the confidence of final victory. This springs, we are told, from faith (1) in God, and (2) in the fact that such a faith unites us to Him. It is derived from the belief that we are "of" and "in" God.

I. THE CHRISTIAN MAY HAVE COURAGE, BECAUSE HE IS OF GOD.

We proceed to inquire what is meant by being "of God," and what, therefore, is the nature of the confidence the Christian feels. There are false, as well as true conceptions of what is meant by a passage such as this, and therefore false, as well as true, grounds of confidence.

1. *Our confidence is not grounded in the past, but in the present.* There are those who suppose that they are to look back for their source of confidence. They look (*a*) to a *past act,* not to a *present Lord;* to a reconciliation worked out for them on the Cross, not to a translation of themselves, by Divine power, into the whole spirit and mind of that great act of Atonement, not to the interweaving, through

And now it is in the world already. The antichristian temper must be in the world, to pave the way for the advent of Antichrist himself.

VER. 4.—**Ye are of God, little children.** For τεκνία see ch. ii. 1. ὑμεῖς is of course emphatic. It opposes the faithful (1) to those who do not confess Jesus, (2) to the world and its ruler. See also note on ch. iii. 10.
—**And have overcome them,** *i.e.*, the false prophets, as displaying "spirits," which are "not of God." The Vulgate reads "eum," *i.e.*, Antichrist; and Wiclif therefore translates here by "him." The idea of conflict and victory, so marked in the Apocalypse, appears occasionally in this Epistle, though it is not brought forward with any degree of prominence until we come to the next chapter. It is, however, involved in the idea of the antagonism between light and darkness, between the children of God and the world, between Christ and the devil, of which we read so much here, and the idea comes from the declaration of Jesus Christ in John xvi. 33: "Be of good cheer, I have overcome the world." Some have compared the perfect here with its use in ch. ii. 13. But here it simply means that the disciples have

the Spirit of Christ, of that Crucifixion into the whole texture of their lives. And (*b*) they look to a past rather than to a present realisation of God's forgiveness and saving power, to a conviction of it once for all, rather than to an abiding conviction of the presence of the latter with them in every moment of temptation, of the former after every fall *truly repented of.*

2. *It is justified by present conduct.* We can do no more here than point to ver. 8. We cannot take to ourselves the promises of this verse, and ignore the explanation of those promises given immediately afterwards. We are only entitled to say "we are of God," if our heart tells us that we are living in love. Imperfectly as yet, no doubt, but still yearning after, striving after, pressing forward towards, more love, and ever reproaching ourselves and craving forgiveness for our past failures, as well as taking care that no unloving spirit is allowed to *remain* within us.

withstood the seductions of the false prophets.—**because greater is he that is in you than he that is in the world.** The fundamental fact of God's indwelling through Christ in all who believe in Him is the source of inner strength whereby all conflict is maintained and victory won. See Luke xi. 21, 22. "He that is in the world" can mean nothing but the devil, who is called the prince (John xii. 31, xiv. 30) and the god (2 Cor. iv. 4) of this world. Cf. also 1 Cor. ii. 12; Eph. ii. 2, vi. 12; Rev. ix. 3, 11. The reason why we have not "in them," as corresponding to "in you," is explained by the next sentence.

VER. 5.—**They are of the world.** Cf. ii. 16; iii. 8, 12, 19, and notes there. "Of the world" means *from* the world, both here, and in the next part of the verse. See also John xv. 19. The whole character and tone of thought of these false prophets and their followers derives its impress from that world which, though it was originally God's order, has rebelled against and overthrown that order, so that the only true description of it is to be found in the words "the whole world lieth in wickedness" (ch. v. 19); or rather, perhaps, "is exposed to the influence of the evil one."—**therefore**

---

3. *It is in God, not in ourselves.* That is to say, it rests entirely on the fact that God is able to save us in every temptation, if we only (1) trust Him implicitly, (2) offer ourselves to Him unreservedly. If we ever fail to overcome temptation, it is not because He cannot save us, but because we will not be saved. We can only trust ourselves to be "of God" when we know that our whole will and purpose is to obey His revealed will, to offer ourselves a continual sacrifice to Him.

II. THE CHRISTIAN HAS, IN ONE SENSE, ALREADY OVERCOME HIS ENEMIES.

The Apostle here has evidently a double meaning, relating (1) to the past (2) to the future. The first is indicated by the perfect tense, the second by the reference to the saving power of God. The first may be discussed here. In what sense can a Christian be said to "have overcome" his enemies? In this, that sin has no longer power over him, except by his voluntary consent thereto (Rom. vi. 14). Before his

speak they of the world, and the world heareth them. Rather *from the world, i.e.,* "from out of the worldly nature" (Ebrard). For the threefold repetition of the word *world,* cf. John iii. 31. But the idea there is of the capacity of seeing only what is visible. The idea here is of men under the influence of a power in opposition to God.

VER. 6.—**We are of God.** Cf. John xvii. 14. This is generally supposed to refer to teachers only. But it is a question whether, both here and in ver. 14, there is not at least a secondary reference to all Christians. Certainly they are all "of God," if there be anything genuine in their Christianity. And as every Christian is bound to "give a reason for the hope that is in him" (1 Peter iii. 15), many to whom the Gospel has not been formally preached by Christ's ministers, may have been able to "hear" the truth. So Calvin: "all who individually called by position and opportunity to bear witness their faith." The Apostle then first (ver. 4) addresses his flock. He next includes them in the same category with himself. See this question further discussed under

---

union with Christ he was under the power of sin. He had no certainty that he could resist it. But from the very moment that he consciously accepts his position as the servant of Christ, from the moment that he realises the power of God in Christ to save him from his sins and reconcile him to his Father, he has overcome the spirits of evil, at least so far as this, that he knows that he is no longer the helpless slave of his own passions, but that he may be their master if and when he wills to be so.

III. HIS TRUST FOR THE FUTURE IS NOT IN HIMSELF BUT IN THE POWER OF GOD.

There are various grounds of trust (1) in our conversion in times gone by, (2) in our progress and perseverance up to the present time, (3) in vague hopes of some possible interference of God on our behalf in the future. The only real ground of hope or confidence lies in our *present realisation* of God (1) as stronger than evil, and (2) as willing to save us from it. Relying on this we may go calmly on from day

ver. 14.—**He that knoweth God heareth us; he that is not of God heareth not us.** Cf. John viii. 47. The present γινώσκων implies a present condition of knowledge, but it neither implies that it is perfect, nor that this knowledge is incapable of being increased. The predestinarian question which Calvin and Düsterdieck force upon our text has really nothing to do with it. "The distinction between 'being of God' and 'not being of God' is a distinction, not of cause, but of result" (Ebrard). "How these two classes are what they are, it is not the purpose of this passage to set forth, nor need we here inquire" (Alford). But what *is* the question in this passage, and what it does not seem to have occurred to any commentator on this passage to inquire into, is this: what is meant by "knowing God" and being "not of God"? St. John in the next sentence shows that the "hearing," *i.e.*, accepting, Christian teaching and "hearing it not," are the tests whereby we may discern the "spirit of truth and the spirit of error." But he does not tell us in what the "knowing God" and the "not being of God" consist. It may be believed that the distinction consists in

---

to day, meeting temptations as they arise, fearing no harm that may happen to us in the future, offering our hearts to God every moment for His inspiration and guidance, firmly convinced that "greater is He that is in us than he that is in the world."

VERS. 5, 6.—*The distinction between the spirit of truth and the spirit of error.*

I. THE DISTINCTION BETWEEN TRUTH AND ERROR IS A PRACTICAL DISTINCTION.

There are those who would make it an *intellectual* distinction. To them it consists, not in the spirit that prompts men's actions, but in the opinions by which they guide their lives. It is not denied but that intellectual error will invariably lead to evil, and that it is our duty to form sound opinions. But it is also our duty to understand how sound opinions are to be formed. We may learn this from John vii. 17, viii. 31. The true way to form right opinions is to set ourselves to obey God's will, and thus we shall be gradually and steadily led

acting up to the light we have, or refusing to do so. He who submits to God's guidance, so far as it is vouchsafed him, may be said, in a sense, to "know God," and such an one will readily welcome any teaching which helps him to know more. He who is "not of God" is he who resists what his own heart teaches him to be the true will of God. And such a man will not listen to the truth when it is proclaimed to him. St. John uses ἀκούω in the sense of *listen*, *i.e.*, to hear and heed.—**Hereby know we the spirit of truth and the spirit of error.** See Isaiah viii. 20, and last note. The words here translated "hereby" are literally "from this," *i.e.*, from the acceptance or rejection of God's truth just mentioned. For "spirit of truth" cf. John xiv. 17, xv. 26, xvi. 13. Dr. Westcott refers to 1 Cor. ii., especially vers. 12, 14. The "spirit of truth" may mean either "the spirit which is true," or "the spirit which proceeds from the truth." Or both. For the Holy Spirit being truly God, truth is an essential characteristic of Him. And inasmuch as He proceedeth from the Father, who is Truth, and from the Son, who has proclaimed that He is the Truth (John xiv. 6), He

---

to the light. If we set ourselves to form sound opinions by argument and not by obedience, we shall not attain them. We shall dispute in a spirit of self-assertion and self-will. When we have got hold of a truth we shall misapply and misinterpret it. We may observe that St. John does not speak of correct doctrines or sound opinions, but of a spirit of truth and a spirit of error, breathed into us by God or God's enemy.

II. IT IS THE DIFFERENCE BETWEEN LIVING FOR GOD AND LIVING FOR THE WORLD. All practical principles of life may ultimately be reduced to two, and thus ascribed to their authors, the spirit of truth and the spirit of error. There are two, and only two, opposing doctrines in existence. The one is the spirit which impels us, in various ways, to make the best of the present life because we know so little about what there is in another. Some it impels to a grosser kind of indulgence, others to a more refined and far-seeking kind of selfishness. But in all it teaches them to bound their horizon by the

may be said also to proceed from the Truth. A third interpretation, not inconsistent with the other two, may be given, namely, that He imparts truth to those who receive Him. The same may be said of the spirit of error. It may be called the spirit of error for three reasons— because it proceeds from error, because it produces error, and because it *is* error. The expression, says Professor Westcott, is unusual; but the idea which prompts the expression is not so. Cf. ch. i. 8, ii. 26. Also 2 Thess. ii. 9–11, and 1 Tim. iv. 1.

---

grave, and to take care, in some way or other, to secure for themselves as ample a share of the blessings and comforts of life as they conveniently can. The other is the spirit which leads us to seek nothing for ourselves, but to offer our whole being to God from Whom it came; to do His will, whatever may befall us: to regard no sorrows, privation, inconveniences, as matters to be complained of, if they come in the path of duty.

III. It distinguishes between the disciples of Christ and the disciples of the evil one. Many tests have been devised for the discovery of the true Christian. One only is the true one. Is he guided by the Spirit of Christ, or is he not? (1) Does he seek to conform his opinions to those of men about him? Does he seek to avoid inconvenience or danger, or is he zealous for the truth, and for it alone? (2) Does he seek to lead an easy life, to cultivate the good opinion of his fellows, to obtain from them what present advantages he can? Or does he set before him steadily what is right as his aim and object? Does he endeavour to attain a standard which is not of this world but of the other? There are many who *call* themselves disciples of Christ. But to be truly His we must renounce the world.

XXI.

LOVE A DIVINE GIFT.

CH. iv. 7.—We here commence a fresh section of the Epistle. Once more the Apostle takes up the duty of love, but from a different and far deeper point of view. The duty of love is enforced in ch. ii. 5–11, as a sign of our belonging to the kingdom of light, and not that of darkness. In ch. iii. 10–18, it is referred to as the necessary proof of our sonship to God. In ch. iii. 23 it is spoken of as a commandment of God, the keeping of which stamps us as abiding in Christ. But here the duty of love is based upon the essential nature of God, and upon the inward fellowship which every believer has with Him by partaking of His Spirit.—**Beloved**. Here, as in ver. 1, we have this form of address as marking a point to which the Apostle desires to draw special attention.—**let us love one another.** "In this in-

---

HOMILETICS.

VERS. 7, 8.—*The real nature of the spirit of truth.*
I. THE SPIRIT OF TRUTH CANNOT CO-EXIST WITH LOVE OF SELF. The question may arise, and *will* arise,—You speak of living for God, but *what is* living for God ? It is possible even to renounce the world and be no nearer God (1 Cor. xiii. 3). It is possible to have a fierce ascetic hatred of this world's goods. It is possible to seek the kingdom of heaven in a spirit of refined selfishness. It is possible to hate and despise those grovelling creatures who seek only for earthly joys.

junction it is obvious that only the love of Christians to each other is first of all meant; yet we see at once, by the general reason given in the great truth that God is love (ver. 8), and sent His Son εἰς τὸν κόσμον (ver. 9), that the universal love of all mankind is no more to be excluded here than it was excluded in ch. iii. 13, seq." (Ebrard). See note on the last-cited passage.—**for love is of God.** St. John first tells us that love comes from God. And then, as he so often does, he leads us insensibly to a higher form of the truth, namely, that "God is love." And since God is love, and since He abides in us by His Spirit (ch. iii. 24), a perpetual stream of love flows from Him to us, and through us, if we will receive it, to the rest of mankind, "especially them that are of the household of faith."—**and every one that loveth is born of God.** The Revised Version prefers "begotten" to "born." Observe the perfect tense. He who loveth must already have received that birth or begetting which is the effect of Christ's coming. Mr. Plummer remarks here, "If a Socrates or a Marcus Aurelius loves his fellow-men, it is by the grace of God that he does so." The passage seems to assert more than this. "*Every one* that loveth," we are told, has not merely received grace from God, but has been "begotten of Him." That is to say, the new birth or begetting

---

It is possible even to serve God in a spirit of Pharisaic pride, of high conceit of ourselves and contempt of others. Is this, *can* it be, the spirit of truth? We reply, *No*; for

II. THE SPIRIT OF TRUTH IS THE SPIRIT OF GOD, AND HE IS LOVE. The contempt of this world is useless for its own sake. The hate of our fellow-creatures is no part of true religion. There can be no true obedience to God where there is an over-estimation of ourselves or contempt of others. So Christ has told us in many a discourse and many a parable. But here we see not only *that* it is, but *why* it is. Religion consists in uniting ourselves to God, and God is Love. If, then,

U

which Christ came to bring into the world, was received before He came, and even by those who rejected Him. The paradox, like many other paradoxes, involves no contradiction. He who believes in the duty of a human being to love his fellows, believes in God far more truly than if he could repeat all the formulæ of the schools. Whosoever has learned to love, has received the first seeds of the life of God. Nay, though perchance he knows it not, he believes on the Son of God, who is love, and came to manifest and to impart love. The full revelation of God's perfections could only be known through God manifest in the flesh. The first stirrings of the Divine life, however, are found in him who has apprehended, however dimly, the truth that God is love, and who has striven to display, in his own life, the likeness to what he has believed of God. If it be asked how such a statement can be reconciled with a passage like John iii. 5, which seems to assert the necessity of a public confession by Christian Baptism; or Acts iv. 12, which asserts the impossibility of salvation without Christ, we may find some light thrown upon the difficulty by ver. 6. The first stirrings of the new and higher life of man (1) have been felt wherever love is present; (2) they are the work of the Son of God. And he in whom they are felt will of necessity be drawn to Christ whenever He is truly presented to him. If they are

---

we are united to God, we must show the results of that union by displaying our likeness to Him. It is not contempt of the world that is to be sought, but the desire to seek the welfare of others before our own. This is God's object; it must, therefore, be ours.

(*a.*) *This is why we are to hate sin.* For all sin is a violation of the law of love. All sin derives its origin from the desire to benefit ourselves at the expense of others. And thus sin can only be put away by the renunciation of all desire for our own gratification at others' expense. Thus, not only immediate gratification, but *all* gratifica-

apparently not so drawn, this may be because, as in the case of a man like Marcus Aurelius, they have never had the doctrines of Christianity fairly presented to them, or, as in the case of many earnest and loving sceptics now, because their assent has been demanded to the formulæ of the schools, and not to the simple statements of Holy Writ. Whensoever the truth, "as it is in Jesus," the truth embodied in His Life and Person, presents itself to their souls, stripped of all the trappings with which man's intellect has encumbered it, they cannot choose but "hear" it, because they have been "begotten of God." But whether this explanation be accepted or not, the declaration stands plainly revealed in the Scriptures. "*Every one* that loveth has been begotten of God." And this *must*, in some way or other, be reconcilable with the doctrines of the need of faith in Christ, of the new birth, and of the efficacy and necessity of the Sacraments.—**and knoweth God.** The tense must be noted here. It is neither the aorist (as in the next verse) nor the perfect (which our English present sometimes approaches in signification). As in the last verse, it signifies a present condition of knowledge which is capable of increase, or, it may be, diminution.

VER. 8.—**He that loveth not knoweth not God.** Here we may either take the aorist (see ch. iii. 1) strictly, in which case it will mean "did not know God" when

---

tion in which others have no share must be distasteful to us. And this, in a sinful world, will constantly involve the renunciation of things at which others greedily snatch, and even of blessings fairly our own, which, but for others' needs, we might legitimately have enjoyed.

(*b.*) *This is the lesson of the Cross.* The Cross presents to us (1) God's love, (2) man's perfection. (1.) It illustrates the love of a Father who desires to keep nothing back, but wills "freely" to "give us all things" (Rom. viii. 32). (2.) It illustrates the Spirit of truth, the Divine Spirit

he professed to do so, *i.e.*, when he entered the Christian Church; or better, less strictly, since the aorist in New Testament Greek frequently answers to the Hebrew imperfect, and is altogether indefinite in point of time, in which case it will mean (Alford, Braune, Plummer) "hath never known Him;" *i.e.*, there can be no knowledge of God without love. This agrees best with what follows.—**for God is love**. "$\dot{\alpha}\gamma\dot{\alpha}\pi\eta$, not $\dot{\eta}\,\dot{\alpha}\gamma\dot{\alpha}\pi\eta$; love is the very essence, not merely an attribute of God" (Alford). Had he said, "*of* the very essence," it would have been more strictly in accordance with the Apostle's language; see below. This root truth of the Gospel, as important an article of faith as any in the Christian creed, would, if firmly grasped, solve not only most of the difficulties of life, but most of the difficulties which beset Christian theology. No doctrine, it may be safely affirmed, which is contrary to this fundamental principle, can possibly be true. Many parts of the Christian creed may seem opposed to this proposition. Yet in reality they are not so. Whatever appears to conflict with it must be so explained as not to put this essential doctrine out of sight. It is to be lamented that this doctrine, standing as it does in the forefront of the Gospel, attested not only by its double repetition here, but by the language of the Saviour Himself, especially in St. John's Gospel,

---

in its contact with the facts of human life. And that Spirit of truth, or love (for they are one and the same), when it dominates our spirits, inculcates the surrender of every blessing at God's call, or our brother's need; the devotion of all our powers to His service, the readiness to surrender even life itself, if that brother's need seem to require it.

VER. 9.—*The manifestation of the love of God.*

I. THIS LOVE WAS MANIFESTED BY THE MISSION OF THE SON.

1. *The world was a fallen world.* From Adam's transgression forward, its tendency was ever downward. God's revelations of Himself,

has been allowed, until lately, to fall so much into the background. Had those who were charged with drawing up the famous Nicene formula, added to the words "God from God, Light from Light," the words "Love from Love," from how many evils would the Church of later times, in all probability, have been saved! Our only danger, now that men have come to understand it at last, is that, in their reaction from a creed which had come to include a great deal of fierceness, severity, and hate, they should be tempted to forget that love, in order to be love, must be reconcilable with righteousness, justice, and truth, and at eternal enmity with all evil. It is surprising how this great truth has been evaded because of the utter incapacity of man's unloving heart to understand it. Expounders of the Scriptures, in past times, have evacuated it of its force by saying that God is "benignissimus;" that He is "the most benevolent of all beings," and the like. They have failed to see that love is an essential attribute of His nature. So again, in other quarters, we have God evaporated into a metaphysical abstraction. He is "the Infinite," *i.e.*, man's conception of infinity. He is "the Absolute," that is, in the strict acceptation of the term, that which is incapable of relation, or, as it has been necessarily watered down to accommodate itself, partially at least, to Christian theology, that

---

in the Law and in heathen philosophy, His sore judgments, from the Flood onward, tended to arrest the declension, but only for a time. See Gen. vi. 5, xiii. 13. The great civilisations of the world ever ended in demoralisation. See Isa. xix., xxiii., xlvii., &c.; Jer. l., &c. New powers were raised up from races as yet uncorrupted. But in their success were the seeds of ruin. Of all the nations of the world, at Christ's coming, the Jews—the only race to whom God had revealed Himself by the Law and by the Prophets—were the only people who had not steadily gone from bad to worse.

which "has no *necessary* relation" to other beings. But, as Haupt accurately points out here, "Love is primarily *under all circumstances* a reciprocal idea, or *idea of relation.*" Professor Westcott here, in a striking note, points out how we owe to St. John the three fundamental ideas of the Godhead, the foundation of all Christian philosophy. God is Spirit (John iv. 24), God is Light (ch. i. 5), and God is Love. See also note on p. 33. And all these, though we find them adumbrated in the Old Testament (as in Gen. i. 1, 2; Psalm iv. 6, xxvii. 1, xxxvi. 9, &c.; Exodus xxxiv. 6; Psalm lxxxvi. 5, 15; Joel ii. 13, &c.) yet appear there rather as attributes of God in relation to man, than as parts of His very essence. Yet light is very strongly insisted on as somewhat more than a mere attribute of God, as we may see from the passages above quoted. Two of these truths, that God was Spirit, and that He was Light, were in some sense discovered before Christ came. Afterwards they were not the peculiar property of the Church, but were common to Christianity and the Gnostic sects. But the last we owe to Christianity alone. And the discovery has proved so far above man's capacity that in eighteen centuries and a half he has scarcely grasped it. It may, perhaps, be a question whether, from the peculiar collocation of the word in St. John's Gospel, we are to regard the word "Spirit"

---

2. *There was need of a Saviour.* He had been predicted from the beginning, "in sundry ways and divers manners." His method was predicted (Jer. xxxi.) A new covenant was to be made, not in the letter, but in the heart. The Gentiles were to partake of it (*N.B.*, Gentiles is frequently, in O. T., equivalent to *peoples of the world.* The antithesis to Jews cannot always be pressed), see Isa. xi. 9, xlix., lx.-lxii.; Jer. i. 5, &c. And their need was evident. If the nation that possessed Moses and the Prophets had become grievously corrupt, how much more the rest of the world? Nor was there any remedy.

in John iv. 24, as bearing the sense of that which is independent of matter, or whether we are to take it as meaning that which breathes or is breathed. If so, it falls in with the Hebrew conception of God as Life—the Living God, as He is frequently called—He who has life in Himself, and is the source of life in others—He who breathed into the nostrils of the noblest of the visible creation the breath of life, so that "man became a living soul" (Gen. ii. 7). With the idea of God as Light is combined that quality of Truth which is claimed by Jesus Christ for Himself (John xiv. 6). For light is that which reveals what is, and truth is that which corresponds to what is. And thus it may be that we have, in this threefold revelation of God, an indication of the special work of each Person in the Blessed Trinity. The essence of the Godhead is, of course, participated in by each Person in the Godhead. But may we not reverently see in the words "God is Spirit," the assertion of God as He is in Himself, the source and fount whence all things, even the other Persons of the Godhead themselves, proceed; in the words, "God is Light" the special function of the Eternal Son, whose work it was to reveal the Father, to communicate Him, to call into being a vast universe of life, which should appreciate, acknowledge, and adore the greatness and goodness of Him who "inhabiteth eternity"? And in the last of

---

Religion could not bring it, for religion, in every country of the world save one, was itself corrupt. Philosophy could not bring it, for it rested, not on the testimony of God, but on the opinions of men. Even God's sore judgments could not bring it. They pointed out the disease, but not the cure. Men knew that they were sinners, but they knew not how to forsake their sin.

3. *The Saviour was God's Only Begotten Son.* The task of salvation was beyond human power. See Ps. xlix. 7. Therefore God sent forth His Only Begotten Son (see Exposition), One who stood in an entirely

these three declarations, "God is Love," may we not discover a special reference to the agency of the Holy Spirit, whose task it is to bring about those mutual relations of harmony and goodwill in the universe, which shall cause it to reflect the nature of Him who made it, whose function it is in the economy of redemption, to impart the Divine influence to the soul of the individual man, and to stir each up to communicate it to his brother? One other remark may be permitted on this deep and inexhaustible subject. St. John says "God is love." But he does not reverse the phrase and say, "love is God." "Love," he says, is "of" or "from God." In other words, love is not a transient phase of God's dealings with man. It is a necessary part of the Divine essence. But God is love and a thousand things beside. The human tongue is powerless to express the innumerable aspects in which His Infinite nature may be viewed. But if there be one word which more than another can express what He is to us, and what, therefore, we are bound to be to all, it is the word used in this never-to-be-forgotten sentence, "God is Love."

VER. 9.—**In this was manifested the love of God toward us.** This great subject of love occupies us as far as ch. v. 3; but, as usual with St. John, the divisions of his subject overlap each other, and the con-

---

peculiar and unique relation to Him, in order to destroy the reign of corruption, reconcile men to God, and make them fit to dwell in His presence for evermore. This Saviour was God Incarnate in the flesh. He only could "condemn sin" adequately "in the flesh," destroy it, bring man's nature out victorious over it, translate man from the distress and degradation he had been in, into a position not of mere innocence, but of triumphant righteousness.

II. HE SAVED US BY GIVING US LIFE.

1. *Sin is death.* We have frequently referred to St. John's habit of

clusion of his teaching on love introduces the subject of the source whence love flows, namely, faith. Here the fact of Christ's coming and the results of that coming, the life which we have by His means, is regarded as the manifestation of God's love. In other places (as in John i. 18, xiv. 6; Col. ii. 9) Christ Himself is pointed out as the manifestation of the fulness of the Divine essence. The Revised Version "in us" is to be preferred to the Authorised Version, which cannot be defended. See also ver. 16. The love of God is manifested in us, because Christ, His Son, who is One with Him (John x. 30), is sent into the world, and He "dwells in our hearts by faith" (Eph. iii. 17). The variety of translation of ἐν τούτῳ in this Epistle has been noticed before.—**because that God sent his only begotten Son into the world, that we might live through him.** Rather *because God hath sent*. The mission of Christ was not a temporary, but an enduring one. God sent His Son into the world; and in the world, by His Spirit, He remains (Matt. xxviii. 20; Rev. v. 6). The word "only begotten," as applied to Christ, only occurs four times in St. John's Gospel, and in this passage. It carries upon the face of it the assertion that the relation of Christ to the Father is an unique relation. And such an idea it expressed to those versed in the Hebrew literature. For it is used

---

viewing things in their tendencies. Viewed in this way, *sin is death*, because it is the road to it. See Ezek. xviii. 4; Rom. vi. 23; 2 Cor. v. 14 (where, perhaps, we should translate "then all died"), &c. In fact, sin has in it the nature of death. The true death is sin (Eph. ii. 1, 5; Col. ii. 13), and the only reason why sin and death are not equivalents while we are in this life is, because the state of sin is not *complete*. Let a man once be given up to sin, and that man is morally and spiritually dead.

2. *Jesus came to give us life.* This doctrine is more fully developed

in the LXX. to render the Hebrew יָחִיד, which is kindred to אֶחָד, one. It is true that sometimes this Hebrew word is rendered by the LXX. ἀγαπητός, and in English by "darling." But the idea of affection comes from the idea of unique relation, and not that of uniqueness from the affection. We may compare the statement in John iii. 16 with this passage. There Christ says that God gave His only begotten Son that all who believe in Him should not perish, but have eternal life. Here we are told that God sent His only begotten Son into the world that we might live through Him. The two statements are identical. Faith makes us partakers of the Life of the only begotten Son of God, and that Life rescues us from the destruction that comes on all that is apart from Him (cf. Ps. xxxvi. 9; also Rom. viii. 10; Eph. ii. 5; Col. ii. 13, iii. 4). Professor Westcott remarks that we are never said to live in Christ, though He *is* said to live in us (Gal. ii. 20). Polycarp, however, as he says, has the expression. And our life (Col. iii. 3) is said to be "hid with Christ in God."

VER. 10.—**Herein is love, not that we loved God, but that he loved us.** The ἐν τούτῳ is referred by most commentators to what follows. "The love to which I am exhorting you consists not in our having in the first instance loved God, but in this; that He loved us, and

---

in ch. v. 12. There we see that He gives us life by giving us Himself. We will not here anticipate that teaching. But what we learn here is that He was sent that we might live through Him. And what is true life? The destruction of sin. We live through Him, because through Him we obtain the strength to mortify every sinful appetite. Nothing but His Divine power can enable us to do this. Our corrupt life needs to be restored by His uncorrupted and incorruptible life. We need His power within us day by day. In fact, we need that continual union with Him that faith alone can effect. It is *He in us*

sent His Son to be a propitiation for our sins." It does not seem to have been observed that this is St. Paul's doctrine in another form. In St. John to do righteousness, to keep God's commandments, and to love, are equivalent to each other (chaps. iii. 10, v. 3; also ii. 29, iv. 7). Thus the doctrine here expressed is precisely the same as in Titus iii. 5. "Not by works of righteousness that we have done, but according to His mercy He saved us." So also Romans iii. 20–22, v. 8–10; Eph. ii. 4, 8, 9; 2 Tim. i. 9. With these we may compare John vi. 44. In other words, the initiative in the work of salvation comes from God, and from Him alone. Until He of His mercy hath given us the power to become His sons (John i. 12), we can do nothing to turn to Him. But this does not exhaust the force of the passage. For the explanation of ἐν τούτῳ the words ἡ ἀγάπη have been paraphrased above "the love to which I am exhorting you." But it would be a mistake to limit their meaning thus. They have a far wider meaning than their relation to the words ἐν τούτῳ would imply. ἡ ἀγάπη means love in the abstract. And what St. John would tell us is that love is a power that comes from God, and has no possible origin in man. "It is in its nature not a shining upward towards God which proceeds from man, but a flame which proceeds from God, and thereby enkindles men" (Ebrard). Haupt has

---

Who alone can avail to give us the life we seek. If then we desire life, we must desire Him.

VER. 10.—*The method of God's manifestation of His love.*

I. THE WORK WAS ALL HIS OWN. We cannot attain to salvation by ourselves. Dead in trespasses and sins, how can we find the power to arise from them? Alienated from God by wicked works, how can we learn to love Him? The impulse must come from without, from above. We must feel that the Fatherly heart yearns for us, even in the depths of sin and sorrow. We must become sensible of its warmth

taken this idea and improved upon it. "All human loving is a flame from the Divine Flame, having in itself no independent existence: 'I love' means no other than that the Divine Love has become in me an overmastering and all-pervading power of life." And, therefore, instead of making constant efforts to kindle in our own hearts a feeling of affection towards God in return for His many mercies, those efforts should rather be directed toward disposing our hearts to receive that full tide of love which flows from Him to all created beings, according to their capacities for its reception. Thus the interpolation of the word "first" in the Vulgate ("but for He first loved us"—Wiclif) weakens the force of the passage. The point here is not the *priority* of God's love, which awakened in us a return (though this idea occurs in ver. 19, where the idea is that of a love which excludes fear), but the *source* from whence all love proceeds, namely, He who, in His essence, is Himself Love.—**and sent his Son to be the propitiation for our sins.** Literally, *and sent his Son, a propitiation for our sins.* See note on ch. ii. 2.

VER. 11.—**Beloved, if God so loved us, we ought also to love one another.** "For the sixth and last time" (Plummer) does St. John use this affectionate expression (the Rec. has ἀδελφοί, however, in ch. ii. 7). See note on ver. 1. The meaning here is not "if God loved us *so much*," we ought also

---

in the icy outer darkness of godlessness. We must see the Eternal Son descending from His heavenly home to seek and to save that which was lost. Thus stirred, our hearts may warm to Him once more.

II. AND IT ISSUES IN FORGIVENESS. We may ask, how can we live through Him? How, that is, can we forsake and conquer sin? Even could we attain to never so great a purity of heart, there is still that dark load of transgression in the past, from which we cannot sever ourselves. It is part of ourselves; we cannot free ourselves of

to love one another, but, "if God love us in *such a manner*," *i.e.*, in the way in which we have been already told (vers. 9, 10) that He loved us, namely, in sending His Son into the world (1) that "we might live through Him," and (2) that He might "be a propitiation for our sins." If God did this for us, if He in this way manifested His love towards us, we also (the καί belongs to ἡμεῖς as well as ὀφείλομεν) ought to love one another. It is not that we are to show love to our brethren without waiting for them to show love to us, because God has set us this example (see note on last verse), for this, as Haupt says, would necessitate the οὕτως again before ὀφείλομεν. But it is that since God has manifested His love to us by giving us of Himself, and by "blotting out the handwriting of our sins, which was against us," there lies on us a moral responsibility to act in His Spirit, and to take care that the same relations exist between ourselves and our brethren which exist between Him and us, and Him and them. As Professor Westcott remarks, it is important to notice the fact that the conclusion drawn from God's love to us is not, as we might have expected, that we should love God in return, but that we should love one another. The reason for this is explained in the next verse when compared with ver. 20.

VER. 12.—**No man hath seen God at any time**. Or perhaps better, **God hath no man ever yet beheld**. The

---

our responsibility for it. The answer is, He came to be a propitiation. Not that He altered the Father's will of love towards us one iota. He came because He was sent. He came to carry out His Father's purpose, which was, is, ever will and must be, one with His own. But he altered man's relation to God. He "bare our sins in His own body on the tree." He took the handwriting of our sins away, nailing it to His cross. He manifested sin as it was, the most shocking insult to God, the cruellest enemy of man, the hateful thing that poisoned all the springs of being here below. He showed that forgiveness did not

theological student should consult Dr. Westcott's exhaustive note on the difference between θεός and ὁ θεός. The former is used when speaking of God as He is in Himself (as in John i. 1, 18), the latter when we think of Him in His relation to ourselves—as He is realised in our consciousness. The one, in short, represents the objective, the latter the subjective idea of God. And thus many supposed contradictions in God's Word are explained. We next note that St. John does not say that no one ever *shall* behold God, which would be to contradict ch. iii. 2 and Matt. v. 8; nor even that no man *can* see Him, though this is certainly asserted of mankind in their present condition in 1 Tim. vi. 16. Next we have to observe that τεθέαται here means somewhat more than the ἑώρακεν of John i. 18. The former verb has the idea of rapt or earnest contemplation. What, then, is the purport of the Apostle's statement here? The key to unlock the connection of thought is undoubtedly ver. 20. And vers. 13, 14, also add their contribution towards the unravelling of the difficulty. The drift of the passage, then, may be supposed to be as follows: "You would naturally suppose that I would lead you, by the thought of God's love, to direct your affections towards Him. And indeed I would do so, were there not danger of leading you to be content with a barren and unreal sentiment. God, as He is in

---

mean indifference to evil, but its conquest. Henceforth all man needed was faith in Him who had gained the victory. In Him, all mankind is justified before God. Henceforth he who unites his will to Christ by faith, is regarded as Christ Himself. No past sins of his are henceforth reckoned to him. His sins are washed away in the blood of Christ, the ever-flowing stream of life which issues from His side. Henceforth God smiles upon his efforts, pardons his weakness, supplies him with the inner fount of strength whereby at last he can "beat down Satan under his feet."

Himself, is beyond the reach of human contemplation. Men have fled from the world and sought to discern Him, but their efforts have been unsatisfactory to themselves and unprofitable to others. But there are ways of discerning God which are more useful in every way. We feel an influence from the unseen, a breath of the invisible Godhead at work within us, and we know that it comes from Him (ver. 13). We cannot gaze on the invisible God. But on that revelation of Him which has taken place in the flesh we *can* gaze and we *have* gazed (τεθεάμεθα—ver. 14). We have done this, either as His first messengers and preachers have done, with the eyes of flesh, or if that vision has not been vouchsafed to us, still the idea of God as revealed to us in the shape of Man is one which our intellects and hearts are alike capable of grasping. Through Him the love of God has been revealed to us (ver. 10). Through Him we can understand how God can dwell in us and be in us and we in Him (ver. 13). And though for the present we are denied the direct vision of God, we can feel that He lives and dwells in us, moulding our minds and purposes into union with His, when we display in our conduct that love which His Spirit within us, and His Image manifested in the world outside us, alike set before us as our true perfection."—**if we love one another, God dwelleth in us, and his love is perfected in us.** Literally,

---

VER. 11.—*What return can we make to God for His love?*

I. WE ARE NOT ASKED TO LOVE GOD IN RETURN, BUT TO LOVE ONE ANOTHER. We are constantly reminded how far the Gospel transcends our human reasonings or instincts. The natural feeling excited by this revelation of God's love would be to make a return to Him; to sacrifice our time, our goods, our persons to Him; to indulge in ascetic practices; to spend days and nights in ecstatic contemplation; to give our goods to build splendid temples to Him. But what He asks is that we should love one another.

II. THE REASON OF THIS. It may be found in the word "so."

If we love one another, God abideth in us, and His love hath been perfected in us, and remains so perfected. This is the only way of giving the force of the perfect participle with ἐστίν, especially if, with ℵ and B, we separate the participle and verb by ἐν ἡμῖν. Much ingenuity has been spent over the simple words ἡ ἀγάπη αὐτοῦ. They have been explained by "His love to us," "our love to Him," "the mutual relation of love between God and us." But surely, with vers. 7 and 8 before us, we cannot go far wrong in interpreting the words of that love which is part of His essential nature (ver. 8), and which we, if we possess it at all, must have received from Him (see ver. 7 and note on ver. 10). If we are living that life of love (ἐὰν ἀγαπῶμεν ἀλλήλους—where observe that the verb is in the *present* tense) God, we may be sure, is abiding in us, and His love—that love which He has shed abroad in our hearts—is already perfected in us. Here, as elsewhere in these notes, we have represented St. John as looking rather to the goal to which the Christian is aiming than at his actual present condition. No one—but One—has succeeded perfectly in leading this life of love. But every single act of love tends to bring each one of us nearer to that consummation. And the more love is made the practical principle of our lives, the nearer we are to that state to which the Lord desired to bring us, when God abides in

---

"If God *so* loved us." That is to say, God flowed out, so to speak, from Himself to us. He not merely cared for us, showed affection to us, He put love in us. He "gave us of His Spirit" (ver. 13). And we therefore must display that Spirit. We must pour out of that we have received. The love which God has put in us must be manifested in our conduct. God asks not for *quid pro quo*, but for our identity of heart with Himself.

VERS. 12, 13.—*The true way of being united to God.*

I. MAN'S SHORTSIGHTEDNESS SUGGESTS MISTAKEN WAYS OF SERVING GOD. There is a warning conveyed in the words "No man

us and we in Him, when we cease to commit sin and have at last come to "do righteousness," when we love our brethren even as Christ hath loved us.

VER. 13.—**Hereby we know that we dwell in him, and he in us, because he hath given us of his Spirit.** We have, in vers. 13–16, a *résumé* of vers. 1–12 ; and, as is usual with St. John, the ideas thus repeated are also strengthened. This verse corresponds to vers. 1–6, the subject being introduced, as we have seen, after St. John's manner, at the end of the preceding section, in ch. iii. 24. Ver. 14 corresponds to ver. 9. The next two verses gather up other threads of the first twelve verses. As the present verse reminds us of the indwelling Spirit that impels us to the confession of Jesus, so ver. 15 reminds us of the necessity of the confession itself (see ver. 2). And as in ver. 14 we are reminded of the Father's love as manifested in the person of His Son, so in ver. 16 we are reminded once more that the love so manifested is a part of His essential nature, and that if union with the Godhead be the result of Christ's coming, the outward sign of that union in ourselves is the possession of a spirit of love (see ver. 8). The recapitulation is occasioned by the necessity of recalling the train of thought in connection with the conclusion to which we are brought by vers. 9–12, namely, that it is not in the ideal contemplation of God, but in the manifestation of His indwelling

---

hath seen God at any time." We are not to be content with a mere ideal contemplation of Him. Some have been so content, but their lives have been barren. For God is beyond the range of our intellectual, moral, spiritual faculties—at least for the present (1 Cor. xiii. 12). To imagine we love Him, because we reason about Him, draw out conclusions from Scripture, Nature, or science about His being, is a mistake. So it is if we inflame ourselves with ardour at His goodness, and seek to pour ourselves out in fervent ejaculations to His name. It is no less a mistake if we try to cultivate our spiritual insight, by losing ourselves in meditations on His nature, His attributes,

X

being, that the true life of God in the soul is to be found. We have seen that the natural train of thought suggested by the commencement of ver. 11 would be "if God so loved us, we ought also to love Him." We have seen also that the Apostle was prevented from drawing this natural conclusion by the fact that God's essential nature was beyond the grasp of our limited faculties. Yet we were not, as he reminds us, to consider ourselves as sundered from that nature. "If we love one another, God abideth in us, and one part at least of His essential nature is perfected in our lives." But if we ask *how* this is, an answer is ready. God dwells in us because there is a presence within us of His Spirit (ver. 13). Nor is this a mere dream of the imagination. We have not seen God, but we have seen Man, the Image of God, in his fullest perfection, endowed, too, with the visible signs of God's presence within Him. He announced Himself as the Saviour of the world, and His claim was attested by the works of mercy He untiringly performed, and by that great and final attestation of His mission which His resurrection placed before us (ver. 14). To Him we testify. And it is to the confession of Him as God manifest in the flesh that we owe the presence of the Spirit in our hearts, and from this presence alone comes the life of love we lead (ver. 15). Our union with, our comprehension of God comes, not from the intellectual insight which

---

His kingdom, His relations with ourselves. So men have done in times past. It was the capital error of St. John's own day. It has penetrated into the Church from which he so earnestly strove to keep it out. If these things are done in order to help us to attain to the true method of serving God, they are not only *most* useful, but even necessary. But if regarded as an end in themselves, they are vain.

II. THE TRUE METHOD OF SERVING HIM. It consists in the placing our wills in a line with His. His will is love to all mankind. Our wills are in a line with His, when we desire to love as He does. And so we are here told (1) that when our wills are thus one with His, He

enables us to grasp the mystery of His being, but from the spiritual oneness with Him which enables us to carry out the purposes which He had in the creation of mankind (ver. 16). This seems to be the connection of thought between vers. 13–16 and what precedes. The more special connection between vers. 12 and 13, which is obviously implied in the turn of the language, must next be drawn out. The Apostle desires to show what evidence we have for the statement that "if we love one another God dwelleth in us, and His love is perfected in us." That evidence, says St. John, is the fact of our possession of the Divine Spirit; and this in turn (ver. 14) is made certain by the revelation of God in His Son. And thus we return to the assertion in ver. 2, that the Spirit of God is discerned by the confession of His Son; only that here we have the acknowledgment of the Spirit connected with the life of love which is His work. The Authorised Version has "dwell" again here. But the Revised Version keeps to "abide," and thus preserves the continuity of thought. "Of (or 'out of') His Spirit," here contrasts with John iii. 34. To Christ alone is the Spirit given without measure. In the case of men in general God "divides to every man severally as He will" (1 Cor. xii. 11).

---

abides within us. He makes no temporary visit to our heart, but takes up His dwelling there. Our union with Him is a real and permanent fact, manifested by our conduct. And we are further told (2) how to discover the signs of this permanent indwelling. If it exists, we shall be conscious of continued impulses toward good, due to the constant presence of His Spirit in the heart. And the presence of that Spirit is due to the humanity of Jesus (ver. 3). The union of the Godhead in His person is the means whereby all men are taken up once more into union with the Divine. Through the humanity of Jesus the Divine Spirit flows into each human heart. And by its impulses to love we recognise its presence within. We know that we dwell in God and God in us, because we feel inspired and mastered by the purpose which God has toward all the world.

XXII.

TEACHING OF CHRISTIAN EXPERIENCE.

CH. iv. 14.—**And we have seen and do testify.** The great majority of commentators suppose St. John and the other Apostles to be meant by "we." But the whole context requires us to understand the words of the consciousness of the whole Christian community. It is impossible to suppose that by "we" and "us" in this whole passage St. John merely means himself and the other Apostles. It is equally impossible to suppose that without a word of explanation of his change of meaning, the Apostle here " brings up in sharp relief the apostolic body whom Christ appointed His witnesses " (Alford, the only recent commentator adopting this interpretation who

---

HOMILETICS.

CH. iv. 14.—*The character of Christian experience.*

I. THE CHRISTIAN DOES NOT BELIEVE, HE KNOWS. The unbeliever is wont to tell the Christian that his is but an opinion, and that one opinion is as likely to be true as another. He asks for evidence, for argument, for logical proof of the truth of Christianity. And he has a right to demand this, *within certain limits.* Man is a reasonable being, and his faith must be a reasonable faith. But reason must keep within its own sphere. It is finite, God is infinite. Reason can apply principles already ascertained, draw conclusions from facts already discovered. But *why* things are, and *how* they are, in their origin, is altogether beyond its province and its power. It knows *that* they are, and can,

seems to have the least idea that any difficulty attaches to it). We must, therefore, with Professor Westcott, understand it of "the experience of the Christian society gathered up in that of its leaders." *They* had seen (gazed on—τεθεάμεθα) Christ with the eyes of flesh. The rest had seen Him through the eyes of those who had beheld His form, till they also could say, καὶ ἡμεῖς τεθεάμεθα καὶ μαρτυροῦμεν. And *what* have Christians seen, and to what do they testify? It is not God's essential nature, but **that the Father sent the Son to be the Saviour of the world,** *i.e.*, to be a continual manifestation of the fact that "God is love." We should rather render "hath sent." The testimony is given to the mission of the Son not as an historic but as an abiding fact. And this further strengthens the interpretation given to the words καὶ ἡμεῖς above. Here the *Father* is spoken of as having sent the Son. In vers. 9, 10 *God* is said to have done so. The two sides of the truth are thus presented to us. In ver. 10 we have the Divine Nature of the Son brought into prominence, here His Sonship. We may, moreover, perceive a subtle corroboration of the interpretation given above, that in these verses we have an explanation of vers. 11, 12. The presence of God in the heart, in spite

---

within certain limits, tell how they are, what they will do, and what they will become. It knows, for instance, certain natural laws, as of motion, gravitation, chemical change, life. But it knows not their cause, their duration, nor can it penetrate beyond a certain distance in its attempts to define them. If it be thus powerless in the affairs of the visible world, is it wonderful if it fail to penetrate the secrets of the world of spirits? Why should it pretend to more wisdom in the spiritual sphere than elsewhere? In the natural world it has been compelled to guess at certain laws, assume their truth, apply them to facts, and if the results correspond with observation, to regard them as established. What other course is open to mortals in the things of the spirit? We must believe first, then act on what we believe, and then we come to know. We know, when we have tried the Gospel

of the fact that immediate comprehension of the Divine essence is denied to us, is proved to us by the intermediate agency (1) of His Spirit within us, and (2) of His Son in the world. Dr. Westcott remarks that the use of the word "Saviour" is characteristic of the later N. T. writings, and is only used once in St. John's Gospel. It is not found even in the central group of St. Paul's Epistles. This is in keeping with what we constantly see with new ideas. They are expressed by verbs, by periphrases, and the like, until necessity demands some noun, some convenient expression to denote the idea. So terms like "Redeemer" are not found in the N. T. applied to Christ, although they have become most common in later times. In the earlier N. T. writings the fact that Christ came to save is constantly insisted on. So we are frequently told that He came to redeem. It would not, therefore, be long before the titles of Saviour and Redeemer would come to be applied to Him. The words "of the world" are significant. They are decisive against the idea that Christ only came to save a few. They must be construed in the light of 1 Tim. ii. 4. Before leaving the subject we may observe another point, which, though once more beneath the sur-

---

and found it answer our expectations. We have applied Christian principles to facts, and found them true. The babe in Christ believes what he is told. He listens to those who "have seen and do testify" that the Father sent the Son to be the Saviour of the world. But when he comes to put his belief into practice, when he tries practically to ascertain whether it is true that Christ came to save, he soon discovers without a doubt that what has been proclaimed to him is no delusion, but literal, sober fact.

II. WHAT THE CHRISTIAN KNOWS. *What* is it then that the Christian sees, and of what can he testify? Of this: that the Father sent the Son to save the world; that Jesus Christ has power to save; that He does save, is saving, and will always save those who trust in Him. He saves them from sin, from "fleshly lusts," from the dominion

face, corroborates the view we have taken of τεθεάμεθα, and of the reference of the passage to the *whole body* of the disciples. It is not "we have beheld *Him*," but "we have beheld His saving power." We have beheld the power of faith in Him to change the heart and life. We have seen men turned "from darkness unto light, and from the power of Satan unto God." We have seen His Spirit thus working in men's hearts, and in the mighty moral revolution which that Spirit has achieved we see the tokens of Divine love.

VER. 15.—**Whosoever shall confess that Jesus is the Son of God, God dwelleth in him and he in God.** Once more we need "abideth" here, as elsewhere. It seems almost certain that Alford is wrong in taking the aorist here in its strict classical sense of a single act. Here, as in other places, it has the sense of the Hebrew imperfect, of a state once commenced and still continuing. Nothing could be more alien to the whole spirit of this Epistle than to imagine that the condition of abiding in Christ could be the result of a "great act, once for all introducing a man into a state of ὁμολογῆσαι." Rather the confession is one not of the lips but of the life. He who is willing

---

of their evil appetites, from bitterness, and spite, and anger, and covetousness, and lying, and all the vices to which man in his natural state is only too prone. He translates them into a kingdom where forgiveness, and favour, and acceptance, and trust, and light, and peace, and love, are the pervading characteristics.

III. HOW THE CHRISTIAN KNOWS IT. He knows it by his own and others' experience. He knows that Jesus Christ *has* saved him over and over again. He knows how, when in secret agony he has wrestled with temptation, and has breathed in his distress a heartfelt prayer to the Saviour, that prayer has been heard. He knows how, when he betakes himself to prayer, to Holy Communion, to communing frequently with God, his prayers are answered; he "grows in grace, and in the knowledge of our Lord and Saviour Jesus Christ." He knows that no other can do it. He looks around him. He sees

to own Jesus publicly as his Lord, and is willing to accept the shame and humiliation as well as the unchanging spirit of self-sacrifice which attaches to such a confession, verily he is a man in whom God is abiding, and who abides in God. For that confession is produced by the action of the Divine Spirit (ver. 2). And such a confession (see next verse) must needs involve the living the same life of love which He, the Son of God, lived, and must testify to the saving power which proceeds from Him. Professor Westcott invites us to compare this statement, not only with that in ver. 2, which we have done already, but with ch. ii. 23. There the confession of Christ is connected with the anti-Christian denial of Him (as indeed in ver. 2). But the point there is the unity of essence, the unity of mind and will, between the Father and the Son, so that the confession or denial of God manifest in the flesh, is a confession or denial of God Himself. Here, as is invariably the case with St. John's repetitions, a deeper truth is reached than before. The confession of Jesus as the Son of God, as the true image and manifestation of His Father—this

---

men who reject Christ the slaves of their own lusts, the votaries of a world that is passing away. Or he finds them given over to a refined selfishness, a polite indifference to all that is high and holy, all that is generous and self-sacrificing. Or he finds them a prey to doubt, darkness, despair; miserable, wretched, unable to believe, because unwilling to trust. Or at best, if he find them satisfied with a creed which acknowledges not Christ, and if he find them, moreover, moral, temperate, kindly, liberal, he finds them still strangers to that nobler, more enthusiastic, more self-devoted life, which, as he sees, is entirely confined to the soldiers of the Cross. Thence alone can spring the impulse to a life of forgetfulness of self in the care of others.' From the time that Christ came to our own, all the higher deeds of heroism, of unremitting toil and devotion for others' good, have been performed by Christian men and Christian women. Nor is it possible, as has been proved over and over again,

confession, when made sincerely, when permitted to mould the life, is at once the token of a life united to God, and the means whereby such a life may be led. The word μένει, as has been before remarked, emphasises the abiding nature of that union, and not merely the union itself.

VER. 16.—**And we have known and believe the love that God hath to us.** "We" here obviously, as before, relates to the whole body of Christian believers. Professor Westcott has some valuable remarks on the relation of faith and knowledge as indicated here, and in John vi. 69, where the words come in reverse order. The truth is that while faith necessarily precedes knowledge, knowledge perfects faith. Without faith the Apostles and the body of the faithful could never have known the things of God; without the knowledge which comes from experience of Christ it may safely be said that no Christian can ever have believed in the sense of that perfect comprehension of Him, that thorough trust in His mercy and goodness, that πληροφορία which constitutes Christian faith in all its fulness. There is a rudimentary and there is a perfect faith. The former precedes knowledge, the latter embodies

---

in the hour of strong temptation, to find any other safeguard than the power of Jesus to "deliver us from evil." And therefore it is that those who have lived *to* Jesus and *for* Jesus, can truly say, not that they are of opinion that Jesus was the Son of God, but that they "have seen and do testify that the Father sent the Son to be the Saviour of the world."

We have already frequently referred to the evidences of God's power in the altered face of the world since Jesus Christ came; and therefore we need not repeat here what has been before said. Only let it be borne in mind that equally in the condition of Christian society and in the experience of the individual life have these words been verified: "We have seen and do testify that the Father sent the Son to be the Saviour of the world."

VER. 15.—*The confession of Jesus the means of salvation.*

We need not here insist again on the fact that God is love, or that

it. It should, however, be observed that the knowledge here spoken of is the knowledge of God's love. "To us" is in R. V. "in us." See note on ver. 9. The margin of R. V. in each place, "in our case," does not rise to the full height of the argument. See ver. 13. It is the inward working of the Spirit of God, communicating His love to us, making it the dominant principle of our lives, and producing a real inward experience of His nature, of which St. John is speaking here.—**God is love ; and he that dwelleth in love dwelleth in God, and God in him.** Here, again, we need the translation "abideth." We have in this sentence the corroboration of our interpretation of the last. The love that God hath is in us, because God Himself is in us, and He is love. If we compare this passage with ver. 8, we see that this is the climax to which the rest is leading. "God is love" is used in ver. 8 as an argument to prove that we ought to walk in love. But the statement itself, St. John feels, requires proof. That proof is found (1) in God's mission of His Son, (2) in the propitiation that Son made for human sin, (3) in the inward witness of the Spirit, producing in us an actual

---

in order to abide in God we must manifest the spirit of love in our own lives. Neither need we carry any further the thought of the last verse, that the experienced Christian has not merely belief but knowledge. And we have explained in the notes how the knowledge which springs from faith leads faith up to a higher stage, until we "see Him who is invisible." We will confine ourselves here, therefore, to developing the meaning of the Apostle in the words, "Whosoever confesseth that Jesus is the Son of God, God dwelleth in him and he in God."

I. IT IS NOT THE CONFESSION OF THE LIPS MERELY. Many confess God with the lips who know not the power of His salvation. They repeat our creeds, they partake of our sacraments, they mingle in our public assemblies, they assist in the management of our religious affairs, they subscribe to our charities, they call themselves members of our body. But they know not the power of their Lord (as they call

experience of the power of God to save us from evil. After mentioning these experimental proofs, St. John repeats the statement, with all the additional weight it has gained, and concludes this section with the assertion that in the abiding life of love alone can true union with God be reached.

Before we pass on to the next section we may, with Professor Westcott, review the various statements we have concerning the abiding in God, which may be regarded as the keystone of St. John's doctrine. (1.) In ch. ii. 6, we see that some have perverted this leading idea in St. John's teaching. One necessary characteristic of the man who abides in God is conformity to Christ's example. (2.) In ch. ii. 10 we are told that love is the key even to the intellectual comprehension of one's position. He that loveth abideth in the light; all others are in darkness. (3.) Young disciples are told (ii. 14) that the "Word" of God abides in them, and that from this they gain their power over evil. (4.) We next have a precept to let that abide in us which we have heard from the beginning (ii. 24). If this abide with us, we abide in the

---

Him) to change their lives. Such there were of old, who "drew near to God with the lips, while the heart was far from Him," from whom even the God-appointed services were an abomination in His eyes. Such were the Pharisees, who pretended to keep the letter of His Law while they hourly violated its spirit. And such there will ever be, as long as it is supposed that by any form of words it is possible to confess Christ.

II. IT IS THE CONFESSION OF THE HEART. And what is meant by this? It is the inner acknowledgment that what the Gospel says is true. And the Gospel says that Jesus is the Son of God. But what is involved in this? That Jesus is the very image and likeness of God. And God is love. Thus Jesus is incarnate love. And as such He desires to save men from all that is not love. The heart must acknowledge this, must respond to it, must place itself in union with it, or the confession is no confession whatever. The first words of the

Son and in the Father. Thus one condition of our thus abiding is the *recognition of revealed truth.* (5.) That which abides in us is spoken of as an " unction ; " the sense of consecration to a Divine purpose which comes from the possession of a Divine spirit (ii. 27, 28). (6.) We come next to an effect of this abiding in God. It protects us from sin (iii. 6), and this (7.) because a seed of Divine life has been given and remains within (iii. 9). This seed is (8.) the seed of eternal life (iii. 15). And next (9.) we have the central truth the Apostle desires to inculcate indicated, and, after his manner, withdrawn until it can be again presented in a clearer light. This life that abides in us is the love of God (iii. 17). And thus (10.) a sign of the presence of this life is the keeping God's commandments (iii. 24), and its witness is the Spirit within us (iii. 25). Love (11.) is another sign that God dwells in us, and this also is the work of His Spirit, who came to save us from all that is unloving (iv. 12, 13). (12.) But all depends on Jesus Christ. The confession of Him as the Revelation of the Father, the Unifier of God and

---

text must be read in connection with the last. The acknowledgment of Jesus must involve the desire to think with Jesus, feel with Jesus, live in Jesus. And that desire has but to be formed and maintained to be more than fulfilled.

III. IT IS THE CONFESSION OF THE LIFE. This and the former go together. There cannot be one without the other. But it is possible to be mistaken about either. We can fancy we are confessing Christ in the heart, when a glance at our lives would undeceive us. Let us examine our lives in every particular, and seek there for the conformity to the image of Christ. Again, it is possible to imagine that we are confessing Christ in the life and yet to be deceived. If we have no inner love to Him, if our hearts are never kindled with the flame of devotion, if we have no pleasure in sacraments, prayers, praises, in study of His Word, in converse with the good and holy, if we do our deeds of charity mechanically, without love and sympathy and brotherly kindness towards those for whom we do them, then we

man, the Perfection of our humanity, is the source of the Divine life that dwells in us. And thus, by a succession of stages, are we led up to the full solution of the mystery of the Divine indwelling. Jesus Christ, *because* He is the Son, *because* He is the Saviour, *because* He has sent His Spirit to subdue all evil in us—all, that is, which is opposed to love—*because* He is Himself verily and truly God, is love itself; and the one decisive sign of the presence or absence of God in the heart, is the presence or absence there of love. The whole secret of Christian assurance consists in this, God is love, and he that dwelleth in love dwelleth in God, and God in him.

With this variety and progressiveness of treatment of the doctrine of the Divine indwelling, we may compare St. John xv., where the inward life is spoken of as flowing in a continuous stream from the Vine itself to the branches, and St. John vi., where it is declared to be fellowship in the flesh and blood, that is, the human nature, of the Lord. These passages, however, give the doctrinal, the Epistle the practical side of the truth; the

---

may suspect that something has gone wrong in our confession; that though we have "the form of godliness," we are strangers to the power thereof; the husk of godliness is there, the life which animates the kernel is dead or dying. Is there any one who desires to know what is meant by confessing that Jesus is the Son of God? Let him ponder well what follows, and he need not be long in doubt. "God is love; and he that dwelleth in love dwelleth in God, and God in him."

VER. 16.—*Why the confession of Jesus results in the Divine indwelling.*

I. BECAUSE JESUS LEADS US TO GOD. The confession of Jesus is the confession of God's Love, manifested in Jesus' life. From that life we learn God's love. We come to know it. We learn to trust in it. We accept it as the great fact which shapes our life. And thus we apprehend the Divine Nature.

former give the fact, the latter its subjective realisation ; the former tell us where the Divine Life is to be sought, the latter whether we have obtained it. And the answer to the question whether we dwell in God and He in us, is to be found in the answer to the question whether or no we are dwelling in love.

II. AND GOD IS LOVE. This *might* be inferred from creation itself. But the Fall has so jarred and crushed the fair world God has made and ourselves that we are scarcely able to discern His Hand in it. So it needed Jesus to show us once more God's nature (*a*) by His Life, and (*b*) by His Death.

XXIII.

CHARACTER OF CHRISTIAN EXPERIENCE.

CH. iv. 17.—St. John now goes on to develop the true doctrine of Christian assurance. Our παρρησία, he tells us, depends on our living the life of love. Nothing else can deprive us of that uneasiness which the presence of sin in the heart never fails to produce. And then, having thus led us up step by step to the real secret of Christian perfection, the Apostle proceeds (ch. iv. 1–12) to point out the one indispensable condition of its possession —faith. **Herein is our love made perfect.** ἐν τούτῳ again, as so frequently before. The question is, does ἐν τούτῳ belong (1) to what precedes, or (2) to our likeness to Christ? (2) has much to recommend it. The perfection

---

HOMILETICS.

CH. iv. 17.—*Fresh light on Christian assurance.*
I. MUTUAL LOVE IS PERFECTED BY OUR DWELLING IN GOD AND HE IN US. The object of Christ in founding His Church must not be held to rest only on our delivery from wrath, but in the infusing into us a spirit of love. Against that there is no law, and therefore there can be no wrath. Thus salvation through Christ is no arbitrary act of God's power or will, but has a moral fitness evident to all. We are delivered from wrath because we are translated into a realm of love. Love surrounds us on every side; we are bathed in an atmosphere of love; we breathe it into us, and it becomes part of us. And this love

of love *might* be held to consist in the likeness of the believer to his Master. But then, beside the awkwardness of "in this . . . because," what is to become of the intermediate clause? If our mutual love is perfected in our likeness to Christ, is it to be supposed that St. John would say that the cause of this was to be found in the desirability that we should have boldness in the day of judgment? Are we to explain it thus:—"In this is love perfected among us, namely, in the fact that we are like Christ; and this is the case in order that we may have boldness in the day of judgment?" If we give ἵνα the sense of result, it yields, it is true, a considerably better sense. But the best way is clearly, with all the best expositors, to connect ἐν τούτῳ with what precedes. "In this," namely, our union with God and God with us, is love perfected among us, so that we may have boldness in the day of judgment, because God sees in us, when thus united in heart and spirit to Him, the likeness of that "Beloved Son, in whom He was well pleased." μεθ' ἡμῶν cannot mean anything else than the mutual affection between Christians existing first in the heart of each individual, and then, as a necessary consequence, in the community; and love must mean love in the abstract, that love which, as

---

is God Himself. We dwell in Him and He in us. And so do all Christians. Hence, therefore, the mutual love that exists among Christians is perfected when God dwells in them and possesses them. The more complete the indwelling, the more complete the possession, and the more complete the result of that possession, the mutual love of those thus possessed by love.

II. WE NEED NOT FEAR THE DAY OF JUDGMENT. The whole tenor of the N. T. proclaims this truth. It is distinctly set forth in such passages as Rom. viii. 1. The statement there is strengthened by John iii. 17, 18, v. 24; Rom. v. 1, 9-11, vi. 7; 2 Cor. v. 19, &c. But the full reason may not be so obvious as it should be. It consists in the identification of ourselves by faith with Jesus Christ, the uniting

we have just been told, sums up all God's relation to His creatures. It is not " our love," however, as A. V. Rather *in this is love perfected among us*, taking μεθ' ἡμῶν with τετελείωται, not with ἡ ἀγάπη. Thus St. John would represent the Christian Church as a body of men looking forward with hope to that coming day of recompense, at the thought of which other men tremble, relying on their oneness in heart and spirit to Him whom the Father " hath sanctified and sent into the world."—**that we may have boldness in the day of judgment.** In regard to παρρησία, see notes on chaps. ii. 28, and iii. 21. The doctrine of Christian assurance is here further developed. If we want assurance or rather boldness in consequence of such assurance that we are Christ's, we shall find it in the fact that we have been conformed to a spirit of love, and in nothing else. Of course the Apostle means that the boldness with which they may then present themselves at the awful tribunal in the last day is to be theirs now, so far as in their conduct they are realising that which alone can give them this boldness. The Apostle bids them look forward to a time when they can cast aside all that leads them to be afraid of God. There is an innate antagonism between love and fear. Fear dis-

---

ourselves with His pure and perfect humanity. " In Him is no sin " (iii. 5). In Him is love, and "love is the fulfilling of the law " (Rom. xiii. 10). His are the deeds of the Spirit, and "against such there is no law" (Gal. v. 23). They who have thus by faith "put on" the Saviour (Rom. xiii. 14 ; Gal. iii. 27, &c.), need not fear the judgment because they have "put off the old man " (Eph. iv. 22 ; Col. iii. 9), and henceforth stand before God, " perfect in Christ Jesus " (Col. i. 28). Nor is this a mere individual affair. We are "one body in Christ" (Rom. xii. 5), and all the members of that body, in so far as by faith they have put on Christ, are free from all fear of His judgment. As has frequently been stated before, St. John regards these Divine truths as realised in the present, whereas, in fact, they are only

Y

appears as soon as ever love has taken entire possession of the heart. Does any one imagine that there is a contradiction between this passage and John iii. 18, v. 24? He will find the two doctrines harmonised in Gal. v. 6. —**because as he is, so are we in this world.** The first question here is, to whom does ἐκεῖνος refer? There can be little doubt that it refers here, as in ch. ii. 6, to Christ. But the question is of little consequence, inasmuch as the identity of essence between the Father and the Son is so plainly affirmed in this Epistle (as, for instance, in ch. ii. 22). Our next point is to observe on the force of ἐστιν. It is not "as He *was*, when among us," but "as He is *now*." "The ground of boldness is present likeness to Christ" (Westcott). And as Haupt says, the explanation of the thought is to be found in John xvii. 11–18. Jesus is no longer in the world. He is with His Father. Those whom He has called are still, however, in the world. But not of it. He has prayed that they "may be sanctified in the truth." With these words in his mind, the Apostle has written here, "As He is," dwelling in the bosom of the Eternal Father, "so also are we," even while we "are in this world." And this because we partake of the life which is in Him. We abide in

---

partially so realised. But the more completely they are made our own by faith, the more nearly do we approach to the ideal state of things he puts before us. Consequently it is in the power of each one of us to bring nearer that blessed time when we all live together in offices of mutual kindness, rejoicing in present favour, and penetrated with the hope of future blessedness.

III. BECAUSE WE ARE FORMED ANEW IN THE IMAGE OF CHRIST. St. John tells us that even here we are like Christ. At the end of a magnificent passage (2 Cor. iii.), St. Paul unfolds to us the process of which St. John puts before us the completion. We gaze intently and steadfastly on the image of Christ, and grow more like Him as we gaze. Even here we may strive to reproduce in our lives, as God has

Him and He in us. The various shifts to which interpreters have been driven in their explanation of this passage, are all due to the impossibility of getting rid of the idea that Christ's work is rather *for* us than *in* us, the conception of a legal and forensic justification instead of a justification consisting in a change of attitude in our whole moral being effected by our appropriation of the Redeemer's life by faith. On the forensic and external theory of justification this passage is unintelligible, and accordingly we have a host of evasive explanations such as the following:—" As He *is* " means "as He *was*." Luther explains, "as He suffered, we also suffer." " As He is the Son of God, so are we, adopted through Him " (Neander). But a comparison of passages, such as chaps. ii. 29, iii. 3, 5, 6, 7, 9, as well as the numerous references both here and in the Gospel to abiding in Him, as well as the parable of the Vine and the branches, will sufficiently justify the explanation given above. The connection of this part of the verse with what precedes, indicated by ὅτι, is given in the words cited above from Professor Westcott. Alford's note is well worth reading.

VER. 18.—**There is no fear in love, but perfect love casteth**

---

called us, some lineaments of the heavenly pattern. This must needs be a most consoling truth. Amid the weaknesses, the sorrows, the annoyances, the petty cares, of our life here, there beams on us the hope from a higher sphere. Our life gathers a dignity and a glory which transfigures its daily cares. For as we learn to endure them, we are mirroring back the likeness of Christ. As He was, so are we "made perfect through suffering" (Heb. ii. 10). As He was wearied with the faithlessness of a "perverse generation" (Matt. xvii. 17), as He endured the "contradiction of sinners" (Heb. xii. 3), so we have to bear the opposition of those who care not for Him. As He " bare the sins of the world " (John i. 29), so we, in our measure, strive to bear them with Him. We complain not if on us falls the weight of care and

out fear. It may seem to be a distinction without a difference, but "fear does not exist in love" would seem a better translation than "there is no fear in love," of the A. V., which the Revisers have also accepted. The A. V. seems to imply that fear and love cannot co-exist in the same person; whereas what is meant is that love and fear are so opposed that the one tends to drive the other out of the mind. As we have frequently remarked before, St. John has before his eyes the ideal condition of perfect union with God to which the believer is ever tending. In that condition no fear exists, nor can exist, for there is no longer cause for fear. Of course St. John is not speaking of that reverent awe which fears to offend (Ps. xix. 9, cxi. 10), but the fear of punishment, of reprobation, of rejection. If we ask how it is that "reverence and godly fear" are so often inculcated on us in Scripture, if fear be opposed to love, we shall find the reply in the words that follow.—**because fear hath torment.** Rather *chastisement*. All the earlier versions, from Wiclif downward, have *peyne* or *paynfulness*. The word, as well as the verb, from which it is derived, is used by Theophrastus of the pruning of a tree (cf. John xv. 2). Aristotle in his "Rhetoric" (i. 10, 17) distinguishes κολάζω from

---

suffering which other men's sins have produced. And though no act of ours can make compensation for sins committed, we offer ourselves thankfully and joyfully to bear the consequences of our own, the agony in wrestling with temptation, the dread of the results that may follow, the shame, the contempt, the lowered estimation in which others hold us, that at least we may display the "mind of Christ" in willingly enduring the consequences of all sin. Far, infinitely far as we fall below His perfections, yet there is a sense in which the most imperfect Christian, if sincere, can feel that even in his case there is a truth in the words, "As He is, so are we in the world."

VER. 18.—*Perfect love casteth out fear.*

I. FEAR AND LOVE MAY CO-EXIST IN THE SAME PERSON. To

τιμωρέομαι in the following way. The latter, he says, has in view the satisfaction for the offence, the former the restoration of the offender. There is no sufficient evidence that it ever bears the meaning "torment." Fear, then (not the fear to offend, but the fear of a deserved punishment), is the direct consequence of the sense of sinfulness. The "fear of the Lord" which St. Paul (2 Cor. v. 11) used to "persuade men," the "fear and trembling" in which (Phil. ii. 12, cf. Eph. vi. 5) he advises us to "work out our own salvation," have to do with that imperfect or transition state in which most Christians are in this life, and from which their progress in Christian love tends to emancipate them.—**He that feareth is not made perfect in love.** These words prove the correctness of the interpretation given above. The Apostle does not say "he that feareth *cannot* love," because love and fear can co-exist, and do co-exist, in all but perfect Christians. What he says is that as long as a man lives in fear of judgment, he thereby proves that he has not been perfected in love. The reference of course is to ver. 17, where nearly the same words are used. And thus it is clear from the context that fear of impending judgment is meant. The exegesis of this passage would be incom-

---

imagine that this is not the case is to misrepresent the Apostle. He does not say that there can be no fear in the mind of the man who has love. What he says approaches far more nearly to the statement that fear is not love. He says that fear is not contained in love. Fear to offend God must always be felt. Fear for the consequences of sin cannot be avoided, even where there is much love in the heart. But the tendency of love is to diminish fear. The more a man is filled with love, the less he is inclined to fear.

II. FEAR IS THE PUNISHMENT OF WRONG-DOING; LOVE INVOLVES THE IMPOSSIBILITY OF WRONG-DOING. This is the Apostle's statement, "Fear hath chastisement." It is the consequence of sin. A man who sins incurs the wrath of God. He must live in the appre-

plete without the mention of Bengel's "unmatched epigram," as Professor Westcott calls it, (his "brief, pointed manner"—Alford) "Varius hominum status, sine timore et amore, cum timore sine amore, cum timore et amore, sine timore cum amore." It is not at all clear why our translators preferred to follow Tyndall and Cranmer here, rather than the Geneva and Rhemish Versions, by omitting the "and" which these last had introduced (Wiclif has the adversative "but"). The Revisers have restored it, making the verse run thus (we have ventured to alter the first sentence): "Fear there is not in love, but perfect love casteth out fear, because fear hath punishment" (or better, *chastisement*), "and he that feareth is not made perfect in love." Thus the last clause, like the former, depends upon the word "because." Perfect love casts out fear, because fear is the outcome of a state of chastisement, and chastisement is a sign of imperfection. He, therefore, who fears, cannot have reached perfection in love, which leaves nothing whatever to be feared, since "love is the fulfilling of the law" (Rom. xiii. 10, cf. also Rom. viii. 15).

VER. 19.—**We love him because he first loved us.** The "Him" here, which all the old versions have introduced,

---

hension of that wrath. And that "certain fearful looking for of judgment and fiery indignation which shall devour the adversaries," is part of his punishment. A certain amount of love, as has been said, is compatible with this state of mind. But perfect love is not. Perfect love is the perfect fulfilling of the law. There can be no fear of punishment in the heart of the man who is doing nothing to incur punishment. And therefore the more perfect the love, the less fear is felt, until the time when fear, in its strict sense—not fear to offend, which is fear of putting oneself into a state in which one is not, but *present dread of consequences*—is impossible.

III. THE PRESENCE OF FEAR IN THE HEART IS A SIGN OF IMPERFECTION. "He that feareth is not made," or "has not been made perfect in love." We most of us detect some signs of uneasiness when

has no authority, and is due to a misapprehension. Cf. ch. iii. 16, note. What the Apostle means is not that we are to be considered as returning an affection which God has shown, but that we have no power to love at all, save from the love of God. The next question is whether (with many commentators and the Vulgate and Rhemish Versions) we should take ἀγαπῶμεν as imperative. The chief reason against it is the entire absence of any hortatory element in this passage. If we ask what is the connection of thought between this verse and what precedes and follows, we find more assistance from Dean Alford and Mr. Plummer than from most other modern commentators. It would seem to be this: There is no place for fear in him who is perfected in love, because the love which he has is from the source of love, namely, God. This gives a perfect confidence to us when we regard God, and when we feel that we are one with Him. But for that oneness to exist, there must be practical proofs of its existence. We must love, or we have no union with God, no ground for confidence. See note on ver. 10. The practical consequence here indicated is still further drawn out in the next verse. If we do *not* love, the ground for our confidence has disappeared.

---

we think of facing the awful judgments of a righteous God. The fear of death falls upon us. All this is the sign that we are not, as yet, made perfect in love. The spiritual life must grow in us. We must gain by degrees the mastery over all habits inconsistent with love. We must train ourselves into resisting all impulses that may do violence to it. As long as one single unkind, or unloving, or selfish thought has even temporary possession of us, we shall continue to tremble. Is is only when "our heart condemns us not" that we "have confidence toward God." Such a blessed condition as this has never yet been reached by mortal man. But blessed are they who approach it more nearly every day. Their fears will lessen, and their hopes brighten, until they reach the "city that hath foundations, whose builder and maker is God."

VER. 20.—**If a man say, I love God, and hateth his brother, he is a liar.** Dean Alford is quite right in saying that they fall into a great error who, like Ebrard, for instance, begin a new section here. As has been already implied, this verse arises naturally out of the last. Our love is a principle implanted within us. And as it comes from One who is love, it is an universal principle. Love cannot be shown to God and denied to those whom He has made and whom He loves. The "if a man say," is, like the expressions in chaps. i. 6, 8, 10, ii. 4, 6, 11, 18, 26, iii. 7, iv. 1, an indication of the fact that influences are at work on Christian souls antagonistic to God's truth, influences against which every Christian must be on his guard. The Apostle is acutely sensible that there is a kingdom of darkness as well as a kingdom of light, and that we need the utmost vigilance, lest our eyes should be blinded to the truth. We *must* love, in consequence of God's love, which is not merely displayed towards us, but if we abide in Him, must have been poured out in us. If we do not love our brother, it is untrue to say, as we are tempted to do, that we love God, because that love which is in Him, and comes from Him, is not in us.—**for he that loveth not his brother**

VER. 19.—*The source of love.*

I. LOVE NOT A WORK ACHIEVED BY MAN, BUT AN IMPULSE DERIVED FROM GOD. See Exposition for the various readings here. Two opposite mistakes have been fallen into on this point. On one side salvation has been regarded as a work achieved by man with God's help; on the other, as a single act of faith which at once and for ever decides a man's future. The first error has led to the most painful efforts, the most rigid and cruel self-tortures, the most wearing anxiety and uncertainty. The other imagines that salvation is not attained by the works of the law, and that therefore any effort to fulfil the will of God is dangerous and deadly, as teaching men to trust in themselves. The truth lies, as usual, between the two. Our salvation does not consist in the fulfilment of a covenant of works, but

whom he hath seen, how can he love God whom he hath not seen? The Sinaitic and Vatican MSS. read here (and the R. V. follows them) "cannot" for "how can he." Even these ancient MSS., as Tischendorf is careful to remind us in his preface, are not without their signs of corruption. The text of the New Testament had already been tampered with in the time of Tertullian and Origen. And here their reading looks like a correction. The received reading, "how can he," was less likely to have been substituted for the direct "cannot" than the contrary. But the oldest Syriac version supports ℵ and B here, so that their reading comes to us on very high authority. But it makes no difference to the sense which reading we take. The meaning is clear, that love must be shown to those whom God loves, it must be displayed in the region of the immediate and visible, if it is love at all. As Ebrard reminds us, it is not that the invisible is harder to love than the visible. The contrary may be more often the case. We may love a human being whom we have not seen more ardently than one who is nearer to us, whose imperfections jar on us from day to day. We may find it far harder to overcome prejudice and dislike, to forgive injuries, than to raise our

---

in the catching of a spirit from on high. That spirit will lead us to crucify the flesh, will nerve us to every effort necessary to stay self within us, and will finally bring our hearts into unison with God. The whole work is His, but wrought out in us. The first impulse comes from Him, and every subsequent struggle of the regenerate will against the works of the flesh is His work. The final result is not absorption in, but perfect union with Him. And He is love. If, therefore, He is in us, love must be in us. Thus it comes to pass that our love is but the stream of which His is the source. "We love, because He first loved us."

II. LOVE IN US IS DERIVED FROM THE LIFE AND DEATH OF CHRIST.

1. *It comes from the contemplation of the life and death of Jesus.* No story has ever had such power to move the human heart as the

hearts in ecstatic adoration to an unseen Father of all. But love, the Apostle reminds us, is a practical principle, not a sentimental enthusiasm. It must be shown, not in the ardour of contemplative feeling, but in the plain and prosaic region of action. It consists in overcoming these dislikes and prejudices of which we have just spoken, in rising superior to the spirit which would revenge injuries, in subduing those selfish impulses which are the direct opposite of love. Even devotion itself may be intensely selfish. Our religion may be no more than the desire to secure heaven for ourselves, happen what may to other people. The intensest fervour in prayer may co-exist with the most absolute devotion to one's own interests. The true test of love is its freeness, its expansiveness, its postponement of our own welfare to that of others. Its most perfect presentment was on the Cross. Thus the highest professions of sanctity, even though evidenced by a life of the most rigid asceticism, or the most utter self-abandonment to the raptures of spiritual contemplation, are but means of self-deceit, if they tempt us to substitute dreams of the invisible for duties in the visible; if they lead us to imagine that there can be any love of God without a corresponding

---

story of Jesus Christ. And that story culminates in His death upon the Cross. To that men look as the supreme embodiment of love. "Greater love hath no man than this, that a man lay down his life for his friends." 2. *But it comes not only from the contemplation, but from the fact of Christ's life.* Christ is living now. His life is poured into us. From it alone can we derive the power to love. It is "Christ in us," which gives "the hope of glory." So true is it that we can only "love, because He first loved us." The Spirit of love which streams forth from Him is the source of all the good deeds which, since He came, have refreshed the world. And all the good deeds of those who have not sought their inspiration from Him are a poor and pale reflection of the unbounded zeal and love of those who have caught the impulse of that Spirit.

love of one's neighbour. The word here translated "seen" is used obviously of ordinary vision. It does not convey the same idea of intensity and earnestness as the word used in vers. 12, 14.

VER. 21.—**And this commandment have we from him, that he who loveth God love his brother also.** "That which is a spiritual necessity is also an express injunction" (Westcott). "From Him" must surely mean God, for our Lord is not mentioned from ver. 15 onward. But we must not forget that the word "God" includes Jesus Christ, nor that all we know of God or God's will comes to us through Him. He is the Word of the Father, through whom every command of the Father comes to us. If we inquire where this command is given, it is sufficient if we find it in substance. We need not look for the exact words. We find it in Deut. vi. 5, and in Lev. xix. 18. We find it in Matt. xxii. 37–39. We find it in John xiii. 34, 35. It is possible, as Professor Westcott tells us, that ἵνα here marks an "injunction directed to an aim." Jesus gave us the commandment *in order that* we might keep it. But it is also possible that here we have only the subject-matter of the commandment itself, and also, after St. John's manner, a fuller development

---

VERS. 20, 21.—*Deeds, not words.*

I. LOVE IS NOT A BEAUTIFUL SENTIMENT, BUT A PRACTICAL PRINCIPLE. The test of true religion is conduct. "Pure religion and undefiled before God and the Father is this; to visit the fatherless and widows in their affliction, and to keep himself unspotted from the world." It might have been otherwise if religion consisted only in the intellectual apprehension of revealed truth. But since it consists in the reception, by faith, of a Person and of a life, it must be far more than this. It must display the characteristics of Him who is thus received and believed. What those characteristics are, is fully unfolded in His Holy Word.

II. WE MUST LOOK FOR THE SIGNS OF ACCEPTANCE IN OUR CONDUCT TO OUR BRETHREN. It is easy to say we love God. It is easy

of the thought contained in ch. ii. 3, 4. The whole commandment is summed up in one word—love, even as another Apostle has said, in words already quoted, "Love worketh no ill to his neighbour, therefore love is the fulfilling of the law," and again, "If there be any other commandment it is summed up in this word, namely, Thou shalt love thy neighbour as thyself" (Rom. xiii. 9, 10). And if any ask in what sense the word "brother" is to be understood here, he will find the answer in Luke x. 29–37.

---

to excite ourselves into an ecstatic admiration for an abstract principle of perfection. To say we love God is easy, but it is very often unreal. For we cannot see God. We do not know Him. We may persuade ourselves that we love Him, but we may be deceiving ourselves. The persuasion in most cases is but a form of words. The true proof of our love for God is the possession of His love. If we possess it, we shall render it back to Him. If we possess it, we shall give evidence of the fact. And this can only be done by displaying it. Our life must be first a struggle with, then a victory over, all that is inconsistent with love. All selfishness, pride, prejudice, littleness must be subdued. All class isolation must as far as possible be overcome. Tenderness, thoughtfulness, willingness to yield, care for the happiness of others rather than our own, such as Christ showed, are the signs of His presence within. If we really love God we must love *love*, for love is Himself.

XXIV.

SOURCE OF THE LIFE OF LOVE.

CH. v.—This chapter may be divided into three portions:—(1) Faith the source of the life of love (vers. 1–12); (2) the true application of faith (vers. 13–17); (3) general summary of the purport of the Epistle (vers. 18–21). The first part divides itself into two heads, (a) the relation between faith and practice, and (b) the grounds on which faith rests. It has been remarked as strange that faith is not so much as mentioned in St. John's Gospel, and only in ch. v. 4 of this Epistle. But the wonder diminishes when we remember that the contents of St. John's Gospel belong to the very early period of the history of Christianity, when facts were not yet formulated into phrases. It is a fact, the significance of which has not been generally appreciated, that whereas the word πίστις

HOMILETICS.

CH. v. 1a.—*The connection of faith and the new birth.*

I. FAITH IS NOT THE CAUSE BUT THE CONSEQUENCE OF THE NEW BIRTH. This statement will be looked upon as a paradox, so firmly is it believed by many that faith is the necessary condition of the new birth. But the paradox, if paradox it be, is plainly asserted here. No other interpretation can be put on St. John's words than this, "Whosoever believeth that Jesus is the Christ has already been born anew from God," *i.e.*, faith is not the cause, but the consequence of the new

does not occur in St. John's Gospel, the word πιστεύω occurs ninety-three times. Thus the position of belief as the ground of the Christian life is most distinctly recognised by St. John. But we do not find in his writings the words which came into use after the doctrines of Christianity had taken hold of the Christian conscience, and thus demanded phrases for the succinct expression of the facts of Christian experience. Thus, though the *ideas* of salvation, justification, reconciliation, redemption, sanctification, are clearly to be found in St. John's Gospel, the *words* which express them will be looked for in vain. There is one exception: σωτηρία is found in ch. iv. 22. The Epistle follows strictly on the lines of the Gospel. And yet the occurrence of such a word as ἱλασμός is sufficient to show that in the Epistle we have passed from the elementary to the doctrinal stage of Christianity. I would simply remark in passing on the evidential force of these facts. I have dealt with them more fully in another work. πίστις occurs, it is true, occasionally in the Synoptic Gospels. But it refers to a more obvious, less esoteric form of faith than that we are here invited to consider. Faith is not, in those Gospels, represented as the foundation of Christian life, though it clearly involves *confidence in a person*, the principle on which Christian faith, in the widest accepta-

---

birth. So St. Paul thinks it necessary to caution us in Eph. ii. 8. "Salvation," he there points out, "is not your work. It is not achieved by your faith. It is a Divine gift. Faith is only the law of its working." Many in our own day make salvation and the new birth man's act, not God's. Man believes, and then God operates. The opposite is the case. With the spiritual as with the natural life, the divinely given germ is the first starting-point, which gathers shape and form by divinely given laws. The natural life develops according to the law of Nature. The spiritual life, if it grows at all, develops according to a spirit of faith. Faith is, no doubt, man's "corre-

tion of the word, is based. There is much to be learned from the position assigned to faith in this Epistle. St. John's method of gradual and almost imperceptible progress in teaching was based on that of his Master. He gives many instances of it in his Gospel. In this Epistle he has taught us (1) that a life has been given us from on high; (2) that this life is one which sheds light on our lives; (3) that it brings with it assurance of pardon; (4) that the light involves not merely intellectual, but moral instruction, and that "love is the fulfilling of the law;" (5) that there are many adverse influences in the world, which it behoves the disciple to resist; (6) that a power is infused into the disciple's heart by which he may rise superior to all evil solicitations; (7) that there is need to make diligent use of this power; (8) that it proceeds from the recognition of Jesus Christ come in our mortal flesh; (9) that this power is nothing less than God Himself, who is Love, dwelling in us, and inspiring His Spirit into us. The next question which naturally arises is, How do we become possessors of this power? The answer is given in the verses which follow (1–12). It is made ours by faith. No definition of faith is given. In fact, no definition of faith is given at all in the New Testament save in Heb. xi. 1. But πιστεύω, πίστις are the New

---

spondence to environment," to use modern scientific language. But even that power is God's gift. Man has nothing of his own beyond the self-determining power which accepts or rejects what God offers him.

II. FAITH PUTS THE PRINCIPLE OF THE NEW BIRTH INTO OPERATION. For (1) the new birth is not, as some imagine, an experience, a sense of reconciliation, an assurance of pardon, or of final salvation. It is the impartation of the σπέρμα θεοῦ (ch. iii. 9)—of the higher Divine life known as spirit. And (2) faith is not simply the belief in a work already done, the acceptance of pardon, the confident expecta-

Testament equivalents to the Hebrew word signifying *reliance*, and they involve the double sense (1) of seeing and (2) of trusting Him who is invisible. The acknowledgment that this mighty power of Divine love exists, and the readiness to throw ourselves upon it for support and guidance, in full confidence that they will be given, is the idea of Christian faith put before us by St. John. This faith rests upon *testimony* (vers. 6–12), and that testimony the inward work of the Spirit carried out (1) by the reanimation of our fainting humanity and (2) by the making us partakers of the humanity of Christ. (This appears to me to be the meaning of the allusions to water and blood.) And it produces boldness, or confidence ($παρρησία$), not only in regard to our own future condition (as in ch. iv. 17), but in the fatherly love and tenderness of God, who will grant every petition of ours (ch. v. 14) which is not in conflict with His wise purposes.

VER. 1.—**Whosoever believeth that Jesus is the Christ, is born of God.** Rather, as before, *every one that believeth that Jesus is the Christ, hath been born* (or *begotten*) *from God*. These words are in close connection with what has gone before. Though they lead to the definition of the place of faith in the Christian scheme, this definition, nevertheless, according to the subtle law of evolution characteristic of St. John's Epistle and Gospel, flows

---

tion of final salvation. Faith is confidence in, reliance on, full persuasion of, the power and goodness of God. His power, in that we are convinced He *can* destroy the empire of sin in us. His goodness, in that we are as firmly persuaded that He *will*. This confidence is the evidence of the presence of the Divine life within us. But it is more. It is (see above) the law of its working. As the heavenly bodies revolve in their orbits according to the law of gravitation, so the Divine life unfolds itself within us according to the law of faith. Nor need this seem strange. If God be good, if in consequence He hates sin,

gradually and imperceptibly from the thought with which the last chapter concludes. The thought unfolds itself thus:—It is a fundamental principle of the Gospel that each disciple should love his brother. And why? Because each is the possessor of a new life, coming direct from God. As Dean Alford contends, these words, "every one that believeth that Jesus is the Christ is born of God," do *not* refer to the individual, but to the community. We are to love our brother because *every* believer shares the gift of the supernatural life (John i. 12, 13). This is made clear by what follows. (See next note.) Our next question is regarding the meaning of πιστεύων. The word has occurred twice before in the Epistle. In ch. iii. 23 it is coupled with love, but not represented as in any sense the channel through which that love flows. It involves the recognition of Jesus Christ, and a full trust and confidence in Him. But there is no specific definition of its character. In ch. iv. 16, it is in one sense yet more restricted, if in another fuller in its scope. It is not belief in God or Christ, but in His love. It is true that this is immediately connected with the assertion that love is of His essence. But what we are in that passage specially asked to contemplate is the action of God towards us, as witnessed to by our experience. Here, however, the nature of faith is clearly set forth. It accepts the truth that

---

if He have power to destroy it, it follows that if we believe all this, we place ourselves in dependence on Him, we rely on His power to overcome sin in us. If, moreover, we believe that this Divine life-principle be really in ourselves, it becomes a moral necessity that in obedience to it, in full trust and persuasion of its presence, we shall set ourselves to work out our own deliverance from sin, in accordance with its promptings. Thus, then, as Jesus said to Nicodemus, the first and essential necessity for those who would enter His kingdom is the new birth. But the second and equally necessary condition is

Jesus is the Christ, and this, of course, involves all the doctrinal statements of ch. iv. He who believes that Jesus is the Christ, believes in Him as the personal manifestation, in human form, of God Himself. We have next to discuss the words, "Hath been begotten of God." In ch. iii. 9 we regarded the words as referring to the *tendencies* of the new life. It may either mean that when the Divine life has reached the stage of maturity, there is no more transgression, or it may regard the man from the point of view of the regenerate life, and lay down the doctrine that so far as that life is concerned he cannot sin, but that whatsoever sin he commits is due not to the operation of that life, but to the "corruption which remaineth, yea, even in them which are regenerate." Whatever its meaning — and the passage is one of serious difficulty — it cannot, without contradicting plain facts, be interpreted to mean the absolute impeccability of every one who has been born again. In the present passage, however, there is considerably less difficulty. The perfect refers to the gift of the Divine life in the first instance, and regards it from the point of view of the gift, not of its development. The Divine life is given once for all when the soul is taken into union with Christ. And the possession of faith in Christ is the clear evidence that this Divine life has been received. He who believes has already been

---

to believe in Christ as having thus regenerated us, so that the new birth may develop into a new life.

VER. 1b.—*The brotherhood of faith.*

I. IT SPRINGS FROM THE POSSESSION OF A DIVINE LIFE. The Apostle assumes that we love Him from whom our life proceeds. We recognise our relation to God. We feel that He is the source of all our being. And we especially thank Him for that second creation which makes us possessors of His higher excellences.

II. IT RECOGNISES THE DIVINE LIFE IN OTHERS AS A BOND OF

begotten of God. Haupt asks why we have πιστεύειν here and not ὁμολογεῖν, as in ch. iv. 15. His answer is that here the Apostle is leading us to consider the inward basis of the Christian life, and not, as there, its outward expression. He further cites John i. 12 to show that we must not confound faith and the Divine life. The former is the means of appropriating the latter the attitude of the human spirit which enables it to receive the heavenly gift, and also, as we have just seen, the sign and evidence of its possession.—**and every one that loveth him that begat, loveth him also that is begotten of him.** Some ancient and modern expositors explain "him that is begotten of Him," of Jesus Christ. But the connection of thought makes it clear that the reference here, as in the former part of the verse, is to the individual Christian. In fact, in this passage and in the succeeding verse we have the converse proposition of that presented to us in ch. iv. 20. The two propositions are not contradictory, but parallel. In the first we are concerned with the Christian life in its manifestation. If a man is not, in his conduct, actuated by love of his neighbour, it is clear that he is not animated by the love of God. Here, however, we are asked to regard the Christian life from the point of view of its origin. He who is conscious that he has been born again of God through the operation of the Holy Spirit ("it is assumed that the child

---

UNION. We know that the same faith which stamps us as having received the new life, stamps others as having received it also. And if we love and prize Christ, and Him who gave Christ above all other things, we cannot fail to love those in whom Christ is to be found. We love them because in them we find Him who is the source of all goodness and truth. One with Him, we are, by a natural and irresistible law, one with each other. And the only possible cause of strife and alienation is the absence of the Divine life, or at best, its failure to pervade the whole man.

will have love for the Author of his being"—Westcott), will feel himself inspired by a love for all in whom he perceives that new life in operation; in all, that is, who are possessed by the spirit of faith in Jesus Christ. Thus the Christian life harmoniously revolves in a perfect circle round God its centre. The love of God involves the love of man: the love of man is the visible manifestation of the love of God. It is important, further, to notice, with Professor Maurice, that here, as in ch. iv. 19, the order is not the ascending from the love of man to the love of God. The love which comes from God is the primary principle of all love. Without it no love were possible. The love of man is its necessary result, the necessary indication of its presence. But the love of man is no more the cause of the love of God than the rise or fall of the barometer is the cause of good or bad weather.

VER. 2.—**By this we know that we love the children of God, when we love God and keep his commandments.** Rather *in this*, as before. This verse still more markedly asserts the converse of the proposition in ch. iv. 20. But its last words supply the explanation. We cannot really love God unless we love our brother. And if we want to know whether we love our brother, we must ask whether we love God. But the keeping of God's commandments is at once the test of our love to God, and

---

VER. 2.—*The test of love—obedience.*
1. THE PARADOXES OF SCRIPTURE. In the Bible we frequently find ourselves confronted by apparent contradictions. Thus (Prov. xxvi. 4, 5) we are told to answer and not to answer a fool according to his folly. Again (Gal. vi. 2, 5) we are told to bear one another's burdens, because every one shall bear his own. Every one is familiar with the contradiction in words between St. Paul and St. James on the subject of justification by works. So here, we have an apparent contradiction to ch. iv. 20. There the love of our neighbour is the test of our love

the mode in which we must display our love to our neighbour. Even in so obvious a duty as the display of love we need direction. The weak compliance which some people mistake for love very often proves to be its exact opposite. "There is," says Haupt, "a purely natural love which is only a sublimated egotism." If we want to know how to display love to our brother, we must seek the source of our inspiration in God. He is love, and to do what He tells us must be to love our neighbour. If, therefore, we want to know whether our course is one of love or not, let us make God the object of all our aspirations, and His Word the guide of all our actions, and we shall not be far wrong. As Professor Westcott reminds us, this truth is emphasised by ὅταν. *Whensoever* we feel that we are actuated by the love of God, and are walking in the way of His commandments, we may be sure that we are fulfilling the great duty of Christian love. The Vatican MS., as well as the Vulgate and other ancient versions, read ποιῶμεν in the place of τηρῶμεν, which is the reading of the Sinaitic MS. and the Rec. text. The editors prefer the former as being an unusual expression, and, therefore, more likely to be corrected to the more usual τηρῶμεν than the contrary. We may compare the expression to "do His commandments" with the still more remarkable expression to "do the truth," in ch. i. 6.

---

to God. Here the love of God and the keeping His commandments are the test of our love to our neighbour. And yet there is no real contradiction in any of these. Truth is many-sided. And every truth has its complement, which confines it to its proper limits, and, so to speak, rounds it off.

II. THE DIRECTION IN WHICH THE TRUE DEFINITION OF BROTHERLY LOVE IS TO BE LOOKED FOR. Man is ignorant. He knows not how to direct his steps. If he tries to show forth love to his neighbour he knows not how to set about it. 1. *Where is he to*

VER. 3 —**For this is the love of God, that we keep his commandments.** The thought of the last verse finds yet more distinct expression here. The keeping of God's commandments *is* the love of God. His commandments are the outward expression of His love, the laws whereby we are kept within its sphere. I have regarded ἵνα here as the sign of the infinitive, as it is in many other places in Scripture. For similar thoughts cf. John xiv. 15, 21, 23, 31; also John xv. 10, and 2 John 6. It is very necessary that this side of the truth should be borne in mind. Had we only ch. iv. 20 before us, we might have imagined that the love of God was a thing that came by practice, and become involved in the Pelagian error that we could of ourselves rise to the level of God's requirements. But such a view is shut out by the present passage, which represents love in us as the expression of the love of God, and God's commandments as the channel in which that expression of love must necessarily flow.—**and his commandments are not grievous.** The reason of this statement is given in the next verse (Alford). Consequently here we are simply concerned with the fact. It had been already declared by Christ in the well-known words, "My yoke is easy, and My burden is light" (Matt. xi. 30). The meaning here, however, is not so much that God's commandments are not difficult to keep, as that they

---

look for direction? To God's commandments set forth in His Holy Word. 2. *Why is this?* Because God is love, and we can only carry out the principle of brotherly love by acting in His Spirit. The directions given us are twofold; precept, and better still, example—the example of Jesus Christ (Phil. ii. 5). Thus a man cannot be loving God unless he be loving his neighbour. Neither can he know how to love his neighbour unless he loves God and seeks direction from Him.

VERS. 3, 4.—*The light yoke of Christ.*
I. HIS YOKE IS LIGHT BECAUSE OF THE NATURE OF HIS COM-

are not burdensome, do not impose a heavy yoke *when kept*. Rather we should say with the Psalmist, "In keeping of them there is great reward" (Psalm xix. 11), *i.e.*, the very fact of keeping them is in itself happiness. It is true that the next verse implies that the difficulty is not so great to the Christian,—not so great as he might be inclined to imagine, seeing that he is provided with a faculty which will enable him to overcome all temptations to break them. But the continuity of thought demands that we should view these words also in connection with what has gone before. There the commandments of God have been regarded as the expression of His love to man, and a guide to us in the manifestation of that love. But they can hardly be this, and also the "heavy burdens, and grievous to be borne," which our Lord speaks of as being imposed by the Pharisees (Matt. xxiii. 4). On the contrary, it is the breach of God's commandments that entails grievous consequences upon us. The more we fulfil God's commandments, the lighter they grow, and the lighter also grow our hearts. Those commandments are the "path of life;" perfectly to fulfil them would be "fulness of joy," the attainment of that "pleasure for evermore" which is declared to be "at God's right hand" (Psalm xvi. 12).

VER. 4.—**For whatsoever is born of God overcometh the**

MANDMENTS. For (1) the keeping of them produces *peace of mind;* (2) it produces an *approving conscience;* (3) it tends to promote unity and peace among mankind; and (4) it grows easier by practice and the formation of holy habits.

II. IT IS LIGHT BECAUSE OF THE POWER HE GIVES US TO BEAR IT. The new life, quickened into operation in us by faith, conquers the world. And this because it is the life of God manifested in Jesus Christ, and imparted to us by the Spirit. A Divine life must be a victorious life. It cannot be otherwise (Luke xi. 22). It is this which makes the fulfilment of God's commands not grievous. By ourselves

world. The neuter here is not, as some have thought, equivalent to *all men*. It rather refers to the power inherent in them, as in John iii. 6, vi. 37, xvii. 2. It is not we who conquer, but the power that dwelleth in us. Or rather, perhaps, we should put it thus. If we conquer, it is through no natural power of our own apart from God, but through His Divine gift, working in each one of us, according to the laws impressed on it by His Providence, and uniting us into one body in Christ. We must observe the present and perfect tenses here, as contrasted with the aorist in the next passage. Whatsoever *has been* born from God *overcomes*, *i.e.*, is in permanent possession of the power to overcome the world. **—and this is the victory that overcometh the world, even our faith.** Literally, *this is the victory which overcame* (or *hath been overcoming*) *the world*. It seems impossible to deny that here the grammar is literally incorrect, but spiritually true. It is not literally true that our faith *overcame* the world. But the Apostle is linking that faith with the past fact from which alone it draws its power. Without connection with that past fact our faith could have no such power. That which overcame the world was the natural life on earth of Jesus Christ (John xvi. 33). To that past fact our faith leads us, in all our struggles with the evil the world contains. With

---

we are utterly incapable of rising to the level of their requirements (Rom. iii. 9, 20, 28). But in His strength we are always able to conquer.

III. FAITH THE SOURCE OF OBEDIENCE. We have but to believe (1) that God is Lord and Ruler of all; (2) that He wills to make us partakers of His glory; (3) that He is ready to impart to us the power we need in order to have victory over sin; and (4) that this power is in His Son;—to attain to perfect obedience. A perfect faith of this kind of necessity produces perfect obedience. If we are not yet victorious over sin, it is because our faith is imperfect. And according

that past fact it unites us, so that the life of Christ is lived over again by each one of us. Hence the deep inner truth suggested by the aorist. Our faith is not a thing of the past but of the present. But it would be utterly ineffective, useless, unless it were in immediate connection with that victory over sin and death achieved by Jesus Christ, a fact literally past, and yet eternally present with His Church. Nor is this the only point in which this passage, viewed literally only, would be misleading. Our faith, regarded in itself, is not the victory. The victory is the victory of Christ, repeated and continued in us. It is, as Professor Westcott says, "the individual appropriation of a victory gained once for all." It should be observed that νίκη occurs here only in the New Testament, and πίστις only here in St. John.

VER. 5.—**Who is he that overcometh the world, but he that believeth that Jesus Christ is the Son of God.** This passage has hidden links of connection with what has preceded. And various truths are implied in it. First, we are informed *why* faith overcomes the world,—because it is faith in the Son of God, in One who possesses Divine power to overcome all that is evil. Next, we are once more taught to look upon God's disordered world as the antagonist to goodness, or, in other words, to love. And thirdly, in connection with ver. 1, we see an addi-

---

to the measure of our faith, so is our approach to Christian perfection. Let us then "reach forward towards the things that are before" (Phil. iii. 13, 14; 2 Pet. i. 5-7).

VER. 5.—*The basis and result of Christian faith.*

I. OUR FAITH IN JESUS AS THE SON OF GOD. Let us consider what is involved in this. 1. It asserts a special character in Jesus Christ. He is not *a* son of God in the sense that all created beings are. He is *the* Son of God in a sense peculiar to Himself. 2. What is implied in sonship? Likeness to the Father. Thus *the* Son of God is one who comes from God, and displays the nature of Him from

tional reason for mutual love in the common antagonism of every true child of God to the tendencies to strife and selfishness which human society presents. This thought, however, is pursued no further. The Apostle turns in the verses which follow to the grounds on which we believe Jesus Christ to be the Son of God. And those grounds, it will be seen, lead us to no barren acceptance of a dogma. It is not belief in the Incarnation, as a formula, but belief in One who has become incarnate. And this belief rests, we learn in what follows, on the inward witness we have (1) of a Spirit, guiding and inspiring us; (2) of an influence, purifying and refreshing us; (3) of a life imparted to us and flowing in our veins. These are felt to be working within us to one and the same purpose, to make us one with God. We cannot leave the subject without pointing out the connection between these two verses on the one hand, and John xvi. 33, and the many passages in which ὁ νικῶν occurs in the Revelation as a mark of the common authorship of the three books. For a similar thought to the one contained in this verse cf. 1 Cor. xv. 57.

---

whom He comes. 3. We find in Jesus Christ all the attributes of His Father: power, wisdom, intelligence, righteousness, glory, love (John i. 14; Col. i. 19, ii. 9; Heb. i. 3; &c.)

II. SUCH A FAITH IS ITSELF VICTORY. See notes on the last two verses. Also Expositions. This faith overcomes the world (1) by uniting us to Christ; (2) because His power, to which it unites us, is Divine. Apart from Christ, we are nothing (John xv. 5). In Him we are partakers of His fulness, and sharers of His victory (John i. 16, xvi. 33).

XXV.

UNION WITH CHRIST.

CH. v. 6.—The Apostle, in the next eight verses, proceeds to explain the grounds on which faith rests. And it is of great importance to observe that, of however much value the historical evidence for Christianity may be, its inward witness is of far greater importance. It is solely to this inward witness that the Apostle refers here. The external evidence is necessary to bring men *to* Christ; the internal witness confirms them *in* Christ. That internal witness is the witness of the Spirit. And this witness is confirmed by two other facts—facts which are not really distinct from the Spirit's witness, but form part of it—the one the cleansing and refreshing influence of the Gospel, the other the intimate union with the humanity of Christ which the Spirit produces in us by means of faith.

HOMILETICS.

CH. v. 6.—(1.) *Jesus Christ cometh by water and by blood.*
The language of the Apostle emphatically intimates that the work of Jesus Christ was a double work, and that he who only regards one part of that work has received only a defective impression of the nature of the Gospel. The first work is the taking away from us what we have—namely, a sinful nature; the second is the giving us

This is he that came by water and by blood. This verse is one full of meaning. And as usual with passages so pregnant, it has given rise to endless diversities of interpretation. It will be convenient to deal with questions of reading and rendering first, and then with questions of interpretation. 1. In regard to reading, it is noteworthy that the Codex Sinaiticus adds "and spirit" after the word "blood." But the addition is clearly made in order to assimilate the passage to ver. 8, as well as to pave the way for the introduction of the words "and the Spirit beareth witness," &c., in this verse. The other uncial MSS., as well as the Syriac and Vulgate, read as the Authorised Version. 2. In regard to rendering, we ought not to fail to observe the difference between δι' ὕδατος here and the ἐν τῷ ὕδατι of the next clause. διά here, without the article, refers to the way in which Jesus Christ was pleased to redeem the world. He came, we are told, He was pleased to work in us, by two means —water and blood. But He did not come to us, or work in us, by the water only, but by the water and by the blood (the article indicating the water and the blood just specified). That is, the method of His working in the soul combined both these *media*, each being an equally necessary element in the work He came to do. 3. The next question that arises is that of interpretation, and we are at once plunged into a sea of difficulties.

---

what we have not—that is, fellowship with the Divine nature. Water may be taken as the type of cleansing from sin (though—see Exposition—it may receive a wider interpretation). Blood is a phrase used to denote the impartation of Christ's righteousness. Let us regard each of these in turn.

I. THE CLEANSING PROCESS.

a. The first step is a sense of reconciliation with God. To express this we have a variety of words in the English Bible. Reconciliation,

First, it is disputed whether there is any reference here to John xix. 34; next, whether there is any reference to the two Sacraments; and thirdly, what is actually meant by the words. We will discuss these questions in the order in which they have been stated. (1.) The reference to John xix. 34 can hardly be denied by any one who reflects on the inward unity of Scripture, and especially on the close connection between St. John's Epistle and his Gospel. The emphatic words with which the Evangelist refers to what he saw, prove beyond a doubt that a mystic meaning attached itself to that which appeared to him to be so wondrous a sight. The occurrence was unquestionably in his eyes typical of some great principle. And when he here (for only a lover of paradox can dispute that the Gospel and Epistle are by the same hand) refers to these very principles, there can be little doubt that he is expounding that of which the incident he reports to us in the Gospel was the type. (2.) We are asked whether the two great Sacraments of the Gospel are here referred to. We may reply that they are referred to in precisely the degree in which they are referred to in the third and sixth chapters of St. John's Gospel. That is to say, the reference is rather to the first principles of the Gospel which these two Sacraments symbolise and apply than directly to the Sacraments themselves. The difficulty has arisen, on the one hand,

---

atonement (both renderings of the word καταλλαγή), justification, adoption, grace, and the like, are used to convey it. All these imply the removal of the alienation between God and man which is the necessary consequence of sin, and the substitution in its place of the confidence (παρρησία), the access (προσαγωγή), the assurance of fatherly love on God's part which has been revealed by Jesus Christ.

  b. The next step is the stirring us up to a conflict with sin. God's object is not merely the removal of the sentence, but of the cause of

from the inability on the part of some to make any distinction between the Sacraments and the eternal truths that underlie them, and on the other hand, from the natural reaction on the part of others which leads them to deny any connection between the outward sign and the thing signified. But as it is impossible for any unprejudiced mind to help seeing some link of connection between the discourses in the third and sixth chapters of St. John and those great ceremonies of the Church which are a kind of visible presentment of the teaching in those chapters, so here, both the order of the words ("water" coming first and "blood" afterwards) and the connection of the first Sacrament with the former, and of the second with the latter, would naturally suggest some reference to the truths symbolised in those Sacraments and embodied in the Saviour's life and work. Those who regard the two Sacraments as at once the expression of two great principles in the Gospel scheme, and as the appointed means whereby those principles are applied to the individual soul, will naturally see here a primary reference to the principles and a secondary reference to the Sacraments as concerned in the application of those principles to the life of the believer.

The first of these two great principles is the work of Christ in cleansing from sin. To this fact of the Christian scheme baptism bears witness. And not only

---

the sentence. The renewed life is entirely irreconcilable with sin, and must be in deadly enmity with it. See chaps. i. 6, 9 (where the word is $ἀφῇ$—see Exposition of this verse), ii. 5, 15, iii. 3, 9, 10, &c., and cf. Rom. vi. throughout, viii. 2, 4, 7, &c. And the object of the renewed life (see Exposition) is the expulsion of sin. The cleansing, or washing, is a process involving the gradual detachment of the soul from all sinful habits.

c. We are sustained in this conflict by the assurance of victory.

does it bear witness to it, but it asserts that the power which will produce this cleansing is already at work within the heart of every one who is admitted into the fellowship of Christ's Church. This cleansing is two-fold in its nature. As the well-known hymn says, we need cleansing from the guilt and from the power of sin. The *guilt* of sin is remitted at the outset of the Christian life. No burden hangs henceforth round the sinner's neck of original sin, nor of any sin repented of. "There is no condemnation to them that are in Christ Jesus," provided their will and purpose is in accordance with His. But cleansing from the *power* of sin is a process, a life-long work, of which baptism represents the initial stage. He who has been baptized need not doubt that this process has been begun in him, and that if his faith remain unimpaired, it will go on to its final completion. Thus baptism is an expression as well as an application of the fact that Jesus Christ came by water. When we come to the other Sacrament, the Body and Blood of Christ are the prominent thought. And not that Body and Blood objectively alone, as an object of contemplation or worship, but subjectively also, as a fact realised within. And the Sacrament of the Lord's Supper involves the recognition of the other great principle of Christianity, namely, that the redeeming work of Christ is carried on simply and solely through

---

See John xvi. 33; 1 Cor. xv. 57; 1 Thess. i. 5; as well as the numerous passages in this Epistle and the Revelation which speak of overcoming. From this point of view water is regarded in its refreshing as well as cleansing aspects. It implies the confidence with which the Christian warrior advances to the battle, armed with the shield of faith; the sustained energy he displays in the conflict; the renewed vigour he evinces when downcast or wearied, when he recurs to the fountain, and is invigorated by fresh draughts of the water of life.

the infusion into the believer, by a process purely spiritual, of the human life of our Saviour Jesus Christ. The blood is the life. And the Blood of Jesus is His life. That life He came to impart to us. We have dwelt too much on the unquestionable truth that His Blood was shed for us. We have allowed ourselves to dwell too little on the equally unquestionable truth that this Blood is imparted to us, inwrought by faith into the very tissue and texture of our lives. And this view will serve also to explain the difference of order here and in St. John's Gospel. There we read of "blood and water," here of "water and blood." This is because there we have the Divine, here the human side of this vital truth. There we have these facts regarded from the point of view of their origin. The Christian Church in her Sacraments, as well as the Apostle in this passage, and our Lord Himself in the two great discourses already referred to, regards them in their application. In the case of each believer the cleansing comes first, the removal of guilt, of the antecedent bar which sin presents to the full union between the spirit and God, and then the consciousness of communion, the reception of life, the "growing together" (Rom. vi. 5) of the believer and his Lord. But from the Divine point of view this order is reversed. The Blood of Christ is that which effects the whole work. "God is one" (Gal. iii.

---

d. But it is the life of Christ which does all. As we have already seen, the water, after all, only represents one particular effect of the gift of the blood. It is the blood which cleanseth us from sin—ch. i. 7; cf. Eph. i. 7; Heb. xii. 24; Rev. i. 5 (where, however, there is a different reading), vii. 14, &c. It is to the blood that we owe our justification, adoption, peace (Rom. iii. 24–26), and all the refreshment and strength which the Christian can receive through his faith. But these ideas are not immediately connected in our minds with blood.

20). It is only the human intellect that requires to divide truth into propositions. The cleansing process is part of the embodying (Eph. ii. 13—20, iii. 6) of the believer into Christ. It is "the Blood of Christ" that "cleanseth from all sin" (ch. i. 7). The water is but a type of that particular truth. It represents, that is, one aspect of the work accomplished by the precious Blood. The Sacraments, then, clearly come within the scope of this passage as the visible ceremonies whereby the fundamental principles of the Gospel are proclaimed and applied to all mankind. (3.) It remains, then, to state what is meant by the words here used. And the answer has been to a great extent anticipated by what has already been said. But the connection between these words and the Christian Sacraments, as symbolising and expressing the relation of the members of Christ to their Head having been admitted, we may proceed to give the words a wider interpretation. The passage has been one full of difficulty to the commentators. The number of explanations has been almost endless. Yet the one here adopted, if not precisely coinciding in all respects with any the writer has seen, is at least in accordance, not perhaps with some modern conceptions, but at least with the doctrine of the Incarnation as it has been taught in the Church from the earliest ages.

The cleansing effects of water have already been

Hence this aspect of the Divine life is represented to us under the figure of water.

    e. Exhortation to confidence in the Christian walk. Vers. 13, 18, 20; Rom. v. 1, &c.

  II. THE UNION OF THE BELIEVER WITH CHRIST.

    a. This was Christ's aim. John xvii. 20, 21 ; Rom. vi. 23 ; Tit. ii. 14, chap. iv. 9, 13, 14, v. 11.

    b. It is carried out by the gift of Himself. So we are taught in

mentioned. But hitherto nothing has been said of its invigorating effects. This aspect of the type of water is also represented to us by the wine of the Lord's Supper. Hence, though the two Sacraments are referred to in this passage by the water and the blood respectively, it is impossible to confine the reference to them. The water also represents the strengthening and refreshing effects of the Life of Christ, the power which is spoken of in the preceding verses as overcoming the world, and as being closely connected with the new birth from on high. It is hardly possible to suppose that the words of Christ, reported with much emphasis by himself, the words, that is, which speak of the Christian as " born again of water and the Spirit," can have been absent from the Apostle's mind. The idea of birth does not involve the idea of cleansing. This last idea is only connected with the former when we conceive of the birth within a sin-stained being of a pure and regenerating influence such as the Life of Christ. Hence, then, the conception of spiritual vigour, as well as the removal of condemnation, must be involved in the mention of water, the idea of a faculty fitting us for conflict and assuring us of victory. But this, true as it is, would only be an one-sided view (a view, nevertheless, very widely diffused. See below). "Not in the water only, but in the water and the blood." The notion is not of a being separate from us cleansing

---

John vi. And this is the truth which underlies the sacrament of Holy Communion. The life the Christian lives is henceforth not his own, but Christ's (Gal. ii. 20). The precious blood is the life of his soul. It is not merely the price paid (1 Pet. i. 18, 19). It is the gift given. (See esp. John vi. 57, with which compare John iii. 16; Heb. ix. 14, x. 10-22. Also Rom. v. 17, 21, and texts cited under head *a*).

c. The necessary condition on our part is faith. It needs not to prove this by Scripture. No doctrine of Holy Writ is more continually

us by any external process of purification, nor even of such a being stirring us up by example, precept, or even assistance, to an energetic conflict with evil. The Apostle's teaching goes deeper. He speaks of inward and vital union with Christ. Christ not only cleanses us as He did the leper, by a touch from without, He cleanses us by His presence within. He not only invigorates us by His example and by His grace, but He strengthens us by the gift of His own self. The explanations of some commentators seem to involve a contracted or mistaken notion not only of the word ἄφεσις, but of the English word "atone." As we have seen, men speak of the former as equivalent to forgiveness. But its more natural meaning is *expulsion*. That the former idea is excluded we would not contend. But we contend for the inclusion of the latter. As the virus of deadly poison is expelled from the body by the antidote, so the poison of sin is expelled from man's composite being by the life of Christ. Sin is first forgiven, no doubt. But it is afterwards destroyed. Its power over the man is taken away, and he stands, not only justified, but purified, sanctified, victorious, by the indwelling of Jesus Christ. So again, the expression "atoning blood" is not used at the present day in its Scriptural and strict English sense as equivalent to "reconciling blood," but involves in modern English ears the idea of reconciling through the endurance of vicarious

---

laid down. But faith, it may be worth while to repeat, is rather the acknowledgment of a fact than the acceptance of a dogma. It is practical rather than intellectual. And as in all other cases, so here, the refusal to recognise facts must bring trouble in its train. If a man will not use the light, he stumbles. If he will not use his ears, he meets with accidents. If he will not admit that he is responsible for his actions, he has that responsibility brought home to him in many very unpleasant ways. So, if he will not admit the existence

punishment. That the sufferings and death of Christ were those of the One Sacrifice for sin is not denied. But we lose sight of half the virtue of that Blood shed, if we merely regard it as offered for us. As the sixth chapter of St. John and the Sacrament of the Lord's Supper most plainly teach, that blood circulates in the veins of every redeemed man. Thus it is not enough to regard it as simply pleading for the forgiveness of our sins. It "atones" by becoming the very life of our life, and its revivifying power effects the expulsion of sin from within us. Thus, then, Jesus came by water and blood. The one typified the removal of the curse from mankind, the free access of all to a gracious and loving Father no longer estranged from us by sin, the quickening and inspiring effects of the new relation between God and man in stirring us up vigorously to live the new life. The other is no type at all, but the plain literal foundation of the Christian religion. The life of Christ is our life. His Blood mystically, yet really, flows in our veins, uniting us in the first instance to His humanity, and through it to the Divine nature itself (2 Peter i. 4). There are many types in the Old Testament of this twofold character of the Divine work, or rather, perhaps, of this method of regarding it first in its effects, and next in its essential character. Of these the most remarkable, perhaps, is the rite of purification in the case of leprosy (Leviticus xiv. 5–7), where the death of the one bird, the dipping of the leper and the living bird in the

---

of a Father, a Saviour, a Divine Spirit, a life proceeding from God, manifested by the Son, infused by the Spirit, he shuts himself out from all its benefits. But like all other gifts of God, the gift of eternal life in Christ is offered to the whole world freely and without stint. It only needs willingness on our part to recognise and to receive it, to enjoy all the blessings which are summed up in the word salvation.

dead bird's blood, and the doing all this in connection with an earthen vessel, and over running water (Heb. *living water*) are singularly corroborative of the interpretation of blood and water given above. The comparison of the last clause in this verse with ver. 11 tends to corroborate the view that has been taken. See note there.—**not by water only, but by water and blood.** The Revised Version translates *not with the water only, but with the water and the blood.* But if the explanation given above is correct it is better to translate ἐν literally, " in." Thus we have the assertion that Jesus comes to the spirit of man not merely in His cleansing and reviving influences, but in His very humanity itself. As has already been said, the belief which St. John here repudiates has nevertheless been very widely diffused. It is impossible to avoid seeing a reference here to those Gnostic heretics who believed that the Spirit first descended on the Saviour at His baptism, and that His Death, which the Church has always regarded as the shedding of His Blood, the sacrifice of Himself, to take away the sins of the world, was, on the contrary, either the act of a phantom, or the ordinary death of a human being—the Æon, or Divine emanation, having left the man Jesus before the agony in the Garden, and returned to His heavenly home. But the error is as prevalent now as it was in the Apostle's day, though in

---

(2.) *There is a Divine witness for these things, even the Spirit of God.*

The soul of man cries out with Zacharias (Luke i. 18), "Whereby shall I know this?" when the wondrous things of God are made known to him. Let us briefly consider on what authority these truths come to us.

I. NATURE WITNESSES TO GOD'S GOODNESS.

So says St. Paul (Acts xiv. 17, xvii. 27 ; Rom. i. 20). So said the Psalmist (Ps. xix. 20). So says the historian of creation (Gen. i. 31). So sang the angels when Christ was born (Luke ii. 14). And so says

another form. The actual entrance of the Saviour Himself into the regenerate man is kept in the background, and an intermediate influence, grace, Divine assistance, something which though given by Christ is not Christ, has taken its place. We need constantly to bear in mind the truth enshrined in fitting words in Cardinal Newman's striking hymn:—

> "And that a higher gift than grace
> Should flesh and blood refine,
> God's presence and His very self
> And essence all Divine."

So, too, the old Gnostic error, derived from the still older philosophical error of the essential evil of matter, still remains among us. Redemption consists, according to this view, not in the salvation of the whole man, but, as the Gnostics taught, in his severance into his component elements. His spirit is saved, his body dies. Thus the great truth the Christian Church has ever taught, that of the resurrection of the body, becomes no more than the Platonic doctrine of the immortality of the soul. And the teaching of such passages as Romans viii. 11, 23; 1 Cor. vi. 19, 20 (and observe the *true* text), xv. 44; Eph. v. 23; Phil. iii. 21; 1 Thess. v. 23; and the like, is lost sight of. The Church of Christ still needs almost as much as ever the caution "not in the water only, but in the water

---

modern discovery, every fresh addition to which is only another proof of the wisdom and beneficence of God.

II. REVELATION TESTIFIES TO CHRIST.

It cannot be denied (1) that revelation falls in with the plan of God's dealings as revealed in the history of man. The argument of Bishop Butler on this point has never been seriously assailed. Again (2) the evidence for revelation is such that it cannot be laughed out of court. The character of Christ (*a*), the indisputable prediction beforehand

and in the blood."—**And it is the Spirit that beareth witness.** It seems that the inversion of thought here, as compared with ver. 8, is due to the allusion to the fact recorded in John xix. 34. The strange and to the Apostle so mysterious incident of which he was the witness, seemed to him to typify most wondrously and most aptly the *modus operandi* of his Master in the redemptive work. And thus we have the two effects of Christ's coming placed before the efficient cause. It is the Spirit from whom we receive the cleansing and refreshing influences of the life of Christ. Nay, it is He who infuses Christ's humanity into us. Our faith, too, rests ultimately upon His presence within. See John iii. 3, 5, xiv. 16–18, xv. 26, xvi. 13, 14; Rom. viii. 2, 9–17, 26, 27; 1 Cor. iii. 16, vi. 19; 2 Cor. iii. 6, 17, 18; Gal. v. 16–18, 22, 25; Eph. v. 9, 18, &c. By a comparison of the various statements of God's Word, we find that the work Jesus Christ came to do is accomplished through the operation of the Spirit. Thus the Spirit beareth witness of Christ by His operations in the heart. The faith that conquers the world is His work. The believer may be attracted to the doctrine of Christ by external evidence, but he can only be built up in it by inward experience. The influence felt by every one who has accepted the message of Christ and begun to act upon it, producing as it does the sense of

---

that the seed of Abraham (Gen. xii. 3), Jacob (Gen. xxviii. 14) and David (2 Sam. vii. 12) should be a source of blessing to mankind, and that to the posterity of the latter an everlasting kingdom was promised (*b*), and the evidence for the resurrection of Christ, which no ingenuity has ever been able to explain away (*c*), are points which insist on the attention of every reasonable man. And (3) the complete change which has taken place, and is still taking place in the state of society wherever the religion of Christ is recognised, is another witness for

pardon, the feeling of inward rest and refreshment, the strong encouragement to conflict with all that is evil, and progress in all that is good, is the best and surest witness to the reality of the revelation of God in Christ. It is this on which the foundation of our faith ultimately rests, the testimony of Christian experience, the evidence of our inward consciousness in regard to the transforming and regenerating power of Christ. Just as the Samaritans (John iv. 42) believed first on the testimony of the Samaritan woman and then—and more permanently—on their own experience of His teaching, so men now believe first on the testimony of others, and then, when they have acted on that testimony, they have practical demonstration of the truth of that to which they have yielded credence. Thus "it is the Spirit that beareth witness." It may perhaps be necessary to call attention once more to the way in which the Authorised Version translates $\mu\alpha\rho\tau\upsilon\rho\iota\alpha$ indifferently by "record," "testimony," "witness," thus somewhat diminishing the emphasis with which St. John dwells on the true character and necessity of the witness for Christ.—**because the Spirit is truth.** This is one of the passages from which the divinity of the Holy Spirit may be inferred. God is truth (Ps. xxxi. 5). Jesus Christ is the truth (John xiv. 6). And the Spirit is truth. It is not said that He is "of," or "from," the truth, that He bears witness to the

---

the truth of His Gospel. This testimony may be rejected. But it is at least testimony which no rational man can pass by unheeded.

III. CONSCIENCE TESTIFIES TO CHRIST.

What St. John intends here to appeal to is not the unconverted, unsanctified conscience, but the believing conscience. It is the universal testimony of those who have accepted and acted on the belief in Christ, that experience has confirmed their faith. We may even call upon unbelievers for a confession of this. The men whose

truth, but that He *is* truth. In other words, He shares the essential nature of the Father and the Son. In this passage we find the ground for relying on His testimony, namely, the conviction of His truth. This is (1) objective, and consists in relying on Him who it is felt will not fail us, since He is the truth itself; and (2) subjective, in that by relying on Him we gain repeated experience that He deserves our trust. We first rely on Him because we are persuaded that He is the truth. We continue to rely on Him because as a fact we find that He is the truth. But the subjective belief depends on the objective. We must first surrender ourselves to the guidance of His power, and then we find out what that inward power or energy is. The rendering which would take ὅτι as "that," and translate "the Spirit beareth witness that the Spirit is truth," need only be noticed to be rejected. St. John may sometimes seem to be arguing in a circle. But he never actually does so, as would be the case if this rendering were adopted. For the Vulgate reading here, "because Christ is the truth," and a remarkable note by Bede on the passage as thus read, see Dr. Westcott's Commentary. The full force of this verse will not be understood till we come to ver. 8, where the Apostle points to the three lines of testimony converging to one end. We have the objective fact, the existence of the Spirit who is truth, on the one hand,

---

lives have been best and worthiest and most devoted, have ever sought their inspiration from Christ. And those, moreover, who have sought from Christ the sense of sin forgiven, the energy to combat sin, encouragement when weary, hope when defeated, perseverance when despondent, have never failed to obtain it. Those who have rested on the sense of oneness with Christ, on the sense of the possession of a new life which is not their own but His, have ever felt—and found —this belief to be one which could not disappoint them. They have

and the two forms His energy in the soul assumes, the water and the blood, on the other, tending to establish that necessary condition of Christian life, Christian faith. But while the three lines of testimony lead to the same end, the Apostle here is careful to remind us that the objective fact is that on which our faith must ultimately rest. Whatever His *modus operandi* in the soul, our faith is faith in a person. "It is the Spirit that beareth witness, because the Spirit is truth."

---

an inward conviction which rests not on opinion, but on fact. Not only do they feel the Spirit bearing witness within them, but they know that "the Spirit is truth."

XXVI.

THE THREE WITNESSES.

CH. v. 7, 8.—*For there are three that bear witness in heaven, the Father, the Word, and the Holy Ghost, and these three are one. And there are three that bear witness on earth, the Spirit, the water, and the blood, and these three agree in one.* The spuriousness of ver. 7 is a fact which, in the present stage of textual criticism, can hardly be said to admit of dispute. A brief summary of the evidence is all that need be offered here. For a fuller statement the reader is referred to those works on New Testament criticism designed for the use of scholars. Especially will the latest view of the critical evidence be found in Professor Westcott's Commentary. The arguments against the genuineness of the verse are as

---

HOMILETICS.

CH. v. 8.—*The threefold witness.*

I. THE WITNESS OF THE SPIRIT. St. John had previously led us to look on the Spirit alone as bearing witness. And thus (see pp. 375-377) he turns our attention to the fact that there *is* a witness. Now he bids us observe what is the nature of this witness, and that we cannot conceive of the Spirit as witnessing (1) apart from Christ, nor (2) apart from the effects of His work. Not apart from Christ, for He is Christ's Spirit (Rom. viii. 9; Gal. iv. 6), and Christ sent Him (John xv. 26; Acts ii. 33). Nor apart from His own work, for the presence of the Spirit is manifested in the fruits of the Spirit (Matt.

follows:—1. It is not found in any Greek manuscript until the 16th century. 2. In spite of its obvious relevancy to the issue, it was never cited in the great Homoöusian controversy, which lasted from about A.D. 318 to 381. 3. It is not quoted by the vast majority of Latin writers, even when the character of their argument demands the citation. This is notably the case with Ambrose, in his *De Spiritu Sancto*, a treatise in which he would naturally quote every passage which in any degree bears on the subject, and in which he actually quotes a good many passages which have a very remote bearing on it. And not only this, but he quotes the passage in which the words in question are now found, leaving those words out, a thing perfectly impossible had he ever heard of them as forming part of the sacred text. The same thing occurs in Leo's letter to Flavian, read publicly at the Fourth Œcumenical Council. And the words are also absent from the whole of the immensely numerous works of Augustine. The arguments for their genuineness are as follows:—1. The passage is found in the authorised edition of the Vulgate, although unknown to Jerome, and originally appearing *after* ver. 8, and then apparently placed in its present position on grounds of logical order. Precisely the same phenomena present themselves in the

---

vii. 16–20; Rom. viii. 1–11; Gal. v. 22). If we ask how we are to distinguish between the witness of the Spirit and that of the water and the blood, the answer is that He witnesses for God by imparting to us the sense that we are under a Divine influence, that we are the children of God (Rom. viii. 16, 17), that we have the right to cry, "Abba, Father." This sense of being under Divine protection and enjoying the Divine favour, is the very first step toward all life in Christ.

II. THE WITNESS OF THE WATER. The water which flowed from the Saviour's side, like the water of which He spake in His discourse to Nicodemus (John iii.) and at the Feast of Tabernacles (John vii.), and the water of baptism, was symbolic of a fundamental Scripture

copies of the more ancient Latin version. 2. It is quoted by Victor towards the end of the fifth century. 3. The words, or something like them, appear in Tertullian and Cyprian, but in such a form that it is difficult to ascertain how much of them is a quotation from Scripture. Possibly the words actually quoted are only the concluding words of ver. 8. The rest are the words of Tertullian himself, and are probably quoted as such by Cyprian from his "master." The way in which they found their way into the text of the Authorised Version is this; Erasmus made a rash promise to introduce them into his text if they could be found in *any* Greek MS. *One* Greek MS. was found to contain them, and accordingly they were introduced into his third edition, from whence they found their way into the texts of Stephens and the Elzevir edition, and thence into our English Bible. The success of the interpolation is easily explained by the convenient formula in which the orthodox doctrine of the Trinity is embodied. In an age less critical, perhaps in some respects less scrupulous than our own, they obtained ready currency. It may be added that their introduction into the sacred text is no doubt due to citations of the passages in Tertullian and Cyprian, in which the words occur in close juxta-

---

truth, the (1) purification and (2) refreshing influences which flow from Christ.

(1.) *Purification*, or removal of the sense of alienation from God. It is hopelessness which leads to recklessness. It is the sense of peace with God which is the starting-point of all effort after holiness (John xvi. 33; Rom. v. 1).

(2.) *Refreshing*. As the sense of peace is a necessary antecedent condition of all efforts after holiness, so it leads to that elasticity and joyousness which enables us to persevere, in spite of failures and discouragements. We know that pardon is not a single act, but a continuous fact. Pardon on repentance is ever being bestowed. We sin

position with the sacred text. By degrees, as these passages became well known, it came to be believed that the additions were part of the Scripture itself, and thus they were introduced by later Latin copyists into the Epistle from which they were supposed to be taken. Internal evidence does not support the retention of the words. Not to insist upon the arguments to be found in Mr. Plummer's excellent note *in loc.*, concerning the connection in which the word Logos appears in Scripture, which, though suggestive, are not immediately decisive, we may observe that the introduction of the words is contrary to the whole drift of the passage. As is remarked in the note at the opening of the chapter, the subject of the Apostle is the inward witness for Christianity in the heart of the believer. That inward witness (ver. 6) is the Spirit. His witness is manifested by the effects in the human spirit of that life of Christ which He came to impart. The introduction of the three Persons of the Blessed Trinity, bearing witness in heaven to the Saviour's work on earth, introduces an altogether foreign element into the argument. It is of course not *impossible* that such a consideration should have been introduced. But any one accustomed to the subtle laws of consecution in accordance with which St. John's

---

daily while yet the corrupt nature remains. We are pardoned daily as we brace ourselves afresh to subdue it. And thus as water refreshes and cheers the way-worn traveller, so does the refreshing effect of peace spur us up to renewed exertion in the journey back to our Father.

Each of these effects of the sense of sonship are present with every Christian who realises his position, who believes, that is, on the Name of the Son of God.

III. THE WITNESS OF THE BLOOD. Our consciousness of the effects of Christ's work cannot be dissociated from our consciousness of His presence within to whom these effects are owing. "Not by water

thoughts are evolved, and his invariable custom of repeating in a slightly modified form propositions of importance once introduced, will feel that this passage is no more entitled to recognition as a part of the Epistle on internal than it is on external grounds. The passage, then, should run as follows:—*For they who are bearing witness are three, the Spirit, the water, and the blood, and the three are unto* (or *into*) *the one.* The words in fact amplify and explain what precedes. St. John has said that Jesus Christ comes, "not by water only, but by water and blood." He proceeds, "and it is the Spirit that beareth witness, because the Spirit is truth." But, he continues, the witnesses in point of fact are three, the Spirit Himself, and the cleansing and invigorating processes He ministers, coming as they do from Christ. He, the Truth itself, makes the presence of His Spirit felt in the heart, first by the sense of pardon, and next by the consciousness of a supernatural power. And both He, and those effects of His work which are thus recognised, tend to the same result, incorporation of each one who is sensible of them into the Divine unity. As has been so frequently insisted on, the pregnant language of the Apostle must be interpreted in its widest signification. εἰς τὸ ἕν means both "*unto*" and "*into* the one." The goal

---

only, but by water and blood." And our consciousness of our possession of this life of His must depend on the feeling that we are being transformed from the likeness of sinful flesh, and conformed to the image of the Son of God (see again Rom. viii. 16, 29, and cf. Rom. xii. 2, and 2 Cor. x. 5). For if the life of Christ dwell in us, it must manifest its presence by its effects. And those effects are our likeness to Christ, displayed in our daily walk.

VER. 9.—*The trustworthiness of the witness.*

This depends on two facts: (1) that it is God's witness, and (2) that it is a witness concerning Christ. The consequence is (3) that we should surrender ourselves to it with perfect confidence.

to which each testimony tends is the same. But the goal is God Himself. And therefore we not only tend *to* Him, but are received *into* Him. The object of Christ's coming is to unite all in Himself to God (1 Cor. xii. 12; Eph. i. 10, ii. 14, iii. 19, iv. 6, &c.) This is the point of the whole Epistle we are now considering. And therefore I am constrained to believe that all interpretations which refer these words to the Truth, or the Gospel, or anything but *God Himself*, fall far short of the mark. The witnesses not only " converge to one goal, that is, the fact already announced, and the consequences deducible from it (vers. 11, 12), that we possess in Jesus Christ eternal life " (Haupt), but even more than this. The witnesses not only testify to us of the fact. They concur in producing it. The work of the Spirit within, the cleansing from sin, the participation in the Life of the Son, *are* eternal life. And so (ver. 11) the Apostle soon goes on to tell us, having, after his manner, led the way to the declaration by what he says here. One other point must be noticed. μαρτυροῦντες is *present*. The three *are* bearing witness in each believer's heart. It is not merely (as we might suppose from the English versions) that it is the *custom* of the Spirit, the Water, and the Blood to bear witness, but that they are at this moment active, energising

---

I. IT IS GOD'S WITNESS. This is the ground of our faith. We believe on Divine testimony. We even give credence to our fellowmen on points on which we believe them to be well-informed. How much more should we believe in Him who cannot lie, and cannot be deceived? There can be no doubt, to those who do not wilfully shut their eyes to facts, that it is a Divine witness. For not only are there the objective facts (1) of the resurrection of Christ, a fact which no human ingenuity has been able to disprove, and (2) of the marked change which from the date of that fact has come over the world, but there is also (3) the witness *within*, the consciousness that a Divine life *is* imparted to the soul, that it *does* convey a sense of pardon and

witnesses for the Living God and His Eternal Son, as ever-existent verities, to each individual human heart capable of receiving their testimony.

VER. 9.—**If we receive the witness of men, the witness of God is greater.** We might at first sight think that a reference is here made to the witness of God in heaven, mentioned in the verse we have rejected as spurious. But further examination does not sustain such a view. The witness of the Spirit, and His effects, is in truth the witness of God, and it is a witness concerning His Son. See vers. 9, 10. We are in the habit of receiving such testimony in our earthly affairs (this is the force of εἰ with an indicative). See John v. 31–47, viii. 17. How much more then shall we rest with confidence on the Divine testimony we find at work within us to certain spiritual facts?—**for this is the witness of God, which he hath testified of his Son.** There are three ways of translating the last ὅτι (ὅτι being the reading of the Sinaitic and Alexandrian MSS. for the Rec. ἥν). We may either (1) take ὅτι as the Authorised Version takes ἥν, as equivalent to "what," or (2) we may translate *for this is the witness of God, because he hath witnessed concerning his Son*, or (3) *for the witness of God is this, that he hath borne witness concerning his Son.*

---

a joyous energy of resistance to the powers of evil, and a manifest fellowship in Christ, a fact of which we are hourly conscious, when we are united to Him by faith.

II. IT IS A WITNESS CONCERNING THE SON OF GOD. This, too, is proved by the Divine characteristics that displayed themselves in the life of Christ—His power, in the realm (*a*) of Nature, (*b*) of grace; His purity (John viii. 46; Heb. iv. 15), His authority (Mark i. 27), His love. (See Scriptures *passim*.) Belief in the Son of God is the secret (ver. 5) which overcomes the world. And that rests upon a Divine testimony, outward, conveyed to us, that is, by others, and inward, borne in, that is, upon our own inward being to the Divine essence as visibly present to the world in Christ.

(1) and (2) would refer back to what has gone before, while (3) refers to what follows. The last of the three renderings is preferred by the best Editors. But the sense of the passage is, in the main, the same, whichever of them is taken. What the Apostle would say is this: that if we seek a proof of the truth of our faith, it is to be found in the Presence of the Son, through the Spirit, within us. The commentators here (Haupt excepted) have hardly kept in view the whole drift of the passage. St. John has passed from the idea of love (ver. 1) to that of obedience (ver. 3). From thence he passes on to the idea of conflict and victory (vers. 4, 5), since obedience can only be obtained through the subjection of the rebellious elements of our fallen nature. But the primary condition on which the victory depends is faith. Faith brings us within the reach of the spiritual influences proceeding from Jesus Christ alone (ver. 6), and depends upon our consciousness of the power of those spiritual influences (vers. 6, 8). But this consciousness comes from God Himself, and is a witness to His Son. It is not till we reach vers. 11, 12, that this truth is fully unfolded. At present we stop short at the truth that our faith is dependent on the inward witness God has

---

III. AND THEREFORE WE MAY REST UPON IT. This is St. John's object, to lead us to put our whole trust in the revelation of God in Jesus Christ. For this reason he appeals to testimony. He bids us listen to the voice of the Spirit. He points out the effects of reconciliation. He dwells on the evidences that the life of Christ dwells within us. And He bids us take courage. All these things are evidences of a voice of God within us, of a Presence of His Son in the world, on which we may safely rest. He gives us confidence amid all the doubts and distresses that assail us, all the temptations that beset us. Our trust is in God, and He will save those who put their trust in Him.

VER. 10.—*The contrast between faith and unbelief.*

1. THE SOURCE OF THE POWER OF FAITH. What, then the Apostle

given us to the Person and Work of His Son. Hence we may either adopt (2) with Haupt, and explain, as he explains, that the witness is God's witness, because it is the fact that He has borne witness concerning His Son, or that His witness is such as ver. 8 describes, because it is a witness concerning His Son. Or if, with Dr. Westcott, we adopt (3), we must explain thus. The witness of God is this: that He has witnessed, by means of the Spirit, the Water, and the Blood, to the redeeming and regenerating energy possessed and displayed by Him whom He hath "sanctified and sent into the world" (John x. 36). Haupt reminds us, in words well deserving of attention, that this testimony is not merely subjective, but objective. "It stands before us as an incontrovertible historical fact. It is with faith in this testimony of God as it is with the miraculous power indwelling in Christ and in Christianity. He who has experienced the miracle of sinful man's renewal needs no other witness for the miracles which the Lord aforetime wrought. But has not he to whom this is *not* a living experience historically before him the great and undeniable miracle that a sunken, dying, ruined world has been awakened through Christ to a new life?" Finally, we may remark a link

---

goes on to ask, is the secret of that power of faith which enables us to overcome the world? It is this:—*faith is the appropriation by the individual of the witness God has given.* Faith is the acceptance of His testimony, the principle which causes us to act on it. Believe on the testimony which God has given, and henceforth the testimony is within. And it will not be long before it manifests its presence by the working of the Divine power that changes the heart.

II. UNBELIEF IS ACCUSATION OF GOD. St. John points out the daring nature of unbelief. God has borne witness concerning His Son. The witness is clear enough to those who will receive it. What it is we have already seen. What is involved in rejecting it we are now told. It is to accuse God of untruth, to insult Him by rejecting His testimony. It is not merely blindness, or misfortune, or excusable

of connection between ver. 5 and the present verse. There, faith in the Son of God is the condition of victory over the world. Here the value of God's testimony consists in this, that it is a testimony concerning His Son. Our faith, therefore, depends upon a truth on which there can be no mistake. Nor can there be any mistake on our part as to His power to sanctify and save Who is demonstrated to be the "Son of God with power, by the resurrection from the dead." Rom. i. 4.

VER. 10.—**He that believeth on the Son of God hath the witness in himself.** This verse is clearly an expansion of ver. 5. He who believes in the Son overcomes the world by virtue of the persuasion he has in his own mind of the reality of the fact in which he believes. He is convinced that He in whom he believes is no other than the Only Begotten of the Father, capable of inspiring him with every "good and perfect gift" which comes from that "Father of all light" (James i. 17). The present ($\pi\iota\sigma\tau\epsilon\acute{u}\omega\nu$) signifies either the habitual, permanent attitude of the soul, or the condition on which alone the witness can be possessed. Most probably the latter, because we are immediately afterwards told what the position of the man is who does not fulfil this condition

---

ignorance. It is downright sin. So manifest, to those who do not wilfully shut their eyes to it, is "the witness God hath borne concerning His Son." We must, therefore, not shrink from telling men plainly of the danger of refusing to believe, as well as of the infinite blessing of hearing the voice of God, and acknowledging the revelation of Him in His Son.

VERS. 11, 12.—*Eternal life in the Son of God.*

We have seen in the Exposition how St. John reaches this great conclusion in his usual meditative and cumulative fashion, and how St. Paul also reaches it as the result of a train of reasoning on spiritual facts. We proceed, therefore, to remark on the nature of the conclusion thus reached in all its fulness. This will be done briefly, because it has been impossible, in this Homiletic Section, altogether

of faith. The Revised Version reads αὐτῷ for the Rec. ἑαυτῷ. The former is probably the true reading, having the support of A and B against ℵ, which supports the Rec. But whether we translate "him" or "himself" makes no difference to the sense. The R. V. also reads τοῦ θεοῦ after μαρτυρίαν, and so does the Vulgate and some other versions.—**He that believeth not God hath made him a liar.** The text is in some confusion here, some MSS. having θεῷ, some υἱῷ, some υἱῷ τοῦ θεοῦ, and so on. But there can be little doubt that θεῷ is the true reading. υἱῷ no doubt comes from the extremely similar passage in John iii. 18, where belief in the *Son* is inculcated, and from the desire to make this part of the antithesis correspond more exactly to the other. But, as Mr. Plummer remarks, St. John's antitheses do not usually correspond exactly. Besides, the whole point of this part of the passage is belief in God. He who believes on the Son of God has God's testimony in himself. Not to believe this testimony is to disbelieve God, and to disbelieve God is to make Him a liar, because *it is a fact* that God has borne witness, and not to believe that witness is neither more nor less than deliberately to give Him the lie. The use of the dative after πιστεύω in this clause, instead

---

to help anticipating the conclusion in considering the steps which led to it.

I. THE GIFT OF GOD IS ETERNAL LIFE.

It may be well to compare the methods by which St. Paul and St. John reach this end. The first does so by the following process. Man is liable to sin, and thus to the wrath of God. He needs deliverance from this sin—a deliverance which he cannot obtain for himself. This deliverance he obtains through the Sacrifice of Christ—a Sacrifice which at once demonstrates the righteousness and justice of God in the past, present, and future. It is faith which makes us partakers of that deliverance, by making us partakers of that righteousness which alone has satisfied the requirements of God's law. Thus we are justified, and thus we obtain peace. And not only so, but we are

of the accusative with εἰς, represents no further difference than there is between our placing reliance *upon*, and trusting *to*, a person.—**because he believeth not the record that God hath given of his Son.** The reason is given here for the statement above. God is made a liar because He has given witness to His Son, and to disbelieve that witness is to impute falsehood to Him. Four points are to be noticed here. The first is that, as elsewhere, the Authorised Version has used a variety of words to translate μαρτυρίαν, thus weakening the emphasis of the passage. Next we are to observe the perfect (A, however, reads ἐπίστευσεν), denoting a definite attitude deliberately taken up on the part of the unbeliever, and a complete and decisive witness given by God to His Son. That such conclusive witness has been given, is simply a matter of experience on the part of Christians. We may further observe that the hypothetical μή in the former part of the verse gives place to οὐ when a definite condition has to be expressed. Lastly, we have πιστεύειν εἰς with μαρτυρίαν here. The dative is the usual form. It implies the giving credence to a statement. The construction with εἰς signifies the reliance on authority. And when we refer back to ver. 8 to see the nature of

---

admitted into a state of things whereby sin, which worketh death, is destroyed, and righteousness, which bringeth life, implanted. We can no longer sin, because we have been set free from its power, and henceforth we live unto God. And this living unto God produces its natural result, holiness, since eternal life, the gift of God, is given us in Jesus Christ our Lord. In the Exposition a short summary has been given of the way St. John reaches the same goal. The new birth in Christ, he shows, is the necessary starting-point of the life of light and love. Faith is the immediate result of that new birth. And faith rests upon the witness of God Himself, given by means of His Spirit, and the experience of Christ's work in the soul. The witness, in short, is the fact that He has given eternal life in His Son Jesus Christ. Thus St. Paul reaches the point through man's experience of

the testimony, we can understand how the construction here is in every way suited to the meaning.

VER. 11.—**And this is the record.** Once more we should translate with Revised Version. *And the witness is this.*—**that God hath given to us eternal life, and this life is in his Son.** Here we come to the climax to which St. John has been slowly leading us—the central thought in which our whole religion is summed up. It was the "Word of life" which (ch. i. 1) he desired to declare to those whom he addressed. He had seen It and known It (ch. i. 2). He knew how It enlightened men's minds in an age of darkness (i. 4), how It purified from sin (i. 7), how It disposed men to mutual love (ii. 9), how It diffused a sense of sonship (iii. 2), how It stirred up opposition to sin and sinners (iii. 5, 10), how It imparted the life of love (iv. 8, 9), how faith gave a strength to that life of love which made it superior to all opposition (v. 5), how God bore witness to His life within the soul by the Water and Blood mystically shed from the Saviour's wounded side (v. 6, 8). And now we are permitted to grasp the truth in its fulness. "The life was manifested" that it might become ours. Eternal, unchangeable life is within our reach. And this life

---

sin and his need of salvation, St. John through his experience of that which redeems from sin, and of the need of remaining in the state of salvation in which we have been placed. But the result is the same. God has given us a changeless life; weak, perishing, dying, as we were, we are saved by being engrafted into that life whose fundamental principle is permanence. Henceforth we need be no more swayed hither and thither by the passions of our human nature, the circumstances of life, the opinions of men. Christ remaineth for ever more as the Rock, and they that are stayed on Him cannot be moved.

II. THAT LIFE IS IN THE SON OF GOD. It needs not to stay now to establish this fact. We have already dealt with it in our treatment of vers. 1, 5, 6, 8. But St. John could not avoid stating it as

can only be obtained in and through the Son of God, who was manifested, as He repeatedly tells us (John vi. 33, 51, x. 10), that we might have life. For ζωή αἰώνιος see ch. i. 2, ii. 26. The ἔδωκεν here refers no doubt to the coming of Christ into the world as the one act which once for all gave eternal life to the world. Had we the perfect, it would fix our thoughts rather on the Divine gift of life. The aorist asks us to contemplate the fact that this gift reached us in the Person of the Son. We should not fail to observe how St. Paul comes to precisely the same conclusion after a long train of argument, in almost the same words. "The gift of God is eternal life in Jesus Christ our Lord." Rom. vi. 23.

VER. 12.—**He that hath the Son hath life, and he that hath not the Son hath not life.** Perhaps we should here render *the* life (*i.e.*, the life which has just been spoken of as in the Son of God). And we should certainly not neglect Bengel's acute remark on the order of the words. τὴν ζωήν is the emphatic portion of the first part of the sentence. It is *life* which he possesses who has the Son. ἔχει is the emphatic word in the second member of the

---

the grand conclusion at which he has been aiming. There is eternal life in Jesus Christ, and in none other. And this because He is the Word of the Father (John i. 1), whose task it was to make that Father known (John i. 18), and He was His Son in such sort that to see Him was to see the Father (John xiv. 9). The gift of God comes in and through His Son, and thus alone. And it comes in this way, because Jesus *is* the Son of God, "of one substance with the Father, who through His having become man, has the power of communicating the otherwise incommunicable life of Him "who dwelleth in the light that no man can approach unto, whom no man hath seen nor can see" (1 Tim. vi. 16).

III. TO HAVE THE SON IS TO HAVE THE LIFE. This is clear from what has been previously said. But what is it to "have the Son"? This: to believe in Jesus Christ as the Son of God, and through faith to receive Him into the soul. Not merely to think of Him, and

sentence. He who has not the Son is destitute of the blessings which flow from Him. And "of the things which have been spoken this is the sum." This is the point to which St. John would lead us. What follows are practical deductions from the central fact. But all that He has said hitherto,—his remarks on light and darkness, on the Church (or believers) and the world, on truth and falsehood, on Christ and Antichrist, on the children of God and the children of the devil, on love and hate, on the spirit of truth and the spirit of error, on conflict with evil, on the testimony of the Spirit —all is summed up in this, the possession of Jesus Christ by those who believe on Him, and the gift to them of eternal life in Him. He who has Him has all. But he who has Him not has nothing—is dead while he liveth. Before passing away from this verse we must not fail to observe that eternal life is not a future but a *present possession* of the believer. That its strength and vigour may differ among different people is not to be wondered at. It could not be otherwise, since it is precisely proportioned to the strength and vigour of our

---

believe in Him as a Deliverer. Not merely to think that the stain and guilt of our sins is removed by His death, that He purifies and refreshes us by the water that flowed from His side. But to realise His life in us ; to feel His blood flowing in our veins, and washing away each impurity as it flows ; to feel ourselves growing daily into closer and more intimate union with Him ; to be ever more fully experiencing the truth that His life is our life, and our life His, until at length we are one with Him.

IV. NOT TO HAVE THE SON IS NOT TO HAVE THE LIFE. There are many ways of deceiving ourselves. We may fancy we are saved because we have experienced the sense of pardon, or because we think there is no need of it, or because we imagine ourselves to have satisfied God's requirements, or because we have access to God through His ministers and receive daily cleansing, or because we are regular in our use of the means of grace. But there is one only test—Have we

faith or realising power. But we must try and escape from the narrow and imperfect conception of eternity as a thing future which is so firmly rooted in the minds of many. Eternal life may, nay *must* be obtained here, if it is to be obtained at all. And its measure is the grasp we have obtained on the fact that God has revealed it to us in His Son.

VER. 13.—**These things have I written unto you that believe in the Name of the Son of God; that ye may know that ye have eternal life, and that ye may believe on the name of the Son of God.** These words should conclude the present section, not commence that which follows. They obviously refer to the *whole of* what has gone before, and explain the object with which the Epistle was written. That object was that the fact of the possession of eternal life by believers in Christ should be one thoroughly understood and grasped by those to whom he was writing. The Revised Version follows a different reading here. The text has no doubt been altered to avoid a supposed obscurity, caused by the

---

the Son? And to this nothing but a life conformed to His life can testify. The desire to bring every thought into obedience to His law, to cast away all that is contrary to His example and His will, to set no other purpose before us than the one he set before Him, to "do the Father's will, and to finish His work," this it is which tells us that we have the Son. Not to have this, is not to have the Son. And not to have the Son is to be an outcast from God, to be tossed about by every current of temptation, to be carried hither and thither, the sport of our own and other men's passions, to have no life beyond the feeble flickering of a lamp in its socket, to be in danger of being banished for ever from the true and eternal light, and of being consigned to that eternal darkness "where is wailing and gnashing of teeth."

VER. 13.—*The certainty of life.*

St. John writes his Gospel that men may *believe*, and have life, his Epistle that men may *know* that they have it. The latter is the application of the principles contained in the former. Without faith in Christ we cannot possess His life. Without knowing that we have that

introduction of a dependent sentence between ὑμῖν and πιστεύουσιν. The Rec. text is supported by some later uncials. ℵ and B omit τοῖς πιστεύουσιν . . . θεοῦ after ὑμῖν, but insert it after αἰώνιον. A reads οἱ πιστεύοντες for τοῖς πιστεύουσιν in the latter place. The sense of the passage is the same whichever of the last two readings we prefer. And that sense is as follows: "I have written these things to you who believe on the Name of the Son of God, in order that you may fully understand the full value of what you receive in Him. You receive the gift of an imperishable life." αἰώνιον, it may be observed, is emphatic in its position. Thus then the truth that St. John wishes to emphasise is that belief in Christ introduces him who has it to no temporary excitement, enthusiasm, influence, but places him in contact with the Divine Nature in its fixedness and unchangeableness. If we take the Authorised Version reading, we are met by an apparent absurdity, which is not, however, so great as it seems. St. John, according to this reading, writes to those who believe on the Name of the Son of

---

life we cannot live it. The spiritual life, therefore, has its outward and its inward side.

I. THE OUTWARD ASPECT OF FAITH. To this we have already referred in the notes on preceding portions of this chapter. (A.) In the first preaching of the Gospel faith rested on *testimony*. 1. *The testimony of facts to Christ*. His life, His miracles, His teaching, all these were God's witnesses either (*a*) to Christ, or still more (*b*) *in* Christ, the witness of His Divinity to His Humanity. 2. *Christ's testimony to Himself*. His claims to Divine authority being otherwise established, we come next to ask what He taught concerning Himself. And it amounts to this: that He was the Only-begotten Son of the Father, one with Him, Who came to make Him known to men, and in Whom the majesty and dignity and holiness of the Father were fitly represented (see N. T. *passim*). 3. *The Apostles' testimony to Christ*. This was their account of what they had seen and heard (ch. i. 1), of what He said, and what they found Him to be. From this threefold testimony men believed in Apostolic times. (B.) We

God in order that they may believe on His Name. But since belief on the part of many was a very imperfect thing, there is no absurdity in endeavouring to lead those to a higher degree of comprehension of what is involved in Christian faith, who have already given in their adhesion to Christ, with, it may be, a very imperfect conception of the true nature of His work. But, as we have seen, this reading is almost certainly not the true one. For ἔγραψα see ch. ii. 12, and for *Name* in place of the thing named see ii. 12, iii. 23. We must not leave this passage without comparing it with John xx. 31. "These things are written that ye may believe that Jesus is the Christ, the Son of God, and that believing ye may have life in His Name." The Epistle marks a more advanced stage of spiritual knowledge. The account of the human life and sayings of Jesus is intended to lead men up to a belief in Him which may lead to life in Him. The Epistle is written to those who have already believed, but who want to be taught more fully what

---

come next to ask, is this the case still? Do men believe still first on testimony? We reply, at least as regards active efficient faith, yes. For (1) the question of baptismal grace does not affect the question. We may believe that at the moment of the child's reception into the Christian Church, he has a title to all the privileges of its membership, that he is brought into new relations to God, and that he has the right to forgiveness of sins, to access to the Father, to union with Him. But (2) the translation of this right into fact rests with himself. The privileges become operative as soon as, and no sooner than, there is the disposition to use them. There needs the response of the human will before potentialities become energies. Thus (3) were the child never *told* of its baptism, never *informed* of the truths on which its salvation depends, the powers vouchsafed to it would remain dormant. It is the instruction the child receives as a member of the Christian Church which wakens these powers into action. And we may observe (4) that the same is true even of *natural* powers. Thus then, faith, the active living faith of the Christian, must still depend for its activity on testimony, the witness of Jesus to Himself in His Church.

II. ITS INWARD ASPECT. But faith has nevertheless an inward

such a belief involves. They need to *know* that they have eternal life in Christ, lest their belief should be a barren acknowledgment of certain facts or acquiescence in certain formulæ, instead of a vital inward union with the source of life. The comparison of these two passages throws very considerable light on the mutual relations of Gospel and Epistle, and would seem to demonstrate the priority of the publication of the former.

---

source. A faith purely historical will never touch the soul. The testimony to Christ is a testimony to certain inward realities. It is as the voice to which the strings which have been tuned respond. If men speak to us of One Who lived and died for man, we must feel that within which tells us that it was for us He lived and died, a power quickening us into a life like His. The Spirit, the Water and the Blood must be ever making their presence felt in the heart, and tending unto the One in Whom all fulness dwells.

III. THE CHRISTIAN LIFE CONSISTS IN THE CONTINUAL HARMONY BETWEEN THE TWO. It is necessary to remember that Christ came to make men one Body in Him. "None of us liveth unto himself and none dieth unto himself" (Rom. xiv. 7). And thus we need that others should witness to us for Christ, should remind us of those eternal truths which have been preached to us, that we may ever grow in the "certainty of those things wherein we have been instructed" (Luke i. 4). And thus, by the mutual ministration of "every joint of supply," do we, imbued with truth in love, grow up in all things unto "the measure of the stature of the fulness of Christ" (Eph. iv. 13-16).

XXVII.

CONCLUSION OF THE EPISTLE.

CH. v. 14.—*And this is the confidence that we have in him, that if we ask anything according to his will he heareth us.* We now enter upon St. John's concluding words of application of the truth to which he has just led us by successive steps. The first consideration to which he invites us is the duty of intercessory prayer for the spread of the life obtainable in Christ. The next is the perfect safety of those who have the life of God, and are disposed to live it. He concludes with a warning to those to whom he speaks not to be carried away by the temptations to return to the life they have forsaken. St. John returns to the idea of boldness or confidence of which he has spoken in ch. ii. 28, iii. 21, iv. 17. But he gives a different turn to the thought here. In ii. 28 he speaks of boldness in itself—the not being ashamed when in God's presence. In iii. 21, this boldness is represented as the result of a clear conscience.

HOMILETICS.

CH. v. 14, 15.—*Confidence that prayer will be heard.*

I. WHATSOEVER WE ASK, WE RECEIVE. See ch. iii. 22; Matt. vii. 8, xxi. 22; John xiv. 15, xv. 7, xvi. 23, 24. It may be well to notice the grounds on which this principle rests. In John xv. 7, it is conditional on abiding in Christ. In ch. iii. 22, it depends upon keeping God's commandments. Here, it rests upon the boldness which comes from the fact that we possess eternal life in the Son

CONCLUSION OF THE EPISTLE. 399

In iv. 17 our boldness in the day of judgment is said to be due to our likeness to Christ, and to the spirit of love we have imbibed from Him. Here a *result* of our boldness is spoken of. We feel that we may venture to approach God. And not only so, but we feel sure that He hears our petitions. There is only one condition to be fulfilled, that we shall not ask what He is not likely to grant (James iv. 3). But this we cannot do when we are penetrated through and through with the life that comes from God through His Son, and especially when for that reason we seek no selfish advantage, but our brother's good. We must not, however, forget to compare ch. iii. 22 with this passage. There, as here, the connection of παρρησία and prayer is pointed out. But there is no condition there, because it is presupposed that our will is one with God's. Here the condition is mentioned, lest liberty and license in prayer should be, as by many they have been, confounded. The "*confidence*" of the Authorised Version is introduced from the Rhemish version. The principal earlier versions have *trust*. ἀκούει here, as in John ix. 31, includes the idea of granting the petition.

VER. 15.—**And if we know that he heareth us, whatsoever we ask, we know that we have the petitions that we desired of him.** The best editors, followed by the Revised Version, connect *whatsoever we ask* with what goes before

---

of God. In truth the acceptance of our prayers depends upon their being offered up in the Spirit of Christ, and this, again, on our being inspired by that Spirit,—in other words, on our believing on Christ, and consequently living His life. When this is the case, it is Christ's Life, not our own, which God recognises in us, and which He receives as pleasing in His sight. We may compare James v. 16, where we are told that the prayer of a righteous man (St. James says little as to the source whence this righteousness is derived—yet see James i. 21), is of great avail when put in action.

rather than with what follows. It is impossible to speak with authority on the point, nor does its settlement one way or other affect the general sense of the passage. The Authorised Version, as usual, has weakened the connection between the two members of the sentence by translating the same word *asked* in the former, and *desired* in the latter part. And the Revised Version has rightly rendered *have asked*, instead of by the simple past tense. In this verse the presence of the condition referred to in the preceding verse is assumed. Granted that our union with Christ gives us the boldness to approach Him, and the desire to unite our will to His, we know that the petitions we have offered in the true spirit of unselfishness and submission are granted as soon as asked.

VER. 16.—**If any man see his brother sin a sin which is not unto death.** Rather, as Revised Version, "*sinning* a sin," the condition of the person who does the act rather than the act itself being implied by the participle. We now perceive more clearly the drift of the Apostle in the previous verses. We have come, many of us, to regard prayer as so entirely a selfish matter that we assume almost as a matter of course that when we ask anything of God, it will be for ourselves. The Apostle has nothing of the kind in his mind. The prayer he is thinking of has nothing selfish in its nature. It is the natural outcome of the life of love which results from the indwelling

---

II. THE CONDITION ON WHICH THIS TRUTH DEPENDS. Our petition must be according to God's Will. See James iv. 4, where the reason why our petitions are not answered is because we wish to spend what we receive on our own pleasures. It may be doubted whether we have any right to expect that any petitions will be answered which are dictated simply with a view to our own happiness. Such petitions may have been answered "in the forbearance of God" in days when men knew not His Will. And so perchance chastisements may be removed from us now for which, in our imperfection, we are not prepared. But

of the Son of God. It consists, therefore, not of petitions for ourselves, but for others. And the Apostle points out the limits of such intercessory prayer, conditioned as it is by the mysterious power of self-determination with which God has endowed every man. Ebrard has some excellent remarks here which deserve to be quoted. He says, "One might be misled into the theoretical notion that *every* prayer for the conversion of a fellow-man *must* be heard and granted. The Apostle here sets aside that erroneous inference. Conversion proceeds in a sphere of its own which touches at all points the domain of human voluntary determination; and in this domain there is a point at which the human will may have so hardened itself against the converting influences of the grace of God, as that God cannot and will not any more save. When this point has been reached, intercession has no assurance of being heard." The Apostle, however, considers first the case in which such intercessions will be heard. And we may ask *in limine*, whether the commentators are entitled here to assume, as they do apparently without exception, that $\dot{\alpha}\mu\alpha\rho\tau\iota\alpha$ is to be translated "*a* sin" here. In the next verse it is translated *sin*. So it is in ch. i. 8, iii. 4, and again, for example, in Rom. v. 13, vii. 7. Is it too much to say that nothing but the rooted idea that there is some particular sin which brings death in its train (the blasphemy against the Holy Ghost, for instance), would have induced so many to assume

---

the utmost that can be permitted is a prayer in the spirit of Matt. xxvi. 39 (which, however, we may profitably remember was *not* answered, being only the cry of weakness of our mortal flesh, which was to be perfected by Divine power). At all events it is not of such prayer, but of prayer for others, that the Apostle speaks here. It is the duty of praying *for others*, not for ourselves, which the Apostle is here enforcing. He makes the common possession by Christians of a common life the ground for insisting on the necessity

that a particular act of sin is spoken of here? But the teaching of the Scripture does not represent death as being the penalty for *any* particular act of sin (see note on ver. 16), but only for a sinful habit of mind. It is ἁμαρτία amounting to ἀνομία—the deliberate and defiant repudiation of God's law, which has this fatal effect. We come next to the words πρὸς θάνατον. We must observe that it is not εἰς θάνατον, that is to say, leading to death and *reaching* that to which it leads, but πρὸς θάνατον, that is, *tending* towards death. The difficulty here is how we can suppose that there is *any* sin which is not πρὸς θάνατον. Every sin tends directly to death. There can be no doubt that the compression of the thought renders the Apostle's language very obscure here. Yet though the language may be obscure, attention to the general drift of the Epistle may serve to clear up the meaning. As we have often seen, St. John is accustomed to look forward to the ultimate result, not only of *actions* but of *conditions*. And it is of the condition of the man, not the tendency of the act, that we may suppose him here to be speaking. Thus ἁμαρτία μὴ πρὸς θάνατον is error of a kind which has not unfixed the whole man from his anchorage on Christ—which is not bearing him irresistibly on to destruction. Rather the case is thus. Error is dragging at the chain, striving to detach the man from his hold on Christ, putting a strain on him which forces him to strive with all his

---

of prayer for each other. And it is prayer of this sort that he wishes us to understand is certain to receive a favourable answer.

VERS. 16, 17.—*The duty of intercessory prayer.*

I. ITS VALUE. It is well worthy of being remembered that *we never utter a prayer for others without bringing down on them a blessing*. How great that blessing is, no tongue can tell. It is here spoken of as *life*. Life, it is true, for those who are not actually on the road to death, but are still in the way of salvation. Yet so far as each act of

might to preserve his union with his Lord. But the anchor holds—faith resists the strain—the will remains firm to Christ and will not be detached. The man is not tending towards death in the whole bent of his disposition and affections. He is in the way of life, and each sin, as it occurs through the frailty which still subsists in him, is repented of, and washed away in the Blood of Christ. See notes on ch. ii. 1, 2. Thus, then, ἁμαρτάνοντα ἁμαρτίαν μὴ πρὸς θάνατον need mean no more than a man in a condition of sinfulness which, though more or less habitual, does not involve the full consent of the will. By assigning to the words a more definite meaning, we involve ourselves in many difficulties which are not suggested by the Apostle's language. Whether ἀδελφόν here and elsewhere is to be confined to the members of the Christian Church is not certain. But, as we have before seen, the probability is that the sense of the words cannot be so confined. See for instance ch. iii. 17. Therefore this part of the verse may be thus paraphrased: "If any one should see another in a condition of sinfulness indeed, but not deadly sinfulness."— **he shall ask, and he shall give him life for them that sin not unto death.** These words are full of difficulties. At first sight it would appear that αἰτήσει and δώσει are to be construed in close connection with each other, and in relation to the same subject. But then two questions arise. Can αὐτῷ in the singular be in apposition to

---

sin is concerned it is a step towards death, and we are told that our prayers may do something to bring the sinner back, may impart a renewed impulse towards that holiness which is life. Even in the case of those who are bent on sin, we receive at least the *offer* of a blessing, though the condition of the soul is such that even God Himself can do no more than make that offer.

II. ITS OBLIGATION. The Apostle is not here giving a command (see Exposition). But his language comes practically to the same thing.

τοῖς ἁμαρτάνουσι in the plural? And can the giving life to the sinner be predicated of any but God? The Authorised Version solves the difficulty by introducing a new subject, θεός, as the nominative to δώσει, and by translating τοῖς ἁμαρτάνουσι, *for* (*i.e., on behalf of*) *those that sin*. But this also involves some violence to the sentence. Tertullian and the Vulgate render freely *dabitur ei vita*, though Tertullian also has *Dominus dabit*. So Revised Version. On the whole, it is best to render *he will ask, and he will give life to him—to them who do not sin unto death*. The "he shall ask," and "he shall give" of the Revised Version savour too much of command. What is meant is that a man who can thus approach the throne of God with confidence will naturally ask what his neighbour most needs. If the expression "he will give him life" seems strong, we may remember that the recognition of secondary causes is not infrequent in the New Testament. James v. 20 is cited by several recent editors. So also Rom. xi. 14; 1 Cor. vii. 16, ix. 20; 1 Tim. iv. 16. This is also the explanation of much of such apparent contradictions as Phil. ii. 12, 13, and Heb. ix. 13, x. 4. What is meant is that the faithful servant of God, in thus offering prayers for those who are within the reach of the saving influences of Christ, will be *the means* of giving life to them. The Apostle speaks first of the person for whom he has supposed prayers to be offered,

---

The man who feels he has access to the throne of grace will certainly, so St. John declares, make use of his privilege, on his brother's behalf. For if we have eternal life in the Son of God we have love towards the brethren. We cannot have one without the other. Interest in our brother's welfare is inseparable from participation in the Divine life. And so it is a matter of course that in our petitions to the throne of grace we shall largely concern ourselves with his wellbeing.

III. ITS RESULT. Our brother's benefit, certainly. As the Exposition shows, St. John is not speaking of those whose error cuts them

and then extends his language so as to embrace all who are in that condition (αὐτῷ—τοῖς ἁμαρτάνουσι). And here we see, perhaps, the meaning of the "whatever we ask" of the last verse. It might seem almost too much to believe that we should have the amazing privilege of contributing to a brother's salvation. Nor does it seem at all clear even to us how so great a thing may be. But so it is. Prayer is a mighty spiritual force, capable of being put into action and of securing results, in the same way as natural forces do. And one employment of the life of love given us in Jesus Christ (v. 11, 12) must therefore be the offering up of intercessory prayer for those who are entangled in the coils of sin, that they may receive strength to recover themselves out of them. Strange as it is, we have here the assurance that it is here that the "prayer of faith can save," not only "the sick" (James v. 15), but the erring. Our last inquiry will be, What is meant by giving life? We must observe first that this life is somewhat strangely said to be given to those who do not sin unto death. The truth is that here again we have a Gospel paradox. The sin is a sin unto death because *every* sin tends to death. It is not a sin unto death because he who commits it is not in a condition tending to death. And giving life must not be interpreted as of *producing* the union between the soul and God, but of *promoting* it by imparting such gifts and

---

off from union with Christ, those, that is, who are deliberately acting in a way to terminate the union. What is the effect of prayers for such persons he does not say, nor need we here inquire. What we are told is that in the case of those whose errors are not such as to cut them off from Christ our prayers will certainly be answered. They will draw down fresh supplies of the Spirit of life on those who need them. Thus by mutual intercessions and mutual acts of brotherly love is the Catholic Church, the Great Communion of Saints, maintained and "increased with the increase of God."

graces flowing from union with Christ as each of us are in a position to bestow on one another according to God's will. See Col. ii. 19. Also Rom. i. 11, 12, xv. 15, 16, 29; 1 Peter iv. 10, where the word is χάρισμα, a special gift of the Spirit.—**There is a sin unto death.** Here Professor Westcott remarks that "a sin unto death" is too definite, and Mr. Plummer reminds us that we have not τις or μία, so that we cannot affirm that any *act* of sin is meant. He further goes on to say that we must get rid of the notion that any such sin can be readily recognised by those among whom the person who commits it lives. So far as this refers to an *act* of sin it is no doubt correct. But the *condition* of sin described by this passage would surely be one readily recognisable as one of antagonism to Christ and Christians. Dr. Westcott points out that the expression was one familiar to the Jews of St. John's day through the teaching of their Rabbis. He gives a number of citations from the Christian Fathers. We find the germ of the idea so prevailed in later ages, of the distinction of sins into venial and mortal where we should expect to find it, in the vehement, impulsive, dogmatic Tertullian. The Eastern Fathers, with Origen at their head, are more careful and balanced in their utterances. But there is a general tendency more or less prevalent in all to turn what St. John said as to the condition of sinfulness into a

---

VERS. 16, 17.—*The sin unto death.*

The Exposition here contains the principal part of what is to be said. But we may sum up the conclusions of the Exposition in Homiletic form.

I. THERE IS NO SUCH THING AS "A" SIN UNTO DEATH. Therefore we may dismiss (*a*) all distinctions between venial and mortal sins, (*b*) all endeavours to discover what this particular sin is, and (*c*) all attempts to discuss it in connection with Mark iii. 28, 29, and the parallel passages. For Mark iii. 30, states distinctly that it is the incapacity to discern between good and evil, and the tendency to

reference to certain particular sins which are "ad damnum" and others which are "ad interitum." Professor Westcott confines the intercessory prayer here mentioned to the members of the Christian Church. Such, undoubtedly, is its primary reference. But, like ἀδελφός, it is capable of being extended further. And though δώσει ζωήν, as we have already contended, refers not to the *original* gift of life, but its subsidiary augmentation, yet though no man can be the origin of his brother's salvation, he may surely, in various ways, contribute largely to it. It would not be contended, for instance, that if the heart of a heathen were disposed towards the life which is in Christ, it were useless to pray for him. It would deprive those engaged in missionary work of great comfort and encouragement, if we refused to let them take heart from this passage, and expect an answer to their prayers on behalf of the heathen, of whom it may be said, as of the scribe in Mark xii. 34, that they are "not far from the kingdom of God." For since all are sinners, all mankind are either ἁμαρτάνοντες πρὸς θάνατον or οὐ πρὸς θάνατον. Let us briefly inquire what is meant by the words. And first of all, Is any sin whatever here referred to which is entirely irremediable in its results? Is Haupt correct when he says that "*the* sin unto death can be no other than consummate enmity to Christ"? I say nothing about those interpretations which explain the

---

substitute the one for the other, which constitutes this sin, that is to say, it is not an *act* but a *state*—a state of alienation from, and opposition to the Spirit of God.

II. THERE IS SIN UNTO DEATH. This is a consideration for warning. There is sin which tends to separate us from Christ and therefore from life. Such sin we may believe to be (*a*) indifference to religious duties and privileges which clearly tends to paralyse the spirit, (*b*) direct and continued disobedience of any plain command of Christ, whether that command be (1) positive, as the direction to receive baptism or to partake of the Holy Communion, or (2) moral,

words of physical death, or of ecclesiastical excommunication. In the present state of theology such explanations scarcely need refutation. But it would seem that Haupt's view is not borne out by the Apostle's language. πρὸς θάνατον is not the same thing as εἰς θάνατον. The former means "tending towards death." It is only the latter which includes the *reaching* death. Why the Apostle says that we are not to pray for a person in this unsettled condition, or whether he says so at all, will be considered in the next note. At present we will confine ourselves to the fact that the Apostle deliberately uses a word which does *not* denote a final condition of the soul. There are conditions of the soul, as of the body, which distinctly tend towards death, and if means are not taken to prevent that result, will lead directly to it. But though the danger is great and even imminent, persons so affected are still within the reach of means. Deliberate sin, no doubt, tends directly to the death of the soul. Still, we cannot assert in every case that no repentance is henceforth possible. Thus, then, it appears that every kind of deliberate sin, as distinct from sin of infirmity, may be within the Apostle's meaning here. Every sort of sin directly tending to break off fellowship with Christ or to prevent our entering into it is of so serious a character as to jeopardise those relations of

---

as the direction to avoid hatred, jealousy, evil speaking, or any other sin, and (c) careless, irreverent, rash language, such as it is to be feared many indulge in, concerning (1) holy things, as Scripture, or the rites of the Church, (2) questions of right and wrong, whereby we are apt to "call evil good and good evil," (3) about holy men and holy causes generally, tending to depreciate holiness or good works. Such sins πρὸς θάνατον are more common among those who call themselves Christians, frequent the house of God, receive Holy Communion, claim the highest privileges of Church membership, than many of us suppose.

affection in which we would fain live with all men. That there are such sins—sins tending to make all fellowship impossible between Christ and the sinner, we have been plainly told in Heb. vi. 4–8, x. 26–31, 2 Pet. ii. 20–22. Of what kind these offences are, our Lord has Himself pointed out in Matt. xii. 31. They are the deliberate refusal to acknowledge God as God, the fixed resolve to reject His voice and disobey His Will. What St. John would here enforce upon us is the very serious nature of offences which have this tendency. There is, he emphatically tells us, a state of sinfulness which tends to death. And this because it is incompatible with the loving relations in which we should strive to live with all mankind. The commentators as a rule rather avoid placing an interpretation on θάνατον. But, as Alford rightly points out, it is the opposite to ζωή. But what form that opposition takes; whether it is that of joyless, loveless, hopeless, remorseful existence in opposition to a life of joy and love, or whether annihilation is meant, we are not told. The only passage which in any way explains the Scripture sense of such words as *die* and *death* is Rev. xx. 14. But into the large question of the future of the lost it is not our purpose to enter. We may remark in conclusion on the full agreement between this passage and Rom. vi. 23.— **I do not say that he should pray for it.** Literally, *not for*

III. THERE IS SIN NOT UNTO DEATH. This is a consideration for comfort. For (*a*) since "the soul that sinneth, it shall die," is a law of God's kingdom, and if "all wrong-doing be sin," we may well be anxious about a single act of sin, lest it should cut us off from Christ. And such souls there are, who go in heaviness throughout the whole course of their lives, because of their deep sense of weakness and transgression. To such it must be an unspeakable comfort to be reminded that "there is sin not unto death." And they may moreover (*b*) be comforted by the thought that the very distress their sins occasion them, if it prompt them to strive after amendment, is a

that do I say that he should ask, *i.e.*, in this case, though there may be *hope*, there can be no *certainty* that his prayers will be answered. There is doubtless some reason for the substitution here of ἐρωτᾷν for αἰτεῖν. The latter implies more humble supplication than the former. And the idea suggested is the more familar request of one admitted to the privilege of ready access to him to whom he makes request. It may be observed (1) that the intercessory prayer of which the Apostle speaks is offered, as we learn from vers. 14, 15, by one united by faith to the life of Christ for all who are or may be possessors of that life ; (2) that there are those whose conduct places them outside that certainty which under all other circumstances the Christian has that his prayer will be answered ; and (3) that we misunderstand the Apostle if we suppose him to forbid prayer even for the most hardened sinner upon earth. He does nothing of the kind. All he says is that he is not speaking of such persons just at present, because in their case at least we do *not* " know that we have the petitions we have asked." His words are, " it is not on behalf of that I am saying we should ask." If we are to understand the passage, we must not treat it as an isolated assertion, but keep the context clearly in view. It is impossible to grasp its meaning unless we keep in mind its close connection with the assertion (1) of the

---

proof that their sin is not unto death. And (c) another source of comfort is open to them in the intercessions of God's people. As Moses' hands, when lifted up to God, gave new strength to Israel in their warfare, so may the feeling that a father or mother, a brother or sister, a true Christian friend, the congregation in which we are wont to worship, the faithful band with whom it is our privilege to " break bread," are offering up heartfelt prayers for us that our hearts may not be " hardened through the deceitfulness of sin " (Heb. iii. 13). And so may we " run with patience the race that is set before us, looking unto Jesus, the author and perfecter of our faith."

union of mankind in Christ, and (2) of the consequent value, duty, and effectiveness of intercessory prayer.

VER. 17.—**All unrighteousness is sin, and there is a sin not unto death.** Rather, *all wrong-doing is sin, and there is sin not unto death.* "There are indeed other cases quite enough," he proceeds, "to which your intercessory prayer may find application. Wherever there is any measure of unrighteousness, there is sin, and fit occasion therefore for intercession" (Haupt). ἀδικία is the opposite to δικαιοσύνη—righteousness or justice. Therefore ἀδικία is any act of unfairness or injustice or unkindness. With this declaration we may compare that of iii. 4. Here sin consists in wrong-doing, there in the disposition to set law aside. The latter definition is theoretical, the former practical. The latter answers the question, What is the true character of sin? What is the principle which lies at the root of it? The former answers the question, How shall I know sin to be sin? What sort of conduct is sinful? The answer is, "Everything which transgresses the golden rule of doing as we would be done by." Into such conduct even the regenerate is frequently betrayed. As St. John has reminded us at the outset, "If we say that we have not sin, we deceive ourselves" (ch. i. 9), and the forgiveness of that sin is "faithful and just" on God's part. If therefore that "mind is to be in us which is also in Christ Jesus" (Phil. ii. 5) we must be constant in intercessions for them that so offend, for in one sense *all* sin tends to

---

VERS. 18-20.—*Three concluding thoughts.*

I. THE KNOWLEDGE THAT A DIVINE POWER PROTECTS US FROM SIN.

1. *This rests on the fact that we have been begotten of God, i.e.*, our confidence is in God, not in ourselves, in the new life, not the old one. We have not yet attained to the condition of which the Apostle speaks. But (*a*) we are tending thither, and (*b*) the practical value of the know-

death. If not, why does the Apostle represent the prayer of the faithful as giving life to the offender. Sin, however, of the kind of which the Apostle is speaking, does not tend to death, because it is in opposition to, not in accordance with, the whole spirit and tendency of the man's life. Regarded in itself, it *does* tend to death. It is an evidence that the principle of death is still at work within the man. If it does not produce its natural results it is because a tide of life stronger than that tending toward death is working in him, cleansing him from all that defiles him. In such persons no sooner is the sin committed than the antagonistic spirit is roused. There is immediate repentance, immediate and determined effort not to offend again in like manner. Only thus can what would otherwise be the paradox of a sin not unto death be maintained. Sin by its very nature is deadly. "The soul that sinneth it shall die" (Ezek. xviii. 4). "The wages of sin is death" (Rom. vi. 23). "Sin, when it is full-grown, bringeth forth death" (James i. 15). It can only be where sin is kept in check by the life of the Spirit that it can be said to be $οὐ\ πρὸς\ θάνατον$. And it is because the prayer of the faithful falls in with, conspires with this life of the Spirit, that it can be said to give life. The truth is well worth remembering in all ages (1) that there is forgiveness for sin committed, even by those in fellowship with Christ, and (2) that the danger of sin lies not so much in the specific act, as in the attitude of opposition to God's

---

ledge is that *whenever we realise* this one source of strength we have it. It is the feebleness of our hold on the truth which is the cause of our many falls. We never fall, but when we forget on Whom it is that we are bidden to rely.

2. *It rests also on the protection of the Son of God.* Since our faith is too feeble to conceive of God (*a*) He has taken man's shape and thus brought Himself within the reach of our capacities. And (*b*) He is

Will it tempts us to take up. (Here, again, we may remark that the μή of the hypothetical clause becomes the οὐ of the direct assertion). Before passing on to the next lesson St. John would have us draw, it will be well to pause and observe with what immense force this recommendation to intercessory prayer is pressed upon us. Step by step through the successive portions of this most weighty Epistle, we are led to the conclusion that the possession of the Son of God, and of life in Him, is the goal to which all Christian faith tends. And the first use the Apostle makes of this most momentous truth, is to impress on us the necessity of praying for one another, and especially in the hour of temptation. Surely there must be something especially solemn in such a duty when presented to us in such a connection. We can hardly escape from the conclusion that intercessory prayer of this particular kind is one of the first duties of every Christian.

VER. 18.—**We know that whosoever is born of God sinneth not; but he that is begotten of God keepeth himself.** The first point to be noticed here is the threefold repetition of οἴδαμεν in this and the two following verses. It gives a special solemnity to this conclusion of the Epistle. Three things are specially singled out as recognised by the Christian consciousness. 1. The knowledge that an inward power enables the Christian to preserve himself from sin. 2. The knowledge that this

---

one of ourselves. If we have been begotten of God, it is through the agency of one Who Himself has been thus begotten. The allusion here may be either (1) to the eternal begetting of the Son by the Father, or (2) to His assumption of human flesh. But whichever it be, "He was not ashamed to call us brethren" (Heb. ii. 11).

3. *The evil one has no power over those over whom Jesus watches.* It is not that he cannot tempt them, for he tempted Him. It is not that we have not sinned, for "in many things we offend all." But it is

inward power is the result of our new birth from on high and our severance thereby from the world (comp. for ἐκ Θεοῦ, ch. iii. 1, 2, iv. 6, &c.) 3. The knowledge that this new birth inspires our understandings and keeps clearly before us the vision of Him that is true. "St. John here recapitulates, not the five main divisions of his Epistle, but *three main aspects and points of his teaching* which pervade more or less the various sections of his Epistle;—our obligation and prerogative of holiness; our opposition to the world; our relation to the Person of Christ."—Ebrard. For (1) see ch. ii. 1, 4, 5, iii. 3–10, 23, 24, v. 2, 3. For (2) see i. 6, ii. 9–11, 15–17, iii. 14, 15, iv. 1–6, v. 10. And for (3) see i. 3, 7, ii. 20, 23, iii. 1, 2, 9, iv. 6–16, v. 1–4, 10–12. The appeal to the Christian consciousness is a remarkable feature of this Epistle. We find it in ch. ii. 21, iii. 2, 5, 14, 15. But it is most emphatically expressed in ch. ii. 20, where the Holy Spirit is indicated as the fountain of Christian knowledge (see note there). St. Paul frequently uses the same expression, but in a very different manner. With him it is the expression of intellectual conviction, either in the form of the conclusions of the sanctified reason, or of the assent to what has been delivered as the doctrine of Christ. In St. John, with the exception of ch. iii. 15, the expression has always some relation to the inward dependence of the believer on God. As usual, our version, following Tyndale, renders γεγεννημένος

---

that He Who conquered sin in our mortal flesh, in our fallen nature, can conquer it in us. And hence, however many the assaults of the evil one may be, we have only to believe that we are in Christ, to overcome them all.

II. THE KNOWLEDGE THAT WE ARE SEPARATED TO A HIGHER LIFE.

1. *We owe our being to God.* The leading thought here is not the protection of God but our deliverance from evil. We have been sepa-

and γεννηθείς by two different words and by the same tense. The Vulgate has *generatio* for γεννηθείς, whence the translation by Wiclif and the Rhemish Version, *the generation of God preserveth him* (*keepith him*, Wiclif). The Revised Version, applying the words ὁ γεννηθείς to Jesus Christ (see ver. 1), renders *We know that whosoever is begotten of God sinneth not, but he that was begotten of God keepeth him*. It is true that *himself* is put in the margin, being the reading of the rec. text with ℵ. But the translation and reading followed by the Revisers in their text (that of A B) presents us with a meaning so much deeper, and corresponding so marvellously, not only with the whole tenor of the Epistle, but with the contrasted idea of the ὁ πονηρός in the last part of the verse, that we should do very ill to reject it. As Professor Westcott remarks, "the phrase ὁ γεννηθείς is unique." But at least it is happy in its uniqueness. It expresses an unique relation, that between the Father and the Son, elsewhere expressed by the almost unique term μονογενής. The Son's generation is an eternal fact, incapable of alteration, addition, or completion. Hence the peculiar fitness of the aorist for the expression of the fact. The word γεννηθείς, involving as it does the same idea as that of γεγεννημένος in the preceding clause, implies that participation in the nature of Christ is the root-principle of salvation through Christ. How he who has just been represented as liable to sin, and needing intercession, should now be spoken of as not

---

rated from the rest of the world by the gift of the Divine Spirit. We enjoy, if we please to live in the light of our new privileges, an immunity from the influences which are fatal to mankind in general. For when the evil one approaches, we can fly to Him in Whose life we live.

2. *The world is in the power of the evil one.* So our Lord calls the evil one the prince of this world (John xii. 31, xiv. 30, xvi. 11). And St. Paul calls him the god of this world (2 Cor. iv. 4). For when the

sinning, and as guarded by a Divine power, is and must remain to a certain extent a difficulty. Yet that difficulty is lessened by the consideration that there are in Scripture two ways of looking at the redeemed. The first regards them as they are in themselves, imperfect, unsettled, the dominion of the Divine Life over their thoughts and appetites as yet incomplete. The next regards them from the point of view of the Divine Life itself, and of the goal to which it is leading them. As far as that Divine life is concerned sin is an impossibility. If sin be committed, it is the effect of the "corruption which doth remain, yea, even in them which are regenerate," and is in no sense the work of the Divine life itself. And further, the presence of the Divine life renders it impossible for the sinner to remain in his sin. Habitual, unrepented sin, and the Divine Life are incompatible, and cannot at the same time inhabit the human heart. But with regard to "sin not unto death," it is but a temporary condition, and yields to the force of that power which makes unrepented sin an impossibility in the heart in which that power is found.—**and that wicked one toucheth him not.** Rather, as Revised Version, "*the* evil one." Toucheth him not should be *layeth not hold of him*. So in John xx. 17. For ὁ πονηρός see ii. 13. The devil may assault, but he cannot prevail. His suggestions may approach the soul, but they cannot find a lodgment within. For a "stronger than he" is keeping

---

wickedness of the world increased God's Spirit ceased to strive with it (Gen. vi. 3). He left man to himself, until the "times of refreshing" should come (Acts iii. 19). Then He separated to Himself a peculiar people, but invited all who would to come and enjoy the salvation He promised "without money and without price." There is no Pharisaical satisfaction in the Apostle's survey of the world—only the highest possible appreciation of the value of the deliverance, and the most earnest hope that men may come forward and claim it, and thus

guard (Luke xi. 22). And while He keeps guard, the goods intrusted to Him (2 Tim. i. 12) shall "be in peace."

VER. 19.—**And we know that we are of God.** This is the second point St. John desires to emphasise. See ii. 29, iii. 1, iv. 5, 6.—**and the whole world lieth in wickedness.** Rather, with the Revised Version and the general *consensus* of modern scholars, *in the evil one*. The Greek demands some notice. First, there is a slight difference between ὅλος ὁ κόσμος in ch. ii. 2 and ὁ κόσμος ὅλος here. The difference is pretty nearly the same as between our "the whole world" and "the world —the *whole* of it." The emphasis here is on ὅλος. In ch. ii. 2 it is on κόσμος. But of course the world here does not include those who have been separated from the world by the new birth which comes from God. *They are delivered from the dominion of evil by the fact that their renewed being comes from God.* The rest of mankind κεῖται ἐν τῷ πονηρῷ. This expression, too, is remarkable. It occurs only here. But it is paralleled by such expressions as ἐν χριστῷ, ἐν τῷ ἀληθινῷ and the like. It is not, however, so strong as ἐκ τοῦ πονηροῦ in ch. iii. 12 (where see note). The force of κεῖται no doubt is that while the believers in Christ are delivered from the malign influences of the evil one, the rest of mankind remain under the dominion of those influences—lie passive under their shadow. Why the whole world should be said to lie in the evil one, and yet Christ should be said

---

be delivered from the yoke under which men have so long groaned. Who would not accept the offer so freely made to all to be "of God," and to escape from the "wickedness" which had made God's beautiful world a desolation?

III. THE KNOWLEDGE THAT JESUS HAS COME TO GUIDE US INTO THE TRUTH.

1. *We are delivered from false conceptions.* The heathen systems were false theologically, for they substituted a host of warring deities,

2 D

in ch. ii. 2 to be a propitiation for all its sins, may be explained by saying that Christ's propitiation is potential, not actual, until appropriated by faith. The absence of the article before ἱλασμός strengthens this view. Until faith becomes active and operative, until it grasps the life and strength which can be found in Christ alone, the individuals who compose the world lie helpless under the yoke of the evil one, unconscious, even, of the blessings which lie within their reach. The passage cited by Haupt and others from Soph. Œd. Col. 258 supports this view of helplessness which we have supposed to be contained in κεῖται ἐν.

VER. 20.—**And we know that the Son of God is come.** Haupt observes that as the two former verses are independent clauses, and that as this verse follows them connected with what goes before by δέ, we should expect to find in it a link of connection with each of them. And such, he adds, is the case. "The previous verses alleged that we know in what relation our Divine sonship places us to sin and to the world: here it is unfolded that we are conscious of the ground of this relation to both." Before His coming we were passive under the power of the evil one. His coming placed us once more in our true relation to Him from Whom we sprang. And this relation involved the possibility of sinlessness, first as a bare possibility only, and then passing through every intermediate stage into the region of realised fact.

---

with human passions, for the one true God. They were false philosophically, for they taught that what God made was evil, incapable of being redeemed, and therefore to be avoided, instead of seeing how man in his complex being could be purified and sanctified. They were false morally, for they had destroyed the true basis of morals, and had substituted for moral truth a chaos of uncertainties. The very best of the heathen systems was nothing more than refined selfishness. None had guessed that the true basis of morals was love.

All this springs from the truth that the Son of God is come into the world.—**and hath given us an understanding.** *An* understanding, not τὴν διάνοιαν, our understanding. διάνοια is properly the process which the mind goes through in order to come to a conclusion. Hence it comes to mean that faculty of the mind which draws conclusions, the power which directs the use of the reason. Here, however, its sphere is limited by what follows. The faculty we have received is that which enables us to know Him Who is true. And this faculty becomes ours by virtue of the Incarnation of the Son of God. ἥκει and δέδωκε are precisely alike in their scope. It is Christ's coming which has endowed us with the faculty of perceiving the true one.—**that we may know him that is true.** Here ℵ A B read γινώσκομεν, and we have the unusual construction of ἵνα with the present indicative. The same construction is apparently found in John xvii. 3, 1 Cor. iv. 16, and in Gal. iv. 17. But in John xvii. 3, Westcott and Hort and the Revisers read γινώσκωσιν. And in the other two cases it has been suggested that in verbs in -οω the indicative and subjunctive are alike in New Testament Greek. See the Notes on Orthography in Westcott and Hort's Greek Testament, p. 167. Possibly here, too, we have an example of what is called *itacism*—a mistake in copying occurring from similarity of *sound*. If we read γινώσκομεν, we must interpret *in order that we may know, as in fact we do,*

---

2. *We are translated into the region of eternal truths.* Delivered from this atmosphere of falsehood, we are not merely told the truth, but it is inwrought into the very fibre and tissue of our being. We are in Him that is true, by our reception through faith of the life of His Son (cf. ἀληθεύοντες ἐν ἀγάπῃ. Eph. iv. 15). And with the vision of truth thus clear before us, we need fear nothing from the delusions around. We have "known the truth, and the truth has made us free" (John viii. 32).

implying that the knowledge is both present and future. But in consideration of the immense number of cases where this itacism occurs, we may accept the Rec. text, in spite of its inferior MS. authority. τὸν ἀληθινόν means the True God as opposed to false gods. See ch. ii. 8, and cf. John xvii. 3. What is implied is that as the moral condition of the world is one of wickedness, so its spiritual condition (cf. Eph. iv. 18) is one of darkness. The understanding (διάνοια) is darkened. The objects of worship acknowledged by the world, the gods of the heathen, the Æons of the Gnostics, are vain things (μάταια), figments of the imagination, unsatisfactory deductions from facts imperfectly understood. Only those who have clung to the Incarnate Son of God have had their eyes directed to the only true and genuine object of worship and of faith, the Creator and the Life of all that is.—**and we are in him that is true.** Not, as the Vulgate and other Latin authorities, *that we may be in Him that is true*, which misses the meaning of the Apostle. St. John has been striving to lead us far beyond the idea of the mere *knowledge* of God. Such knowledge when possessed is the result of something more glorious and perfect still—union with Him. We not only know the source of truth, and have risen beyond the delusions to which other men are a prey, but we are actually ourselves living *in* Him who is alone genuine and true—in One who exists, not subjectively in our imperfect conceptions, but

---

VER. 21.—"*Little children, keep yourselves from idols.*"

We may in these days dismiss the thought of worship of actual images of wood and stone such as the heathen worship, and such as the members of the Roman Catholic Church treat with a veneration hardly to be distinguished from adoration. We however have idols —false conceptions—of our own, which Lord Bacon has divided into four classes.

I. THE IDOLS OF THE TRIBE. These are the things which society

objectively, above and beyond them.—**in his Son Jesus Christ.** These words are explanatory of the former, and teach the same truth as ch. ii. 23 and ver. 11. We are in the True One only in and through our union with the Flesh and Blood of His only-begotten Son.—**This is the true God and eternal life.** A lively controversy has raged over these words. It is certain that they are not so clear that they can be controversially adduced against those who do not believe in the Godhead of our Lord Jesus Christ. But their position in the sentence affords a strong presumption in favour of the doctrine. It is hardly possible that such incautious language would have been used by one who believed that between the Father and the Son an infinite interval existed. The real truth is that we cannot distinguish between the Nature of the Father and that of the Son. We cannot accept rash statements such as that of Dean Alford, who, when he endeavoured to show that οὗτος *must* be understood of the Father, and not of the Son, declares that the "latter is indeed ἡ ζωή, but not ἡ ζωὴ αἰώνιος." For whatever we predicate of the Father, we predicate also of the Son, His Fatherhood alone excepted. The Son is the revelation, the expression of the Father. He and His Father are one (John x. 30). We cannot come to the Father but by Him (John xiv. 6). Whosoever hath seen Him hath seen the Father (John xiv. 9). To know Jesus Christ whom He hath sent is to know the only true God

---

worships, rank, fame, wealth, genius, the arts of the demagogue, plausibility, bold assertion, clap-trap, appeals to the passions or the whims of the hour rather than the reason.

II. THE IDOLS OF THE CAVE. These are the false conceptions of life a man forms for himself, the love of pleasure, of notoriety, of gain; the opinions hatched for the sake of fame or popularity, or even, as is often the case, out of a man's prejudices and tempers, the creations of the false and distorted medium through which we view the things around us.

and to receive life eternal (John xvii. 3). And so we are led to the only sound and secure basis for faith, conduct, life, as distinguished from the uncertainties and falsehoods abroad in the world, the true God, revealed in His Son Jesus Christ. The close connection of thought between these last words of the Apostle and our Lord's last prayer before His Passion, as recorded by the same Apostle, cannot fail to strike every one who studies the two in the original. They afford a spiritual coincidence of the most remarkable kind. It is to the convictions so deeply impressed on himself under circumstances so extraordinary that the Apostle desires to lead his disciples. It is on those truths, above all others, that he desires their minds to repose. If we ask why ἀληθινὸς θεός has the article, the answer would seem to be sufficiently obvious. ἀληθινός is what is true, as opposed to what is false. It is to Him, not as an abstract conception, but as a concrete reality, not as what He is in Himself, but as what He is to us, that the Apostle would lead all men by his words here. And this is brought out by the emphatic warning with which he concludes the Epistle, testifying as it does to the terrible perils with which Christians were and are environed—perils which make it necessary that our faith should be no languid acquiescence in facts which have no interest for us, but robust and energetic, as becomes those who are battling with the temptations of a world which is still in the grasp of the powers of evil.

III. THE IDOLS OF THE MARKET-PLACE. Never were these more numerous or more hideous than to-day. The fever for speculation, the desire to be rich without trouble, the gambling of the Stock Exchange, the adulteration of goods, the shameless puffery, the deliberate manufacture of worthless articles, the amassing of a fortune through the schemes of "bubble" companies, the readiness to make profit by unlawful means, to treat our fellow-men as counters wherewith to play the game of life—the tone, in short, of commercial morality of

Ver. 21.—**Little children, keep yourselves from idols.** Rather, "from *the* idols," εἴδωλα, figments of the imagination, the false conceptions of Divinity abroad in the world, which confuse men's minds and lead them from what is good to what is evil. These conceptions of the mind, presented in visible shape, became what later times have known as *idols.* For τεκνία, see ch. ii. 1. φυλάσσω implies more careful guardianship than τηρέω. The latter has rather the *result* in view, the effect of careful protection of oneself, namely, safety, while φυλάσσω rather gives the idea of danger to be guarded against. And this is precisely the Apostle's point, and the reason he concludes, not with the glorious truth of the last verse, with which he might well have brought his teaching to an end, but with words of solemn warning suited to the dangerous position in which the persons he addressed were placed. Snatched from the perils of a world lying in darkness, endowed with the priceless gift of eternal life, yet with that gift at present undeveloped and unassimilated, and with those perils encompassing them on all sides, they stood in need of all their energy, courage, and watchfulness lest they should lose the blessings with which they had been endowed. The idols were to be found wherever they went. The idol temples rose in multitudes in every city and every country throughout the world. The household gods of the heathen faced them in every house. The rites of heathendom forced

---

the day, stamps the idols of the market-place as more destructive in these times than any other of the Christian life.

IV. The idols of the theatre. Such are the conceptions of the so-called philosophy of the day, questioning as it does the existence of a Personal God, substituting a mysterious nonentity, or the ideal of Humanity, or an unsolvable riddle, or an unchangeable and impersonal order for the God of the Bible, and endeavouring to foster every doubt and every difficulty which may serve to hinder men's belief in Him. The truth is in the world, and it can make us free. But there

themselves on them at every public or private gathering, on every occasion of business or pleasure. With those rites were entwined the principles from which they had been delivered; behind them stood the force of habit, the ties of family and social affection. It was no easy matter in those days for Christians to stand firm. They needed constant reminding of "Him that is true," and of the close relation in which they stood to Him, if they were to resist influences at once so all-pervading and so subtle. And what the Apostle said to them he says still to us. His words have been interpreted of the dangers of to-day. And justly so. For they contain a principle applicable to all time. Every age has its own dangers, its falsehoods masquerading in the garb of truth, its delusions, striving to substitute the love of the visible, convenience and profit, doctrines that save trouble, and observances that dispense with the surrender of self, for "Him that is True," in whom we "live and move and have our being" in Jesus Christ, and to Whom we are bound to offer every desire and every thought, to be saturated with His Spirit of love. Still does the spirit of self interpose to prevent the sacrifice of self to God. The vain delusions of a decaying world claim the homage we owe to Him alone. And still, therefore, do Christians need that the echo of perhaps the last words ever penned by Apostle of Christ should resound through the ages;—**Little children, guard yourselves from the idols.**

---

needs now, as ever, the conscious surrender of ourselves to its influence, the deliberate rejection of the falsehoods around, which would poison the springs of our life. Yes, now, and as then, and until evil is crushed for ever, will the Apostle's warning need to be repeated, "Little children, guard yourselves from the idols."

NISBET'S THEOLOGICAL LIBRARY.

Extra Crown 8vo.

NEW VOLUMES.

ST. JOHN'S FIRST EPISTLE. A Commentary with Homiletical Suggestions. By the Rev. J. J. LIAS, M.A. 7s. 6d.

DANIEL I.—VI.: An Exposition of the Historical Portion of the Writings of the Prophet Daniel. By the Very Rev. R. PAYNE SMITH, D.D., Dean of Canterbury. 6s.

FUTURE PROBATION. A Symposium on the question, "Is Salvation Possible after Death?" By the Rev. STANLEY LEATHES, D.D., Principal CAIRNS, D.D., LL.D., Rev. EDWARD WHITE, Rev. STOPFORD BROOKE, M.A., Rev. F. LITTLEDALE, LL.D., Rev. J. PAGE HOPPS, Right Rev. the BISHOP OF AMYCLA, &c. 6s.

RECENTLY PUBLISHED.

I.

THE ATONEMENT:

A Clerical Symposium.

By the Ven. Archdeacon FARRAR, D.D., Professor ISRAEL ABRAHAMS, Rev. Dr. LITTLEDALE, Rev. G. W. OLVER, Principal RAINY, D.D., the BISHOP OF AMYCLA, and Others. 6s.

"We recommend our readers to purchase the work. Although the papers are naturally argumentative and not devotional, the record of the efforts of different minds to grasp the doctrine of the Atonement cannot but be helpful."—*Literary Churchman.*

II.

INSPIRATION:

A Clerical Symposium on In what Sense and Within what Limits is the Bible the Word of God?

By the Ven. Archdeacon FARRAR, the Revs. Principal CAIRNS, Professor STANLEY LEATHES, D.D., Prebendary ROW, Professor J. RADFORD THOMSON, Right Rev. the BISHOP OF AMYCLA, and Others. 6s.

"The volume is an interesting one, written throughout in a temperate and scholarly spirit, and likely to prove useful to the higher stamp of theological students."—*Church Times.*

LONDON: J. NISBET & CO., 21 BERNERS STREET.

NISBET'S THEOLOGICAL LIBRARY—Continued.

III.
ZECHARIAH:
HIS VISIONS AND HIS WARNINGS.

BY THE LATE REV. W. LINDSAY ALEXANDER, D.D. 6s.

"Of sterling value. Those who have found difficulty in grasping the brief and mysterious parables of the Hebrew Prophet, will derive great help in their study of this prophecy from Dr. Alexander's careful and painstaking discussion."—*Literary Churchman.*

"This book will stand any comparison with the few other well-known commentaries on Zechariah's Prophecy, and is a valuable addition to expository and critical literature."—*Clergyman's Magazine.*

IV.
FOUR CENTURIES OF SILENCE;
Or, *FROM MALACHI TO CHRIST.*

BY THE REV. R. A. REDFORD, M.A., LL.B.,

Professor of Systematic Theology and Apologetics, New College, London. 6s.

"Carefully and intelligently done. The critical views expressed appear to us generally just. His account of Philo is particularly good."—*Literary Churchman.*

"It would be difficult to speak too highly of the wide reading, the careful and discriminating thought, and the wise and cautious judgments by which, throughout, the work is characterised. Every chapter is full of most interesting information and discussion."—*British Quarterly Review.*

V.
IMMORTALITY:

A Clerical Symposium on What are the Foundations of the Belief in the Immortality of Man? 6s.

By the Rev. Prebendary Row, M.A., Rabbi HERMANN ADLER, Professor G. G. STOKES, F.R.S., Rev. Canon KNOX-LITTLE, Right Rev. BISHOP OF AMYCLA, Rev. Principal JOHN CAIRNS, D.D., Rev. EDWARD WHITE, and Others.

"A work of great and absorbing interest, marked by extreme ability. No intelligent and competent reader can fail to find the volume a most deeply interesting one."—*Literary Churchman.*

LONDON: J. NISBET & CO., 21 BERNERS STREET.

NEW AND RECENT WORKS

IN

THEOLOGICAL AND BIBLICAL SUBJECTS.

ATONEMENT AND LAW; or, Redemption in Harmony with Law as Revealed in Nature. By JOHN M. ARMOUR. Crown 8vo, 5s.

ST. PAUL THE AUTHOR OF THE LAST TWELVE VERSES OF THE SECOND GOSPEL. By HOWARD HEBER EVANS, M.A., Author of "St. Paul the Author of the Acts of the Apostles and the Third Gospel." Crown 8vo, 2s. 6d.

AUTHORSHIP OF THE FOUR GOSPELS. From a Lawyer's Point of View. External Evidences. By WILLIAM MARVIN, Ex-Judge of the District Court of the United States for the Southern District of Florida, &c. Crown 8vo, 3s. 6d.

THE DOCTRINE OF ENDLESS PUNISHMENT. By WILLIAM G. T. SHEDD, D.D., Professor of Systematic Theology in Union Theological Seminary, New York. 5s.

AN EXPOSITORY COMMENTARY ON THE BOOK OF JUDGES. By the Rev. A. R. FAUSSET, D.D., Canon of York. Demy 8vo, 10s. 6d.

HORÆ PSALMICÆ. STUDIES IN THE CL. PSALMS: Their Undesigned Coincidence with the Independent Scripture Histories Confirming and Illustrating Both. By Canon FAUSSET, D.D. Second Edition. Demy 8vo, 10s. 6d.

CLOUDS CLEARED. A Few Hard Subjects of New Testament Teaching Explained. By the Rev. CLAUDE SMITH BIRD, M.A., Author of the "Life of the Rev. Chancellor Bird." Small crown 8vo, 2s.

THE EMPIRE OF THE HITTITES. By WM. WRIGHT, D.D. With Decipherment of Hittite Inscriptions by Professor SAYCE. LL.D.; A Hittite Map by Col. Sir CHARLES WILSON, F.R.S., and Captain CONDER, R.E.; and a Complete Set of Hittite Inscriptions by W. H. RYLANDS, F.S.A. Second Edition, with Twenty-seven Plates. Royal 8vo, 17s. 6d.

METAPHORS IN THE GOSPELS: A Series of Short Studies. By the Rev. DONALD FRASER, D.D. Crown 8vo, 6s.

SYNOPTICAL LECTURES ON THE BOOKS OF HOLY SCRIPTURE. By the Rev. DONALD FRASER, D.D. New Edition.

THE HEBREW FEASTS IN RELATION TO RECENT CRITICAL HYPOTHESES REGARDING THE PENTATEUCH. By the Rev. W. H. GREEN, D.D. Crown 8vo, 5s.

LONDON: J. NISBET & CO., 21 BERNERS STREET.

New Series of Text-Books for Bible Students.

Just Published, the First Volume, small crown 8vo, 1s.

LESSONS ON THE
I. NAMES AND TITLES OF OUR LORD.
II. PROPHECIES CONCERNING OUR LORD, AND THEIR FULFILMENT.

The Fifty-two Lessons forming a Year's Course of Instruction for Bible-Classes, Sunday-Schools, and Lectures.

By FLAVEL S. COOK, D.D., Chaplain of the Lock, London.

Published Monthly, price 7d.,

THE BIBLICAL ILLUSTRATOR;

OR, ANECDOTES, SIMILES, EMBLEMS, AND ILLUSTRATIONS,

EXPOSITORY, SCIENTIFIC, GEOGRAPHICAL, HISTORICAL, AND HOMILETIC.

Gathered from a Wide Range of Home and Foreign Literature on the Verses of the Bible.

Edited by the Rev. J. S. EXELL.

THE MEN OF THE BIBLE.

Crown 8vo, 2s. 6d. each.

ABRAHAM: His Life and Times. By the Rev. W. J. DEANE, M.A.

In Preparation.

MOSES: His Life and Times. By the Rev. Canon G. RAWLINSON, M.A.
GIDEON: His Life and Times. By the Rev. J. M. LANG, D.D.
ELIJAH: His Life and Times. By the Rev. Professor W. MILLIGAN, D.D.
SOLOMON: His Life and Times. By the Ven. Archdeacon FARRAR, D.D.
ISAIAH: His Life and Times. By the Rev. Canon S. R. DRIVER, M.A.
JEREMIAH: His Life and Times. By the Rev. Canon T. K. CHEYNE, M.A.
JESUS THE CHRIST: His Life and Times. By the Rev. F. J. VALLINGS, M.A.

Several of the above Volumes will be ready early in 1887.

LONDON: J. NISBET & CO., 21 BERNERS STREET.

WORKS BY THE REV. G. S. BOWES.

I.

CONVERSATION: Why don't we do more Good by it? Crown 8vo, 2s. 6d.

"A book much needed and very valuable. The illustrative stories are apt and well selected. Most families and friendly circles would be the better for reading this sensible book."—*Literary World.*

"A timely book, full of interesting and suggestive matter, calculated to revive the lost art of conversation."—*Family Churchman.*

"To devout and earnest Christians this will be acceptable as a wise and good book."—*Queen.*

"The author is well known through his valuable 'Illustrative Gatherings.' He has handled a large and difficult theme in a very practical and useful manner."—*Church Bells.*

II.

ILLUSTRATIVE GATHERINGS FOR PREACHERS AND TEACHERS. A Manual of Anecdotes, Facts, Figures, Proverbs, Quotations, &c. Eleventh Edition, First and Second Series. Small crown 8vo, 3s. 6d. each.

"Full of valuable matter, well arranged for reference."—*Rock.*

III.

SCRIPTURE ITSELF THE ILLUSTRATOR: A Manual of Illustrations, gathered from Scriptural Figures, Phrases, Types, Derivations, Chronology, Texts, &c. Fourth Edition. Small crown 8vo, 3s. 6d.

IV.

IN PROSPECT OF SUNDAY: A Collection of Analyses, Arguments, Applications, Counsels, Cautions, &c. Third Thousand. Crown 8vo, 5s.

"Mr. Bowes is well known as the author of some very useful books which clergymen and others engaged in Scriptural teaching have welcomed to their profit. His former books supplied numerous apt illustrations; the present furnishes arguments and inferences from scripture arranged under appropriate headings. The use of it would not supersede labour on the part of him into whose hands it falls, but it would serve to direct the young and inexperienced how to gather out of the Word of God the lessons which it teaches. It would, therefore, be a very convenient present to a young clergyman, or the teacher of a Bible-class, while it would be found very suggestive for private meditation."—*Record.*

"It is full of holy thought of a kind which begets thought. It has our warmest commendation."—*Sword and Trowel.*

"The work cannot fail to prove a valuable addition to any teacher or preacher."—*Rock.*

V.

INFORMATION AND ILLUSTRATION: Helps gathered from Facts, Figures, Anecdotes, Books, &c., for Sermons, Lectures, and Addresses. Crown 8vo, 5s.

"This is a storehouse of anecdote and fact of no ordinary merit. The compiler is himself manifestly a man of exceptional good taste and judgment, and wherever we have tested his book, we have found its fragments of fact and incident just of the kind which a public speaker would desire."—*Baptist.*

"We think the present work gives abundant evidence that Mr. Bowes has peculiar fitness for the task he undertook. His work will be found very helpful to writers and speakers who are seeking for apt illustrations and important facts."—*Christian.*

"This is one of those useful books Mr. Bowes gives us from time to time, and like his 'Illustrative Gatherings' and other works, is full of valuable matter, well arranged for reference. Facts, anecdotes, arguments, and opinions are here set forth under appropriate headings, and thus a repository of material ready for use is provided for teachers and preachers, who will certainly find these pages worthy of attention, while ordinary readers will peruse the work with interest on account of the variety and attractive character of its contents."—*Rock.*

LONDON: J. NISBET & CO., 21 BERNERS STREET.

BOOKS RECENTLY PUBLISHED BY
JAMES NISBET & CO.

THE "ST. PAUL'S EDITION."

THE CHRISTIAN YEAR. Thoughts in verse for the Sundays and Holy Days throughout the Year. By the Rev. JOHN KEBLE, M.A. With the Collects, and MEDITATIONS SELECTED FROM THE WRITINGS OF THE REV. H. P. LIDDON, D.D., D.C.L., Canon of St. Paul's, &c. Extra crown 8vo, gilt top, 7s. 6d.

MOMENTS ON THE MOUNT: A Series of Devotional Meditations. By the Rev. GEORGE MATHESON, D.D., Author of "The Natural Elements of Revealed Theology." Third Edition. Crown 8vo, 3s. 6d.

"This little volume is not one to be read through at a sitting, and then laid aside. Rather each meditation is to be pondered over, and to be enjoyed singly and separately, and to be dwelt upon until it becomes a permanent possession. Their suggestiveness can hardly fail to stimulate to Biblical and Theological research. They will create, if they do not satisfy, the thirst for religious knowledge."—*Scotsman.*

"Each study is suggestive, and we rise from the perusal of the book deeply impressed with the evidence it furnishes of the purity and depth of the author's spiritual experience."—*Glasgow Herald.*

OVER THE HOLY LAND. By the Rev. A. J. WYLIE, LL.D., Author of "History of Protestantism." Crown 8vo, 7s. 6d.

"One of the most interesting books on Palestine which it has been our privilege to read."—*Edinburgh Courant.*

"Dr. Wylie's observations on the true sites of the holy places at Jerusalem will be read with interest, as well as his disquisitions on the present physical desolation of the country, and the possibility and method of restoring it to its ancient fertility. Some of his descriptions of scenery are very striking and effective."—*Record.*

THROUGH BIBLE LANDS: A Narrative of a Recent Tour in Egypt and the Holy Land. By PHILIP SCHAFF, D.D. With Illustrations. Crown 8vo, 6s.

ST. AUGUSTIN, MELANCHTHON, NEANDER. Three Biographies. By PHILIP SCHAFF, D.D., Author of "Through Bible Lands," "Christ and Christianity," &c. Crown 8vo, 4s. 6d.

CLOUDS CLEARED. A Few Hard Subjects of New Testament Teaching Explained. By the Rev. CLAUDE SMITH BIRD, M.A. Small crown 8vo, 2s.

THE PERSON OF CHRIST: The Perfection of His Humanity Viewed as a Proof of His Divinity. By PHILIP SCHAFF, D.D. Small crown 8vo, 3s. 6d.

"A very readable and helpful book."—*Church Standard.*

CHRIST AND CHRISTIANITY. Studies in Christology, Creeds and Confessions, Protestantism and Romanism, Reformation Principles, Sunday Observance, Religious Freedom and Christian Union. By PHILIP SCHAFF, D.D. Demy 8vo, 10s. 6d.

"The paper on 'Christ His own Witness' is an excellent and comprehensive statement of that one of the grounds of faith which has, happily, come into exceptional prominence in our own day. Theological students will find two invaluable bits of historical analysis in 'Christ in Theology' and 'Creeds and Confessions of Faith,' as lucid as they are brief."—*British Quarterly Review.*

LONDON: J. NISBET & CO., 21 BERNERS STREET.

BOOKS RECENTLY PUBLISHED—Continued.

A VOLUME OF SERMONS: By the Rev. EUGENE BERSIER, D.D. With a Personal Sketch of the Author by the Rev. F. HASTINGS. Crown 8vo, 7s. 6d.

"Bersier may perhaps claim to be the greatest living pulpit orator of Paris. Not only is his preaching vigorous, fervid, and evangelical, but he is unconventional in the structure of his sermons, and practical in his allusions to contemporary life and his interpretation of it."—*British Quarterly Review.*

"Marked by vigour and coherence of thought, as well as by rare force, fervour, and elevation in expression."—*Scotsman.*

LIFE AND LETTERS OF THE LATE REV. ADOLPHE MONOD, Pastor of the Reformed Church of France. By one of his Daughters. With Portrait. Crown 8vo, 6s.

"To all who have interested themselves in the spread of Protestantism in France, and more particularly in the history of the Reformed Church there, the publication of this translation will be hailed with unfeigned delight. To those who desire to become acquainted with the life of one of the most devoted of men, and one who, in the course of his eventful ministry, passed through deep spiritual experiences of no ordinary kind, the perusal of this biography will afford an unusual degree of satisfaction."—*Daily Review.*

MODERN ATHEISM; or, The Heavenly Father. By M. ERNEST NAVILLE. Translated by the Rev. HENRY DOWNTON. Crown 8vo, 6s.

"The author has few rivals on the Continent in the graces of polished eloquence, and his arguments are stated with that peculiar clearness and elegance of illustration which give a charm and freshness to the best kind of French literature."—*Record.*

THE BOOK OF DANIEL; or, The Second Volume of Prophecy. Translated and Expounded, with a Preliminary Sketch of Antecedent Prophecy. By the Rev. JAMES G. MURPHY, D.D., Professor of Hebrew, &c. Small crown 8vo, 3s.

"With a perfect mastery of the literature of his subject, Dr. Murphy gives his readers results rather than references, and brings within most moderate compass all that the ordinary Bible student needs to know. Through the visions of the prophet the reader proceeds with confidence, for he feels that all through he has the advantage of a most capable and trusty guide."—*Presbyterian Churchman.*

FOR THE WORK OF THE MINISTRY. A Manual of Homiletical and Pastoral Theology. By W. G. BLAIKIE, D.D., LL.D., Professor of Apologetics and of Ecclesiastical and Pastoral Theology, New College, Edinburgh. Fourth Edition. Crown 8vo, 5s.

"A volume which displays a considerable amount of wide and varied reading, much thought and ability, great good feeling, and an earnest and charitable desire to further the attainment of the highest ends of all right human thought and action."—*Guardian.*

THE PUBLIC MINISTRY AND PASTORAL METHODS OF OUR LORD. By Professor W. G. BLAIKIE, D.D., LL.D. Crown 8vo, 6s.

"Should be very acceptable and profitable, not only to those whose life-work is the ministry of the Gospel, but also to those who in other ways take their share of active service for the spiritual good of men, and we heartily commend it to them."—*Messenger.*

ROCK *VERSUS* SAND; or, The Foundations of the Christian Faith. By J. MONRO GIBSON, D.D., Author of "The Ages before Moses," &c. Small crown 8vo, 1s. 6d.

"Able and timely expositions of the basis of Christian Faith. The plan adopted is novel, and the arguments cogent and conclusive."—*Christian Age.*

LONDON: J. NISBET & CO., 21 BERNERS STREET.

THE HOMILETIC MAGAZINE.

Papers on the following subjects will appear during the year 1887:—

EARLY SCANDINAVIAN RELIGION AND BIBLICAL THEOLOGY. By RASMUS B. ANDERSON, Minister of the United States to the Court of Denmark.

POSITIVISM AS A RELIGION. By Rev. J. RADFORD THOMSON, M.A.

PAULINE THEOLOGY. By Rev. J. OSWALD DYKES, D.D.

ST. PAUL'S EPISTLE TO THE COLOSSIANS. By Rev. JAMES MORISON, D.D.

ST. PAUL'S EPISTLE TO THE EPHESIANS. By Rev. A. F. MUIR, M.A.

UNCONSCIOUS PROPHECIES. By Rev. A. MACKENNAL.

Rev. DAVID DAVIES on the WELSH HWYL, &c. &c.

SPECIAL PAPERS ON PREACHERS AND PREACHING. Sermonic Outlines for the Church's Year.

ALSO A

NEW SYMPOSIUM on "THE REUNION OF CHRISTENDOM: IS IT DESIRABLE? IS IT POSSIBLE?" Articles promised by H. E. CARDINAL MANNING, Ven. ARCHDEACON FARRAR, D.D., Rev. HENRY ALLON, D.D., and others.

Published Monthly, Price One Shilling,

THE HOMILETIC MAGAZINE.

"A mass of very valuable literature to ministers."—*British Quarterly.*

"The *Homiletic Magazine* is a very cheap publication, and in its new form will no doubt obtain a more extended circulation."—*Christian World.*

"The *Homiletic Magazine* is a useful and serviceable periodical. . . . The present and past Numbers of this Quarterly must be admitted to supply an abundant fund of all that is best and freshest in the religious thought of the present day. . . . The names of the principal contributors—names well known and highly appreciated in theological circles more or less wide—afford a sufficient guarantee for the general excellence and quality of the several articles."—*Scotsman.*

"It suggests texts, affords hints for their treatment, illustrates the art of pulpit division and arrangement, and throws light of an interesting kind on many themes, old and new. It devotes a large proportion of its space to exposition proper—the 'Expository Section' being, in our judgment, the strongest feature of the Magazine. In the Numbers before us we have excellent papers by a host of the ablest and best-known scholars of the time. . . . It is a rich collection of papers on Biblical subjects."—*Glasgow Herald.*

The Magazine is published in America on the same day as in England.

ANNUAL SUBSCRIPTION, 12s., payable in advance.

LONDON: J. NISBET & CO., 21 BERNERS STREET.

www.ingramcontent.com/pod-product-compliance
Lightning Source LLC
Chambersburg PA
CBHW020535300426
44111CB00008B/677